Programming
Windows® Services

Implementing Application Servers

Programming Windows® Services

Implementing Application Servers

Randy C. Morin

Wiley Computer Publishing

John Wiley & Sons, Inc.

NEW YORK · CHICHESTER · WEINHEIM · BRISBANE · SINGAPORE · TORONTO

Publisher: Bob Ipsen

Editor: Marjorie Spencer

Assistant Editor: Margaret Hendrey

Managing Editor: Micheline Frederick

Text Design & Composition: North Market Street Graphics

Library of Congress Cataloging-in-Publication Data:

0471-38576-X

Printed in the United States of America.

10 9 8 7 6 5 4 3 2 1

This book is dedicated to my wife Bernadette, for bringing my daughter Adelaine into this world. Thank you.

CONTENTS

I have to ask forgiveness from my daughter Adelaine, as I spent a lot of time writing this book that I should have spent playing with her. But whenever writer's block set in, I was quickly watching *Teletubbies* and *Blue's Clues* by her side. In fact, even as I write this acknowledgement, she is sleeping at my side. She fell asleep while watching her favorite episode of *Blue's Clues*, "Blue's Birthday." As soon as she was fast asleep, I quickly changed the channel to the Senators versus Islanders NHL hockey game and started writing the dedication and acknowledgment. So, thanks to Adelaine for sleeping those few hours at a time, so I could squeeze out a couple more paragraphs each time.

I also have to thank my wife Bernadette, who takes out the garbage so that I can spend a couple extra minutes behind the keyboard, who calls me at 11 P.M. to tell me that I have to come home from work and that I'm working too hard. I'm intentionally taking Tuesday and Thursday off work this past week and the next two in order to make up for some of the extra time I've been spending at work trying to get those alerts triggered.

I'm currently working for 724 Solutions as the development manager for the content server team. One of our servers has been problematic; this results in long hours at work. I think I've got it fixed now—but I've said that before.

I also have to thank my entire family: my dad Ed, my mom Jean, my brother Wade, my two sisters, Miche and Jackie, my sister-in-law Lori, my brother-in-law John, my wife's parents, Ernie and Ruth, and my daughter's godparents, Mildred and Paul. Also, my friends: Bruce, Valentin, Jules, and Dave. A person is defined by his or her family and friends and acquires their good habits and bad. Fortunately, my family and friends have more good habits than bad.

I also have to apologize to my hockey team, the Cobalt Silver Kings. I've attended only one game this year and used the extra time to write more. Like I've said every week this year, I'll make it to the next game. See you guys on Wednesday at the Rinx.

I've been a co-author and contributing author before. I've also helped many authors by reviewing their books. But this is the first book that I've written entirely on my own. I'd like to thank Marjorie Spencer for giving me this opportunity. I'd also like to thank all the staff at Wiley that have helped put this book together.

And thanks to this 486SLC33 Epson laptop that I've been writing with. In the age of Pentiums running at hundreds of megahertz, a 486 running Windows 3.1 still remains my primary computer. The battery is long dead. And I can't compile code with it. Maybe my wife will buy me a Pentium laptop for Christmas. I hope she reads this.

Happy Y2K everybody!

The software development projects that I've been engaged in over the last few years have had the same evolutionary pattern about them. They start off writing simple dialog-based application servers. Error and trace logs are saved in simple text log files. Communication between application servers and clients is based on some proprietary RPC, likely over sockets. Application servers are configured by editing INI files.

Eventually, everybody realizes that the GUIs in their application server are pretty much mute. So the dialog-based application server is replaced with a GUI-less application server. Double-clicking the executable module starts this GUI-less application server. The operator logs off the physical computer and the application server terminates. Oops.

A new paradigm is considered where the process outlives the user's login session. This is where everything is converted to Windows Services. Everybody takes that first step to professionalize his or her application servers. Unfortunately, all the Windows Services are created in isolation and no commonality exists between the application servers.

The next step has everybody converting from text-based log files to using the Windows Event Log. From proprietary socket-based RPCs to object-oriented RPCs such as COM and CORBA. From INI files to the Microsoft Management Console. From zero commonality to completely reusable application frameworks.

The amount of time wasted going through this evolution is very costly and can mean the difference between the success and failure of your project. I suffered through this enough times myself that I figured my countless failures (and some successes) could be the start of a great programming book. And here we are.

I gathered all my notes from the last few years and wrote them down in a literary manner. Added some clean pictures and explanations and called up Wiley. Six months later, you're reading how to avoid all the mistakes I've encountered over the last few years.

This is what this book is about. A somewhat quick and in-depth tutorial to get you started immediately using Windows Services and all that they have to offer. Don't struggle through those evolutionary blues. Start here. Read this book.

Randy Charles Morin works as a software development manager for 724 Solutions (www.724.com) in Toronto, Ontario, Canada. This company develops Internet-based banking solutions for large banks. Its product is available with the Bank of Montreal in Canada as Veev (www.veev.bmo.ca). Randy has previously co-authored three books (*COM/DCOM Primer Plus*, *COM/DCOM Unleashed*, and *SQL Server 7.0 Programming Unleashed*) and authors a software development Web site (www.kbcafe.com).

Randy lives in Brampton, Ontario, Canada, with his pregnant wife Bernadette and his 22-month-old daughter Adelaine. He spends a great deal of time cheering his Toronto Maple Leafs to victory, but is still waiting for Toronto's first Stanley Cup in his lifetime.

CHAPTER 1

Introduction

The biggest development in Microsoft Windows in the last few years is the introduction of Windows NT application servers. Application servers and servers in general have been the exclusive domain of Unix. A lot of effort has gone into development of Unix application servers. And from those efforts a lot of expertise has been attained.

Many Unix applications servers have been programmed as system processes called daemons that run in the background even when no user is logged into the Unix machine. NT Services attempt to replicate exactly this behavior.

NT application servers are a newer breed and few NT programmers have any expertise in developing application servers. Most NT application servers

Definition Daemon

The word *daemon* comes from the Greek word *daimon*, meaning spirit. The interpretation in computer science is that the daemon process is hidden, like a spirit. I've heard NT Services and daemons also referred to as long-lived processes. The implication here is that the short-lived processes are those that are started and stopped by the interactive user and long-lived processes are those that live beyond the lifetime of the interactive user's session.

tend to be very ad-hoc efforts that evolve over time as the programmers begin understanding which NT features are best suited to their application servers.

Unfortunately, NT application servers tend to evolve over their lifetimes since they are usually developed by programmers with little to no experience with Windows NT. In this book, I will attempt to convey all the expertise that I have so that other less-experienced programmers don't have to make the same mistakes that I've made over and over.

But this book is not about NT application servers, it's about NT Services. This is true. My objective is to explain NT application servers as implemented using NT Services. There are many types of NT Services, one of which is also an application server. If the objective is to implement an NT Service that is not an application server, then don't worry, the concepts explained herein remain the same. If the objective is to implement an application server, then this is the right book.

What's in This Book

I've selected a broad range of topics that should help guide NT Service developers in their efforts. In the second chapter of this book, I explain all the small details of programming and manipulating a basic NT Service. I also provide a template with which the developer can create NT Services with a variety of programming tools such as Visual Basic, C++, and Delphi.

In Chapter 3, I demonstrate how to develop NT Services that use sockets, DCOM, CORBA, and other distributed transports to communicate with the outside world.

The fourth chapter shows the reader how to develop professional NT Services by using the NT Event Log to log the information, warnings, and errors. The NT Event Log is a critical part of any NT Service as it is a convenient aid in providing feedback to the computer operator when an NT Service fails.

The fifth chapter demonstrates how to add polish to an NT Service by using various techniques to configure an NT Service, such as how to write a Control Panel applet, a Microsoft Management Console add-on, and much more.

Chapter 6 concentrates on the arduous task of securing the application server using NT Security and configuring the NT Service to work with the different security services available on the NT platform.

In the last chapter, I provide examples of using various techniques to debug services. Since services are started by the Service Control Manager (SCM) and cannot be started within the debugger, it is much more difficult to track down bugs. Therefore, I've allocated an entire chapter to aid the developer in tracking down those nasty bugs.

Application Servers

An application server is a midtier server in a multitier architecture. Until recently, all client-server applications were designed with two tiers (see Figure 1.1): a client tier that housed the interactive application and a server tier that housed the data. The server tier was typically a database management system such as Oracle, Sybase SQL Server, or DB2.

More recently architectures follow a new paradigm in development in which the application uses a multitier design. The multitier design attempts to redistribute the application over a greater number of servers. The redistribution can help the designer meet other design requirements. Some design requirements that are more easily met in multitier architectures are a thinner client application and improved scalability of the application.

The most basic of multitier designs is the three-tier architecture (see Figure 1.2). In the three-tier architecture, the three tiers are the client, application, and data. The middle-tier servers in this model are often referred to as application servers.

The advantage of the three-tier architecture is scalability. In the old two-tier model, the only reason to scale the servers was to use replication to create more and more server tiers. This was not very efficient and required a client to maintain a lot of state in order to boost performance.

In the three-tier model, application logic is moved from the client and database into a middle application tier. This middle application tier reduces both the complexity of the client and the load on the database. As new users are added, the application can be scaled by introducing more application servers (see Figure 1.3).

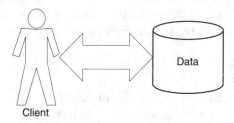

Figure 1.1   Two-tier architecture.

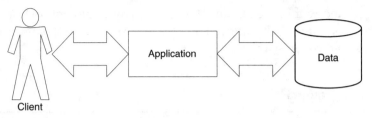

Figure 1.2 Three-tier architecture.

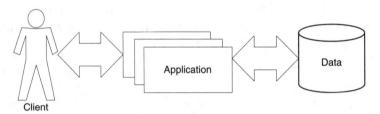

Figure 1.3 Multiple application servers.

Because the database has less load, it can support more concurrent users before designers have to resort to replication. Additionally, because application logic was moved from the client, the client becomes thinner. A thinner client has enormous advantages—just look at the success of the new breed of thin clients, such as Web browsers and mobile phones. The thin client can reside in a much less powerful client device.

Book Conventions

It is very important to know the book conventions since they may not be appropriate for direct use in a production application.

Coding Style

The coding style of the author is my own and basically reflects most of the generally accepted coding standards. But on occasion, I deviate from generally accepted coding practices. If readers find these practices unacceptable, then it is their responsibility to modify the code to fit into their organization's vision.

Error Checking

In a production application, every new operation should be checked for allocation failures, every exception should be handled as soon as possible, and every HRESULT return should be checked for call failures. And all of these errors should be reported in the error log. I have failed everywhere to check these return codes. This was done intentionally to simplify the presentation of code fragments to the reader.

An effort has been made to present frameworks that implement a complete range of error checking. But no effort has been made to add error checking to code snippets. I expect more from developers of production applications.

Services Control Panel Applet

Before beginning with the how-to of programming NT Services, here's a quick introduction to a developer's best friend in programming NT Services, the Services Control Panel applet. The applet is an SCM controller that allows the user to start, stop, pause, continue, and configure the startup of NT Services. The Service Control Panel applet is shown in Figure 1.4.

The applet can be started by selecting Settings | Control Panel from the Start menu and double-clicking the Service icon. Alternatively, I've found it useful to put a shortcut in my Start menu. To add the Services Control Panel applet

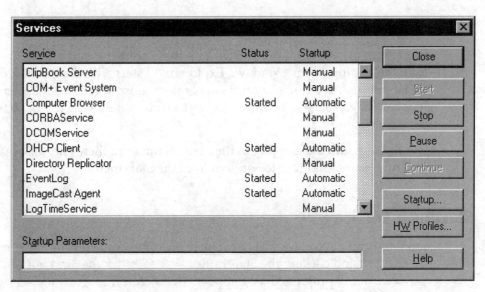

Figure 1.4 Services Control Panel applet.

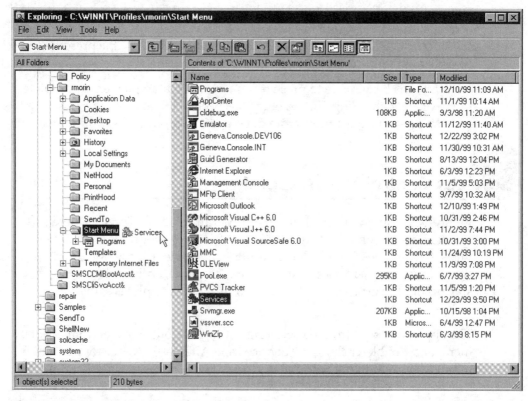

Figure 1.5 Copy Services Control Panel applet shortcut.

shortcut to the Start menu, right-click on the Start menu and select Explore from the pop-up menu. Windows Explorer will start with the Start Menu folder selected. Select the Control Panel folder in Explorer. Drag the Services item from right-pane listview to the Start Menu folder in the left-pane tree-view (see Figure 1.5).

Once I have added the applet to the Start menu, I can then start the applet by selecting Start | Shortcut to Services from the Start menu.

Starting a Service

From the applet I can start a service that is stopped by selecting the service in the listview and clicking the Start button. When I click the Start button, the Service Control progress dialog appears (see Figure 1.6) while the service is starting.

Figure 1.6 Starting a service.

I can also start a service with command-line parameters by typing the command-line parameters in the Startup Parameters text control before clicking on the Start button.

Stopping a Service

I can stop a service that is already started by selecting the service in the listview and clicking the Stop button. A message box will appear confirming that I want to stop the services (see Figure 1.7).

Select Yes and the Service Control progress dialog will appear while the service is being stopped (see Figure 1.8).

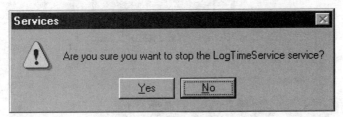

Figure 1.7 Stopping a service message box.

Figure 1.8 Stopping a service.

Pausing a Service

You can pause a service that is already started by selecting the service in the listview and clicking the Pause button. A message box will appear confirming that you want to pause the services (see Figure 1.9).

Select Yes and the Service Control progress dialog will appear while the service is being paused (see Figure 1.10).

Restart a Paused Service

I can restart a paused service by selecting the service in the listview and clicking the Continue button. The Service Control progress dialog appears while the service is being unpaused (see Figure 1.11).

Startup

Additionally, I can configure a service by selecting the service in the listview and clicking the Startup button. The Startup dialog appears (see Figure 1.12).

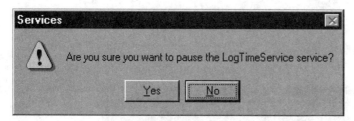

Figure 1.9   Pausing a service message box.

Figure 1.10   Pausing a service.

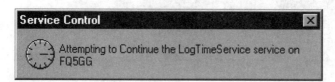

Figure 1.11   Continuing a service.

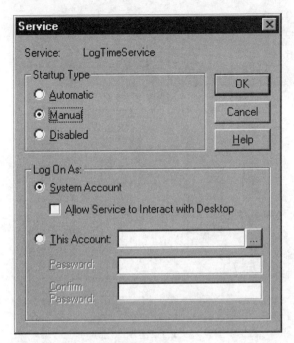

Figure 1.12 Startup dialog.

There are three Startup Types available for a service: Automatic, Manual, and Disabled. Automatic startup informs the SCM that the user wishes to start the service when the computer is initially booted. Manual startup means that the user must manually start the service; it is not started when the computer is initially booted. Last, Disabled startup means that the service can no longer be started.

The Startup dialog also allows the user to specify the username that will be used when starting the service. Normally services are started with the Local System Account and take on the security context of the Local System Account. But it is sometimes advisable to start a service with another username. If I select the This Account radio button and click the . . . (ellipsis) button, I can select an alternate username with which to start the service (see Figure 1.13).

If I do select an alternate username to start the service, I will have to specify the password for that user. Remember also that if the password changes for the specified user, then the service can no longer start. It is therefore advisable to set up special accounts for services, for which the password does not expire and cannot be changed.

If I select the Local System Account as the startup user, I may also select the Allow Service to Interact with Desktop checkbox. If the service displays a

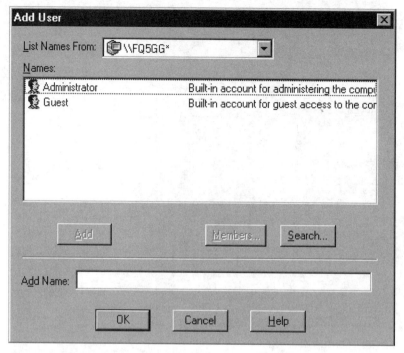

Figure 1.13 Select User Account dialog.

message box or any window, it will not be visible to the interactive user unless this checkbox is selected.

Development Principles

Beyond just describing how to code, slash, or hack together an NT Service, I'd like to explain five development principles that I use everyday to increase the quality of my work. I call these my five development principles. The five principles are as follows:

- KISS
- Reuse versus rewrite
- Statelessness leads to scalability
- Architecture is experience and knowledge
- Bleeding edge

KISS

I don't know how many times I've used this principle myself. Every day and all the time are the appropriate times for using this godsend. KISS: Keep it simple, stupid. The retro-argument, "It's complex but I understand it," never holds true. It only takes one careless bus driver to turn a complex design into an unmanageable design. Remember that nearly every design is eventually passed on to a less-senior developer, whether by bus accident or vertical-horizontal promotion. It should also be obvious to managers why KISS takes the risk out of horizontal promotions, which usually means an employee quits one job to take a similar job with another company.

Even when the complex programmer doesn't get hit by a bus, the usual outcome is that the design becomes increasingly complex over time when the original programmer starts doubting him- or herself and starts wondering what the intention of the originally design was. Eventually this leads to a design so complex that the original developer loses the ability to manage the complexity and suddenly is hit by another bus—stress—and quits.

Another retro-argument is that the design is complex but efficient. This is usually not true either. I've seen many designs that are professed to be more efficient, but that yield little or no gain and sometimes are less efficient than the simple solution.

Reuse versus Rewrite

I have never met a programmer yet who understands the difference between reuse and rewrite. These verbs may appear contrary enough that they would not be confused, but they often are. The typical confusion begins with a development project that has implemented two or more versions of the same class. Then a developer mentions the possibility of reuse and the designers huddle for the arduous task of making one reusable component that fits the needs of all. Two weeks later, they decide that the class must be rewritten from scratch because all of the existing classes were not good enough. So, rather than reusing an existing class, in the end, they are simply creating a new class from scratch.

The idea that programmers can write reusable components is a fallacy. They can't. They cannot anticipate future requirements in a class. And if they try to do this, then they'll likely end up with a thick class that implements more functionality than is required. They also end up with a class that is more complex than required. It is also likely that their thick class will end up being rewritten in the near future since it will someday not meet some oblique requirement that it misses.

The cycle becomes endless. Rather than extending an existing class to meet new requirements, the temptation of writing a new class that has both the existing and new requirements turns into a battle of time. By the time a class is stable, new requirements encourage programmers to write a newer class. And so on.

The advantage of reuse is not that the class may be reused in the future. The advantage of reuse is that the class may be reused now. Writing a class that is reusable is more difficult and requires more time than writing a nonreusable class. This directly implies that writing reusable classes costs more in time and resources than writing nonreusable classes. There is no gain. None! Really! The gain of reuse only occurs in the future when that class is reused. If that class is never reused, then nothing is gained. If developers continuously write more string classes, then they are losing big time.

When programmers see the opportunity for reuse, their best bet is to take an existing class, restructure it, inherit from it, and add to it as they see fit to meet new requirements. They shouldn't anticipate future requirements. Nor should they rewrite the class from scratch.

Statelessness Leads to Scalability

Statelessness? Who art thou and what art thou beckoning? *Statelessness* is really a misnomer. No servers, except the most simple of servers, are stateless. In order to be stateless, they'd have to return the same results given the same request without any regard to time. This is true statelessness. What most people and also what I'm referring to in this section as *statelessness* is the ability of a server to share state with the rest of the world, rather than maintain state internally. This concept may be hard to grasp, so I'll try to sum it up with an example.

A server that returns the time of day is truly not stateless. If the server keeps track of that time of day internally within its own process, then this time of day will require synchronization with the world time. This is considered extremely stateful. If the server uses the system time of the local machine, then synchronization will be less important. This type of server is considered less stateful, because it does not maintain the state internally, but rather it relies on an outside source to maintain the state.

The advantage of reducing statefulness is scalability. Imagine that there is one time server that maintains its state (time) internally. Now imagine that there is a second time server that also maintains its state (time) internally. These times may not be synchronized. As more and more servers are added (a process called scaling), the likelihood of one server being unsynchronized increases. Now imagine that each server retrieves the state (time) from a shared system clock. The times will never be unsynchronized regardless of the scaling.

Time, of course, is not really an issue when it comes to synchronization, as most users have grown used to correctly setting the computer's clock. On the other hand, it's amazing how many times I've encountered systems that had requirements to have accurate time and were rarely accurate.

One really important resource that must be synchronized is a database. I'm not talking about a DBMS (database management system); I'm talking about a database. The data managed by a DBMS is a database. So, too, is the information held in memory by an application. These databases are state. Synchronization is important and redundancy is bad. If a developer wanted to scale an application server process that maintained a database in active memory, then synchronization again would become a problem, just like it was a problem with the time server.

The best bet to increase the statelessness of an application server is to move the database from active memory into a database, so that it may be shared by several instances of the application server processes.

Beware, of course; there is a down side. In-memory data is occasionally faster than data persisted in a DBMS. But when I say *occasionally*, I'd like to point out that occasionally usually means those occasions when speed is not relevant or when the design is faulty.

Example

As an example of faulty design, I once wrote a class that loaded an entire database record by record into memory. My first instance of the server had an average processing time of about 15 minutes. This was because the Rogue Wave DBTools SQL Server 6.5 access library was very deficient in loading bulk data. After converting the routines to use open database connectivity (ODBC), the average processing time was reduced to 17 seconds. The faulty design was in the data access classes. Removing the faulty design improved performance 5,000 percent.

Architecture Is Experience and Knowledge

It's rare to visit a house built in the last 20 years that doesn't have a bathroom. What about a house that was built 50 years ago? What about 100? Amazing that over the years people have drawn the conclusion that in-house plumbing is a good idea. It took a long time for this conclusion to be reached. Actually, it really wasn't time, it was experience and knowledge. Eventually, as architects became more experienced and more knowledgeable, they realized that in-house plumbing was first possible and then a necessity.

This is true of all architectural fields, especially the software architecture field. Ten years ago, the multitier architecture was an unknown. As more software architects had good experiences with this architecture, they adopted it. And using these multitier architectures has proven to be very beneficial to software development projects.

If architects don't actually know what multitier architecture is, then it is unlikely that they will implement it. Architects occasionally implement architectures that they are not familiar with and most of the time they implement them incorrectly. This is because they have no knowledge of the pitfalls of the architecture. They likely ran down every pitfall until the project was dead.

This is where knowledge and experience are extremely important in architecture. Architects should make certain that they are knowledgeable and experienced with the architecture they are attempting to implement. I've encountered numerous architects that read in a magazine about a new architecture and the next day propose this architecture as the basis for their next project. This is foolish, and typical. Typical, because most architectures deal in the theoretical (magazine articles) and not the practical (experience).

I have been burned many times by architectural decisions that were made by architects or designers that had no real experience in the field in which they were making decisions. As an example, many architects chose the route of implementing multitiered servers. I was the first person to jump on board the multitier bandwagon. But these architects began making bad decisions because of lack of experience. They had never implemented these architectures before and in the end they had applications that required two hours to initialize themselves or that were not scalable or that processed a maximum of three transactions per second.

Acronym Bingo

Most architects can throw acronyms around faster than Nolan Ryan's fastball. In order to pass the time in meetings, I invented a game called acronym bingo. Simply add to a list all the popular acronyms that everybody in a particular workplace likes to use. The list should be about 25 acronyms in length to accurately simulate a bingo card. Keep one card for every architect or designer that is attending the meeting. Whenever one of the architects uses one of the acronyms, cross it off that person's list. The first architect or designer that uses five different acronyms from your bingo card wins. Call out "Bingo!" and announce the winner.

Almost every architectural design will have some benefits. As an example, if a project architect decides to use an RS-232-based transport between the servers, it may be hard to believe this architectural decision has any benefit. Well, it can. By limiting the transport to RS-232, the architect automatically reduces the possible transport-based problems down to the set of problems relevant to the RS-232 transports.

A worse architectural decision is to allow any transport mechanism. I've been on projects that used TCP/IP, HTTP, DCOM, RMI, and CORBA. Each transport protocol had its own problems and my team experienced all of them. And trust me, Murphy is right when he says everything that can go wrong will go wrong. Had we decided on just one transport, then the set of problems would have been limited to something reasonable.

Assuming that designers make an architectural decision to limit the transport to one protocol, they then have the opportunity to acquire a large set of knowledge within their development groups that is focused on this technology. If developers have expertise in this transport, they'll likely run into very few problems. On the other hand, if they use several transports, then the development groups will never develop any real expertise in any one of the transports. And they'll experience several times the problems and headaches. This same logic of focusing a development group's expertise applies to all the development tools that may be used.

Bleeding Edge

The last principle is bleeding edge. Sort of rhymes with leading edge, doesn't it? This is not a coincidence. Leading edge technology is often referred to as bleeding edge, because new technologies are usually low quality.

Everybody wants to work on leading edge projects. Projects that use the latest technology, the fastest technology. But leading edge projects have an extremely large failure rate. The cause is that they use newer technologies that are not proven or experienced. If it's a new technology, then how can anyone know the pitfalls? Because nobody has experience with the new technology, it is not possible to avoid the pitfalls and bypass the bugs. This leads to thousands of hours of wasted time developing workarounds for the pitfalls and bugs of the new technology.

I usually find it more comforting to join the second wave of adopters of a technology. This allows the first wave of adopters to experience the pains of the new technology. I can then usually rely on Usenet and listserv postings to avoid the pains. If a company is one of the first 10 to adopt a new technology, don't be proud. Be fearful.

My worst experiences with bleeding edge technology have been while using alternative languages. Delphi, Java, and Basic have always been a major cause of problems in projects that I've tackled. At some point in the design of a C++ application, somebody mentions that this one component would be more easily developed in Java or VB or Delphi rather than C++. Why? Because Java has this new bleeding edge feature called RMI. Because VB is integrated with MTS. Because Delphi has awesome support for Automation.

Focusing developers' skill sets is more important than using bleeding edge technology. They'll always win in the long run with a focused skill set.

Summary

That chapter was easy. In the next chapter I dive deep into the guts that make an application an NT Service.

CHAPTER 2

Programming NT Services

S o, what is an NT Service? An *NT Service* is a process that may be started when the NT Workstation Server is initially booted and prior to an interactive user logging into the Workstation Server. An NT Service is a process that continues to exist even when an interactive user logs out of the NT Workstation Server.

The advantage of NT Services is obvious. These processes do not interfere with the interactive user of the NT Workstation Server and neither does the interactive user activity interfere with the operation of the NT Service. Well, that's not entirely true. Interactive users may steal process cycles and system resources from NT Services and vice versa. But generally users stay away from stopping and starting NT Services and NT Services typically do not interact with the users' desktops.

One of the biggest fears about non-NT Service processes is inadvertently stopping them using the system menu, Ctrl+C, or killing tasks in the task manager. An interactive user typically should not be able to easily stop an application server. Making the starting and stopping of NT Services much more explicit allows the interactive users to browse a computer system without making the additional effort of avoiding the console window or windowed application that, if killed, would generally cost users respect with their peers.

Generally, before the advent of NT Services, zero junior operators were tasked with operating an NT server that had a 24-hour-a-day application server available to the interactive user. I think every junior operator has made the mistake at least once (likely more) of inadvertently stopping the process that he or she has been charged with baby-sitting.

But don't get over-zealous as even NT Service processes can inadvertently be stopped. Don't reboot the NT Workstation Server. This obviously stops all NT Services. This may seem like trivial information, but I've experienced a situation in which I should have explained this to a junior operator that was working along my side. I left him alone for only five minutes.

The situation is better than before NT Services, as only my overconfidence convinced me not to warn the junior operator in advance. Prior to NT Services, I would have warned the junior up front, as it was inevitable that he'd stop that critical process when my back was turned.

NT Services are shielded from the interactive users through a component called the Service Control Manager (SCM, see Figure 2.1). The SCM has entry points available to other applications that can be used to start and stop an NT Service. Starting and stopping NT Services without the SCM intervening is generally not possible.

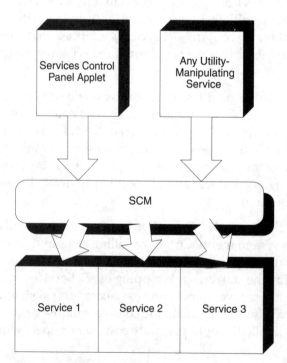

Figure 2.1 SCM and services.

Funneling all starting and stopping of NT Services through the SCM effectively makes it more difficult for the user to inadvertently start and stop services.

Another advantage of NT Services is the ability to start and stop these processes remotely. I don't know how many times I've had to walk to the computer room to safely start up or shut down some process. NT Services are easily started remotely and operators don't need PC-Anywhere (or something similar) to do it. In the Chapter 5 on configuration, I talk about the various utilities that are available to the operator to start, stop, and configure NT Services, both locally and remotely.

The rest of this chapter shows you how to create and manipulate NT Services using various programming tools.

Programming NT Services

NT Services are usually programmed in C++. A lot of effort and money has been invested in expertise with this combination of skills and a lot of literature is available on NT Services programming in C++. I'll begin by explaining how to develop an NT Service using C++ and provide a basic framework for creating NT Services in C++. Once I've discussed the basic concepts in C++, I'll show you how to implement an NT Service with other programming tools.

WinMain

Like all NT applications, the entry point to an NT Service is the WinMain function. The minimal NT application is shown in Listing 2.1.

Don't get me wrong, though. WinMain is not the only entry point available to NT Services. An NT Service may also have the main-styled entry point that may prove more convenient for programmers who require parsing of the command-line input parameters. NT applications with the main entry point are sometimes called console applications.

```
int WINAPI WinMain(HINSTANCE hinstance,
HINSTANCE /* hprevious */, LPSTR lpCmdLine, int /* nShowCmd */)
{
   return 0;
}
```

Listing 2.1   Minimal NT application.

NOTE

NT applications with the main entry point are not the same as console applications, but for the sake of convenience I will occasionally refer to NT applications with the main entry point as console applications. When an NT Service has the main entry point, it is clearly not a console application, so please excuse my language misuse for the rest of this chapter.

The minimal NT console application is shown in Listing 2.2.

```
int main(int argc, char** argv)
{
return 0;
}
```

Listing 2.2   Minimal NT console application.

ServiceMain

Normally you would initialize and run your application in the WinMain function. NT Services differ in their implementation of the WinMain function in that they must redirect the SCM to the ServiceMain entry point. I've provided an example of calling the ServiceMain entry point in Listing 2.3.

```
int WINAPI WinMain (HINSTANCE hinstance,
HINSTANCE /* hprevious */, LPSTR lpCmdLine, int /* nShowCmd */)
{
  SERVICE_TABLE_ENTRY servicetableentry[] =
    { {"MyService", ServiceMain }, {NULL, NULL} };
  ::StartServiceCtrlDispatcher(servicetableentry);
  return 0;
```

Listing 2.3   Calling ServiceMain.

When I call the StartServiceCtrlDispatcher function, the SCM creates a second thread where it calls the ServiceMain entry point.

```
BOOL StartServiceCtrlDispatcher( LPSERVICE_TABLE_ENTRY lpServiceStart
Table);
```

If I run the executable compiled using the code in Listing 2.3 from the command line, the StartServiceCtrlDispatcher function will return the following message after 15 seconds:

ERROR_FAILED_SERVICE_CONTROLLER_CONNECT

TIP

If either StartServiceCtrlDispatcher or RegisterServiceCtrlHandler return ERROR_SERVICE_DOES_NOT_EXIST from GetLastError, most likely the NT Service was not installed properly. This can be valuable information for the operator, so when this error occurs, make certain to report this error and the possible cause in the error log.

The NT Service should perform all static initialization in the ServiceMain. The minimal ServiceMain implementation is shown in Listing 2.4.

```
SERVICE_STATUS servicestatus;
SERVICE_STATUS_HANDLE servicestatushandle;
void WINAPI ServiceCtrlHandler (DWORD dwControl);
void WINAPI ServiceMain (DWORD argc, LPTSTR * argv)
{
  servicestatus.dwServiceType = SERVICE_WIN32;
  servicestatus.dwCurrentState = SERVICE_START_PENDING;
  servicestatus.dwControlsAccepted = SERVICE_ACCEPT_STOP;
  servicestatus.dwWin32ExitCode = 0;
  servicestatus.dwServiceSpecificExitCode = 0;
  servicestatus.dwCheckPoint = 0;
  servicestatus.dwWaitHint = 0;

servicestatushandle =
  ::RegisterServiceCtrlHandler("MyService",
    ServiceCtrlHandler);
  if (servicestatushandle == (SERVICE_STATUS_HANDLE)0)
{
  return;
  }

// Initialize the service here
// ...

servicestatus.dwCheckPoint = 0;
servicestatus.dwWaitHint = 0;
servicestatus.dwCurrentState = SERVICE_RUNNING;
::SetServiceStatus(servicestatushandle, &servicestatus);

// You can use this thread or exit

  return;
}
```

Listing 2.4 Minimal ServiceMain implementation.

The ServiceMain should immediately call the RegisterServiceCtrlHandler function to register the ServiceCtrlHandler callback function with the SCM.

TIP

An interesting piece of knowledge that may help when programming very complex initializations of NT Services is that the service name is passed as the null-terminated string in the argv input parameter of the ServiceMain function.

I found this out when I was tasked with writing a generic service loader that loaded different configurations and libraries (dynamic link libraries, DLLs) depending on the name of the service. During initialization in the ServiceMain, I cross-referenced the name of the service to the configuration file and passed the configuration file name to the initialization procedures.

```
SERVICE_STATUS_HANDLE RegisterServiceCtrlHandler(
LPCTSTR lpServiceName, LPHANDLER_FUNCTION lpHandlerProc );
```

The RegisterServiceCtrlHandler function returns a SERVICE_STATUS_HANDLE that is used to notify the SCM of the service's state of well-being and capabilities.

```
BOOL SetServiceStatus ( SERVICE_STATUS_HANDLE hServiceStatus, LPSER-
VICE_STATUS lpServiceStatus);
```

Calling the SetServiceStatus function with the returned SERVICE_STATUS_HANDLE and a SERVICE_STATUS structure enables me to perform this SCM notification.

```
typedef struct _SERVICE_STATUS
{
  DWORD dwServiceType;
  DWORD dwCurrentStatus;
  DWORD dwControlsAccepted;
  DWORD dwWin32ExitCode;
  DWORD dwServiceSpecificExitCode;
  DWORD dwCheckPoint;
  DWORD dwWaitHint;
} SERVICE_STATUS, *LPSERVICE_STATUS;
```

The dwServiceType member is almost always SERVICE_WIN32_OWN_PROCESS, but other values are sometimes used.

The dwCurrentState member variable informs the SCM of the state of the service. A service has three steady states: stopped, running, and paused. It also has four transition states: start pending, stop pending, continue pending, and pause pending. Figure 2.2 is a state diagram showing the movement between states of a service.

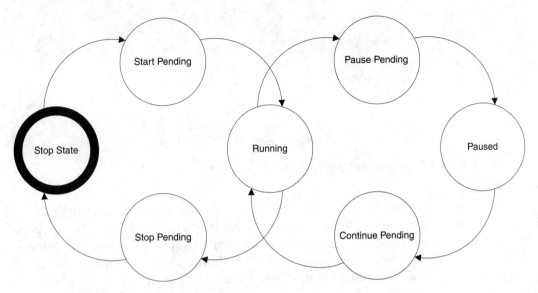

Figure 2.2 NT Service states.

This state diagram does not include any state transitions caused by abnormal operation. If the service was in the start pending state and the initialization of the service failed, then it would transition to the stopped state. The numeric equivalents of the state constants are shown in Listing 2.5.

These constants are pretty much self-explanatory. They match the states one for one that are shown in Figure 2.2.

The dwControlsAccepted member of the SERVICE_STATUS structure describes the capabilities of the service. The numeric equivalents of the bit mask flags are shown in Listing 2.6.

```
//
// Service State -- for CurrentState
//
#define SERVICE_STOPPED           0x00000001
#define SERVICE_START_PENDING     0x00000002
#define SERVICE_STOP_PENDING      0x00000003
#define SERVICE_RUNNING           0x00000004
#define SERVICE_CONTINUE_PENDING  0x00000005
#define SERVICE_PAUSE_PENDING     0x00000006
#define SERVICE_PAUSED            0x00000007
```

Listing 2.5 Numeric state constants.

```
//
// Controls Accepted   (Bit Mask)
//
#define SERVICE_ACCEPT_STOP              0x00000001
#define SERVICE_ACCEPT_PAUSE_CONTINUE    0x00000002
#define SERVICE_ACCEPT_SHUTDOWN          0x00000004
#define SERVICE_ACCEPT_PARAMCHANGE       0x00000008
#define SERVICE_ACCEPT_NETBINDCHANGE     0x00000010
```

Listing 2.6 ControlsAccepted bit mask values.

The SCM can send messages to the service to stop, pause, and continue the service. Services can tell the SCM with this flag whether they can be stopped, paused, or continued. If the SCM is not instructed to send those control messages, then it won't send them. In fact, the buttons to trigger these control messages will be grayed in the Service Control Panel applet.

TIP

Although the SCM application programming interface (API) allows for custom user-defined control messages, this seems to be more of a kludge than a reasonable implementation mechanism. Before using a custom control message, I ask myself if it would be more appropriate to send the notification using sockets, remote procedure calls (RPCs), DCOM, Common Object Request Broker Architecture (CORBA), or some other interprocess communication (IPC) mechanism.

The dwWin32ExitCode and dwServiceSpecificExitCode members of SERVICE_STATUS are used to report an exit code to the SCM. The dwService SpecificExitCode is ignored unless dwWin32ExitCode is equal to ERROR_SERVICE_SPECIFIC_ERROR.

The dwCheckPoint member of SERVICE_STATUS should be incremented between calls to SetServiceStatus to indicate to the SCM the progress of the initialization.

The dwWaitHint member of SERVICE_STATUS is the amount of time in milliseconds that the SCM should wait between calls to SetServiceStatus during initialization. If this time expires before calling SetServiceStatus, the SCM will terminate the service.

A very intelligent way of initializing a service is to break the initialization into small steps that can be reported to the SCM. As an example, if I have five initialization steps, then between each step the service should call SetServiceStatus to inform the SCM that it is still initializing. Listing 2.7 shows an example of calling the SCM between initialization steps.

```
void WINAPI ServiceMain(DWORD argc, LPTSTR * argv)
{
  servicestatus.dwServiceType = SERVICE_WIN32;
  servicestatus.dwCurrentState = SERVICE_START_PENDING;
  servicestatus.dwControlsAccepted = SERVICE_ACCEPT_STOP;
  servicestatus.dwWin32ExitCode = 0;
  servicestatus.dwServiceSpecificExitCode = 0;
  servicestatus.dwCheckPoint = 0;
  servicestatus.dwWaitHint = 0;

  servicestatushandle =
   ::RegisterServiceCtrlHandler("MyService",
     ServiceCtrlHandler);
  if (servicestatushandle == (SERVICE_STATUS_HANDLE)0)
  {
   return;
  }

  // start initialization

  servicestatus.dwCheckPoint++;
  servicestatus.dwWaitHint = 10000;
  ::SetServiceStatus(servicestatushandle, &servicestatus);

  DoStep1();

  servicestatus.dwCheckPoint++;
  ::SetServiceStatus(servicestatushandle, &servicestatus);

  DoStep2();

  servicestatus.dwCheckPoint++;
  ::SetServiceStatus(servicestatushandle, &servicestatus);

  DoStep3();

  // end initialization

  servicestatus.dwCheckPoint = 0;
  servicestatus.dwWaitHint = 0;
  servicestatus.dwCurrentState = SERVICE_RUNNING;
  ::SetServiceStatus(servicestatushandle, &servicestatus);

  // You can use this thread or exit

  return;
}
```

Listing 2.7   Calling SetServiceStatus during initialization.

Before each initialization step, I increment dwCheckPoint and call SetService-
Status. I could also have reset dwWaitHint before each call to SetServiceStatus
in order to provide a more accurate interval for each of the initialization steps.

Before exiting ServiceMain, I set dwCurrentState to SERVICE_RUNNING
and call SetServiceStatus. This tells the SCM that the service has completed
its initialization and is ready for action.

ServiceCtrlHandler

During the initialization in the ServiceMain function, the NT Service registered the ServiceCtrlHandler. The ServiceCtrlHandler receives notification
events from the SCM. The call to StartServiceCtrlDispatcher caused the SCM
to create a second thread where it invoked the ServiceMain function. The primary thread is used to receive notifications from the SCM and these notifications are forwarded to the ServiceCtrlHandler function. The call stacks of the
two threads in the startup of an NT Service are depicted in Figure 2.3.

The minimal ServiceCtrlHandler implementation is shown in Listing 2.8.

In the minimal implementation of ServiceCtrlHandler, the service simply sets
dwCurrentState to SERVICE_RUNNING and calls SetServiceStatus. In this
implementation, the service ignores the dwControl notification parameter. In
a more complete implementation, the service should check the parameter to
determine what event was triggered and perform whatever logic necessary to
handle the event. Listing 2.9 shows a complete implementation of Service-
CtrlHandler.

In this implementation, the ServiceCtrlHandler handles five different notifications: pause, continue, stop, shutdown, and interrogate. All services must
minimally handle the interrogate notification. Listing 2.10 shows all the possible control messages.

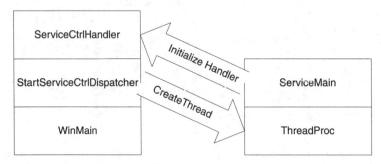

Figure 2.3   NT Service threads.

```
void WINAPI ServiceCtrlHandler (DWORD dwControl)
{
  servicestatus.dwCurrentState = SERVICE_RUNNING;
  ::SetServiceStatus(servicestatushandle, &servicestatus);
  return;
}
```

Listing 2.8   Minimal ServiceCtrlHandler implementation.

```
void WINAPI ServiceCtrlHandler (DWORD dwControl)
{
  switch (dwControl)
  {
  case SERVICE_CONTROL_PAUSE:
    servicestatus.dwCurrentState = SERVICE_PAUSE_PENDING;
    ::SetServiceStatus(servicestatushandle, &servicestatus);
    DoPause();
    servicestatus.dwCurrentState = SERVICE_PAUSED;
  break;
  case SERVICE_CONTROL_CONTINUE:
    servicestatus.dwCurrentState = SERVICE_CONTINUE_PENDING;
    ::SetServiceStatus(servicestatushandle, &servicestatus);
    DoContinue();
    servicestatus.dwCurrentState = SERVICE_RUNNING;
  break;
  case SERVICE_CONTROL_STOP:
  case SERVICE_CONTROL_SHUTDOWN:
    servicestatus.dwCurrentState = SERVICE_STOP_PENDING;
    ::SetServiceStatus(servicestatushandle, &servicestatus);
    DoStop();
    servicestatus.dwCurrentState = SERVICE_STOPPED;
  break;
  case SERVICE_CONTROL_INTERROGATE:
    servicestatus.dwCurrentState = SERVICE_RUNNING;
  break;
  }
  ::SetServiceStatus (servicestatushandle, &servicestatus);
  return;
}
```

Listing 2.9   Complete ServiceCtrlHandler implementation.

```
//
// Controls
//
#define SERVICE_CONTROL_STOP            0x00000001
#define SERVICE_CONTROL_PAUSE           0x00000002
#define SERVICE_CONTROL_CONTINUE        0x00000003
#define SERVICE_CONTROL_INTERROGATE     0x00000004
#define SERVICE_CONTROL_SHUTDOWN        0x00000005
#define SERVICE_CONTROL_PARAMCHANGE     0x00000006
#define SERVICE_CONTROL_NETBINDADD      0x00000007
#define SERVICE_CONTROL_NETBINDREMOVE   0x00000008
#define SERVICE_CONTROL_NETBINDENABLE   0x00000009
#define SERVICE_CONTROL_NETBINDDISABLE  0x0000000A
```

Listing 2.10 ServiceCtrlHandler control messages.

The SERVICE_STATUS::dwControlsAccepted member variable was set previously with very similar flags. A service must also handle all the notification events that it enumerated in this member variable.

NOTE

In Windows 2000, a new function is available called RegisterServiceCtrlHandlerEx. This function allows programmers to pass context data to their ServiceCtrlHandlerEx callback function. The ServiceCtrlHandlerEx callback function also has additional control codes.

Controlling Services

Because all manipulation of NT Services is performed through the Service Control Manager, Microsoft made available a small API that programmers can use to talk to the SCM. The functions in this API are explained in this section.

Service Control Manager COM Component

Opening and closing the SCM is done using the OpenSCManager and Close-ServiceHandle functions.

```
SC_HANDLE OpenSCManager( LPCTSTR lpMachineName, LPCTSTR lpDatabaseName,
DWORD dwDesiredAccess );
BOOL CloseServiceHandle( SC_HANDLE hSCObject );
```

An important thing to remember is to never close the SC_HANDLE with the CloseHandle function. Listing 2.11 shows how this is done.

```
SC_HANDLE handle = ::OpenSCManager(NULL, NULL, SC_MANAGER_ALL_ACCESS);
...
::CloseServiceHandle(handle);
```

Listing 2.11 Opening and closing the SCM.

The first parameter of OpenSCManager is the name of the computer on which I wish to open the SCM. If I leave this parameter as NULL, then it opens the SCM on the local machine. The second parameter allows me to specify alternative SCM databases. If the second parameter is NULL, then the default SCM database is used.

In the call to OpenSCManager, I pass as the third parameter the desired access that I wish to acquire with the handle. If operators do not have administrative rights, then they will not be allowed to open the SCM with SC_MANAGER_ALL_ACCESS as the CreateService and LockServiceDatabase functions are reserved for administrative users. Listing 2.12 shows the enumeration of these access rights.

```
//
// Service Control Manager object specific access types
//
#define GENERIC_READ                 (0x80000000L)
#define GENERIC_WRITE                (0x40000000L)
#define GENERIC_EXECUTE              (0x20000000L)

#define SC_MANAGER_CONNECT           0x0001
#define SC_MANAGER_CREATE_SERVICE    0x0002
#define SC_MANAGER_ENUMERATE_SERVICE 0x0004
#define SC_MANAGER_LOCK              0x0008
#define SC_MANAGER_QUERY_LOCK_STATUS 0x0010
#define SC_MANAGER_MODIFY_BOOT_CONFIG 0x0020

#define SC_MANAGER_ALL_ACCESS     (STANDARD_RIGHTS_REQUIRED    | \
                                   SC_MANAGER_CONNECT          | \
                                   SC_MANAGER_CREATE_SERVICE   | \
                                   SC_MANAGER_ENUMERATE_SERVICE | \
                                   SC_MANAGER_LOCK             | \
                                   SC_MANAGER_QUERY_LOCK_STATUS | \
                                   SC_MANAGER_MODIFY_BOOT_CONFIG)
```

Listing 2.12 Enumeration of SCM access rights.

Table 2.1   SCM Access Rights and Functions

SCM ACCESS RIGHTS	SCM FUNCTION
SC_MANAGER_CONNECT	OpenService
SC_MANAGER_CREATE_SERVICE	CreateService
SC_MANAGER_ENUMERATE_SERVICE	EnumServiceStatus
SC_MANAGER_LOCK	LockServiceDatabase
SC_MANAGER_QUERY_LOCK_STATUS	QueryServiceLockStatus
GENERIC_READ	EnumServiceStatus QueryServiceLockStatus
GENERIC_WRITE	CreateService
GENERIC_EXECUTE	OpenService LockServiceDatabase

Table 2.1 shows which access rights are required to call each of the SCM functions.

Once I've opened a handle to the SCM, I can use that handle to open a service using the OpenService function.

```
SC_HANDLE OpenService( SC_HANDLE hSCManager, LPCTSTR lpServiceName,
DWORD dwDesiredAccess );
```

Again, I won't forget to use the CloseServiceHandle function (not CloseHandle) to close the handle to the service. Listing 2.13 shows how to open a service.

The parameters of the OpenService call are trivial. The first parameter is the handle to the SCM. The second parameter is the key name of the service.

Each service has two names, the key name and the display name. The key name should be small, as it is used to identify the service in the Windows Registry when opening a handle to the service and to reference the service as

```
SC_HANDLE handle = ::OpenSCManager(NULL, NULL, SC_MANAGER_ALL_ACCESS);
SC_HANDLE hService = ::OpenService(handle, servicename.c_str(),
  SERVICE_ALL_ACCESS);
...
::CloseServiceHandle(hService);
::CloseServiceHandle(handle);
```

Listing 2.13   Opening a service.

a dependent. I try to keep the key name to eight or less characters with no spaces. The display name should be a very accurate name, so that applications such as the Services Control Panel applet display a name that makes sense to the operator.

The third parameter is the access rights that I wish to acquire with the service handle. Listing 2.14 presents the enumeration of access rights that can be acquired for a service.

Table 2.2 shows which access rights are required to call each of the NT Service functions.

```
//
// Service object specific access type
//
#define GENERIC_READ                    (0x80000000L)
#define GENERIC_WRITE                   (0x40000000L)
#define GENERIC_EXECUTE                 (0x20000000L)

#define DELETE                        (0x00010000L)
#define READ_CONTROL                  (0x00020000L)
#define WRITE_DAC                     (0x00040000L)
#define WRITE_OWNER                   (0x00080000L)

#define SERVICE_QUERY_CONFIG            0x0001
#define SERVICE_CHANGE_CONFIG           0x0002
#define SERVICE_QUERY_STATUS            0x0004
#define SERVICE_ENUMERATE_DEPENDENTS    0x0008
#define SERVICE_START                   0x0010
#define SERVICE_STOP                    0x0020
#define SERVICE_PAUSE_CONTINUE          0x0040
#define SERVICE_INTERROGATE             0x0080
#define SERVICE_USER_DEFINED_CONTROL    0x0100

#define SERVICE_ALL_ACCESS        (STANDARD_RIGHTS_REQUIRED      | \
                                   SERVICE_QUERY_CONFIG          | \
                                   SERVICE_CHANGE_CONFIG         | \
                                   SERVICE_QUERY_STATUS          | \
                                   SERVICE_ENUMERATE_DEPENDENTS  | \
                                   SERVICE_START                 | \
                                   SERVICE_STOP                  | \
                                   SERVICE_PAUSE_CONTINUE        | \
                                   SERVICE_INTERROGATE           | \
                                   SERVICE_USER_DEFINED_CONTROL)
```

Listing 2.14 Enumeration of service access rights.

Table 2.2 SCM Access Rights and Functions

NT SERVICE ACCESS RIGHTS	NT SERVICE FUNCTION
SERVICE_QUERY_CONFIG	QueryServiceConfig
SERVICE_CHANGE_CONFIG	ChangeServiceConfig
SERVICE_QUERY_STATUS	QueryServiceStatus
SERVICE_ENUMERATE_DEPENDENTS	EnumDependentServices
SERVICE_START	StartService
SERVICE_STOP	ControlService (stop only)
SERVICE_PAUSE_CONTINUE	ControlService (pause and continue only)
SERVICE_INTERROGATE	ControlService (interrogate only)
SERVICE_USER_DEFINED_CONTROL	ControlService (custom control messages only)
DELETE	DeleteService
READ_CONTROL	QueryServiceObjectSecurity
WRITE_DAC	SetServiceObjectSecurity
WRITE_OWNER	SetServiceObjectSecurity
GENERIC_READ	QueryServiceConfig QueryServiceStatus EnumDependentServices
GENERIC_WRITE	ChangeServiceConfig
GENERIC_EXECUTE	StartService Control Service

Starting and Stopping Services

With the service handle I can then start and stop services using the StartService and ControlService functions.

```
BOOL StartService( SC_HANDLE hService, DWORD dwNumServiceArgs, LPCTSTR
  *lpServiceArgVectors );
BOOL ControlService( SC_HANDLE hService, DWORD dwControl, LPSERVICE_STA-
  TUS lpServiceStatus );
```

To start a service, I call the StartService function and pass a handle to the service. To stop a service, I call the ControlService function and pass a handle to the service and the SERVICE_CONTROL_STOP flag. Listing 2.15 shows how to start and stop a service.

The StartService function takes optional parameters for specifying startup command-line parameters that will be passed to the service's ServiceMain

```
void StartService (const std::string & servicename)
{
  SC_HANDLE handle = ::OpenSCManager(NULL, NULL,
                          SC_MANAGER_ALL_ACCESS);
  SC_HANDLE hService = ::OpenService(handle, servicename.c_str(),
          SERVICE_ALL_ACCESS);
  ::StartService (hService, 0, NULL);
  SERVICE_STATUS servicestatus;
  ::ControlService(hService, SERVICE_CONTROL_STOP, &servicestatus);
  ::CloseServiceHandle(hService);
  ::CloseServiceHandle(handle);
}
```

Listing 2.15 Start and stop a service.

function. Both of these function parameters may be zero and NULL, if no command-line parameters need to be passed to the service's ServiceMain function.

The ControlService function sends a control message to a service. The control messages are shown in Listing 2.10 earlier in the chapter. The third parameter of the ControlService function is the SERVICE_STATUS structure where the SCM will place the latest status information received from the active service.

Registering Services

Everything I've discussed so far is useless if the SCM doesn't know the service exists. The next step is to use the functions I discussed so far and three new functions, QueryServiceStatus, DeleteService, and CreateService, in order to install and uninstall services.

```
BOOL QueryServiceStatus( SC_HANDLE hService, LPSERVICE_STATUS lpSer-
    viceStatus );
BOOL DeleteService( SC_HANDLE hService );
SC_HANDLE CreateService( SC_HANDLE hSCManager,
   LPCTSTR lpServiceName, LPCTSTR lpDisplayName,
   DWORD dwDesiredAccess, DWORD dwServiceType,
   DWORD dwStartType, DWORD dwErrorControl,
   LPCTSTR lpBinaryPathName, LPCTSTR lpLoadOrderGroup,
   LPDWORD lpdwTagId, LPCTSTR lpDependencies,
   LPCTSTR lpServiceStartName, LPCTSTR lpPassword );
```

To uninstall a service, the first thing I should do is find out if it's running and, if so, stop it. I can determine the status of a service using the QueryServiceStatus function. I can then stop the service using the DeleteService function. Listing 2.16 shows how to uninstall a service.

```
void UninstallService(const std::string & servicename)
{
  SC_HANDLE handle = ::OpenSCManager(NULL, NULL,
                         SC_MANAGER_ALL_ACCESS);
  SC_HANDLE hService = ::OpenService(handle, servicename.c_str(),
                         SERVICE_ALL_ACCESS);
  SERVICE_STATUS status;
  ::QueryServiceStatus(hService, &status);
  if (status.dwCurrentState != SERVICE_STOPPED)
  {
    ::ControlService(hService, SERVICE_CONTROL_STOP, &status);
  }
  ::DeleteService(hService);
  ::CloseServiceHandle(hService);
  ::CloseServiceHandle(handle);
};
```

Listing 2.16   Uninstall a service.

To install a service, I simply have to call the CreateService function with the appropriate arguments. Listing 2.17 shows an example of installing a service.

It is important to formulate the appropriate parameters when using the CreateService function. The second and third parameters I've left as the service name. A professional-looking NT Service would typically have a small key

```
void InstallService(const std::string & servicename)
{
  SC_HANDLE handle = ::OpenSCManager(NULL, NULL,
                         SC_MANAGER_ALL_ACCESS);
  char szFilename[256];
  ::GetModuleFileName(NULL, szFilename, 255);
  std::stringstream ss;
  ss << "\"" << szFilename << "\"";
  char dependencies []="NtLmSsp\0EventLog\0\0";
  SC_HANDLE hService = ::CreateService(handle,
    servicename.c_str(), servicename.c_str(), SERVICE_ALL_ACCESS,
    SERVICE_WIN32_OWN_PROCESS, SERVICE_AUTO_START,
    SERVICE_ERROR_IGNORE, ss.str().c_str(), NULL, NULL,
    dependencies, NULL, NULL);
  ::CloseServiceHandle(hService);
  ::CloseServiceHandle(handle);
};
```

Listing 2.17   Install a service.

name as the second parameter and a more descriptive display name as the third parameter. In the next few paragraphs, I'll show how to convert between long display names and short key names (see Listing 2.18).

The fourth parameter in the CreateService function is the access rights I wish to acquire with the service handle. (Return to the preceding discussion of OpenService for a more complete description of these rights.)

The fifth parameter is the type of service I am installing. This is similar to the SERVICE_STATUS::dwServiceType variable that I used earlier in the chapter.

The sixth parameter is the startup type of the service. Generally, I use SER-VICE_DEMAND_START, but on occasion I use SERVICE_AUTO_START. Both auto-start and demand-start allow the user to manually start the service using the SCM. Auto-start additionally tells the SCM to start the service whenever the computer is restarted.

```
//
// Start Type
//

#define SERVICE_BOOT_START          0x00000000
#define SERVICE_SYSTEM_START        0x00000001
#define SERVICE_AUTO_START          0x00000002
#define SERVICE_DEMAND_START        0x00000003
#define SERVICE_DISABLED            0x00000004
```

The seventh parameter determines what action should be taken when the service fails to start. The SERVICE_ERROR_IGNORE is the safest of options, as it does not affect the system as a whole. The higher the error type, the greater the effect on the local system. The SERVICE_ERROR_NORMAL type pops up a message box for an operator response. This type of interaction is meaningless in a production environment where the operator is not constantly looking at the screen during the startup. The best bet is to stick with the ignore error control type and notify the operator using SNMP (Simple Network Monitor Protocol) or some other type of monitor protocol.

```
//
// Error control type
//
#define SERVICE_ERROR_IGNORE        0x00000000
#define SERVICE_ERROR_NORMAL        0x00000001
#define SERVICE_ERROR_SEVERE        0x00000002
#define SERVICE_ERROR_CRITICAL      0x00000003
```

The eighth parameter is the key name of the service. This name can later be used to reference the service. The OpenService function also requires this parameter to find the service in the SCM database. The ninth parameter of the CreateService function is the long name of the service. The tenth parameter allows me to specify a startup sequence by service group. Startup groups tend to be quite difficult to manage, so I don't suggest using them.

The eleventh parameter is a dependency list. The dependency list is used by the SCM to ensure that dependent services are not started until all services that they depend on are started. If I attempt to start a service that has dependencies that are not yet started, the SCM will attempt to start the dependencies before it starts the dependent service. I typically put NtLmSsp, the NT authentication service, and EventLog, the NT Event Log, in the dependency list since most of my services depend on these services.

The last two parameters of CreateService are the username and password that will be used for authentication and authorization of security-restricted calls made by the service. When the service is initially started, the SCM will place the service in a process that has the security credentials of the username. It will also fail to load the service if the incorrect username-password is provided. If these two parameters are NULLed, then the SCM loads the service in a process that has the security credentials of the local system account. For more information on NT Security and the local system account, see Chapter 6 on security later in this book.

When I call the CreateService function, the SCM creates entries in the Windows Registry. Programmers might find themselves trying to add or change

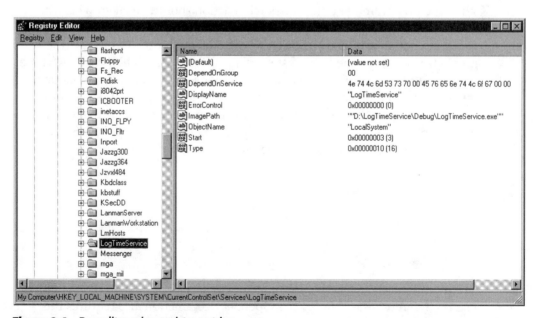

Figure 2.4 Regedit service registry entries.

their service's configuration by manually modifying the registry. If they do attempt this, they must remember that the entries are only read by the SCM when the computer is rebooted. They'll likely have to reboot the computer before the entries are recognized by the SCM. Figure 2.4 shows examples of SCM entries in Regedit.

The LogTimeService key has eight values in its root. These values match the parameters in the call to CreateService. The lpServiceName parameter of the CreateService call is the subkey name, that is, LogTimeService. The lpDisplayName parameter is the value of the DisplayName setting. The dwServiceType parameter is the value of the constant SERVICE_WIN32_OWN_PROCESS, that is, 0x10, the value of the Type setting. The dwStartType parameter is the value of the constant SERVICE_AUTO_START, that is, 0x3, the value of the Start setting. The dwErrorControl parameter is the value of the constant SERVICE_ERROR_IGNORE, that is, 0x0, the value of the ErrorControl setting. The lpBinaryPathName parameter is now the value of the ImagePath setting. And so on.

More Service Control Manager Functions

GetServiceDisplayName and GetServiceKeyName are not very useful functions unless I am trying to manage a group of services or provide an interactive SCM client.

```
BOOL GetServiceDisplayName( SC_HANDLE hSCManager,
  LPCTSTR lpServiceName, LPTSTR lpDisplayName,
  LPDWORD lpcchBuffer );
BOOL GetServiceKeyName( SC_HANDLE hSCManager,
  LPCTSTR lpDisplayName, LPTSTR lpServiceName,
  LPDWORD lpcchBuffer );
```

An interesting tool I've developed with GetServiceKeyName is shown in Listing 2.18. This tool converts a display name to a key name. I use it to quickly determine the key name when I'm looking for service dependencies.

In order to call the GetServiceKeyName function, I had to acquire a handle to the SCM first. I can then call GetServiceKeyName with the handle to the SCM and the display name of the service as input parameters. The output is placed in the third and fourth parameters, a character buffer and a length indicator.

It is not always possible to configure a service properly when it is first installed. In order to change the configuration once it has been installed, the QueryServiceConfig and ChangeServiceConfig functions can be used to read and write such changes.

```cpp
int main(int argc, char* argv[])
{
 if (argc < 2)
 {
  std::cout << "Usage: getkeyname displayname"
  << std::endl;
  return 0;
 }

 std::stringstream displayname;
 for (int i=1;i<argc;i++)
 {
   if (!displayname.str().empty())
   {
    displayname << " ";
   }
   displayname << argv[i];
 }

 char sz[256];
 DWORD dw = 255;
 SC_HANDLE handle = ::OpenSCManager(NULL, NULL,
                         SC_MANAGER_ALL_ACCESS);
 ::GetServiceKeyName(handle, displayname.str().c_str(), sz,
  &dw);
 ::CloseServiceHandle(handle);

 std::cout << "Key name = " << sz << std::endl;

 return 0;
}
```

Listing 2.18 GetServiceKeyName.

```cpp
BOOL QueryServiceConfig( SC_HANDLE hService,
   LPQUERY_SERVICE_CONFIG lpServiceConfig, DWORD cbBufSize,
   LPDWORD pcbBytesNeeded );
BOOL ChangeServiceConfig( SC_HANDLE hService,
   DWORD dwServiceType, DWORD dwStartType,
   DWORD dwErrorControl, LPCTSTR lpBinaryPathName,
   LPCTSTR lpLoadOrderGroup, LPDWORD lpdwTagId,
   LPCTSTR lpDependencies, LPCTSTR lpServiceStartName,
   LPCTSTR lpPassword, LPCTSTR lpDisplayName );
```

A common task is switching a service's startup mode between auto-start and demand-start. The ChangeServiceConfig function may be used to switch a service's startup mode. Listing 2.19 is the source code that programmatically toggles a service's startup mode.

```
int main(int argc, char* argv[])
{
 if (argc != 2)
 {
  std::cout << "Usage: togglestartupmode keyname"
  << std::endl;
  return 0;
 }

 SC_HANDLE handle = ::OpenSCManager(NULL, NULL,
                         SC_MANAGER_ALL_ACCESS);
 SC_HANDLE hService = ::OpenService(handle, argv[1],
                         SERVICE_ALL_ACCESS);

 QUERY_SERVICE_CONFIG cfg;
 DWORD dw;
 ::QueryServiceConfig(hService, &cfg,
     sizeof(cfg), &dw);
 switch(cfg.dwStartType)
 {
 case SERVICE_AUTO_START:
  std::cout << "Toggle to demand start" << std::endl;
  cfg.dwStartType = SERVICE_DEMAND_START;
  break;
 case SERVICE_DEMAND_START:
  std::cout << "Toggle to auto start" << std::endl;
  cfg.dwStartType = SERVICE_AUTO_START;
  break;
 default:
  std::cout << "Invalid start type" << std::endl;
  return 0;
 }
 ::ChangeServiceConfig(hService, SERVICE_NO_CHANGE,
  cfg.dwStartType, SERVICE_NO_CHANGE, NULL, NULL, NULL,
  NULL, NULL, NULL, cfg.lpDisplayName);

 ::CloseServiceHandle(hService);
 ::CloseServiceHandle(handle);

 return 0;
}
```

Listing 2.19   Toggling a service's startup mode.

The QueryServiceConfig and ChangeServiceConfig functions can be used to change any of the service configuration members of the QUERY_SERVICE_CONFIG structure.

```
typedef struct _QUERY_SERVICE_CONFIG {
    DWORD   dwServiceType;
    DWORD   dwStartType;
    DWORD   dwErrorControl;
    LPSTR   lpBinaryPathName;
    LPSTR   lpLoadOrderGroup;
    DWORD   dwTagId;
    LPSTR   lpDependencies;
    LPSTR   lpServiceStartName;
    LPSTR   lpDisplayName;
} QUERY_SERVICE_CONFIG, *LPQUERY_SERVICE_CONFIG;
```

The members of the QUERY_SERVICE_CONFIG structure are very similar to the parameters of the call to CreateService. They are also similar to the value in the Registry for the service.

If programmers get into managing a large amount of services, they may be interested in the functions that give them access to a large amount of SCM detail: EnumDependentServices, EnumServicesStatus, QueryServiceLockStatus, LockServiceDatabase, and UnlockServiceDatabase.

```
BOOL EnumDependentServices( SC_HANDLE hService,
    DWORD dwServiceState, LPENUM_SERVICE_STATUS lpServices,
    DWORD cbBufSize, LPDWORD pcbBytesNeeded,
    LPDWORD lpServicesReturned );
BOOL EnumServicesStatus( SC_HANDLE hSCManager,
    DWORD dwServiceType, DWORD dwServiceState,
    LPENUM_SERVICE_STATUS lpServices, DWORD cbBufSize,
    LPDWORD pcbBytesNeeded, LPDWORD lpServicesReturned,
    LPDWORD lpResumeHandle );
BOOL QueryServiceLockStatus( SC_HANDLE hSCManager,
    LPQUERY_SERVICE_LOCK_STATUS lpLockStatus, DWORD cbBufSize,
    LPDWORD pcbBytesNeeded );
SC_LOCK LockServiceDatabase( SC_HANDLE hSCManager );
BOOL UnlockServiceDatabase( SC_LOCK ScLock );
```

I particularly like using EnumServicesStatus to provide on overview of the status of services on a particular machine. Listing 2.20 is the source code for another utility I use to quickly dump the status information of each service.

This is likely similar to the code that WinMsd and the Service Control Panel applet use to display the status of the various services. The EnumServicesStatus function can be used to retrieve the status of several services at a time. Programmers must maintain a handle (resumehandle) and pass it to the EnumServicesStatus function to indicate which service statuses have already been returned.

When I create a service with the CreateService function, NT assigns a SECURITY_DESCRIPTOR to the service. I can both query and modify the descriptor using the QueryServiceObjectSecurity and SetServiceObjectSecurity functions.

```
int main(int argc, char* argv[])
{
 ENUM_SERVICE_STATUS enumeration[10];
 DWORD bytesneeded, servicesreturned;
 DWORD resumehandle = 0;

 SC_HANDLE handle = ::OpenSCManager(NULL, NULL,
                              SC_MANAGER_ALL_ACCESS);

 while (::EnumServicesStatus(handle, SERVICE_WIN32,
         SERVICE_STATE_ALL, enumeration,
         sizeof(ENUM_SERVICE_STATUS)*10,
         &bytesneeded, &servicesreturned, &resumehandle) ||
 ::GetLastError() == ERROR_MORE_DATA)
 {
  for (int i=0;i<servicesreturned;i++)
  {
   std::cout << enumeration[i].lpServiceName
                        << "\t";
   switch (enumeration[i]
                    .ServiceStatus.dwCurrentState)
   {
   case SERVICE_STOPPED:
    std::cout << "Stopped";
    break;
   case SERVICE_START_PENDING:
    std::cout << "Start Pending";
    break;
   case SERVICE_STOP_PENDING:
    std::cout << "Stop Pending";
    break;
   case SERVICE_RUNNING:
    std::cout << "Running";
    break;
   case SERVICE_CONTINUE_PENDING:
    std::cout << "Continue Pending";
    break;
   case SERVICE_PAUSE_PENDING:
    std::cout << "Pause Pending";
    break;
   case SERVICE_PAUSED:
    std::cout << "Paused";
    break;
   }
   std::cout << std::endl;
  }
  if (resumehandle == 0)
```

Continues

Listing 2.20 Dump service status information.

```
    {
      break;
    }
  };

  ::CloseServiceHandle(handle);
  return 0;
}
```

Listing 2.20 Dump service status information *(Continued)*.

```
BOOL QueryServiceObjectSecurity( SC_HANDLE hService,
     SECURITY_INFORMATION dwSecurityInformation,
     PSECURITY_DESCRIPTOR lpSecurityDescriptor,
     DWORD cbBufSize, LPDWORD pcbBytesNeeded );
BOOL SetServiceObjectSecurity( SC_HANDLE hService,
     SECURITY_INFORMATION dwSecurityInformation,
     PSECURITY_DESCRIPTOR lpSecurityDescriptor );
```

In Chapter 6, I discuss security in detail. At that time, I'll explain SECURITY_
DESCRIPTOR structures and how they determine who can interact with
securable objects.

NOTE
Windows 2000 has four new functions for working with NT Services. These new functions add little value to the existing ancestral functions that I've already explained. They are ChangeServiceConfig2, EnumServicesStatusEx, QueryServiceConfig2, and QueryServiceStatusEx.

Multiservice Processes

Several of the services are implemented in the module services.exe located in the System32 directory. The services implemented in this one module (NT 4.0, SP5) are the Alerter, Browser, DHCP, EventLog, LanmanServer, Lanman-Workstation, LmHost, Messenger, NtLmSsp, and PlugPlay. That's a lot of services in one module. But beyond being in the same module these services also share a common process. How a service shares its process space with other services is explained in the next few paragraphs.

When I called CreateService, I passed the parameter SERVICE_WIN32_OWN_
PROCESS. This function parameter implies that the services will not share their process space with other services. This parameter is the service type and can actually contain any of the values shown in Listing 2.21.

```
//
// Service Types (Bit Mask)
//
#define SERVICE_KERNEL_DRIVER          0x00000001
#define SERVICE_FILE_SYSTEM_DRIVER     0x00000002
#define SERVICE_ADAPTER                0x00000004
#define SERVICE_RECOGNIZER_DRIVER      0x00000008

#define SERVICE_DRIVER            (SERVICE_KERNEL_DRIVER | \
                                  SERVICE_FILE_SYSTEM_DRIVER | \
                                  SERVICE_RECOGNIZER_DRIVER)


#define SERVICE_WIN32_OWN_PROCESS      0x00000010
#define SERVICE_WIN32_SHARE_PROCESS    0x00000020
#define SERVICE_WIN32             (SERVICE_WIN32_OWN_PROCESS | \
                          SERVICE_WIN32_SHARE_PROCESS)


#define SERVICE_INTERACTIVE_PROCESS    0x00000100


#define SERVICE_TYPE_ALL          (SERVICE_WIN32   | \
                                  SERVICE_ADAPTER  | \
                                  SERVICE_DRIVER   | \
                                  SERVICE_INTERACTIVE_PROCESS)
```

Listing 2.21   Service types.

One such service type is SERVICE_WIN32_SHARE_PROCESS. If I specify this service type, then the SCM will attempt to start all services contained within the module in the same process space. Listing 2.17 provides a function to install a service that does not share its process space. Listing 2.22 shows an alternate function for installing a service that does share its process space.

There are a few more things required in order to share one process space among many services. For each service implemented in the module, I'll have to provide an entry in the SERVICE_TABLE_ENTRY array that tells the SCM the location of the service's entry point. Listing 2.23 shows an example of multiple entries in the SERVICE_TABLE_ENTRY array.

Alternatively, the two services may also have two separate service entry points. Listing 2.23 shows an example of setting the SERVICE_TABLE_ENTRY array for two services that have separate service entry points.

An important element not to miss in this code is that the SERVICE_TABLE_ ENTRY array must be terminated with a NULL entry. This is true whether there is one or more than one entry.

```cpp
void InstallServiceWithSharedProcess(const std::string & servicename)
{
  SC_HANDLE handle = ::OpenSCManager(NULL, NULL,
                            SC_MANAGER_ALL_ACCESS);
  char szFilename[256];
  ::GetModuleFileName(NULL, szFilename, 255);
  std::stringstream ss;
  ss << "\"" << szFilename << "\"";
  char dependencies []="NtLmSsp\0EventLog\0\0";
  SC_HANDLE hService = ::CreateService(handle,
      servicename.c_str(), servicename.c_str(),
      SERVICE_ALL_ACCESS, SERVICE_WIN32_SHARE_PROCESS,
      SERVICE_AUTO_START, SERVICE_ERROR_IGNORE, ss.str().c_str(),
      NULL, NULL, dependencies, NULL, NULL);
  ::CloseServiceHandle(hService);
  ::CloseServiceHandle(handle);
};
```

Listing 2.22   Install a service with shared process.

When the ServiceMain routine is called, the service name will be passed as
the first argv array element. If two or more services share a service entry
point, then I can differentiate which service is being started using the service
name passed in as the first argv array element.

The last thing to consider is which service is receiving a control message in
the ServiceCtrlHandler function. The only way to tell is to register different
service control handler functions for each service that will share the process
space. Listing 2.24 shows how to register separate control handler functions
from a common ServiceMain function using the service name that is passed
in as the first argv array element.

```cpp
int WINAPI WinMain(HINSTANCE hinstance,
  HINSTANCE /* hprevious */, LPSTR lpCmdLine, int /* nShowCmd */)
{
  SERVICE_TABLE_ENTRY servicetableentry[] =
    { {"MyFirstService", ServiceMain },
    {"MySecondService", ServiceMain }, {NULL, NULL} };
  ::StartServiceCtrlDispatcher(servicetableentry);
  return 0;
}
```

Listing 2.23   Multiple SERVICE_TABLE_ENTRYs.

```
void WINAPI ServiceMain(DWORD argc, LPTSTR * argv)
{
 //...

 if (std::string("MyFirstService") == argv[0])
 {
  servicestatushandle =
    ::RegisterServiceCtrlHandler("MyFirstService",
     ServiceCtrlHandler1);
 }
 else if (std::string("MySecondService") == argv[0])
 {
  servicestatushandle =
    ::RegisterServiceCtrlHandler("MySecondService",
     ServiceCtrlHandler2);
 }
 else
 {
  return;
 }

 //...
 return;
}
```

Listing 2.24   Multiple ServiceCtrlHandler and common ServiceMain.

If I implemented two or more separate service entry-points, then registering two or more separate service control handler functions is really easy. Listing 2.25 shows two service entry points that register two separate service control handler functions.

I'm not a big fan of services sharing process spaces, so I won't speak of it again in this book. However, there are some reasons why sharing process space is important. Some service might need to share large amounts of active memory. The active memory could be shared across processes using memory maps, but a less-complex implementation might be to move the two services into the same process space.

The disadvantage of sharing process space is that failures in one service may have a negative effect on the other service that shares the same process space. Assuming two services have separate process spaces, then failures in one would likely be localized to the one process and the one service.

```
void WINAPI ServiceMain1(DWORD argc, LPTSTR * argv)
{
 //...

 servicestatushandle =
  ::RegisterServiceCtrlHandler("MyFirstService",
     ServiceCtrlHandler1);

 //...
 return;
}

void WINAPI ServiceMain2(DWORD argc, LPTSTR * argv)
{
 //...

 servicestatushandle = ::RegisterServiceCtrlHandler(
    "MySecondService", ServiceCtrlHandler2);

 //...
 return;
}
```

Listing 2.25   Multiple ServiceCtrlHandler and multiple ServiceMain.

The next section presents a reusable framework for implementing NT Services. This reusable framework must be extended if services are to share common process space.

Generic C++ Service

In this section, I present a reusable C++ class that can be used to develop services. Once this reusable framework is completed, it is easy to create a large amount of NT Services with very little coding required. Listing 2.26 shows the C++ class declaration for the reusable NT Service framework.

I'm a fan of using C++ namespaces. Using namespaces has a lot of advantages. The big advantage is that programmers do not have to worry about creating unique identifiers that don't conflict with other libraries. My class is called Service. I'm sure other classes have the same name, but I don't have to worry about conflicts because my class is contained within a namespace.

```
namespace NtService
{

class Service
{
public:
  Service();
  Service(const Service & rhs);
  Service(const std::string & servicename);
  virtual ~Service();
  Service & operator=(const Service & rhs);
  void Start(char * commandline);
  // Event Handlers
  virtual void OnInitialize();
  virtual void OnRun();
  virtual void OnInterrogate();
  virtual void OnPause();
  virtual void OnContinue();
  virtual void OnStop();
  virtual void OnInstall();
  virtual void OnUninstall();
  // Notify SCM
  void Stopped();
  void Paused();
  void Running();
  void StartPending(DWORD dwWaitHint = 10000);
  void StopPending();
  void PausePending();
  void ContinuePending();
  // State Accessor
  bool IsPaused();
  // Configuration
  void AcceptPause(bool b = true);
};

}; // end namespace NtService
```

Listing 2.26 Service class.

A very important part of architecture is to build simple interfaces, not complex ones. That was my intent when developing this class. The interface in C++ is typically everything that would be found in the class's header file. In my Service class, I've limited the class to 23 methods and very few method parameters, so it should be quite easy to use. Listing 2.27 shows the implementation (the guts).

```
namespace
{

SERVICE_STATUS servicestatus;
SERVICE_STATUS_HANDLE servicestatushandle;
std::string servicename;
bool paused = false;
NtService::Service * service = NULL;

void WINAPI ServiceCtrlHandler(DWORD dwControl)
{
  switch (dwControl)
  {
  case SERVICE_CONTROL_PAUSE:
   service->OnPause();
  break;
  case SERVICE_CONTROL_CONTINUE:
   service->OnContinue();
  break;
  case SERVICE_CONTROL_STOP:
  case SERVICE_CONTROL_SHUTDOWN:
   service->OnStop();
  break;
  case SERVICE_CONTROL_INTERROGATE:
   service->OnInterrogate();
  break;
  }
};
void WINAPI ServiceMain(DWORD argc, LPTSTR * argv)
{
  servicestatus.dwServiceType = SERVICE_WIN32;
  servicestatus.dwCurrentState = SERVICE_START_PENDING;
  servicestatus.dwControlsAccepted = SERVICE_ACCEPT_STOP;
  servicestatus.dwWin32ExitCode = 0;
  servicestatus.dwServiceSpecificExitCode = 0;
  servicestatus.dwCheckPoint = 0;
  servicestatus.dwWaitHint = 0;

  servicestatushandle =
   ::RegisterServiceCtrlHandler(servicename.c_str(),
                      ServiceCtrlHandler);
  if (servicestatushandle == (SERVICE_STATUS_HANDLE)0)
  {
   return;
  }

  service->OnInitialize();  service->Running();
  service->OnRun();
```

Continues

Listing 2.27   Service implementation.

```
   return;
};

};

namespace NtService
{

Service::Service()
{
   service = this;
};

Service::Service(const std::string & _servicename)
{
 servicename = _servicename;
   service = this;
};

Service::Service(const Service & rhs)
{
  // NO STATE
};

Service::~Service()
{
};

Service & Service::operator=(const Service & rhs)
{
  // NO STATE
  return *this;
};

void Service::Start(char * commandline)
{
  char * seps = " -/\t\n";
  char * token = ::strtok(commandline, seps );
  int i=0;
  while( token != NULL )
  {
   // Register as Service
   if (::_stricmp(token, "service")==0)
   {
      OnInstall();
      return;
   }

   // Unregister as Service
   if (::_stricmp(token, "unregserver")==0)
   {
```

Continues

Listing 2.27

```
  OnUninstall();
    return;
  }

  /* Get next token: */
  token = ::strtok( NULL, seps );
  }

  SERVICE_TABLE_ENTRY servicetableentry[] =
  {
  { const_cast<char *>(servicename.c_str()), ServiceMain },
  { NULL, NULL }
  };
  ::StartServiceCtrlDispatcher(servicetableentry);
};

// Event Handlers
void Service::OnInitialize()
{
  // Do nothing
  StartPending();
};

void Service::OnRun()
{
  // Do nothing
};

void Service::OnInterrogate()
{
  if (IsPaused())
  {
   Paused();
  }
  else
  {
   Running();
  }
};

void Service::OnPause()
{
  Paused();
};

void Service::OnContinue()
{
  Running();
};

void Service::OnStop()
```

Continues

Listing 2.27 Service implementation *(Continued)*.

```
{
  Stopped();
};

void Service::OnInstall()
{
  Service::OnUninstall();
  SC_HANDLE handle = ::OpenSCManager(NULL, NULL,
        SC_MANAGER_ALL_ACCESS);
  char szFilename[256];
  ::GetModuleFileName(NULL, szFilename, 255);
  std::stringstream ss;
  ss << "\"" << szFilename << "\"";
  char dependencies []="NtLmSsp\0EventLog\0\0";
  SC_HANDLE hService = ::CreateService(handle,
      servicename.c_str(), servicename.c_str(),
      SERVICE_ALL_ACCESS, SERVICE_WIN32_OWN_PROCESS,
      SERVICE_DEMAND_START, SERVICE_ERROR_IGNORE,
      ss.str().c_str(), NULL, NULL, dependencies, NULL, NULL);
  ::CloseServiceHandle(hService);
  ::CloseServiceHandle(handle);
};

void Service::OnUninstall()
{
  SERVICE_STATUS status;
  SC_HANDLE handle = ::OpenSCManager(NULL, NULL,
SC_MANAGER_ALL_ACCESS);
  SC_HANDLE hService = ::OpenService(handle, servicename.c_str(),
        SERVICE_ALL_ACCESS);
  ::QueryServiceStatus(hService, &status);
  if (status.dwCurrentState != SERVICE_STOPPED)
  {
    ::ControlService(hService, SERVICE_CONTROL_STOP, &status);
  }
  ::DeleteService(hService);
  ::CloseServiceHandle(hService);
  ::CloseServiceHandle(handle);
};

// Notify SCM
void Service::Stopped()
{
  servicestatus.dwCurrentState = SERVICE_STOPPED;
  ::SetServiceStatus(servicestatushandle, &servicestatus);
  paused = false;
};

void Service::Paused()
```

Continues

Listing 2.27

```
{
  servicestatus.dwCurrentState = SERVICE_PAUSED;
  ::SetServiceStatus(servicestatushandle, &servicestatus);
  paused = true;
};

void Service::Running()
{
  servicestatus.dwCurrentState = SERVICE_RUNNING;
  ::SetServiceStatus(servicestatushandle, &servicestatus);
  paused = false;
};

void Service::StartPending(DWORD dwWaitHint)
{
  servicestatus.dwCurrentState = SERVICE_RUNNING;
  servicestatus.dwWaitHint = dwWaitHint;
  ::SetServiceStatus(servicestatushandle, &servicestatus);
};

void Service::StopPending()
{
  servicestatus.dwCurrentState = SERVICE_STOP_PENDING;
  ::SetServiceStatus(servicestatushandle, &servicestatus);
};

void Service::PausePending()
{
  servicestatus.dwCurrentState = SERVICE_PAUSE_PENDING;
  ::SetServiceStatus(servicestatushandle, &servicestatus);
};

void Service::ContinuePending()
{
  servicestatus.dwCurrentState = SERVICE_CONTINUE_PENDING;
  ::SetServiceStatus(servicestatushandle, &servicestatus);
};

// State Accessor
bool Service::IsPaused()
{
  return paused;
};

// Configuration
void Service::AcceptPause(bool b)
{
  servicestatus.dwControlsAccepted |=
    SERVICE_ACCEPT_PAUSE_CONTINUE;
};

}; // end namespace NtService
```

Listing 2.27 Service implementation *(Continued)*.

As this code shows, the Service class does not maintain any state data. All the state data is saved in global variables in the implementation.

TIP

Saving state data as global variables is not generally considered good practice. In this case, I made an exception since this improved encapsulation without loss of functionality. This should only be done with classes that do not have per-object state.

The servicestatus and servicestatushandle variables are used in the call to the SetServiceStatus function.

```
SERVICE_STATUS servicestatus;

SERVICE_STATUS_HANDLE servicestatushandle;
```

The servicename is used during the initialization and installation routines: ServiceMain, Start, Install, and Uninstall.

```
std::string servicename;
```

The paused variable is used to signal whether the service is paused or not. This would allow classes derived from Service to implement the capability to pause and continue.

```
bool paused = false;
```

The service variable is simply a pointer to this. The self-pointer was required in order to pass the object instance to the global functions: ThreadProc, ServiceCtrlHandler, and ServiceMain.

```
NtService::Service * service = NULL;
```

The next global function is ServiceCtrlHandler. In this function, I simply interpret the dwControl parameter and pass the control message to the appropriate notification method: OnPause, OnContinue, OnStop, and OnInterrogate. I can reimplement any of these notification handlers by overriding the corresponding virtual method.

```
void WINAPI ServiceCtrlHandler(DWORD dwControl)
{
  switch (dwControl)
  {
  case SERVICE_CONTROL_PAUSE:
   service->OnPause();
  break;
  case SERVICE_CONTROL_CONTINUE:
   service->OnContinue();
  break;
  case SERVICE_CONTROL_STOP:
  case SERVICE_CONTROL_SHUTDOWN:
   service->OnStop();
  break;
```

```
  case SERVICE_CONTROL_INTERROGATE:
    service->OnInterrogate();
  break;
  }
};
```

The ServiceMain function is similar to the one shown earlier in the chapter in Listing 2.7. The only differences are that this one uses the servicename variable when calling RegisterServiceCtrlHandler instead of hard-coding the service name and the OnInitialize virtual method is called. I can override the OnInitialize method to perform implementation-specific initialization.

```
void WINAPI ServiceMain(DWORD argc, LPTSTR * argv)
{
  servicestatus.dwServiceType = SERVICE_WIN32;
  servicestatus.dwCurrentState = SERVICE_START_PENDING;
  servicestatus.dwControlsAccepted = SERVICE_ACCEPT_STOP;
  servicestatus.dwWin32ExitCode = 0;
  servicestatus.dwServiceSpecificExitCode = 0;
  servicestatus.dwCheckPoint = 0;
  servicestatus.dwWaitHint = 0;

  servicestatushandle =
    ::RegisterServiceCtrlHandler(servicename.c_str(),
                      ServiceCtrlHandler);
  if (servicestatushandle == (SERVICE_STATUS_HANDLE)0)
  {
    return;
  }

  service->OnInitialize();
  service->Running();
  service->OnRun();
  return;
};
```

The parameterized constructor should always be called at least once at the start of the service. If I derive a subclass from Service, my subclass should call the parameterized constructor in order to pass the service name to the framework.

```
Service::Service(const std::string & _servicename)
{
        servicename = _servicename;
    service = this;
};
```

The start method scans the command line for the -service and -unregserver parameters. If it encounters either of these command-line parameters, then it runs the Install or Uninstall routines. If it does not encounter either of these command-line parameters, then it calls StartServiceCtrlDispatcher to start the service.

```
void Service::Start(char * commandline)
{
  char * seps = " -/\t\n";
  char * token = ::strtok(commandline, seps );
  int i=0;
  while( token != NULL )
  {
   // Register as Service
   if (::_stricmp(token, "service")==0)
   {
        OnInstall();
        return;
   }

   // Unregister as Service
   if (::_stricmp(token, "unregserver")==0)
   {
        OnUninstall();
     return;
   }

   /* Get next token: */
   token = ::strtok( NULL, seps );
  }

  SERVICE_TABLE_ENTRY servicetableentry[] =
  {
   { const_cast<char *>(servicename.c_str()), ServiceMain },
   { NULL, NULL }
  };
  ::StartServiceCtrlDispatcher(servicetableentry);
};
```

The OnInitialize, OnRun, OnInterrogate, OnPause, OnContinue, and OnStop virtual methods can be overridden to perform custom handling of these events. If I override any of these virtual methods, then I can't forget to call the appropriate state functions to inform the SCM of the service's state. If I do not call these functions appropriately, then I may experience instances in which the SCM shuts the service down because it hasn't received appropriate status messages.

```
// Event Handlers
void Service::OnInitialize()
{
  // Do nothing
  StartPending();
};

void Service::OnRun()
{
  // Do nothing
};
```

```
void Service::OnInterrogate()
{
  if (IsPaused())
  {
   Paused();
  }
  else
  {
   Running();
  }
};

void Service::OnPause()
{
  Paused();
};

void Service::OnContinue()
{
  Running();
};

void Service::OnStop()
{
  Stopped();
};
```

The last few functions represent the events that may be triggered with an NT Service. When the service is initially started, the OnInitialize method is called. After the service is initialized, the OnRun method is called. When the Pause, Continue, or Stop buttons are clicked in the Services Control Panel applet, the OnPause, OnContinue, and OnStop methods are called, respectively. I can implement these events by overriding the virtual functions.

The installation routines are similar to those presented in Listing 2.17. If I want to add my own install and uninstall code, then I override this virtual method. If I override the OnInstall or OnUninstall method, I can still call the parent method to perform the basic service installation.

```
void Service::OnInstall()
{
  Service::OnUninstall();
  SC_HANDLE handle = ::OpenSCManager(NULL, NULL,
  SC_MANAGER_ALL_ACCESS);
  char szFilename[256];
  ::GetModuleFileName(NULL, szFilename, 255);
  std::stringstream ss;
  ss << "\"" << szFilename << "\"";
  char dependencies []="NtLmSsp\0EventLog\0\0";
  SC_HANDLE hService = ::CreateService(handle,
```

```
        servicename.c_str(), servicename.c_str(),
        SERVICE_ALL_ACCESS, SERVICE_WIN32_OWN_PROCESS,
        SERVICE_DEMAND_START, SERVICE_ERROR_IGNORE,
        ss.str().c_str(), NULL, NULL, dependencies, NULL, NULL);
    ::CloseServiceHandle(hService);
    ::CloseServiceHandle(handle);
};

void Service::OnUninstall()
{
    SERVICE_STATUS status;
    SC_HANDLE handle = ::OpenSCManager(NULL, NULL,
                        SC_MANAGER_ALL_ACCESS);
    SC_HANDLE hService = ::OpenService(handle,
        servicename.c_str(), SERVICE_ALL_ACCESS);
    ::QueryServiceStatus(hService, &status);
    if (status.dwCurrentState != SERVICE_STOPPED)
    {
      ::ControlService(hService, SERVICE_CONTROL_STOP, &status);
    }
    ::DeleteService(hService);
    ::CloseServiceHandle(hService);
    ::CloseServiceHandle(handle);
};
```

The Stopped, Paused, Running, StartPending, StopPending, PausePending, and ContinuePending functions can be use to inform the SCM of the service's status. Before I leave any notification methods, I should update my status with the SCM by calling one of these notification methods.

```
void Service::Stopped()
{
    servicestatus.dwCurrentState = SERVICE_STOPPED;
    ::SetServiceStatus(servicestatushandle, &servicestatus);
    paused = false;
};

void Service::Paused()
{
    servicestatus.dwCurrentState = SERVICE_PAUSED;
    ::SetServiceStatus(servicestatushandle, &servicestatus);
    paused = true;
};

void Service::Running()
{
    servicestatus.dwCurrentState = SERVICE_RUNNING;
    ::SetServiceStatus(servicestatushandle, &servicestatus);
    paused = false;
};

void Service::StartPending(DWORD dwWaitHint)
{
```

```
   servicestatus.dwCurrentState = SERVICE_RUNNING;
   servicestatus.dwWaitHint = dwWaitHint;
   ::SetServiceStatus(servicestatushandle, &servicestatus);
};

void Service::StopPending()
{
   servicestatus.dwCurrentState = SERVICE_STOP_PENDING;
   ::SetServiceStatus(servicestatushandle, &servicestatus);
};

void Service::PausePending()
{
   servicestatus.dwCurrentState = SERVICE_PAUSE_PENDING;
   ::SetServiceStatus(servicestatushandle, &servicestatus);
};

void Service::ContinuePending()
{
   servicestatus.dwCurrentState = SERVICE_CONTINUE_PENDING;
   ::SetServiceStatus(servicestatushandle, &servicestatus);
};
```

IsPaused and AcceptPause are helper methods that aid the programmer in determining whether the service is paused and informing the SCM that it accepts pause notifications.

```
bool Service::IsPaused()
{
   return paused;
};

void Service::AcceptPause(bool b)
{
   servicestatus.dwControlsAccepted |=
     SERVICE_ACCEPT_PAUSE_CONTINUE;
};
```

Now that there is a C++ framework in place, I can instantiate the service by simply creating the object and calling the Start method. This can be done in one line of code (see Listing 2.28).

```
int WINAPI WinMain(HINSTANCE hinstance,
  HINSTANCE /* hprevious */, LPSTR lpCmdLine, int /* nShowCmd */)
{
   NtService::Service("MyService").Start(lpCmdLine);
   return 0;
}
```

Listing 2.28 Start your service.

The service in Listing 2.28 is quite boring. It allows me to start and stop a service. The service simply creates a thread and terminates the thread immediately. That's it. In order to provide implementation that actually does something beyond acting like a service, I could derive a subclass from the Service class and override one or more of the virtual methods.

To demonstrate how to derive a service implementation from the Service class, I will create a service that appends the current time to a file. Listing 2.29 shows the code for this service.

A very minimal program indeed. The framework pretty much handles everything for me, so I can concentrate on the implementation. I enabled pausing in this service by calling AcceptPause in the OnInitialize routine and by checking the IsPaused method before I did any real activity. I can also call the

```
class LogTimeService : public NtService::Service
{
public:
  LogTimeService()
    :NtService::Service("LogTimeService") {};
  virtual void OnRun()
  {
   std::ofstream of;
   of.open("d:\\logtime.log");
   while (true)
   {
     if (!IsPaused())
   {
      of << ::GetTickCount() << std::endl;
   }
     ::Sleep(1000);
   }
  }
  virtual void OnInitialize()
  {
   AcceptPause();
  }
};

int WINAPI WinMain(HINSTANCE hinstance,
  HINSTANCE /* hprevious */, LPSTR lpCmdLine, int /* nShowCmd */)
{
  LogTimeService().Start(lpCmdLine);
  return 0;
}
```

Listing 2.29   LogTimeService.

AcceptPause method at any time to enable pausing, as well as disable pausing by calling the AcceptPause method with the false parameter.

Later in the book, I write a socket server with this framework. In this service, I implement more functionality in order to demonstrate other benefits of the framework.

Visual Basic Services

Let me start by saying that I don't consider Visual Basic an appropriate language for creating NT Services. Before programmers attempt to make a Visual Basic NT Service, they should take another day to reflect on this decision. Visual Basic is not an appropriate language for creating such components. But when push comes to shove, some programmers will ignore this sane advice and proceed with the development of yet another Visual Basic NT Service. Don't tell me later that I didn't warn you.

Don't NT Service My Visual Basic

Why the naysayer? Why do I preach against implementing NT Services in Visual Basic? Because VB is a high-level language and most VB developers work at that level. That is, there is little expertise in working with the SCM directly. If programmers run into trouble, there is nobody out there that can help them. Whereas, if they took the time and wrote their services in C++, they'd find a thousand times the expertise.

Since some will ignore my advice, I might as well demonstrate how to do the evil VB NT Service the correct way. The first thing I'll have to do is import all the NT Service symbol definitions into a .BAS module. Listing 2.30 shows the constant definitions that I'll need to program NT Services with VB.

```
Option Explicit

Private Const SERVICE_WIN32_OWN_PROCESS = &H10&
Private Const SERVICE_WIN32_SHARE_PROCESS = &H20&
Private Const SERVICE_WIN32 = SERVICE_WIN32_OWN_PROCESS + _
  SERVICE_WIN32_SHARE_PROCESS
```

Continues

Listing 2.30 Constant definitions.

```
Private Const SERVICE_ACCEPT_STOP = &H1
Private Const SERVICE_ACCEPT_PAUSE_CONTINUE = &H2
Private Const SERVICE_ACCEPT_SHUTDOWN = &H4
Private Const SERVICE_ACCEPT_PARAMCHANGE = &H8
Private Const SERVICE_ACCEPT_NETBINDCHANGE = &H10&

Private Const SC_MANAGER_CONNECT = &H1
Private Const SC_MANAGER_CREATE_SERVICE = &H2
Private Const SC_MANAGER_ENUMERATE_SERVICE = &H4
Private Const SC_MANAGER_LOCK = &H8
Private Const SC_MANAGER_QUERY_LOCK_STATUS = &H10
Private Const SC_MANAGER_MODIFY_BOOT_CONFIG = &H20
Private Const SC_MANAGER_ALL_ACCESS = (STANDARD_RIGHTS_REQUIRED Or _
                          SC_MANAGER_CONNECT Or _
                          SC_MANAGER_CREATE_SERVICE Or _
                          SC_MANAGER_ENUMERATE_SERVICE Or _
                          SC_MANAGER_LOCK Or _
                          SC_MANAGER_QUERY_LOCK_STATUS Or _
                          SC_MANAGER_MODIFY_BOOT_CONFIG)

Public Const STANDARD_RIGHTS_REQUIRED = &HF0000
Private Const SERVICE_QUERY_CONFIG = &H1
Private Const SERVICE_CHANGE_CONFIG = &H2
Private Const SERVICE_QUERY_STATUS = &H4
Private Const SERVICE_ENUMERATE_DEPENDENTS = &H8
Private Const SERVICE_START = &H10
Private Const SERVICE_STOP = &H20
Private Const SERVICE_PAUSE_CONTINUE = &H40
Private Const SERVICE_INTERROGATE = &H80
Private Const SERVICE_USER_DEFINED_CONTROL = &H100
Private Const SERVICE_ALL_ACCESS = (STANDARD_RIGHTS_REQUIRED Or _
  SERVICE_QUERY_CONFIG Or _
  SERVICE_CHANGE_CONFIG Or _
  SERVICE_QUERY_STATUS Or _
  SERVICE_ENUMERATE_DEPENDENTS Or _
  SERVICE_START Or _
  SERVICE_STOP Or _
  SERVICE_PAUSE_CONTINUE Or _
  SERVICE_INTERROGATE Or _
  SERVICE_USER_DEFINED_CONTROL)

Private Const SERVICE_BOOT_START As Long = &H0
Private Const SERVICE_SYSTEM_START As Long = &H1
Private Const SERVICE_AUTO_START As Long = &H2
Private Const SERVICE_DISABLED As Long = &H4
Private Const SERVICE_DEMAND_START As Long = &H3

Private Const SERVICE_ERROR_IGNORE As Long = &H0
```

Continues

Listing 2.30

```
Private Const SERVICE_ERROR_NORMAL As Long = &H1
Private Const SERVICE_ERROR_SEVERE As Long = &H2
Private Const SERVICE_ERROR_CRITICAL As Long = &H3

Private Enum SERVICE_CONTROL
  SERVICE_CONTROL_STOP = &H1
  SERVICE_CONTROL_PAUSE = &H2
  SERVICE_CONTROL_CONTINUE = &H3
  SERVICE_CONTROL_INTERROGATE = &H4
  SERVICE_CONTROL_SHUTDOWN = &H5
End Enum

Private Enum SERVICE_STATE
  SERVICE_STOPPED = &H1
  SERVICE_START_PENDING = &H2
  SERVICE_STOP_PENDING = &H3
  SERVICE_RUNNING = &H4
  SERVICE_CONTINUE_PENDING = &H5
  SERVICE_PAUSE_PENDING = &H6
  SERVICE_PAUSED = &H7
End Enum
```

Listing 2.30 Constant definitions *(Continued).*

Listing 2.31 shows the structure definitions that I'll need to program NT Services with VB.

Listing 2.32 shows the function definitions that I'll need to program NT Services with VB.

```
Private Type SERVICE_TABLE_ENTRY
  lpServiceName As String
  lpServiceProc As Long
  lpServiceNameNull As Long
  lpServiceProcNull As Long
End Type

Private Type SERVICE_STATUS
  dwServiceType As Long
  dwCurrentState As Long
  dwControlsAccepted As Long
  dwWin32ExitCode As Long
  dwServiceSpecificExitCode As Long
  dwCheckPoint As Long
  dwWaitHint As Long
End Type
```

Listing 2.31 Structure definitions.

```
Private Declare Function StartServiceCtrlDispatcher _
  Lib "advapi32.dll" Alias "StartServiceCtrlDispatcherA" _
  (lpServiceStartTable As SERVICE_TABLE_ENTRY) As Long
Private Declare Function RegisterServiceCtrlHandler _
  Lib "advapi32.dll" Alias "RegisterServiceCtrlHandlerA" _
  (ByVal lpServiceName As String, ByVal lpHandlerProc As Long) _
  As Long
Private Declare Function SetServiceStatus _
  Lib "advapi32.dll" (ByVal hServiceStatus As Long, _
  lpServiceStatus As SERVICE_STATUS) As Long
Private Declare Function OpenSCManager _
  Lib "advapi32.dll" Alias "OpenSCManagerA" _
  (ByVal lpMachineName As String, ByVal lpDatabaseName As String, _
  ByVal dwDesiredAccess As Long) As Long
Private Declare Function CreateService _
  Lib "advapi32.dll" Alias "CreateServiceA" _
  (ByVal hSCManager As Long, ByVal lpServiceName As String, _
  ByVal lpDisplayName As String, ByVal dwDesiredAccess As Long, _
  ByVal dwServiceType As Long, ByVal dwStartType As Long, _
  ByVal dwErrorControl As Long, ByVal lpBinaryPathName As String, _
  ByVal lpLoadOrderGroup As String, ByVal lpdwTagId As String, _
  ByVal lpDependencies As String, ByVal lp As String, _
  ByVal lpPassword As String) As Long
Private Declare Function DeleteService _
  Lib "advapi32.dll" (ByVal hService As Long) As Long
Declare Function CloseServiceHandle _
  Lib "advapi32.dll" (ByVal hSCObject As Long) As Long
Declare Function OpenService _
  Lib "advapi32.dll" Alias "OpenServiceA" _
  (ByVal hSCManager As Long, ByVal lpServiceName As String, _
  ByVal dwDesiredAccess As Long) As Long
```

Listing 2.32 Function definitions.

All the identifiers are VB equivalents of what I've been describing in the first sections of this chapter. An important consideration beyond converting C++ to VB is to find where the NT Service functions are located.

In the Win32 API documentation, each function has a QuickInfo section that notes which Import Library to use when linking these functions. Usually there is a one-to-one mapping of Import Libraries to DLLs. In the case of the NT Service API, the Import Library is advapi32.lib and, consequently, the DLL is advapi32.dll.

I can verify this fact by running Quick View against the DLL. The advapi32.dll is found in the system32 directory. If I right-click on the DLL and select Quick View from the pop-up menu, then the Quick View utility will display the header information for the module. If I scan the Export Table in the header, I find all the NT Service API functions. As shown in Figure 2.5, the StartServiceCtrlDispatcher function is exported from the advapi32.dll module.

Another important consideration is aliasing all the Win32 functions in order to use the ANSI (non-Unicode) versions of the Win32 functions. In order to provide for both ANSI and Unicode functions, Microsoft reimplemented all Win32 functions that had strings for both ANSI and Unicode. The ANSI functions were prefixed with an *A* and the Unicode functions were prefixed with a *W*.

When programming in C++ Win32, programmers generally don't have to consider the different ANSI and Unicode functions because the functions are redefined using preprocessor macros. Listing 2.33 shows how the OpenSC-Manager function is redefined.

If the UNICODE preprocessor constant is defined, then OpenSCManager is defined as the Unicode version of this function. Otherwise, it is the non-Unicode version.

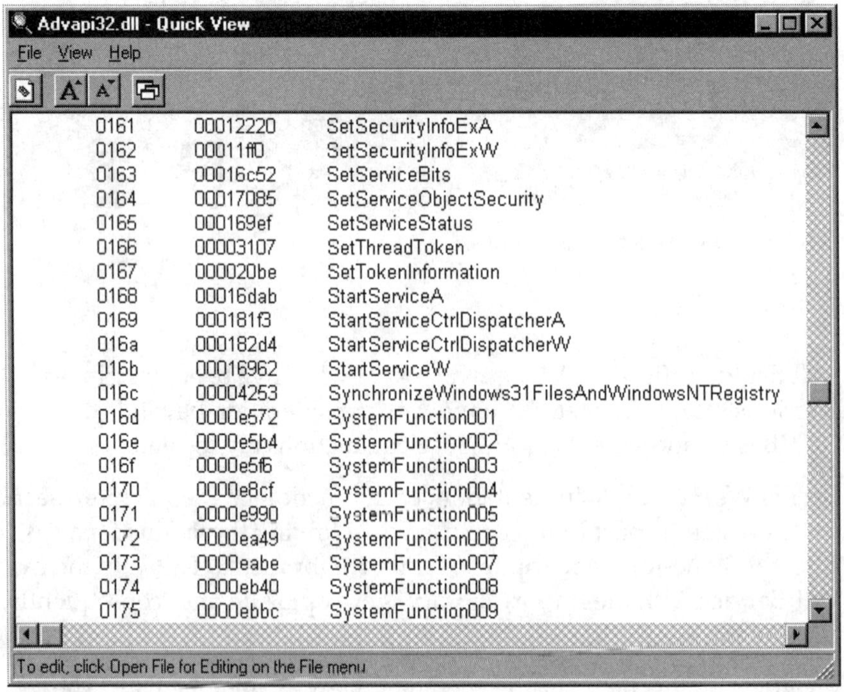

Figure 2.5 Quick View of advapi32.dll.

```
WINADVAPI
SC_HANDLE
WINAPI
OpenSCManagerA(
    LPCSTR  lpMachineName,
    LPCSTR  lpDatabaseName,
    DWORD   dwDesiredAccess
    );
WINADVAPI
SC_HANDLE
WINAPI
OpenSCManagerW(
    LPCWSTR lpMachineName,
    LPCWSTR lpDatabaseName,
    DWORD   dwDesiredAccess
    );
#ifdef UNICODE
#define OpenSCManager   OpenSCManagerW
#else
#define OpenSCManager   OpenSCManagerA
#endif // !UNICODE
```

Listing 2.33   Unicode and ANSI OpenSCManager.

Getting back to writing the VB NT Service, I create a second .BAS file where I can put the implementation. An example implementation is present in Listing 2.34.

I'm not going to explain this Visual Basic service in much detail as it is simply a C++-to-Visual Basic translation of code that I've been explaining throughout this chapter.

```
Private Const servicename As String = "MyService"
Private servicestatushandle As Long
Private servicestatus As SERVICE_STATUS

Sub Main()
  Dim handle As Long
  Dim hService As Long
  Dim servicetableentry As SERVICE_TABLE_ENTRY
  Dim b As Boolean
```

Continues

Listing 2.34   Example VB implementation.

```
Dim commandline As String

commandline = Trim(LCase(Command()))
Select Case commandline
Case "service"
   handle = OpenSCManager(vbNullString, vbNullString, _
   SC_MANAGER_CREATE_SERVICE)
   hService = CreateService(handle, servicename, _
   SERVICE_NAME, SERVICE_ALL_ACCESS, _
   SERVICE_WIN32_OWN_PROCESS, _
   SERVICE_DEMAND_START, SERVICE_ERROR_NORMAL, _
   App.Path & "\" & App.EXEName, vbNullString, _
   vbNullString, vbNullString, vbNullString, _
   vbNullString)
   CloseServiceHandle hService
   CloseServiceHandle handle
Case "unregserver"
   handle = OpenSCManager(vbNullString, vbNullString, _
   SC_MANAGER_CREATE_SERVICE)
   hService = OpenService(handle, servicename, _
   SERVICE_ALL_ACCESS)
   DeleteService hService
   CloseServiceHandle hService
   CloseServiceHandle handle
Case Else
   servicetableentry.lpServiceName = servicename
   servicetableentry.lpServiceProc = _
   FncPtr(AddressOf ServiceMain)
   b = StartServiceCtrlDispatcher(servicetableentry)
End Select
End Sub

Sub ServiceMain(ByVal dwArgc As Long, ByVal lpszArgv As Long)
   Dim b As Boolean

   servicestatus.dwServiceType = SERVICE_WIN32_OWN_PROCESS
   servicestatus.dwCurrentState = SERVICE_START_PENDING
   servicestatus.dwControlsAccepted = SERVICE_ACCEPT_STOP
   servicestatus.dwWin32ExitCode = 0
   servicestatus.dwServiceSpecificExitCode = 0
   servicestatus.dwCheckPoint = 0
   servicestatus.dwWaitHint = 0

  servicestatushandle = RegisterServiceCtrlHandler(servicename, _
    AddressOf ServiceCtrlHandler)
   servicestatus.dwCurrentState = SERVICE_START_PENDING
   b = SetServiceStatus(servicestatushandle, servicestatus)

   'DoInitialization
```

Continues

Listing 2.34 Example VB implementation *(Continued)*.

```
        servicestatus.dwCurrentState = SERVICE_RUNNING

    b = SetServiceStatus(servicestatushandle, servicestatus)
End Sub

Sub ServiceCtrlHandler(ByVal fdwControl As Long)
    Dim b As Boolean

    Select Case fdwControl
    Case SERVICE_CONTROL_STOP
        servicestatus.dwCurrentState = SERVICE_STOP_PENDING
        b = SetServiceStatus(servicestatushandle, servicestatus)
        servicestatus.dwCurrentState = SERVICE_STOPPED
    Case SERVICE_CONTROL_INTERROGATE
    Case Else
    End Select
    b = SetServiceStatus(servicestatushandle, servicestatus)
End Sub

Function FncPtr(ByVal fnp As Long) As Long
    FncPtr = fnp
End Function
```

Listing 2.34

NTSRVOCX and Visual Basic

Another approach to creating NT Services in Visual Basic is to use the NTSR-VOCX created by Mauricio Ordonez of Microsoft Consulting Services. NTSR-VOCX is an ActiveX control for creating NT Services.

As a nonbeliever in creating VB services, I won't go into any detail on using this ActiveX control. But in case programmers want to pursue the option, I thought I'd mention its existence. One definite advantage of using NTSR-VOCX is that it is an ActiveX control and can span development tools. That is, programmers can create services using this control with almost any development tool: Visual C++, C++Builder, VB, Java, and more.

The big disadvantage of the ActiveX control is that programmers don't have access to the underlying code of the control. This makes it very difficult to debug, especially when there are differences between the expectations of the developer using the control and the results of using the control.

Java Services

Microsoft created a Java package called com.ms.service that attempts to aid Java developers in creating NT Services in Java. The com.ms.service.Service class is very similar to the C++ framework I developed earlier in this chapter.

Programmers can simply derive a subclass from the com.ms.service.Service class and implement the constructor and up to four abstract member functions. The four abstract member functions that are called when the stop, shutdown, pause, and continue message are sent to the service are as follows:

- handleShutdown. On success, return true.
- handleStop. On success, return true.
- handlePause. On success, call setPaused and return false.
- handleContinue. On success, call setRunning and return false.

Another important thing to remember when using the com.ms.service.Service class is that the constructor must call setRunning in order to inform the SCM that it is ready for action. The setRunning function has two variant implementations, one with no argument and one that accepts a bit mask that may contain zero or more values from ACCEPT_PAUSE_CONTINUE, ACCEPT_SHUTDOWN, and ACCEPT_STOP. These three values have the same meaning as the values in Listing 2.6 discussed earlier in this chapter.

Just as I called SetSystemStatus with a pending argument in C++, I should also call the CheckPoint member function of com.ms.service.Service in order to inform the SCM that I am still alive. The CheckPoint function has one parameter denoting the maximum amount of milliseconds of processing the

```
import com.ms.service.*;

public class MyService extends Service
{
  static Thread thread = null;

  public MyService(String[] args)
  {
   CheckPoint(10000); // give me 10 seconds to initiatlize
   thread = new Thread((Runnable) new MyThread());
   thread.start();
   setRunning(ACCEPT_STOP);
  }

  protected boolean handleStop()
  {
   thread.stop();
   thread = null;
   return true;
  }
}
```

Listing 2.35 MyService.java.

service expects to use before it will make another call to CheckPoint or call setRunning or setPaused. Listing 2.35 shows a complete implementation of a Java NT Service.

The implementation of the NT Service in Java is quite simple. In the Java service, I've created a separate thread that performs the actual operations of the service. Listing 2.36 shows the implementation of the MyThread class.

The separate thread is a class MyThread that simply loops endlessly while writing Hello to a log file once every second.

Installing com.ms.service

Installing the service component for Java is quite easy. First, install the Microsoft Software Development Kit (SDK) for Java from http://msdn .microsoft.com/visualj/downloads/sdk.asp. Unzip the bin\jntsvc\service .zip file into the \Winnt\Java\TrustLib directory.

```java
import java.io.*;

public class MyThread implements Runnable
{
  public void run()
  {
    try
    {
      File file = new File("d:\\", "logfile.log");
      BufferedWriter writer = new BufferedWriter(
        new OutputStreamWriter(new FileOutputStream(file)));
      while (true)
      {
        writer.write("Hello");
        writer.newLine();
        writer.flush();
        Thread.sleep(1000);
      }
    }
    catch(IOException e)
    {
    }
    catch(InterruptedException e)
    {
    }
  }
}
```

Listing 2.36   MyThread.java.

```
C:\WINNT\System32\cmd.exe                                          _ □ ×
D:\Program Files\Microsoft SDK for Java 3.2\jntsvc>jntsvc /?

Microsoft NT (R) Service Generator for Java Version 5.00.3167
Copyright (C) Microsoft Corp 1996-1998. All rights reserved.

Usage: JNTSVC [options] [@command file] files

options:
  /BASE:<dir>                Set base directory.
  /OUT:<filename>            Set output file name.
  /R                         Recurse into sub-directories.
  /R-                        Do not Recurse into sub-directories (default).
  /U                         Verbose output.
  /SVCMAIN:<classname>       Set main class file. Required. May be followed
                             by one or more service-specific options.

service-specific options:
  /SERVICENAME:<filename>    Set service name.
  /DISPLAYNAME:<filename>    Set service display name.
  /EVENTSOURCE:<name>        Set event source name in error log.
  /CLASSPATH:<path>          Set any additional class paths required.
  /INSTALLPARAMS:<params>    Set installation parameters.  When the service
                             is installed, the service's static 'installService'
                             method will be invoked with this string.
  files                      List of class files needed to run service.

  Note that multiple services are supported, but that each must be preceeded
  by a /SVCMAIN switch specifying the service class name.

Eg. JNTSVC *.class /OUT:Services.EXE /SVCMAIN:MyService1
    "/SERVICENAME:Unique Name" /SVCMAIN:MyService2

D:\Program Files\Microsoft SDK for Java 3.2\jntsvc>_
```

Figure 2.6 Java service command-line help.

Once the SDK has been installed, the jntsvc (Java to NT Service) tool that creates an executable for the Java service is ready to be used. Jntsvc is a command-line tool with very simple parameters. Figure 2.6 shows the command-line parameters available with the jntsvc tool.

Programmers can use the jntsvc utility to compile an executable that is used to configure and manipulate the Java NT Service. To generate such an executable from the code I've presented in this chapter, programmers can run the jntsvc command-line shown in Figure 2.7.

After generating the Java executable, programmers can use the command-line options of this executable to configure the service. If the executable is run with the /? command-line parameter, programmers can preview all the options they have using this generated executable (also in Figure 2.7).

Delphi Services

NT Services can be developed in nearly any language. One of the easiest implementations is Delphi. Delphi has always been a favorite development tool of mine. This stems from the thousands of programs I wrote in Borland-

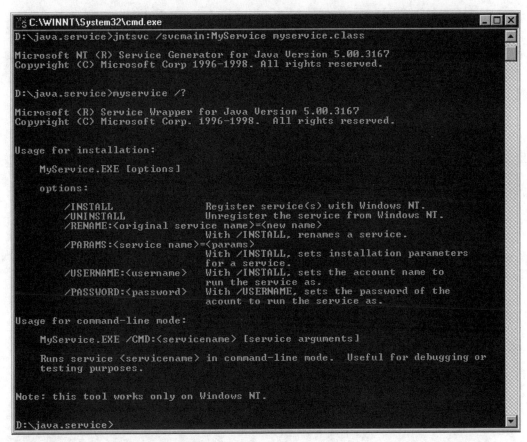

Figure 2.7 Java NT Service command-line option.

Turbo Pascal as a youth. I'm sure many others had those same experiences. We all still vote for Delphi as the number one development tool, but we're now C++ developers and Pascal is just not that popular.

But Delphi remains one of the best development tools on the market and is used by at least a handful of developers. For that handful of remaining Pascaling developers, here's the how-to in Delphi. Listing 2.37 shows a simple NT Service implemented in one Delphi module.

I must apologize, but I didn't write any installation and uninstallation routines. In the end, I decided that they would only take up half of the listing with code that has very little real content and that they should be trivial enough that readers should be able to create them. If readers do create their own services, I suggest they write these routines.

```
program MyNtService;

uses Windows, SysUtils, WinSvc;

{$R *.RES}

type

var servicetable : array[0..1] of TServiceTableEntry;
  servicestatus : TServiceStatus;
  servicestatushandle : SERVICE_STATUS_HANDLE;
  finished : Boolean;

procedure ServiceMain(args : LongInt; argv : argArray); stdcall;
var file : Text;
begin
  servicestatus.dwServiceType := SERVICE_WIN32_OWN_PROCESS;
  servicestatus.dwCurrentState := SERVICE_START_PENDING;
  servicestatus.dwControlsAccepted := SERVICE_ACCEPT_STOP;
  servicestatus.dwWin32ExitCode := 0;
  servicestatus.dwServiceSpecificExitCode := 0;
  servicestatus.dwCheckPoint := 0;
  servicestatus.dwWaitHint := 0;
  servicestatushandle :=
   RegisterServiceCtrlHandle(PChar("MyDelphiService",
     @ServiceCtrlHandler);
  SetServiceStatus(servicestatushandle, servicestatus);

  while ExecuteDelay(1000) do
  begin
   AssignFile(f, "d:\file.log");
   try
     Append(f);
   except
     Rewrite(f);
   end;
   WriteLn(f, "Tick");
   CloseFile(f);
  end;

  result := 0;
end;

procedure ServiceCtrlHandler(msg : LongInt); stdcall;
begin
  case msg of
   SERVICE_CONTROL_STOP:
   begin
     servicestatus.dwCurrentStatus := SERVICE_STOPPED;
```

Continues

Listing 2.37 Delphi service sample.

```
      SetServiceStatus(servicestatushandle, servicestatus);
    end;
  end;
end;

begin
    servicetable[0].lpServiceName := PChar("MyDelphiService");
    servicetable[0].lpServiceProc := @ServiceMain;
    servicetable[1].lpServiceName := nil;
    servicetable[1].lpServiceProc := nil;
    StartServiceStrlDispatcher( servicetable[0] );
end.
```

Listing 2.37

Again, it wouldn't be that helpful for me to step through this code listing. The listing is very similar to what I've already presented in the sections on C++ and Visual Basic. In this implementation, I write Tick to a log file every second. Admittedly, my examples are lacking in originality, but I thought I'd keep all the services very simple in this chapter.

One important part of the listing is the inclusion of the WinSvc Pascal source file. This step is shown in part in Listing 2.38.

```
{*********************************************************}
{                                                         }
{     Delphi Run-time Library                    }        }
{     Windows 32bit API Interface Unit                }   }
{                                                         }
{     Copyright (c) 1996,98 Borland International    }    }
{                                                         }
{*********************************************************}

unit WinSvc;

{$ALIGN ON}
{$MINENUMSIZE 4}
{$WEAKPACKAGEUNIT}

interface

uses Windows;
```

Continues

Listing 2.38   WinSvc.

```
//
// Constants
//

const

//
// Controls
//
  {$EXTERNALSYM SERVICE_CONTROL_STOP}
  SERVICE_CONTROL_STOP         = $00000001;
  {$EXTERNALSYM SERVICE_CONTROL_PAUSE}
  SERVICE_CONTROL_PAUSE        = $00000002;
  {$EXTERNALSYM SERVICE_CONTROL_CONTINUE}
  SERVICE_CONTROL_CONTINUE     = $00000003;
  {$EXTERNALSYM SERVICE_CONTROL_INTERROGATE}
  SERVICE_CONTROL_INTERROGATE  = $00000004;
  {$EXTERNALSYM SERVICE_CONTROL_SHUTDOWN}
  SERVICE_CONTROL_SHUTDOWN     = $00000005;

type

//
// Service Status Structure
//

  PServiceStatus = ^TServiceStatus;
  {$EXTERNALSYM _SERVICE_STATUS}
  _SERVICE_STATUS = record
   dwServiceType: DWORD;
   dwCurrentState: DWORD;
   dwControlsAccepted: DWORD;
   dwWin32ExitCode: DWORD;
   dwServiceSpecificExitCode: DWORD;
   dwCheckPoint: DWORD;
   dwWaitHint: DWORD;
  end;
  {$EXTERNALSYM SERVICE_STATUS}
  SERVICE_STATUS = _SERVICE_STATUS;
  TServiceStatus = _SERVICE_STATUS;

//
// Function Prototype for the Service Main Function
//

{$IFDEF STRICT}
  {$EXTERNALSYM LPSERVICE_MAIN_FUNCTIONA}
  LPSERVICE_MAIN_FUNCTIONA = procedure (dwNumServicesArgs: DWORD;
```

Continues

Listing 2.38 WinSvc *(Continued).*

```
    lpServiceArgVectors: PLPSTRA) stdcall;
  {$EXTERNALSYM LPSERVICE_MAIN_FUNCTIONW}
  LPSERVICE_MAIN_FUNCTIONW = procedure (dwNumServicesArgs: DWORD;
    lpServiceArgVectors: PLPSTRW) stdcall;
  {$EXTERNALSYM LPSERVICE_MAIN_FUNCTION}
  LPSERVICE_MAIN_FUNCTION = LPSERVICE_MAIN_FUNCTIONA;
{$ELSE}

//
// Prototype for the Service Control Handler Function
//

{$IFDEF STRICT}
  {$EXTERNALSYM LPHANDLER_FUNCTION}
  LPHANDLER_FUNCTION = procedure (dwControl: DWORD) stdcall;
{$ELSE}
  {$EXTERNALSYM LPHANDLER_FUNCTION}
  LPHANDLER_FUNCTION = TFarProc;
{$ENDIF}
  THandlerFunction = LPHANDLER_FUNCTION;

///////////////////////////////////////////////////////////////////
// API Function Prototypes
///////////////////////////////////////////////////////////////////

{$EXTERNALSYM ControlService}
function ControlService(hService: SC_HANDLE; dwControl: DWORD;
  var lpServiceStatus: TServiceStatus): BOOL; stdcall;

implementation

const
  advapi32 = 'advapi32.dll';

function ControlService;       external advapi32 name 'ControlService';

end.
```

Listing 2.38

I didn't think I should present the entire listing here as it would waste a dozen or more pages. I cut 90 percent of the listing for the sake of brevity. I've provided here one set of constants, one structure, and one function. For those writing their services in Pascal, I suggest that they familiarize themselves with the entire WinSvc source listing.

Summary

So now you think you can write an NT Service, eh? (Yes, I'm Canadian.) Hold your horses—an NT Service is nothing much until it does something beyond existing. In the next chapter, I'll show how to build upon this knowledge to implement various types of NT Services. The rest of this book talks about implementation details that allow programmers to add IPC (interprocess communication), security, and debugging functionality to their already complete NT Services.

CHAPTER 3

Implementation

The next step in writing an NT Service is to incorporate the infrastructure with a business or system function. If the service is an application server, then it likely is a processor for some business function. A very likely architecture is having some client communicate via some remote communication protocol with the application server. This architecture is depicted in Figure 3.1.

This chapter presents some frameworks for developing NT Services using various remote communications protocols. The what-is how-to advantages and disadvantages of each protocol are also presented. In particular, I will outline two important features, fail-over and load balancing, and how to incorporate these features into the framework.

The remote communication protocols that I address are Sockets, RPC, DCOM, CORBA, and MSMQ. These protocols and other remote communica-

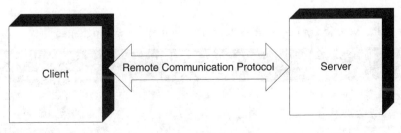

Figure 3.1   Client-application server architecture.

tion protocols can be grouped into three broad categories: byte-oriented transports, function-oriented transports, and objected-oriented transports.

The division of these remote communication protocols is an evolution that closely resembles the evolution of programming languages (see Table 3.1).

Programming languages began with simple Machine Language (ML) and gradually evolved into Assembler (ASM). Both are byte-oriented protocols in that each instruction is individually coded and contains one to a few bytes of data. Eventually the functional programming paradigm evolved and such languages as Pascal and C were created. The evolution continued into the object-oriented paradigm in which C++ and Java are now the mainstream development tools.

The future of network communication may also lie in the same direction as the future of programming languages. The current trend in programming is toward fourth-generation languages that are based on intuitive designs rather than logical designs. The same trend in network communication may evolve from some of the intuitive design concepts such as Extensible Markup Language (XML) as opposed to logical API-style designs.

It is my opinion that fourth-generation languages have failed to replace third-generation languages such as C, C++, Pascal, and Java because they are performance handicapped over the Internet. This may also prove true of XML.

Byte-oriented transports are transports that move one byte at a time from the source to the destination. Sockets are the most popular of these byte-oriented protocols and are the only byte-oriented protocol that I will address in this book. Other byte-oriented protocols include named pipes, IPX, and SPX, but I don't consider these protocols to be viable in an Internet-based society.

Function-oriented transports are usually layered on top of byte-oriented transports and hide the nitty-gritty movement of bytes from the source to the destination. Function-oriented transports can provide some advantages in hiding the underlying byte protocol, providing automatic marshaling of data and automatic handling of trivial and recoverable error conditions. The most popular function-oriented transport is RPC. Other function-oriented proto-

Table 3.1 Evolution of Communications and Programming Languages

	PROGRAMMING LANGUAGES	COMMUNICATION PROTOCOLS
Object-Oriented	C++, Java	CORBA, DCOM
Function-Oriented	C, Pascal	RPC, MSMQ
Bytes-Oriented	ML, ASM	Sockets, TSAP

cols include HyperText Transport Protocol (HTTP), Simple Mail Transport Protocol (SMTP), File Transport Protocol (FTP), Microsoft Message Queue Server (MSMQ), and MQ Series. I specifically address both RPC and MSMQ in this book.

The last type of transport is the object-oriented transport. This transport allows developers to seamlessly integrate remote objects into their development architectures. The two most popular object-oriented transports are DCOM and CORBA. Both are explained in this book.

Sockets Internet Protocol

I really hope that I don't need to define sockets, but, in case I do, *sockets* is the protocol used to talk over the Internet, also known as Internet Protocol (IP). Wrong! Sockets have nothing to do with the Internet. Sockets are an API for programming over any transport layer, but which happen to be used almost exclusively with the Internet (IP). To fully understand this, it is best if I explain the International Organization for Standardization's Open Systems Interconnection (ISO OSI) Reference Model. This model divides the communication model into seven distinct layers (see Figure 3.2).

The seven layers are the physical, data-link, network, transport, session, presentation, and application layers. The IP protocol is a network-layer implementation and, like most other network-layer communication protocols, can be both connection-oriented and connectionless. The two transport layers that are usually implemented over IP are TCP (connection-oriented) and UDP (connectionless). The API between any of the seven layers of the Reference Model is known as a Service Access Point (SAP). The API to the trans-

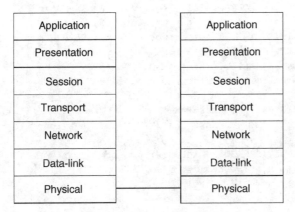

Figure 3.2 ISO OSI Reference Model.

port layer is known specifically as a Transport SAP (TSAP). Sockets are a TSAP implementation and could be implemented over any transport. But sockets are almost exclusively implemented over TCP/IP and UDP/IP.

The connection-oriented IP protocol is very popular and is known as Transmission Control Protocol (TCP). An important thing to remember is that TCP is a connection-oriented protocol normally layered on top of the IP protocol. TCP can and is implemented on top of other communication protocols including the SPX protocol. The connectionless IP protocol is less known and is called User Datagram Protocol (UDP).

Socket Programming

I develop my sample socket server using the TCP/IP protocol and the Winsock library. Remember that TCP/IP is a connection-oriented protocol. A TCP/IP server needs to use the functions in Listing 3.1 to receive client requests and to send client responses.

When programming in Winsock, the first thing I must do is to initialize the Winsock library by calling the WSAStartup function. The WSAStartup function takes one input parameter and one output parameter. The input parameter indicates the version of Winsock that I wish to use. The output parameter is a structure indicating the version and capabilities of the Winsock driver.

```
typedef struct WSAData {
    WORD            wVersion;
    WORD            wHighVersion;
    char            szDescription[WSADESCRIPTION_LEN+1];
    char            szSystemStatus[WSASYS_STATUS_LEN+1];
    unsigned short  iMaxSockets;
```

```
int PASCAL FAR WSAStartup(WORD wVersionRequired, LPWSADATA lpWSAData);
SOCKET PASCAL FAR socket (int af, int type, int protocol);
int PASCAL FAR bind (SOCKET s, const struct sockaddr FAR *addr,
 int namelen);
int PASCAL FAR listen (SOCKET s, int backlog);
SOCKET PASCAL FAR accept (SOCKET s, struct sockaddr FAR *addr,
 int FAR *addrlen);
int PASCAL FAR recv (SOCKET s, char FAR * buf, int len, int flags);
int PASCAL FAR send (SOCKET s, const char FAR * buf, int len,
 int flags);
int PASCAL FAR shutdown (SOCKET s, int how);
int PASCAL FAR closesocket (SOCKET s);
int PASCAL FAR WSACleanup(void);
```

Listing 3.1   TCP/IP server Winsock functions.

```
    unsigned short      iMaxUdpDg;
    char FAR *          lpVendorInfo;
} WSADATA;
```

The important member of the WSAData structure is the wVersion member. This WORD value indicates the version of Winsock that I will be using. If this is not equal to the version I requested in the input parameter to WSAStartup, then I may encounter problems.

When the application exits, I should call WSACleanup to free resources held by the Winsock library. Listing 3.2 shows a sample of using the startup and cleanup functions.

```
void main()
{
WORD w = MAKEWORD(2,0);
WSADATA wsadata;
int i = ::WSAStartup(w, &wsadata);
// Do stuff
// ...

::WSACleanup();
};
```

Listing 3.2 Winsock startup and cleanup.

Once I've initialized the Winsock library, I can create a server socket. The socket function is used to create sockets. The function has three parameters: the address family, the socket type, and the transport protocol. The socket function returns a socket handle that is used with other socket functions. The address family may be any of the values in Listing 3.3. For Internet applications, the address family should be AF_INET.

```
#define AF_UNSPEC 0   /* unspecified */
#define AF_UNIX   1   /* local to host (pipes, portals) */
#define AF_INET   2   /* internetwork: UDP, TCP, etc. */
#define AF_IMPLINK 3  /* arpanet imp addresses */
#define AF_PUP    4   /* pup protocols: e.g. BSP */
#define AF_CHAOS  5   /* mit CHAOS protocols */
#define AF_IPX    6   /* IPX and SPX */
```
Continues

Listing 3.3 Address families.

```
#define AF_NS     6          /* XEROX NS protocols */
#define AF_ISO    7          /* ISO protocols */
#define AF_OSI    AF_ISO     /* OSI is ISO */
#define AF_ECMA   8          /* european computer manufacturers */
#define AF_DATAKIT 9         /* datakit protocols */
#define AF_CCITT  10         /* CCITT protocols, X.25 etc */
#define AF_SNA    11         /* IBM SNA */
#define AF_DECnet 12         /* DECnet */
#define AF_DLI    13         /* Direct data link interface */
#define AF_LAT    14         /* LAT */
#define AF_HYLINK 15         /* NSC Hyperchannel */
#define AF_APPLETALK 16      /* AppleTalk */
#define AF_NETBIOS  17       /* NetBios-style addresses */
#define AF_VOICEVIEW 18      /* VoiceView */
#define AF_FIREFOX  19       /* FireFox */
#define AF_UNKNOWN1 20       /* Somebody is using this! */
#define AF_BAN    21         /* Banyan */
#define AF_MAX    22
```

Listing 3.3   Address families *(Continued)*.

The socket type may be any of the values in Listing 3.4. The SOCK_STREAM type is used for connection-oriented socket protocols and the SOCK_DGRAM type is used for connectionless socket protocols. For TCP/IP communication, I should specify the SOCK_STREAM type.

```
#define SOCK_STREAM    1     /* stream socket */
#define SOCK_DGRAM     2     /* datagram socket */
#define SOCK_RAW       3     /* raw-protocol interface */
#define SOCK_RDM       4     /* reliably delivered message */
#define SOCK_SEQPACKET 5     /* sequenced packet stream */
```

Listing 3.4   Socket types.

The last parameter is the transport protocol. Listing 3.5 shows the available transport protocols.

If I specify IPPROTO_IP transport and the socket type is SOCK_STREAM, then TCP is used as the transport. Alternatively, I could have specified IPROTO_TCP to use the TCP transport. Listing 3.6 shows an example of creating a TCP/IP socket.

```
#define IPPROTO_IP      0       /* dummy for IP */
#define IPPROTO_ICMP    1       /* control message protocol */
#define IPPROTO_IGMP    2       /* group management protocol */
#define IPPROTO_GGP     3       /* gateway^2 (deprecated) */
#define IPPROTO_TCP     6       /* tcp */
#define IPPROTO_PUP     12      /* pup */
#define IPPROTO_UDP     17      /* user datagram protocol */
#define IPPROTO_IDP     22      /* xns idp */
#define IPPROTO_ND      77      /* UNOFFICIAL net disk proto */
#define IPPROTO_RAW     255     /* raw IP packet */
#define IPPROTO_MAX     256
```

Listing 3.5 Transport constants.

Once I've established the socket, I have to name the socket by calling the bind function. The bind function takes three parameters: The socket handle that was retrieved from the socket function call, a sockaddr structure, and the sockaddr structure length.

```
struct sockaddr {
  u_short sa_family; /* address family */
  char sa_data[14]; /* up to 14 bytes of direct address */
};
```

The first member of the sockaddr structure determines the content of the second member. For an Internet address, I should set the sa_family member to AF_INET. If the first member is AF_INET, then the structure takes on a new form, sockaddr_in.

```
void main()
{
 WORD w = MAKEWORD(2,0);
 WSADATA wsadata;
 int i = ::WSAStartup(w, &wsadata);

 SOCKET socket = ::socket(AF_INET, SOCK_STREAM,
 IPPROTO_TCP);
 // Do stuff
 // ...

 ::WSACleanup();
};
```

Listing 3.6 Create a socket.

```
struct sockaddr_in {
    short sin_family;
    u_short sin_port;
    struct in_addr sin_addr;
    char sin_zero[8];
};
```

Communication over IP happens between two Internet addresses and over a port. The port makes it easy for two Internet addresses to distinguish two different communications channels. The port is specified in the sin_port member of the sockaddr_in structure and the Internet address is specified in the in_addr structure.

```
struct in_addr {
    union {
        struct { u_char s_b1,s_b2,s_b3,s_b4; } S_un_b;
        struct { u_short s_w1,s_w2; } S_un_w;
        u_long S_addr;
    } S_un;
};
```

The sin_zero member is filler to make the sockaddr_in structure the same size as the sockaddr structure. Some Internet address constants that have special meaning are shown in Listing 3.7.

```
#define INADDR_ANY          (u_long)0x00000000
#define INADDR_LOOPBACK     0x7f000001
#define INADDR_BROADCAST    (u_long)0xffffffff
#define INADDR_NONE         0xffffffff
```

Listing 3.7 Special Internet addresses.

When writing a TCP/IP server, I can specify INADDR_ANY as the address. Listing 3.8 continues the example by binding the socket.

Now that I have a bound-named socket, I have to listen for client connections. Listening for client connections is done using the listen function. The listen function takes two parameters: the socket handle and the maximum number of pending connections. For the maximum queue length, I can specify the SOMAXCONN constant. Listing 3.9 extends the example to listen on the socket.

If the number of maximum pending connections is exceeded, then the client connection and subsequent attempts to connect will be rejected until the server accepts a pending connection. The client will receive a connection-refused error when the server rejects connections in this manner.

```
void main()
{
WORD w = MAKEWORD(2,0);
WSADATA wsadata;
int i = ::WSAStartup(w, &wsadata);
SOCKET socket = ::socket(AF_INET, SOCK_STREAM,
        IPPROTO_TCP);

sockaddr_in name;
name.sin_family = AF_INET;
name.sin_port = 12345;
name.sin_addr.s_addr = htonl(INADDR_ANY);
::bind(socket, (sockaddr *)&name, sizeof(name));
// Do stuff
// ...

::WSACleanup();
};
```

Listing 3.8 Bind to a socket.

The server accepts a pending connection by calling the accept function. This function takes three parameters: an input parameter of the socket handle I am listening on and two output parameters, the sockaddr structure and the sockaddr structure length. The function returns a new socket handle that can then be used to communicate with the client. The sockaddr output parameter

```
void main()
{
WORD w = MAKEWORD(2,0);
WSADATA wsadata;
int i = ::WSAStartup(w, &wsadata);
SOCKET socket = ::socket(AF_INET, SOCK_STREAM,
        IPPROTO_TCP);

sockaddr_in name;
name.sin_family = AF_INET;
name.sin_port = 12345;
name.sin_addr.s_addr = htonl(INADDR_ANY);
::bind(socket, (sockaddr *)&name, sizeof(name));

::listen(socket, SOMAXCONN);
// Do stuff
// ...

::WSACleanup();
};
```

Listing 3.9 Listen on a socket.

```
void main()
{
 WORD w = MAKEWORD(2,0);
 WSADATA wsadata;
 int i = ::WSAStartup(w, &wsadata);
 SOCKET socket = ::socket(AF_INET, SOCK_STREAM,
                IPPROTO_TCP);
 sockaddr_in name;
 name.sin_family = AF_INET;
 name.sin_port = 12345;
 name.sin_addr.s_addr = htonl(INADDR_ANY);
 ::bind(socket, (sockaddr *)&name, sizeof(name));
 ::listen(socket, SOMAXCONN);

 int n = sizeof(name);
 ::accept(socket, (sockaddr *)&name, &n);
 // Do stuff
 // ...

 ::WSACleanup();
};
```

Listing 3.10 Accept a connection.

is the name of the client. For TCP/IP, the name of the client is the client's
Internet address and port. Listing 3.10 extends the example again to accept
client connections.

It is very important to note that the accept function returns a new socket handle. This is done to allow the first socket handle to continue listening for
additional client connections while the second socket handle communicates
with the newly connected client.

Once the TCP/IP client and server are connected, they may freely begin calling the send and recv functions to transfer data. The send and recv functions
take four parameters: the socket handle, the buffer contents to be transferred,
the size of the buffer, and a set of flags. The standard message flags are
shown in Listing 3.11.

```
#define MSG_OOB 0x1       /* process out-of-band data */
#define MSG_PEEK 0x2      /* peek at incoming message */
#define MSG_DONTROUTE 0x4 /* send without using routing tables */
```

Listing 3.11 Message flags.

```
void main()
{
WORD w = MAKEWORD(2,0);
WSADATA wsadata;
int i = ::WSAStartup(w, &wsadata);
SOCKET listen = ::socket(AF_INET, SOCK_STREAM, IPPROTO_TCP);
sockaddr_in name;
name.sin_family = AF_INET;
name.sin_port = 12345;
name.sin_addr.s_addr = htonl(INADDR_ANY);
::bind(listen, (sockaddr *)&name, sizeof(name));
::listen(listen, SOMAXCONN);
int n = sizeof(name);
SOCKET socket = ::accept(listen, (sockaddr *)&name, &n);

char buffer[256];
::recv(socket, buffer, sizeof(buffer), 0);
::send(socket, buffer, sizeof(buffer), 0);

::WSACleanup();
};
```

Listing 3.12 Receive and send data.

This growing example is nearly complete with the sending and receiving of data (see Listing 3.12).

Finally, once I've finished sending and receiving data, I can close the socket. Closing a socket is a little more complex than it needs to be. I must first call the shutdown function, and if it succeeds, I call the closesocket function. The shutdown function takes two parameters: the socket handle and the type of shutdown desired. The shutdown constants are shown in Listing 3.13.

```
#define SD_RECEIVE   0x00
#define SD_SEND      0x01
#define SD_BOTH      0x02
```

Listing 3.13 Shutdown constants.

It's actually recommended that programmers first call shutdown with SD_SEND to inform the other socket that they are no longer sending bytes. Then they call shutdown again with SD_RECEIVE to inform the other socket that they are no longer receiving bytes. And they can call shutdown a third time with SD_BOTH before closing the socket. The closesocket function takes

```
void main()
{
 WORD w = MAKEWORD(2,0);
 WSADATA wsadata;
 int i = ::WSAStartup(w, &wsadata);
 SOCKET listen = ::socket(AF_INET, SOCK_STREAM,
          IPPROTO_TCP);

 sockaddr_in name;
 name.sin_family = AF_INET;
 name.sin_port = 12345;
 name.sin_addr.s_addr = htonl(INADDR_ANY);
 ::bind(listen, (sockaddr *)&name, sizeof(name));
 ::listen(listen, SOMAXCONN);
 int n = sizeof(name);
 SOCKET socket = ::accept(listen, (sockaddr *)&name, &n);
 char buffer[256];
 ::recv(socket, buffer, sizeof(buffer), 0);
 ::send(socket, buffer, sizeof(buffer), 0);
 ::shutdown(socket, SD_SEND);
 ::shutdown(socket, SD_RECEIVE);
 ::shutdown(socket, SD_BOTH);
 ::closesocket(socket);
 ::closesocket(listen);
 ::WSACleanup();
};
```

Listing 3.14 Minimal socket server.

one parameter, the socket handle. Listing 3.14 shows a complete example of a minimal socket server.

I didn't call shutdown on the listening socket. This is because there was yet no bound client to the socket. This is typical of any listening socket. Additionally, it would be nice if the socket server could service more than one client at a time. In order to service more than one client, I must spawn threads for each socket connection, so that I may continue accepting additional client connections with the primary thread. Listing 3.15 shows how I may extend the socket server to accept additional requests. This complete example is a little ludicrous because it loops infinitely and spawns threads with reckless abandon.

An important function of Winsock that I've yet to explain is the WSAGet-LastError.

```
int WSAGetLastError (void);
```

```
DWORD WINAPI ThreadProc(void * p)
{
 SOCKET socket = *(SOCKET *)p;
 char buffer[256];
 ::recv(socket, buffer, sizeof(buffer), 0);
 ::send(socket, buffer, sizeof(buffer), 0);
 ::shutdown(socket, SD_SEND);
 ::shutdown(socket, SD_RECEIVE);
 ::shutdown(socket, SD_BOTH);
 ::closesocket(socket);
};
void main()
{
 WORD w = MAKEWORD(2,0);
 WSADATA wsadata;
 int i = ::WSAStartup(w, &wsadata);
 SOCKET listen = ::socket(AF_INET, SOCK_STREAM, IPPROTO_TCP);
 sockaddr_in name;
 name.sin_family = AF_INET;
 name.sin_port = 12345;
 name.sin_addr.s_addr = htonl(INADDR_ANY);
 ::bind(listen, (sockaddr *)&name, sizeof(name));
 ::listen(listen, SOMAXCONN);
 while (true)
 {
  int n = sizeof(name);
  SOCKET socket = ::accept(listen, (sockaddr *)&name, &n);
  DWORD dw;
  HANDLE thread =
  ::CreateThread(NULL, 0, ThreadProc, &socket, 0, &dw);
  ::CloseHandle(thread);
 };
 ::closesocket(listen);
 ::WSACleanup();
};
```

Listing 3.15   Complete socket server.

If any of the functions mentioned in the section return an error, then I can use WSAGetLastError to retrieve a more colorful description of the error. The complete list of Winsock 2 error codes is shown in Listing 3.16.

The errors are broken into three separate sets. The first set of errors is the translation of Microsoft C errors into Winsock error codes. The second set of errors is the translation of Berkeley socket errors into Winsock error codes. The third set of errors is the extended Winsock error codes.

```
/*
 * All Windows Sockets error constants are biased by WSABASEERR
 * from the "normal"
 */
#define WSABASEERR      10000
/*
 * Windows Sockets definitions of regular Microsoft C error
 * constants
 */
#define WSAEINTR                (WSABASEERR+4)
#define WSAEBADF                (WSABASEERR+9)
#define WSAEACCES               (WSABASEERR+13)
#define WSAEFAULT               (WSABASEERR+14)
#define WSAEINVAL               (WSABASEERR+22)
#define WSAEMFILE               (WSABASEERR+24)

/*
 * Windows Sockets definitions of regular Berkeley error
 * constants
 */
#define WSAEWOULDBLOCK          (WSABASEERR+35)
#define WSAEINPROGRESS          (WSABASEERR+36)
#define WSAEALREADY             (WSABASEERR+37)
#define WSAENOTSOCK             (WSABASEERR+38)
#define WSAEDESTADDRREQ         (WSABASEERR+39)
#define WSAEMSGSIZE             (WSABASEERR+40)
#define WSAEPROTOTYPE           (WSABASEERR+41)
#define WSAENOPROTOOPT          (WSABASEERR+42)
#define WSAEPROTONOSUPPORT      (WSABASEERR+43)
#define WSAESOCKTNOSUPPORT      (WSABASEERR+44)
#define WSAEOPNOTSUPP           (WSABASEERR+45)
#define WSAEPFNOSUPPORT         (WSABASEERR+46)
#define WSAEAFNOSUPPORT         (WSABASEERR+47)
#define WSAEADDRINUSE           (WSABASEERR+48)
#define WSAEADDRNOTAVAIL        (WSABASEERR+49)
#define WSAENETDOWN             (WSABASEERR+50)
#define WSAENETUNREACH          (WSABASEERR+51)
#define WSAENETRESET            (WSABASEERR+52)
#define WSAECONNABORTED         (WSABASEERR+53)
#define WSAECONNRESET           (WSABASEERR+54)
#define WSAENOBUFS              (WSABASEERR+55)
#define WSAEISCONN              (WSABASEERR+56)
#define WSAENOTCONN             (WSABASEERR+57)
#define WSAESHUTDOWN            (WSABASEERR+58)
#define WSAETOOMANYREFS         (WSABASEERR+59)
#define WSAETIMEDOUT            (WSABASEERR+60)
#define WSAECONNREFUSED         (WSABASEERR+61)
```

Continues

Listing 3.16 Winsock 2 error constants.

```
#define WSAELOOP               (WSABASEERR+62)
#define WSAENAMETOOLONG        (WSABASEERR+63)
#define WSAEHOSTDOWN           (WSABASEERR+64)
#define WSAEHOSTUNREACH        (WSABASEERR+65)
#define WSAENOTEMPTY           (WSABASEERR+66)
#define WSAEPROCLIM            (WSABASEERR+67)
#define WSAEUSERS              (WSABASEERR+68)
#define WSAEDQUOT              (WSABASEERR+69)
#define WSAESTALE              (WSABASEERR+70)
#define WSAEREMOTE             (WSABASEERR+71)

/*
 * Extended Windows Sockets error constant definitions
 */
#define WSASYSNOTREADY         (WSABASEERR+91)
#define WSAVERNOTSUPPORTED     (WSABASEERR+92)
#define WSANOTINITIALISED      (WSABASEERR+93)
#define WSAEDISCON             (WSABASEERR+101)
#define WSAENOMORE             (WSABASEERR+102)
#define WSAECANCELLED          (WSABASEERR+103)
#define WSAEINVALIDPROCTABLE   (WSABASEERR+104)
#define WSAEINVALIDPROVIDER    (WSABASEERR+105)
#define WSAEPROVIDERFAILEDINIT (WSABASEERR+106)
#define WSASYSCALLFAILURE      (WSABASEERR+107)
#define WSASERVICE_NOT_FOUND   (WSABASEERR+108)
#define WSATYPE_NOT_FOUND      (WSABASEERR+109)
#define WSA_E_NO_MORE          (WSABASEERR+110)
#define WSA_E_CANCELLED        (WSABASEERR+111)
#define WSAEREFUSED            (WSABASEERR+112)
```

Listing 3.16

Sample Socket Service

The next task is to incorporate this socket server code into the NT Service framework. Additionally, I will clean up some of the code presented in this section so that it works with the service framework. Listing 3.17 shows the complete NT socket service using the NT Service framework.

The last sample is really only a combination of two previous examples with additional error handling and reporting. The most important part of this sample to digest is the cleanup that is performed when the service is stopped. All socket handles are being placed in a global array. When the service is stopped, I force the shutdown of all local sockets. This is important, as I don't want the client socket to wait endlessly because the server socket was not properly shutdown.

I've seen examples where socket connections with a life expectancy in milliseconds were open for 15 hours because the client and server socket appli-

```
namespace
{
 SOCKET g_listen;
 std::map<int, SOCKET> msockets;
 int count = 0;
 CriticalSection cs;
 bool stop = false;

 DWORD WINAPI ThreadProc(void * p)
 {
  SOCKET socket = *(SOCKET *)p;
  cs.Lock();
  int cookie = count++;
  msockets[cookie] = socket;
  cs.Unlock();
  char buffer[1];
  while (!stop)
  {
   if (::recv(socket, buffer, sizeof(buffer), 0)
            == SOCKET_ERROR)
   {
    break;
   }
   if (::send(socket, buffer, sizeof(buffer), 0)
            == SOCKET_ERROR)
   {
    break;
   }
  }
  cs.Lock();
  ::shutdown(socket, SD_SEND);
  ::shutdown(socket, SD_RECEIVE);
  ::shutdown(socket, SD_BOTH);
  ::closesocket(socket);
  msockets.erase(cookie);
  cs.Unlock();
 };
};

class SocketService : public NtService::Service
{
public:
 SocketService()
  :NtService::Service("SocketService") {};
 virtual void OnRun()
 {
  while (!stop)
```

Continues

Listing 3.17 NT socket service.

```
   {
     int n = sizeof(name);
     SOCKET socket = ::accept(g_listen, (sockaddr *)&name, &n);
     DWORD dw;
     HANDLE thread =
     ::CreateThread(NULL, 0, ThreadProc, &socket, 0, &dw);
     ::CloseHandle(thread);
   }
 }
 virtual void OnInitialize()
 {
   WORD w = MAKEWORD(2,0);
   WSADATA wsadata;
   int i = ::WSAStartup(w, &wsadata);
   listen = ::socket(AF_INET, SOCK_STREAM, IPPROTO_TCP);
   sockaddr_in name;
   name.sin_family = AF_INET;
   name.sin_port = 12345;
   name.sin_addr.s_addr = htonl(INADDR_ANY);
   ::bind(g_listen, (sockaddr *)&name, sizeof(name));
   ::listen(g_listen, SOMAXCONN);
   Running();
 }
 virtual void OnStop()
 {
  stop = true;
  cs.Lock();
  for (std::map<int, SOCKET>::iterator i = msockets.begin();
    i != msockets.end(); i++)
 {
    ::shutdown(i->second, SD_SEND);
    ::shutdown(i->second, SD_RECEIVE);
    ::shutdown(i->second, SD_BOTH);
    ::closesocket(i->second);
  }
  ::closesocket(listen);
  ::WSACleanup();
  cs.Unlock();
 }
};

int WINAPI WinMain (HINSTANCE hinstance,
 HINSTANCE /* hprevious */, LPSTR lpCmdLine, int /* nShowCmd */)
{
 SocketService().Start(lpCmdLine);
 return 0;
}
```

Listing 3.17

cations simply didn't like reporting their statuses to each other. The server socket was long dead, but the client maintained the connection for hours because a thread was hung.

Sample Socket Client

A TCP/IP client needs to use the functions in Listing 3.18 to send server requests and receive server responses.

The only functions I didn't discuss while building the server are inet_addr, gethostbyaddr, gethostbyname, and connect. The middle two functions, gethostbyaddr and gethostbyname, serve very similar purposes. They are used to return host information given a host address or host name. Both return a hostent structure.

```
struct hostent {
  char FAR * h_name;         /* official name of host */
  char FAR * FAR * h_aliases;   /* alias list */
  short h_addrtype;          /* host address type */
  short h_length;            /* length of address */
  char FAR * FAR * h_addr_list; /* list of addresses */
};
```

The h_name member is the official name of the host. The h_aliases member is an array of aliases used by the host. The h_addrtype member is the type of address being returned and may be any of the types listed in Listing 3.3. The h_length member is the length of each address presented in the h_addr_list.

```
int PASCAL FAR WSAStartup (WORD wVersionRequired,
            LPWSADATA lpWSAData);
SOCKET PASCAL FAR socket (int af, int type, int protocol);
unsigned long inet_addr (const char FAR * cp);
struct hostent FAR * PASCAL FAR gethostbyaddr(
     const char FAR * addr, int len, int type);
struct hostent FAR * PASCAL FAR gethostbyname(
     const char FAR * name);
int PASCAL FAR connect (SOCKET s,
     const struct sockaddr FAR *name, int namelen);
int PASCAL FAR recv (SOCKET s, char FAR * buf, int len,
 int flags);
int PASCAL FAR send (SOCKET s, const char FAR * buf, int len,
 int flags);
int PASCAL FAR shutdown (SOCKET s, int how);
int PASCAL FAR closesocket (SOCKET s);
int PASCAL FAR WSACleanup(void);
```

Listing 3.18 TCP/IP socket client functions.

The last member, h_addr_list, is an array of host addresses. Normally, a host only has one address.

The gethostbyname function takes one parameter, a c-style character string that is the name of the host. Listing 3.19 shows an example of its usage. If either gethostby functions fail, they will return NULL.

The gethostbyaddr function takes three parameters: a structure representing the address of the host, the size of the structure, and the address type. For Internet addresses, the structure should be of type in_addr and the address type should be AF_INET.

The inet_addr function can be used to determine whether an address is an Internet address. The inet_addr function takes one input parameter and returns an in_addr structure. If the Internet address is not valid, then the in_addr structure has the value of INADDR_NONE. This indicates that the address is not an Internet address and can hint at the usage of either of the gethostby functions. Listing 3.19 shows how to use the three functions, inet_addr, gethostbyname, and gethostbyaddr, to retrieve the hostent structure.

If the GetHostAddress function returns NULL, then I can be pretty sure that the address didn't exist. This GetHostAddress function will return a valid hostent structure regardless of whether the address is specified in IP form or Uniform Resource Locator (URL) form.

Nearly every Internet resource can be addressed using either its IP or URL address. As an example, a Web site can be loaded in Internet Explorer (IE) using either form. In the address bar of IE, if I type www.kbcafe.com, the

```
hostent * GetHostAddress(const std::string & str)
{
 hostent * retval;
 in_addr inaddr;
 inaddr.s_addr = ::inet_addr(str.c_str());
 if (inaddr.s_addr == INADDR_NONE)
 {
  retval = ::gethostbyname(str.c_str());
 }
 else
 {
  retval = ::gethostbyaddr((const char *)&inaddr, sizeof(inaddr),
          AF_INET);
 }
 return retval;
}
```

Listing 3.19 gethostbysomething usage.

KBCafe Web site will appear. From a command prompt, if I type getipfromurl www.kbcafe.com, I can return to IE and enter the IP address that was output from the getipfromurl utility and the same KBCafe Web site appears. This is because IE is using the same or similar functions to map the string address into a real host address.

The client is very simple. First, I acquire a handle to a socket by calling the socket function (Listing 3.20). Then I connect this socket to a server socket by calling the connect function. Then I call the send and recv functions as I see fit until my client has finished its doings.

```cpp
int main(int argc, char * argv[])
{
 // get param[1] as server IP
 if (argc != 2)
 {
 std::cout << "usage:\tsocketclient [IP]" << std::endl;
 return 1;
 }

 HOSTENT * hostent = GetHostAddress(argv[2]);

 // get socket
 SOCKET socket;
 socket = ::socket(AF_INET, SOCK_STREAM, IPPROTO_TCP);

 sockaddr_in sa;
 sa.sin_family = AF_INET;
 sa.sin_port = 12345;
 sa.sin_addr.s_addr = *((u_long *)hostent->h_addr_list[0]);

 // connect to sever
 ::connect(socket, (sockaddr *)&sa, sizeof(SOCKADDR));

 // send request
 std::string request = "Hello";
 ::send(socket, request.c_str(), request.length(), 0);

 // printout request
 std::cout << "Request = " << request << std::endl;

 // receive response
 char response[256];
 ::recv(socket, response, 256*sizeof(char), 0);

 // printout response
 std::cout << "Response = " << response << std::endl;

 return 0;
}
```

Listing 3.20 Socket client.

Fail-Over and Load Balancing

Because sockets are simply an API into the transport layer, they do not incorporate many session management features. When a connection between two sockets is established, I can use the socket handle to represent the session. But beyond giving me a session handle, the socket handle, there is no functionality that makes it easy to implement fail-over or load balancing.

The easiest way to implement fail-over and load balancing in sockets is to implement connection-oriented sockets where the session connection is held open for brief periods of time.

To perform fail-over and load balancing, a proxy sits between the server and the clients (see Figure 3.3).

The proxy maintains a list of server addresses and simply round-robins through the server addresses to balance the load. When a connection to a server fails, the proxy temporarily discards the server address and continues with the next address in the list. The disadvantage of this technique is the brief duration of sessions. The brief duration makes it difficult for servers to maintain client state data. The workaround for this disadvantage is to create a stateless communication protocol between the client and server. Stateless communication is not always possible or easy.

If, for instance, I do implement a stateless communication protocol, then I can also benefit from the ability to recover processing threads by simply restarting the server. If I find that a particular socket server is not responding, I can rectify the situation by simply restarting the server. This is best implemented using a PING request. When the socket server receives the PING request, it immediately returns the PING response without any meaningful processing. If the PING client doesn't receive the expected response, the socket server is cycled, that is, shut down and restarted.

HTTP

HTTP (HyperText Transfer Protocol) is a connection-oriented socket protocol that was designed to transmit HyperText Markup Language (HTML) over the Internet. This protocol is now being used for much more than transmitting HTML. As a connection-oriented socket protocol, it is very well suited for implementing the fail-over and load-balancing strategies described here. Most HTTP traffic is stateless, that is, session data is usually only maintained for the brief lifetime of the connection. Some HTTP traffic uses a technique of passing cookies to maintain state.

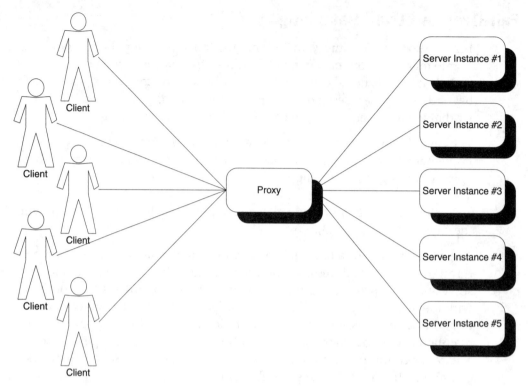

Figure 3.3 Proxy fail-over and load balancing.

I can implement this ping strategy in the socket server by adding code that checks if the transaction is a PING request and if so, sends a PING response. I've modified the ThreadProc function in the socket service to respond properly to PING requests (Listing 3.21).

The PING client must send a PING request to the socket server, receive the PING response, and compare it to the expected response. Assuming there are no errors, it can exit safely. If there are errors, then the PING client must stop and start the socket service. This PING client is shown in Listing 3.22.

The PING client creates a socket and attempts to connect to the socket server. When the connection is established, I should display some kind of generic message that the socket server can interpret as an attempt to ping. The socket server should respond with a second generic message that tells the client that it received the PING request. If the client received the PING request, it should terminate normally. If the client does not receive the PING, then I may decide to take measures to restart the server. In my example, I use the SCM functions to stop and restart the service.

```
DWORD WINAPI ThreadProc(void * p)
{
 SOCKET socket = * (SOCKET *)p;
 cs.Lock();
 int cookie = count++;
 msockets[cookie] = socket;
 cs.Unlock();
 char buffer[1];
 while (!stop)
 {
  if (::recv(socket, buffer, sizeof(buffer), 0)
                      == SOCKET_ERROR)
  {
   break;
  }
  if (::send(socket, buffer, sizeof(buffer), 0)
                      == SOCKET_ERROR)
  {
   break;
  }
 }
 cs.Lock();
 ::shutdown(socket, SD_SEND);
 ::shutdown(socket, SD_RECEIVE);
 ::shutdown(socket, SD_BOTH);
 ::closesocket(socket);
 msockets.erase(cookie);
 cs.Unlock();
};
```

Listing 3.21   PING socket service.

A PING client like this could be scheduled to run every few minutes to ensure that when the service croaks measures are taken to restart it without having to rely on the intervention of the operator. It might also be wise to add additional code in this PING client to send an SMTP (Simple Mail Transport Protocol) message or page to the operator.

Web Server

Now that I've demonstrated the details of programming a socket server, I'm going to ask the question, Do I really want to write my own socket server? There are many commercial socket servers that are very well tested. One such Web server is IIS (Internet Information Server). This Web server is very stable

```
int main(int argc, char * argv[])
{
 // get param[1] as server IP
 if (argc != 2)
 {
  std::cout << "usage:\pingclient [IP]" << std::endl;
  return 1;
 }

 HOSTENT * hostent = GetHostAddress(argv[2]);

 // get socket
 SOCKET socket;
 socket = ::socket(AF_INET, SOCK_STREAM, IPPROTO_TCP);

 sockaddr_in sa;
 sa.sin_family = AF_INET;
 sa.sin_port = 12345;
 sa.sin_addr = ((LPIN_ADDR)hostent->h_addr_list;
 // connect to server
 ::connect(socket, (sockaddr *)&sa, sizeof(SOCKADDR));

 // send request
 std::string request = "PING";

 ::send(socket, request.c_str(), request.length(), 0);

 std::cout << "Request = " << request << std::endl;

 // receive response
 char response[256];
 ::recv(socket, response, 256*sizeof(char), 0);
 std::cout << "Response = " << response << std::endl;

 if (std::string(response) == "PING")
 {
  std::cout << "SUCCESSFUL PING" << std::endl;
  return 0;
 }

 // Restart the service
 SC_HANDLE scm = ::OpenSCManager (NULL, NULL,
        SC_MANAGER_ALL_ACCESS);
 SC_HANDLE service = ::OpenService(scm, "SomeService",
        SERVICE_ALL_ACCESS);
 SERVICE_STATUS status;
 ::ControlService(service, SERVICE_CONTROL_STOP, &status);
 ::StartService(service, NULL, NULL);
 ::CloseServiceHandle(service);
 ::CloseServiceHandle(scm);

 return 0;

}
```

Listing 3.22   PING client.

and has had a lot of success. For the last couple of projects I've worked on, IIS was one of the more stable components.

DCOM

Distributed Component Object Model (DCOM) is an object-oriented transport. Object-oriented transports are the best of the breed because they seamlessly integrate with existing object architectures.

The great advantage of object-oriented transports is how they can make a call to a remote object look exactly like a call to a local object. Programmers can build local servers with stub local objects and gradually incorporate the full functionality of the real remote objects, as they become available. This promotes near optimal parallel development of components.

This type of transport also provides programmers with a pluggable design. Switching between a first-generation component and a second-generation component is a one-line change.

COM is the most widely used object framework. Every Visual Basic application is also a COM application, because all Visual Basic classes are COM classes. Other tools such as Microsoft Foundation Classes (MFCs) and Active Template Library (ATL) have made the development of COM objects in C++ almost trivial. But COM has one shortcoming: It only works within the boundaries of one computer. In order to overcome this, Microsoft introduced DCOM. DCOM allows COM objects to communicate across computer networks.

A great thing about DCOM is that every COM object is also a DCOM object. This is easily accomplished because COM uses a light version of MS-RPC (Microsoft Remote Procedure Calls) as its transport. This version is light because it lacks networking capabilities. The transport only works between two processes on the same machine. It is then easy to plug DCOM into the equation by removing the light RPC and replacing it with a full implementation of RPC that is capable of networked operation.

Remote Procedure Calls

Remote Procedure Calls (RPCs) was a widely used protocol for calling and marshaling function parameters across process and computer boundaries. The protocol varies widely in its implementation, as there is little standardization in implementation. There did exist an attempt to standardize the APIs for an RPC. This standard was known as Distributed Computing Environment (DCE) RPC and was created by Open Software Foundation (OSF), an organization that was created in order to define open standards.

It should be remembered that DCE RPC is only a standard and many implementations, mostly incompatible, exist across a multitude of platforms. In this book, I will use Microsoft's implementation of RPC (Ms-RPC).

Distributed Computing Environment

Beyond simply being a function-oriented transport, the DCE RPC standard defined additional functionality including security, directory services, time services, threading, and marshaling.

Interface Definition Language

In order to provide for parameter marshaling, the DCE standard introduced a language called Interface Definition Language (IDL). DCE IDL provides a standard mechanism for creating implementation-independent declarations of function calls. Listing 3.23 shows a sample IDL file.

```
/*
-----------------------------------------------------------------
File:     varpc.idl
Purpose:  RPC Interfaces for Visual Studio Analyzer Eventing
System:   Visual Studio Analyzer Analysis.
Copyright: (c) 1997, Microsoft Corporation
      All Rights Reserved
Tabs:     2,2
-----------------------------------------------------------------
*/

import "vaevt.idl";

[
uuid(6c736d30-e80d-11d0-96e7-00a0c90f27e2),
version(1.0)
]
interface IRPC_MicrosoftVisualStudioAnalyzer
{
  long VSAOpenConnection    ([out] long *vaaId);
  long VSACloseConnection   ([in] long vaaId);
  long VSABeginSession      ([in] long vaaId,
    [in, string] wchar_t *guidSourceID,
    [in, string] wchar_t *strSessionName);

  long VSAEndSession        ([in] long vaaId);
  long VSAIsActive          ([in] long vaaId);
```

Continues

Listing 3.23 Sample IDL.

```
long VSAFireEvent      ([in] long vaaId,
 [in, string] wchar_t *guidEvent,
                       [in] long prgCount,
                       [in, string, size_is(prgCount)]
                            wchar_t *prgKeys[],
                       [in, string, size_is(prgCount)]
                            wchar_t *prgValues[],
 [in] long dwTimeLow,
    //The local time of the event, or 0. (Low 32 bits)
 [in] long dwTimeHigh,
    //The local time of the event, or 0. (High 32 bits)
 [in] VSAEventFlags dwFlags // See above
 );

 long VSARegisterSource (
 [in, string] wchar_t *strVisibleName,
 [in, string] wchar_t *guidSourceID);

 long VSAIsSourceRegistered(
        [in, string] wchar_t *guidSourceID);

 long VSARegisterStockEvent(
        [in, string] wchar_t *guidSourceID,
        [in, string] wchar_t *guidEventID);

 long VSARegisterCustomEvent(
        [in, string] wchar_t *guidSourceID,
        [in, string] wchar_t *guidEventID,
        [in, string] wchar_t *strVisibleName,
        [in, string] wchar_t *strDescription,
        [in] long nEventType,
        [in, string] wchar_t *guidCategory);

 long VSARegisterEventCategory (
        [in, string] wchar_t *guidSourceID,
        [in, string] wchar_t *guidCategoryID,
        [in, string] wchar_t *guidParentID,
        [in, string] wchar_t *strVisibileName,
        [in, string] wchar_t *strDescription);

 long VSAUnregisterSource (
        [in, string] wchar_t *guidSourceID);
}
```

Listing 3.23

The IDL shown here is an interface to the Visual Studio Analyzer. Don't
worry about what the Analyzer is or does. The important thing is to note the
characteristics of this IDL file. The functions contained within the interface
are functions supported by the RPC interface. Unlike COM and CORBA IDL,
which are explained later, the functions within the interface do not belong to

an object, but are c-styled functions. Each function can be called independently without reference to an object.

The IDL source can be processed into proxy and stub code. The proxy code is then linked to the client and the stub code is linked to the server to provide seamless remote function calls, also known as remote procedure calls.

Universally Unique IDs

Another DCE introduction was the Universally Unique IDs (UUIDs). UUIDs are 128-bit numbers that were used to uniquely identify interfaces. The concept of UUIDs was extended in DCOM to provide for a much greater range of implementations for Unique IDs (UIDs).

Synchronous Calls

A very large advantage as well as disadvantage of RPC is that the protocol is said to be synchronous. That is, the client sends a request to the server and blocks until the server replies to the client with a response. When a thread is blocked, it is doing nothing. This can't be good. On the other hand, synchronous calls are not nearly as complex as asynchronous calls; that is, the simplicity of synchronous over asynchronous protocols is also an advantage.

Security

DCE Security is another important feature of RPC. DCE RPC uses a security provider called Kerberos. The Windows 2000 operating system has plans to adopt the Kerberos security provider as its default security provider. Once Windows 2000 incorporates the Kerberos standard, it will also be available for use by MS-RPC.

Plain COM

Implementing a COM server is quite difficult. To facilitate the implementation of COM technologies, Microsoft has provided a large set of APIs and frameworks that make developing with COM less difficult. A COM object is very similar to a C++ object that has a purely abstract interface. Listing 3.24 shows an example of a C++ program using a purely abstract interface to call functions in a C++ object.

The IBeerBottle interface is identical to a COM interface, except that COM interfaces are typically declared in COM IDL and must be derived from the IUnknown interface (see Listing 3.25). COM IDL is an object-oriented implementation of DCE IDL.

The IUnknown::AddRef and IUnknown::Release methods are used by an implementation to perform reference counting. The IUnknown::QueryInter-

```cpp
class IBeerBottle
{
public:
 virtual void Open() = 0;
 virtual void Drink() = 0;
 virtual int GetMiliLiters() = 0;
};

class MyBeerBottle : public IBeerBottle
{
 bool m_open;
 int m_mililiters;
public:
 MyBeerBottle()
 : m_open(false), m_mililiters(350) {};
 void Open()
 {
  m_open = true;
 };
 void Drink()
 {
  if (m_open)
  {
   m_mililiters -= 50;
  }
 };
 int GetMiliLiters()
 {
  return m_mililiters;
 };
};

int main()
{
 IBeerBottle * beer = new MyBeerBottle();
 beer->Open();
 beer->Drink();
 std::cout << "Liters left = " << beer->GetMiliLiters()
               << std::endl;
 delete beer;
 return 0;
}
```

Listing 3.24 C++ abstract interfaces.

face method is used to cast one interface pointer into another interface pointer implemented by the object.

The MyBeerBottle class is similar to a COM class, except that COM classes usually have factory classes. Factory classes are a standard design pattern

```
interface IUnknown
{
 HRESULT QueryInterface(
    [in] REFIID riid,
    [out, iid_is(riid)] void **ppvObject);
  ULONG AddRef();
  ULONG Release();
};
```

Listing 3.25   IUnknown IDL.

```
interface IClassFactory : IUnknown
{
 [local] HRESULT CreateInstance(
    [in, unique] IUnknown * pUnkOuter,
    [in] REFIID riid,
    [out, iid_is(riid)] void **ppvObject);

 [local] HRESULT LockServer(
    [in] BOOL fLock);
};
```

Listing 3.26   IClassFactory IDL.

where the factory class exists solely to construct classes of one or more class types. COM factory classes have a common factory class interface, IClassFactory (see Listing 3.26).

The IClassFactory::CreateInstance method is used to create an actual object instance. The implementation of the main function in Listing 3.24 is also nearly identical to what would be done in COM. Rather than call the new operator, COM objects are created by calling the CoGetClassFactory function to retrieve the factory class, followed by IClassFactory::CreateInstance method to create the class instance. Listing 3.27 shows a derivation of the beer application that uses COM classes that inherit from the IUnknown and IClassFactory building blocks.

The first part of Listing 3.27 is the interface and class IDL declaration. It is very important to understand the difference between a COM interface and a COM class. The COM interface defines a contract that is used by the client to call on the COM class. If a COM class advertises that it implements a particular interface, then it must expose all the methods of that interface.

```
[
 object,
```

```
[
 object,
 uuid(D1E057E0-5198-11d3-B6CA-00C04F8B72E7),
 pointer_default(unique)
]
interface IBeerBottle : IUnknown
{
 HRESULT Open();
 HRESULT Drink();
 HRESULT GetMiliLiters([out] int * i);
};


[
    uuid(AD092D00-C13A-11d3-9C2B-747106C10000),
    version(1.0)
]
library BEERBOTTLELib
{
 [
  uuid(A5440680-519C-11d3-B6CA-00C04F8B72E7),
 ]
 coclass BeerBottle
 {
  [default] interface IBeerBottle;
 };
};

class MyBeerBottle : public IBeerBottle
{
 bool m_open;
 int m_mililiters;
 long m_references;
public:
 MyBeerBottle()
 : m_open(false), m_mililiters(350), m_references(0) {};
 ULONG STDMETHODCALLTYPE AddRef()
 {
  ::InterlockedIncrement(&m_references);
  return m_references;
 }
 ULONG STDMETHODCALLTYPE Release()
 {
  ::InterlockedDecrement(&m_references);
  if (m_references == 0)
  {
   delete this;
```

Continues

Listing 3.27 Beer application in COM.

```
    }
   return m_references;
  }
  HRESULT STDMETHODCALLTYPE QueryInterface(REFIID riid,
          void ** ppv)
  {
   if (riid == IID_IUnknown)
   {
    *ppv = static_cast<IUnknown*>(this);
    AddRef();
    return S_OK;
   }
   if (riid == IID_IBeerBottle)
   {
    *ppv = static_cast<IBeerBottle*>(this);
    AddRef();
    return S_OK;
   }
   *ppv = NULL;
   return E_NOINTERFACE;
  };
  HRESULT STDMETHODCALLTYPE Open()
  {
   m_open = true;
   return S_OK;
  };
  HRESULT STDMETHODCALLTYPE Drink()
  {
   if (m_open)
   {
    m_mililiters -= 50;
    return S_OK;
   }
   return S_FALSE;
  };
  HRESULT STDMETHODCALLTYPE GetMiliLiters(int * i)
  {
   *i = m_mililiters;
   return S_OK;
  };
 };

class MyBeerBottleFactory : public IClassFactory
{
 long m_references;
public:
 ULONG STDMETHODCALLTYPE AddRef()
```

Continues

Listing 3.27   Beer application in COM *(Continued).*

```
{
 ::InterlockedIncrement(&m_references);
 return m_references;
}
ULONG STDMETHODCALLTYPE Release()
{
 ::InterlockedDecrement(&m_references);
 if (m_references == 0)
 {
  delete this;
 }
 return m_references;
}
HRESULT STDMETHODCALLTYPE QueryInterface(REFIID riid,
        void ** ppv)
{
 if (riid == IID_IUnknown)
 {
  *ppv = static_cast<IUnknown*>(this);
  AddRef();
  return S_OK;
 }
 if (riid == IID_IClassFactory)
 {
  *ppv = static_cast<IClassFactory*>(this);
  AddRef();
  return S_OK;
 }
 *ppv = NULL;
 return E_NOINTERFACE;
};
HRESULT STDMETHODCALLTYPE CreateInstance(
        IUnknown * pUnkOuter, REFIID riid, void ** ppv )
{
 if (pUnkOuter != 0)
 {
  *ppv = 0;
  return CLASS_E_NOAGGREGATION;
 }
 MyBeerBottle * object = new MyBeerBottle;
 if (object == 0)
 {
  return E_OUTOFMEMORY;
 }
 object->AddRef();
 HRESULT hr = object->QueryInterface (riid, ppv);
```

Continues

Listing 3.27

```
  object->Release();
  return hr;
};
HRESULT STDMETHODCALLTYPE LockServer(BOOL bLock)
{
  return E_NOTIMPL;
}
};

int main()
{
 ::CoInitialize(NULL);
 MyBeerBottleFactory * beerfactory =
     new MyBeerBottleFactory;
 IClassFactory * factory = NULL;
 beerfactory->QueryInterface(IID_IClassFactory,
          (void **)&factory);
     DWORD dw;
 ::CoRegisterClassObject(CLSID_BeerBottle, factory,
  CLSCTX_LOCAL_SERVER, REGCLS_MULTIPLEUSE, &dw);

 {
  IClassFactory * factory = NULL;
  ::CoGetClassObject( CLSID_BeerBottle, CLSCTX_ALL, 0,
   IID_IClassFactory, (void **)&factory );
  IBeerBottle * beer = NULL;
  factory->CreateInstance(0, IID_IBeerBottle,
             (void **)&beer);
  factory->Release();
  beer->Open();
  beer->Drink();
  int i=0;
  beer->GetMiliLiters(&i);
  std::cout << "Liters left = " << i << std::endl;
  beer->Release();
 }

 ::CoRevokeClassObject(dw);
 ::CoUninitialize();
 return 0;
};
```

Listing 3.27 Beer application in COM *(Continued).*

```
uuid(D1E057E0-5198-11d3-B6CA-00C04F8B72E7),
pointer_default(unique)
]
interface IBeerBottle : IUnknown
{
HRESULT Open();
```

```
HRESULT Drink();
HRESULT GetMiliLiters([out] int * i);
};
```

All COM IDL declarations are broken into two components: the header and the body. The header must include the object attribute to denote that the declaration is a COM interface and not an RPC interface. The uuid attribute is the unique identifier that is used to reference the interface.

I used the GenGuid tool provided with MsDev and the SDK to generate new uuids for my interface. I will also use this tool again to generate new uuids for my coclass (see the following) and my AppID (see the following section on CLSID and AppID).

```
[
 uuid(A5440680-519C-11d3-B6CA-00C04F8B72E7),
]
coclass BeerBottle
{
 [default] interface IBeerBottle;
};
```

The class IDL declaration is also split into header and body. The header must also contain a uuid attribute that defines the unique identifier that is used to reference the class.

The IDL declarations should be placed in an IDL file and compiled using the MIDL (Microsoft IDL) compiler. The output of the MIDL compiler is the four files, myinterface.h, dlldata.c, myinterface_i.c, and myinterface_p.c. The header files will contain the necessary declarations in order to use and create the COM objects. The dlldata.c source is the glue necessary to build a proxy-stub DLL. The myinterface_i.c defines the IID and CLSID constants used to identify interfaces and classes. The myinterface_p.c is the marshaling code needed to marshal calls made through the interface.

I will not include the entire content of these four files generated by the MIDL compiler in this book. (Readers can generate their own if they want to look at the entire content.) But I would like to draw attention to some of the content of these files. Listing 3.28 shows the C++ definition for the IBeerBottle interface found in the myinterface.h file.

As this listing shows, the interface is defined as an abstract C++ class. A constant IID_IBeerBottle is defined that I may use to reference the interface. Listing 3.29 shows the constant definitions for the IBeerBottle interface and BeerBottle classes found in the myinterface_i.c file.

The two constant definitions were generated from the uuid found in the IDL interface and class declarations. I am now ready to create an NT Service that implements the MyBeerBottle class.

```
EXTERN_C const IID IID_IBeerBottle;

MIDL_INTERFACE("D1E057E0-5198-11d3-B6CA-00C04F8B72E7")
IBeerBottle : public IUnknown
{
public:
  virtual HRESULT STDMETHODCALLTYPE Open( void) = 0;

  virtual HRESULT STDMETHODCALLTYPE Drink( void) = 0;

  virtual HRESULT STDMETHODCALLTYPE GetMiliLiters(
    /* [out] */ int __RPC_FAR *i) = 0;
};
```

Listing 3.28 C++ definition of the COM interface.

Sample COM Service

I'll reuse the IDL declarations and the two classes I created in Listing 3.30. From there, I only have to override the OnRun methods of the generic Nt-Service framework.

The OnRun method loads the COM library and registers the class factory object and waits for incoming messages to the thread. Pretty simple. The service framework is taking care of everything else.

I call four COM-specific functions in the OnRun method. The CoInitialize function loads the COM library and starts the apartment. (I explain apartments later in the chapter.) I then call the CoRegisterClassObject function to register the new object with the COM.

When the message loop terminates, I clean everything up by first calling the CoRevokeClassObject function to deregister the object with COM. Finally, I call the CoUninitialize function to stop the apartment and unload the COM library.

Two additional files are needed in order for COM to properly activate and access the service's COM object. The first is the proxy-stub DLL needed in order to marshal method calls between the service and its clients. The second is the registration file necessary to configure the COM class in the Windows Registry to run in a service.

```
const IID IID_IBeerBottle =
{0xD1E057E0,0x5198,0x11d3,{0xB6,0xCA,0x00,0xC0,0x4F,0x8B,0x72,0xE7}};
const CLSID CLSID_BeerBottle =
{0xA5440680,0x519C,0x11d3,{0xB6,0xCA,0x00,0xC0,0x4F,0x8B,0x72,0xE7}};
```

Listing 3.29 IDL constant definitions.

```
class DCOMService : public NtService::Service
{
 DWORD dw;
public:
 DCOMService()
  :NtService::Service("DCOMService") {};
 virtual void OnRun()
 {
 ::CoInitialize(NULL);
 MyBeerBottleFactory * beerfactory =
          new MyBeerBottleFactory;
 IClassFactory * factory = NULL;
 beerfactory->QueryInterface(IID_IClassFactory,
            (void **)&factory);
 ::CoRegisterClassObject(CLSID_BeerBottle, factory,
  CLSCTX_LOCAL_SERVER, REGCLS_MULTIPLEUSE, &dw);

     MSG msg;
     while (GetMessage (&msg, 0, 0, 0))
     {
        DispatchMessage(&msg);
     }

     ::CoRevokeClassObject(dw);
     ::CoUninitialize();
 }
};
int WINAPI WinMain(HINSTANCE hinstance,
 HINSTANCE /* hprevious */, LPSTR lpCmdLine, int /* nShowCmd */)
{
 DCOMService().Start(lpCmdLine);
 return 0;
}
```

Listing 3.30 DCOM service.

Proxy Stub

The proxy-stub DLL is necessary in order to convert COM method call parameters to data streams that can be sent across the wire or transferred between processes. To create this file, I need to compile all the marshaling code generated earlier with MIDL into a proxy-stub DLL. Listing 3.31 shows a make file that will compile the proxy stub.

Earlier I generated four files, dlldata.c, myinterace_p.c, myinterface_i.c, and myinterface.h. These are the files that will be used as input for the make to produce the output, the proxy-stub DLL, myinterfaceps.dll.

```
myinterfaceps.dll: dlldata.obj myinterface_p.obj \
        myinterface_i.obj
 link /dll /out:myinterfaceps.dll /def:proxystub.def \
        /entry:DllMain dlldata.obj myinterface_p.obj \
        myinterface_i.obj kernel32.lib rpcndr.lib rpcns4.lib \
        rpcrt4.lib \ rpcrt4.lib oleaut32.lib uuid.lib

.c.obj:
cl /c /Ox /DWIN32 /D_WIN32_WINNT=0x0400 \
             /DREGISTER_PROXY_DLL &<

clean:
 @del myinterfaceps.dll
 @del myinterfaceps.lib
 @del myinterfaceps.exp
 @del dlldata.obj
 @del myinterface_p.obj
 @del myinterface_i.obj
```

Listing 3.31 Proxy-stub make file.

One additional file beyond the four already identified is required. The proxy-stub (DEF) module DEFinition file is shown in Listing 3.32.

```
LIBRARY    "MyInterfacePS"

DESCRIPTION 'Proxy/Stub DLL'

EXPORTS
 DllGetClassObject    @1 PRIVATE
 DllCanUnloadNow      @2 PRIVATE
 GetProxyDllInfo      @3 PRIVATE
 DllRegisterServer     @4 PRIVATE
 DllUnregisterServer   @5 PRIVATE
```

Listing 3.32 Proxy-stub module DEFinition file.

The DEF file defines the entry points into the proxy-stub DLL. The DllGet-ClassObject and DllCanUnloadNow functions are described later in this chapter. The DllRegisterServer and DllUnregisterServer functions are called to register and unregister the DLL.

Once I've created the proxy-stub DLL, I must register this proxy stub on every machine that uses the interface. It must be registered along with the COM service and with all clients that call the interfaces to the COM service. To register the proxy stub, I can use the RegSvr32 utility.

When I invoke the RegSvr32 utility, it loads the proxy-stub DLL and calls the DllRegisterServer exported function. I can also unregister the proxy-stub DLL with this tool by calling RegSvr32 with the /u command-line parameter. The code to simulate this registration and unregistration is shown in Listing 3.33.

```
void RegSvr32(const std::string & str)
{
 HINSTANCE handle = ::LoadLibrary(str.c_str());
 FARPROC dllentrypoint = ::GetProcAddress(handle,
  "DllRegisterServer");
 (*dllentrypoint)();
};

void UnRegSvr32(const std::string & str)
{
 HINSTANCE handle = ::LoadLibrary(str.c_str());
 FARPROC dllentrypoint = ::GetProcAddress(handle,
  "DllUnregisterServer");
 (*dllentrypoint)();
}

void main(int argc, char ** argv)
{
 if (argc != 2 && argc != 3)
 {
  std::cout << "Usage:\n\tMyRegSvr32 {-u} {dll-name}"
   << std::endl;
  return;
 }

 if (std::string(argv[1]) == "-u" ||
  std::string(argv[1]) == "/u")
 {
  if (argc != 3)
  {
   std::cout << "Usage:\n\tMyRegSvr32 {-u}"
                     " {dll-name}" << std::endl;
   return;
  }

  ::UnRegSvr32(argv[2]);
 }
 else
 {
  ::RegSvr32(argv[1]);
 }
};
```

Listing 3.33 RegSvr32 simulated code.

This simulated code does very little. First, I check if the first command-line parameter was -u. If the first parameter was -u, then I call the function to unregister the server; otherwise, I call the function to register the server.

In the RegSvr32 function, I load the DLL, get the address of the DllRegisterServer function, and call it. I do the same in the UnRegSvr32 function, except I call the DllUnregisterServer function, rather than the DllRegisterServer function.

CLSID and AppID

I also need to configure the CLSID and AppID of the COM class service in the registry (see Listing 3.34).

To configure a COM class, I must add a CLSID in the HKEY_CLASSES_ROOT\CLSID key in the Windows Registry. In the IDL (see Listing 3.27), the coclass had a uuid attribute. This uuid attribute is the unique class ID that is used to reference the class. This uuid is added as a subkey below the CLSID key. Only two settings are required in this subkey: the name and the AppID.

The AppID was generated using the GenGUID tool previously described in this chapter. When calls are made to the CoCreateInstance, the COM library will use this AppID value in the CLSID subkey to find the AppID subkey in HKEY_CLASSES_ROOT\AppID subkey. This indirection was added to the COM object configuration in order for several COM classes to share a common configuration at the application level (see Table 3.2).

I also need to configure the AppID to point to the service name, so that the COM Service Control Manager (SCM) knows which service to activate and call when the object is created. The LocalService value denotes the name of the service where the coclass objects will be created.

Sample COM Client

The client application is quite simple. I will create one instance of the Beer-Bottle object, call a couple of methods, and verify the results are correct. Listing 3.35 presents this simple client.

```
[HKEY_CLASSES_ROOT\CLSID\{A5440680-519C-11d3-B6CA-00C04F8B72E7}]
@="BeerBottle class"
"AppID"_"{5B1A9640-51D7-11d3-B6CA-00C04F8B72E7}"

[HKEY_CLASSES_ROOT\AppID\{5B1A9640-51D7-11d3-B6CA-00C04F8B72E7}]
@="DCOMService"
"LocalService"="DCOMService"
```

Listing 3.34   COM service registry settings.

Table 3.2 CLSID to AppID Indirection

HKEY_CLASSES_ROOT			
CLSID			
	{00020906-0000-0000-C000-000000000046}]		
		AppID = {00020906-0000-0000-C000-000000000046}	
HKEY_CLASSES_ROOT			
AppID			
	{00020906-0000-0000-C000-000000000046}]		

I start by loading the COM library by calling the CoInitialize function. The second thing to do is to load the class factory object that will create the BeerBottle object. The CoGetClassObject function returns the class factory instance. I can then call the IClassFactory::CreateInstance method to create the BeerBottle object instance. I then release the class factory by calling the IUnknown::Release method.

Now that I have the object instance, I can call methods of the instance, IBeerBottle::Open, IBeerBottle::Drink, and IBeerBottle::GetMiliLiters. When I am

```cpp
int main(int argc, char* argv[])
{
    ::CoInitialize(NULL);

    IClassFactory * factory = NULL;
    ::CoGetClassObject( CLSID_BeerBottle, CLSCTX_ALL,
     0, IID_IClassFactory, (void **)&factory );
    IBeerBottle * beer = NULL;
    factory-> CreateInstance(0, IID_IBeerBottle,
            (void **)&beer);
    factory->Release();
    beer->Open();
    beer->Drink();
    int i=0;
    beer->GetMiliLiters(&i);
    std::cout << "Liters left = " << i << std::endl;
    beer->Release();

    ::CoUninitialize();
    return 0;
}
```

Listing 3.35 COM client.

finished, I call the IUnknown::Release method to destroy the object and CoUninitialize to unload the COM library.

The output of the program is "Liters left = 300." This is correct. I won't explain why, as I don't have any intent on explaining how drinking beer works. Had one of the function or method calls failed, they would have returned an HRESULT value indicating the failure.

Note that I called the Release method on both the class factory object and the actual object, but I never called the AddRef method on these objects. It would be logical to assume that the referencing counting on these classes would be incorrect. In fact, they aren't. When the CoGetClassFactory function and the CreateInstance method are called, the AddRef method call can be assumed.

Active Template Library

Programming raw COM objects is rather cumbersome. I've excluded a lot of topics because of this complexity, yet the section on COM will remain the largest in the book. In order to make COM server development as easy as possible, Microsoft created a set of C++ templates known as the Active Template Library (ATL) that makes COM server development somewhat easier, but still not easy.

In tandem with the ATL Object Wizard, COM server development does become easy. A little point-and-click action can bring COM servers into being in a matter of minutes. Remember all the code I wrote creating the COM BeerBottle class? The ATL Object Wizard can do the same with the click of a few buttons.

Here I'll recreate the BeerBottle class in ATL. I load MsDev and select File | New from the menu bar. The Project Wizard appears (see Figure 3.4).

Then I select the ATL COM AppWizard in the Projects tab. I add an appropriate Project name and Location and click on the OK button. After I click the OK button, the ATL COM AppWizard appears (see Figure 3.5).

I select the Service (EXE) Server Type radio button and click the Finish button. The other two options in this wizard are to create a COM DLL and a COM EXE (one that is not a service). I explain COM DLLs later in this chapter. I will not address COM EXEs except as NT Services. The New Project Information dialog should appear (see Figure 3.6).

The New Project Information dialog explains what files the code generator will be creating. The first file, myatlservice.dsp, is the DevStudio project file that I'll use to create the COM service. The wizard will also create a C++ source file (cpp) and a COM IDL file (idl) and make a file for the proxy stub.

The C++ source file will contain the C++ code needed to create the service EXE. The IDL file will contain the interface descriptions that I'll use to gener-

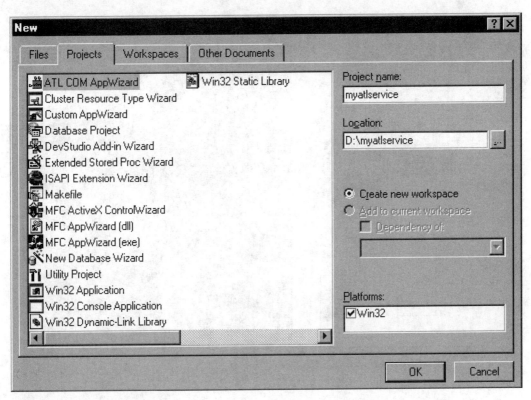

Figure 3.4   Project Wizard.

ate the proxy-stub header and source. The make file will turn the proxy-stub source into a proxy-stub DLL.

I click OK to confirm the project creation. The Wizard will then generate all the source files that are necessary to create the base ATL service with no objects. To add objects to the ATL service, I select Insert | New ATL Object from the menu bar. The ATL Object Wizard should appear (see Figure 3.7).

I select the Objects Category, the Simple Object, and click the Next button. The ATL Object Wizard Properties appear (see Figure 3.8).

In the Names tab, I add the desired Short Name and the Wizard will automatically fill the other seven text boxes in the tab. The Class field is the name of the C++ class that will be generated. The H and CPP File fields will be the filenames where this class will be contained. The CoClass field is the name that will identify the class in the IDL file. The Interface field is the name that will identify the interface in the IDL file. The Prog ID field is a short name that will be associated with the CLSID in order to give the class a more human-readable name.

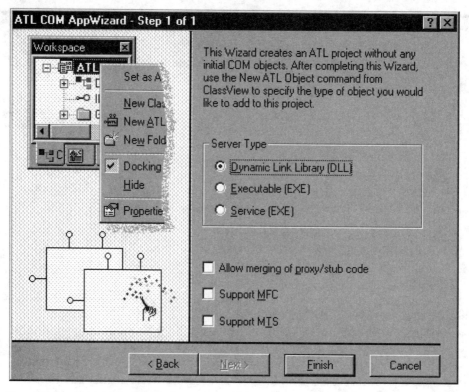

Figure 3.5 ATL COM AppWizard.

Next, I'll switch to the Attributes tab. In the Attributes tab, I must ensure that I have selected the same default settings as seen in Figure 3.9 and then click on the OK button.

The Threading Model may be Single, Apartment, Both, and Free. This determines how threading is handled in the COM server. I explain COM threading in detail later in the chapter. The Interface type may be Dual or Custom. A Dual interface is one that is both a custom interface and an automation interface. A Custom interface is a COM custom interface that is not also an automation interface. The Aggregation options are Yes, No, and Only. A COM object that supports aggregation may be inherited using aggregation inheritance. I won't explain this in the book, as it is not relevant to NT Services.

The last three attributes are either selected or not. They are support of IError-Info, IConnectionPoints, and a free-threaded marshaler. The IErrorInfo interface is used in COM Automation to communicate rich error information between COM clients and servers. The IConnectionPoint interface is used by COM to implement a very rich callback mechanism. Last, the free-threaded marshaler provides the call marshaler with an alternate threading strategy.

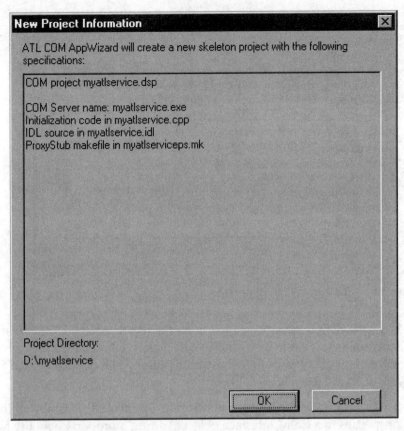

Figure 3.6 New Project Information dialog.

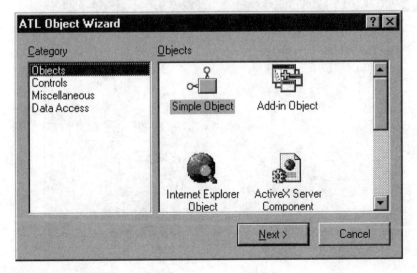

Figure 3.7 ATL Object Wizard.

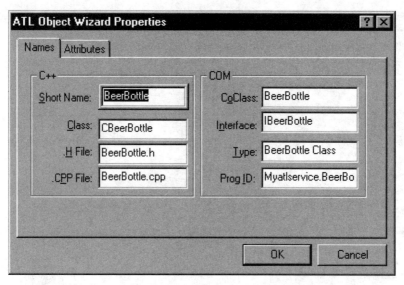

Figure 3.8 ATL Object Wizard Properties.

The Wizard will now generate code for the BeerBottle object. I then must add methods to the BeerBottle interface. To add these methods, I simply right-click on the interface that will declare these methods and select Add Method from the pop-up menu (see Figure 3.10).

A second COM option was given in this pop-up menu, that is, the ability to add properties to a COM interface object. Adding a property actually has the

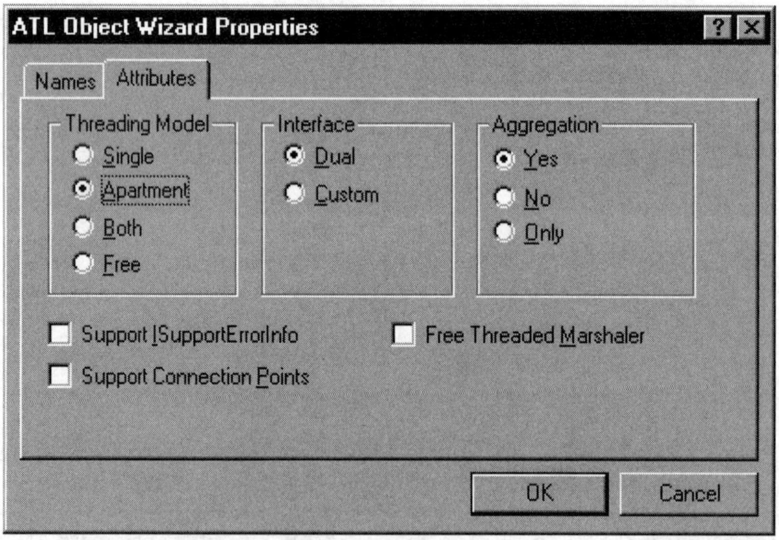

Figure 3.9 ATL Object Wizard Attributes tab.

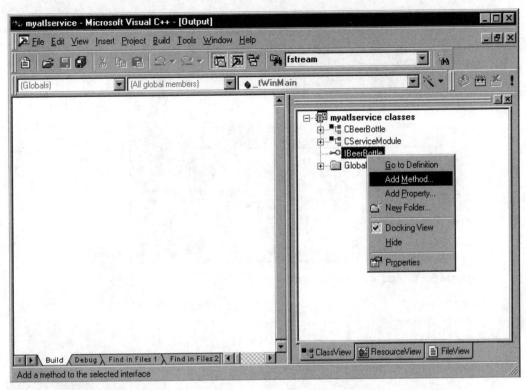

Figure 3.10 Add Method.

effect of adding two methods, one to access the data and one to set the data of the property.

After I select Add Method from the pop-up menu, the Add Method to Interface dialog appears (see Figure 3.11).

After I fill in the Method Name and Parameters, I click the OK button. The Parameters field must be filled in the same manner as the parameters would appear in the IDL file. The Wizard will add method templates to the existing class that implements the interface (see Listing 3.36).

Now I have all the COM code I need to complete the implementation of the class. After I add member variables to the class (CBeerBottle) and complete the implementations of the functions, I have a complete ATL-COM-NT Service.

Because developing COM objects in ATL is so easy, I will build all COM objects for the rest of this book using ATL. In most major sections of this book, I'll present the user with a COM object that simplifies usage of the technology I'm describing.

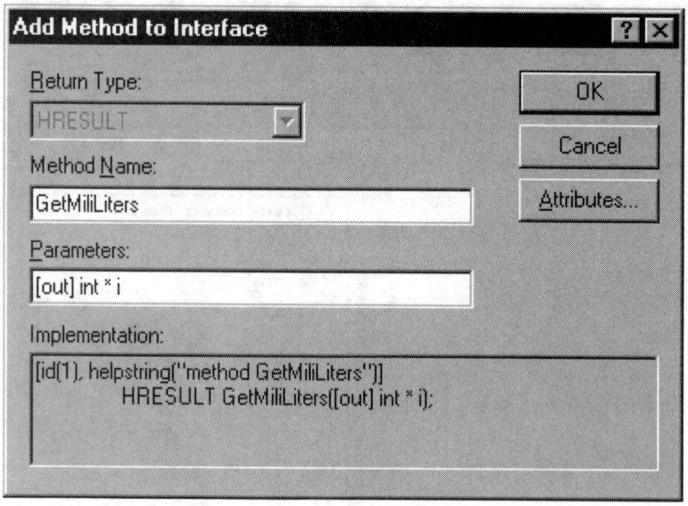

Figure 3.11   Add Method to Interface.

```
// BeerBottle.cpp : Implementation of CBeerBottle
#include "stdafx.h"
#include "Myatlservice.h"
#include "BeerBottle.h"

/////////////////////////////////////////////////////////////////////
// CBeerBottle

STDMETHODIMP CBeerBottle::Open()
{
 // TODO: Add your implementation code here

 return S_OK;
}

STDMETHODIMP CBeerBottle::Drink()
{
 // TODO: Add your implementation code here

 return S_OK;
}

STDMETHODIMP CBeerBottle::GetMiliLiters(int *i)
{
 //TODO: Add your implementation code here

 return S_OK;
}
```

Listing 3.36   Method templates.

Object Linking and Embedding DataBase

Object Linking and Embedding DataBase (OLEDB) is an interface specification developed by Microsoft and implemented over COM. OLEDB was introduced as a replacement for Microsoft's legacy Open DataBase Connectivity (ODBC) specification.

Both ODBC and OLEDB are data access layers that abstract the type of database management system. The differences between ODBC and OLEDB are that ODBC is a thick abstraction layer and is function-oriented, whereas OLEDB is a paper thin abstraction layer and is object-oriented. The primary advantage of using OLEDB rather than ODBC is that OLEDB's thinner abstraction layer is much faster.

Both ODBC and OLEDB are very complex interfaces. This was by design, as both interfaces were designed to be complete. A general rule of thumb is that completeness in an interface is directly proportional to complexity. As completeness increases so does complexity.

In order to reduce the complexity of programming using ODBC and OLEDB, Microsoft has established several class libraries that wrap and attempt to simplify calls to these data access layers. These include the MFC (Microsoft Foundation Class) ODBC classes, DAO (Data Access Objects), RDO (Remote Data Objects), and ADO (Active Data Objects). The MFC ODBC, DAO, and RDO class libraries are now obsolete and have been replaced by the next generation of data access objects, ADO.

Active Data Objects

An implementation of COM that makes interacting with databases very easy is Active Data Objects (ADO). ADO is a very simple database interface that sits on top of OLEDB (see Figure 3.12).

A very popular use of ADO is to access an MS-SQL Server back end. As shown in Figure 3.12, ADO calls are implemented as calls to OLEDB and then to the MS-SQL Server's native transport protocol, Tabular Data Stream (TDS).

ADO is not only for exclusive use with application servers that are DCOM-based. ADO can also be used with any NT-based application server. If developers have no intent of moving their application servers to platforms other than NT, then I suggest that they use ADO as their database-access class.

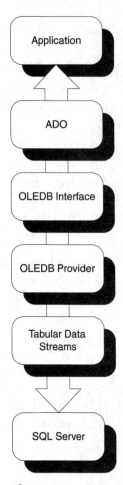

Figure 3.12 ADO and OLEDB.

The big advantage of using ADO is that the ADO data model is very simple and very small; I think I've already mentioned the advantages of KISS. The ADO data model is depicted in Figure 3.13.

There are seven classes in the ADO data model: Connection, Command, Parameter, Recordset, Error, Property, and Field. ADO simplicity derives from the fact that it has only seven classes.

The Connection class is used to manage database connections, manage transactions, and execute commands. The pseudo-IDL for the Connection class is summarized in Listing 3.37.

The actual IDL for the Connection class is too complex to be presented in this chapter, so I've simplified it for this presentation. The Open

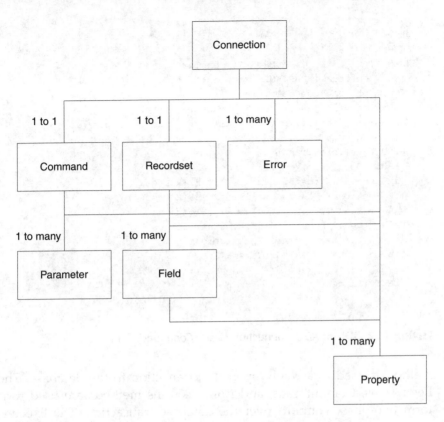

Figure 3.13 ADO data model.

```
{
properties:
 BSTR ConnectionString;
 long CommandTimeout;
 long ConnectionTimeout;
 BSTR Version; // read-only
 Error[] Errors; // read-only
 BSTR DefaultDatabase;
 long IsolationLevel;
 long Attributes;
 CursorLocation[] CursorLocation;
 ConnectMode[] Mode;
 BSTR Provider;
 long State; // read-only

                                                Continues
```

Listing 3.37 IDL for ADO Connection class.

```
methods:
 HRESULT Close();
 HRESULT Execute( [in] BSTR CommandText,
  [out, optional] VARIANT* RecordsAffected,
  [in, optional, defaultvalue(-1)] long Options,
  [out, retval] _Recordset** ppiRset);
 HRESULT BeginTrans([out, retval] long* TransactionLevel);
 HRESULT CommitTrans();
 HRESULT RollbackTrans();
 HRESULT Open( [in, optional, defaultvalue("")] BSTR ConnectionString,
  [in, optional, defaultvalue("")] BSTR UserID,
  [in, optional, defaultvalue("")] BSTR Password,
  [in, optional, defaultvalue(-1)] long Options);
 HRESULT OpenSchema( [in] SchemaEnum Schema,
  [in, optional] VARIANT Restrictions,
  [in, optional] VARIANT SchemaID,
  [out, retval] _Recordset** pprset);
 HRESULT Cancel();
};
```

Listing 3.37   IDL for ADO Connection class *(Continued)*.

method is used to actually open the connection to the database. The BeginTrans, CommitTrans, and RollbackTrans methods are used to perform two-phase commits over the database transaction. The Execute method is used to send a SQL statement over the connection to the database. Listing 3.38 shows an example using the ADO connection interface from Visual Basic.

I'm presenting the ADO examples in VB since I've found that writing ADO in VB is really simple and that there is a lot of knowledge already in the market on how to use ADO with VB. I don't suggest that programmers mix and match VB and C++. They should stick to one or the other in order to focus their acquisition of knowledge.

The Command class is used to execute SQL queries, both Data Manipulation Language (DML) and Data Definition Language (DDL) on a connection to a

```
Private connectionADO As Connection
Set connectionADO = New Connection
connection.Provider = "SQLOLEDB"
connection.Open "server=myserver;Database=MyDatabase",_
    "user", "password"
```

Listing 3.38   Using the ADO Connection interface.

database. This Command class is also used to set query parameters and to retrieve query results. Listing 3.39 shows pseudo-IDL for the ADO Command class.

I generally use ADO commands when I'm interested in passing parameters with a SQL query. I can create the parameters with the CreateParameter method and send both the SQL command and parameters through the current connection with the Execute method. Listing 3.40 shows an example using the ADO command interface.

The Parameter class is used to set the query parameters of a command object. Listing 3.41 shows pseudo-IDL for the ADO Parameter class.

The parameter object is not interesting at all but it does allow me to specify my parameters with a great deal of detail. Instead of calling the CreateParameter method of the Command class, I can also add parameters to a SQL query by passing parameter objects as parameters to the Execute method of the Command class. Listing 3.42 shows an example using the ADO parameter interface.

```
interface _Command : _ADO
{
properties:
  Connection ActiveConnection;
  BSTR CommandText;
  long CommandTimeout;
  bool Prepared;
  Parameter[] Parameters; // read-only
  CommandType[] CommandType;
  BSTR Name;
  long State; // read-only

methods:
  HRESULT Execute( [out, optional] VARIANT* RecordsAffected,
    [in, optional] VARIANT* Parameters,
    [in, optional, defaultvalue(-1)] long Options,
    [out, retval] _Recordset** ppiRs);
  HRESULT CreateParameter(
    [in, optional, defaultvalue("")] BSTR Name,
    [in, optional, defaultvalue(0)] DataTypeEnum Type,
    [in, optional, defaultvalue(1)]
    ParameterDirectionEnum Direction,
    [in, optional, defaultvalue(0)] long Size,
    [in, optional] VARIANT Value,
    [out, retval] _Parameter** ppiprm);
  HRESULT Cancel();
};
```

Listing 3.39 IDL for ADO Command class.

```
Private commandADO As Command
Dim rowsaffected As Long
Set commandADO = New Command
commandADO.CommandText = "INSERT INTO favorites(name, url)" &_
 " VALUES ("KBCafe", "http://www.kbcafe.com")
commandADO.ActiveConnection = connectionADO
commandADO.Execute rowsaffected,,adExecuteNoRecords
```

Listing 3.40   Using the ADO command interface.

```
interface _Parameter : _ADO
{
properties:
 BSTR Name;
 VARIANT Value;
 DateType[] Type;
 ParameterDirection[] Direction;
 unsigned char Precision;
 unsigned char NumericScale;
 long Size;
 long Attributes;

methods:
 HRESULT AppendChunk([in] VARIANT Val);
};
```

Listing 3.41   IDL for ADO Parameter class.

```
commandADO.CommandText = "INSERT INTO favorites(name, @url)" &_
    " VALUES ("KBCafe","http://www.kbcafe.com")
commandADO.ActiveConnection = connectionADO
commandADO.Parameters("@url") = strUrl
commandADO.Execute rowsaffected,,adExecuteNoRecords
```

Listing 3.42   Using the ADO parameter interface.

The Recordset class is used to retrieve the query results generated by a command object. Listing 3.43 shows pseudo-IDL for the ADO Recordset class.

Although the Recordset class has a lot of methods that make it very complete, I limit my concern to the MoveNext methods and Fields property. Listing 3.44 shows an example using the ADO recordset interface.

```
interface _Recordset : _ADO
{
properties:
 Position[] AbsolutePosition;
 Connection ActiveConnection;
 BOOL BOF; // read-only
 VARIANT Bookmark;
 long CacheSize;
 CursorType[] CursorType;
 BOOL EOF; // read-only
 Field[] Fields; // read-only
 LockType[] LockType;
 long MaxRecords;
 long RecordCount; // read-only
 BSTR Source;
 Position[] AbsolutePage;
 EditMode[] EditMode; // read-only
 VARIANT Filter;
 long PageCount; // read-only
 long PageSize;
 BSTR Sort;
 long Status; // read-only
 long State; // read-only
 CursorLocation[] CursorLocation;
 MarshalOptions[] MarshalOptions;
 IUnknown * DataSource;
 Command ActiveCommand; // read-only
 BOOL StayInSync;
 BSTR DataMember;

methods:
 HRESULT AddNew( [in, optional] VARIANT FieldList,
  [in, optional] VARIANT Values);
 HRESULT CancelUpdate();
 HRESULT Close();
 HRESULT Delete(
  [in, optional, defaultvalue(1)] AffectEnum AffectRecords);
 HRESULT GetRows( [in, optional, defaultvalue(-1)] long Rows,
  [in, optional] VARIANT Start,
  [in, optional] VARIANT Fields,
  [out, retval] VARIANT* pvar);
 HRESULT Move( [in] long NumRecords,
  [in, optional] VARIANT Start);
 HRESULT MoveNext();
 HRESULT MovePrevious();
 HRESULT MoveFirst();
```

Continues

Listing 3.43 IDL for ADO Recordset class.

```
HRESULT MoveLast();
HRESULT Open( [in, optional] VARIANT Source,
 [in, optional] VARIANT ActiveConnection,
 [in, optional, defaultvalue(-1)] CursorTypeEnum CursorType,
 [in, optional, defaultvalue(-1)] LockTypeEnum LockType,
 [in, optional, defaultvalue(-1)] long Options);
HRESULT Requery([in, optional, defaultvalue(-1)] long Options);
HRESULT _xResync(
 [in, optional, defaultvalue(3)] AffectEnum AffectRecords);
HRESULT Update( [in, optional] VARIANT Fields,
 [in, optional] VARIANT Values);
HRESULT _xClone([out, retval] _Recordset** ppvObject);
HRESULT UpdateBatch(
 [in, optional, defaultvalue(3)] AffectEnum AffectRecords);
HRESULT CancelBatch(
 [in, optional, defaultvalue(3)] AffectEnum AffectRecords);
HRESULT NextRecordset( [out, optional] VARIANT* RecordsAffected,
 [out, retval] _Recordset** ppiRs);
HRESULT Supports( [in] CursorOptionEnum CursorOptions,
 [out, retval] VARIANT_BOOL* pb);
HRESULT Find( [in] BSTR Criteria,
 [in, optional, defaultvalue(0)] long SkipRecords,
 [in, optional, defaultvalue(1)]
  SearchDirectionEnum SearchDirection,
 [in, optional] VARIANT Start);
HRESULT Cancel();
HRESULT Save( [in, optional] BSTR FileName,
 [in, optional, defaultvalue(0)]
  PersistFormatEnum PersistFormat);
HRESULT GetString(
 [in, optional, defaultvalue(2)] StringFormatEnum StringFormat,
 [in, optional, defaultvalue(-1)] long NumRows,
 [in, optional] BSTR ColumnDelimeter,
 [in, optional] BSTR RowDelimeter,
 [in, optional] BSTR NullExpr,
 [out, retval] BSTR* pRetString);
HRESULT CompareBookmarks( [in] VARIANT Bookmark1,
 [in] VARIANT Bookmark2,
 [out, retval] CompareEnum* pCompare);
HRESULT Clone(
 [in, optional, defaultvalue(-1)] LockTypeEnum LockType,
 [out, retval] _Recordset** ppvObject);
HRESULT Resync(
 [in, optional, defaultvalue(3)] AffectEnum AffectRecords,
 [in, optional, defaultvalue(2)] ResyncEnum ResyncValues);
};
```

Listing 3.43 IDL for ADO Recordset class *(Continued).*

```
Private recordsetADO As Recordset
Set recordsetADO = New Recordset
recordsetADO.Open "SELECT * FROM favorites", connectionADO
```

Listing 3.44   Using the ADO recordset interface.

The Error class is the error statement generated by the OLEDB provider. As each command is executed, error results are saved in the error collection of the connection object. Listing 3.45 shows pseudo-IDL for the ADO Error class.

```
interface Error : IDispatch
{
properties:
 long Number; // read-only
 BSTR Source; // read-only
 BSTR Description; // read-only
 BSTR HelpFile; // read-only
 BSTR HelpContext; // read-only
 BSTR SQLState; // read-only
 long NativeError; // read-only;
};
```

Listing 3.45   IDL for ADO Error class.

I usually set up a special function that allows me to spill all database errors to the log file. I'm also usually very diligent about dumping all the information regardless of whether I think it would be useful.

The Field class is the individual fields contained with a recordset. When recordsets are returned from command execution, the recordsets point to one record in the result set at a time. The individual fields within the record are saved in the field collection of the recordset object. Listing 3.46 shows pseudo-IDL for the ADO Field class.

Again, the Field class has a lot of members that make the class very complete. Programmers can usually limit their attention to the Value property when using Field objects.

COM Techniques

Implementing a simple COM Server is far from a complete solution. There is quite a bit about COM that users will learn as they dig into the experience.

```
interface Field : _ADO
{
properties:
  long ActualSize; // read-only
  long Attributes;
  long DefinedSize;
  BSTR Name; // read-only
  DataType[] Type;
  VARIANT Value;
  unsigned char Precision;
  unsigned char NumericScale;
  VARIANT OriginalValue; // read-only
  VARIANT UnderlyingValue; // read-only
  IUnknown * DataFormat;

methods:
  HRESULT AppendChunk([in] VARIANT Data);
  HRESULT GetChunk( [in] long Length,
            [out, retval] VARIANT* pvar);
};
```

Listing 3.46 IDL for ADO Field class.

The examples I've provided generally do not discuss many of the enhancements that COM has acquired over the last couple of years. Most programmers are likely familiar with acronyms such as MTS and COM+, but what these utilities provide and how to use them is a mystery to most.

Automation

COM interfaces are static interfaces that should not change over time. Once an interface is defined, changing it will almost always invalidate any existing clients. Because COM interfaces are static, Microsoft introduced Automation in order to provide for a dynamic object interface.

In the Automation model all function calls occur over the IDispatch interface (see Listing 3.47).

To be more specific, method calls are burrowed through the IDispatch:: Invoke method. All methods of a class are assigned a dispatch ID. This dispatch ID is then passed as the dispIdMember parameter. The return value is passed in the pVarResult method parameter, and the method parameters are wrapped into the pDispParams method parameter. This provides for a complete dynamic interface.

```
[
  object,
  uuid(00020400-0000-0000-C000-000000000046),
  pointer_default(unique)
]
interface IDispatch : IUnknown
{
  HRESULT GetTypeInfoCount( [out] UINT * pctinfo );

  HRESULT GetTypeInfo( [in] UINT iTInfo,
        [in] LCID lcid,
        [out] ITypeInfo ** ppTInfo );

  HRESULT GetIDsOfNames( [in] REFIID riid,
        [in, size_is(cNames)] LPOLESTR * rgszNames,
        [in] UINT cNames,
        [in] LCID lcid,
        [out, size_is(cNames)] DISPID * rgDispId );

  HRESULT Invoke( [in] DISPID dispIdMember,
        [in] REFIID riid,
        [in] LCID lcid,
        [in] WORD wFlags,
        [in, out] DISPPARAMS * pDispParams,
        [out] VARIANT * pVarResult,
        [out] EXCEPINFO * pExcepInfo,
        [out] UINT * puArgErr );
}
```

Listing 3.47 Dispatch interface.

There are two ways of binding to dynamic interfaces. The first is called early binding and occurs when the client is being compiled. The three Get functions of the IDispatch interface allow a client to query the structure of the dynamic interface. The structure of the dynamic interface is saved in the .TLB (Type LiBrary) file. During the compilation of the client module, the development tool can read the type library using the Get methods of IDispatch, so that function calls at run time do not require run-time acquisition of type library information. The second method of binding to dynamic interfaces is called late binding and occurs when the Get methods of IDispatch are called at run time.

The advantage of early binding is that method calls are faster because the type library has already been processed. The disadvantage of early binding is that method calls that were bound during compilation must be static for the lifetime of the module.

Dynamic invocations using IDispatch are typically slower than equivalent custom interface calls because of the additional overhead of querying the dynamic interface and marshaling function parameters. But these disadvantages are not relevant in a distributed environment using early binding.

NOTE
In the context of this discussion, *distributed environment* is defined as a environment in which the COM calls are occurring across process and even machine boundaries.

The marshaling of parameter data that must occur in an IDispatch::Invoke call is not additional overhead in a distributed environment. Regardless of whether the marshaling occurs before the call to IDispatch::Invoke or in the proxy stub, the marshaling must occur. So, there is little or no performance gain in using custom interfaces in a distributed environment. The little performance gain might be the optimized marshaling code in the proxy stub versus any nonoptimized marshaling occurring before the call to the IDispatch:: Invoke function.

Type Library Marshaling

In order to query the structure of the dynamic interface, dynamic classes expose this structure in their type library. This type library may be a .TLB file and it may also be an embedded resource in a DLL or EXE module. Beyond allowing a client to query the structure, the type library can also be used to perform the marshaling of call parameters within the proxy stub. This type of marshaling is called type library marshaling and has superseded standard marshaling in popularity.

With standard marshaling, the proxy and stub communicate over RPC with each other. This relationship is depicted in Figure 3.14.

Definitions

Standard marshaling is when COM uses the proxy-stub DLL, generated using the MIDL compiler, to marshal the interface calls. *Type library marshaling* is when COM uses the type library, generated using the MIDL compiler, to marshal the interface calls. A third type of marshaling that will not be explained in this book is custom marshaling. *Custom marshaling* is when COM uses a custom marshaling DLL to marshal the interface calls.

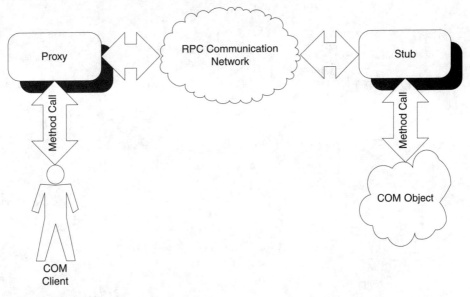

Figure 3.14 Standard marshaling.

A call from a COM client is made on the object's proxy, which is located in the same apartment as the COM client. This gives the feel to the COM client that the COM object is actually local to the apartment. The fact that the client is not aware of whether the object is local to its apartment or is remote is called location transparency.

The proxy's task is to wrap (marshal) the parameters of the method call. Once wrapped, a frame is sent to the stub over RPC. The stub then unmarshals the parameters and performs the actual method call on the COM object. The returned parameters are then marshaled and returned to the proxy over RPC. The proxy unmarshals these parameters and returns the result to the client.

Type library marshaling is slightly different from standard marshaling. In type library marshaling, the methods of the class are described in a resource called a type library. All COM objects that use type library marshaling use a common proxy and stub that are called the Automation proxy and Automation stub. They are named such because they were borrowed from Microsoft's Object Linking and Embedding (OLE) Automation technology. Type library marshaling is depicted in Figure 3.15.

Instead of the proxy and stub having knowledge of how to marshal and unmarshal calls to one set of COM classes, the Automation proxy and stub have knowledge of how to generically marshal and unmarshal method calls.

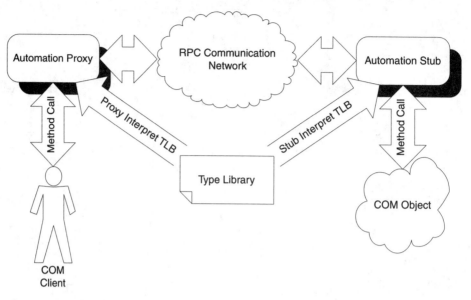

Figure 3.15 Type library marshaling.

The Automation proxy and stub then read the COM class type information from the type library in order to perform the marshaling and unmarshaling.

Threading

In NT 4.0, there were two threading models that a COM server may adopt in its implementation. The models are the multithreaded apartment (MTA) model and the single-threaded apartment (STA) model. In either model, a COM object exists in the context of an apartment. The difference between MTA and STA is that in an MTA, each apartment may have one or more threads while in an STA, the apartment may contain only one thread. The choice of using either model should be carefully matched to the requirements of the object being implemented.

Objects that exist in an STA inherently exist in only one thread. This eliminates concurrency problems that would normally arise in a multithreaded environment. For this reason, STAs are often easier to implement, especially for programmers who are less experienced in developing thread-safe objects.

The downside of STAs is twofold. The STA object is single-threaded and the STA object must synchronize method calls from outside threads on a message queue. The disadvantage of a single-threaded object is not always obvious. But consider an object with one method that is called from numerous threads. Now consider that this method call executes a query on a remote database. While the query is sent to the remote database and until the query results are returned, the entire object is blocked. If this remote query blocks for 10 milliseconds, then the object will sleep (or do nothing) even when outstanding calls are waiting, clearly not an efficient use of CPU cycles. Since an MTA object is multithreaded, multiple calls will occur on the object simultaneously. While one call is blocked waiting for returned query results, another may be preparing the next query. This is a more efficient use of CPU cycles.

The second disadvantage of STA objects is that method calls from outside threads must be synchronized on a message queue. The additional time spent managing this message queue is a drain on CPU cycles. In an MTA, an object may be called from various threads, but as long as the threads all exist in the same apartment, the method calls continue to completion without having to switch thread contexts or place the call on some queue.

The process flow of calls from remote, out-of-process, out-of-apartment, and in-apartment threads is illustrated in Figure 3.16.

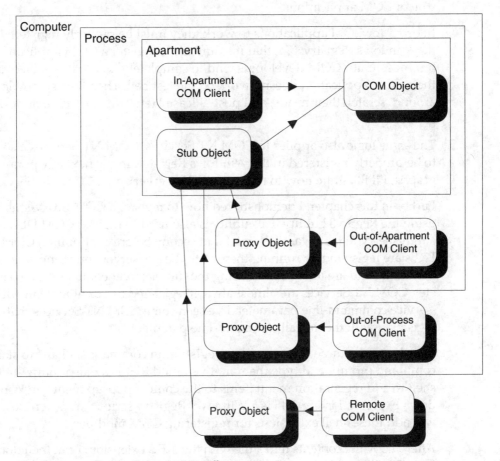

Figure 3.16 Process flow of COM calls.

As the diagram shows, all COM method calls that occur between apartments are marshaled, whereas method calls that occur within apartments are not marshaled. In the STA world, then, all calls between threads are marshaled, whereas in the MTA world, two threads can share an apartment and calls between them would not require marshaling. Because of these disadvantages, MTA objects are the only way to go when developing a high-performance object.

Configuration

It is often the case that newbie COM developers run into a lot of configuration problems when they move their applications from the confines of their single desktop computer and onto a test bed or production environment. Non-COM Win32 applications are usually installed by copying the modules to the hard disk, which makes them immediately available. The same is not true of COM applications.

In order for COM applications to work, they must be properly registered in the Windows Registry. Not that it's difficult to register a COM application, but most junior COM developers tend to completely ignore this subject until their COM application doesn't work on the test bed. Then they scramble around, scratch their heads, and post "Please Help" on a listserve or newsgroup.

The same logic also applies to COM NT Services. COM NT Services also need to be properly registered in the Windows Registry. In the next few paragraphs, I'll illustrate how to register a COM server and a COM NT Service.

Earlier in this chapter, I demonstrated how to register a COM proxy-stub DLL using the RegSrv32 utility. This utility is also used to register COM DLLs. (As a refresher, you may want to reread that section before continuing.) COM EXEs are registered by running them with the -regserver command-line parameter and are unregistered using the -unregserver command-line parameter. COM NT Services are almost always registered by running them with the -service command-line parameter. I've seen some COM NT Services that are registered with the -install command-line parameter.

In order to run these command-line registration commands, I have to start a command prompt and type them in. I've found that I can also configure the shell to add registration menu items to the context pop-up menus in Windows Explorer. Listing 3.48 is a Windows Registry script that, when executed, will add these shell extensions for registering COM modules.

After I copy the contents into a file with the .REG extension, I can then double-click the file in Windows Explorer to add the entries to the Windows Registry.

```
REGEDIT4

[HKEY_CLASSES_ROOT\.dll]
@="dllfile"

[HKEY_CLASSES_ROOT\dllfile]
@="Application Extension"

[HKEY_CLASSES_ROOT\dllfile\shell\Register DLL\command]
@="RegSrv32.EXE %1"

[HKEY_CLASSES_ROOT\dllfile\shell\Unregister DLL\command]
@="RegSrv32.EXE -u %1"

[HKEY_CLASSES_ROOT\.exe]
@="exefile"

[HKEY_CLASSES_ROOT\exefile]
@="Application"

[HKEY_CLASSES_ROOT\exefile\shell\Register EXE\command]
@="%1 /regserver"

[HKEY_CLASSES_ROOT\exefile\shell\Register Service\command]
@="%1 /service"

[HKEY_CLASSES_ROOT\exefile\shell\Unregister EXE\command]
@="%1 /unregserver"
```

Listing 3.48   Regserver shell.

If the entries are correctly added to the Windows Registry, I should see the dialog shown in Figure 3.17.

If these entries are added to the Windows Registry, then I can register and unregister COM modules simply by right-clicking the file in Windows Explorer (see Figure 3.18).

Note that these context menu items will appear for all DLLs, EXEs, and services. Programmers shouldn't get overzealous using this tool. If they choose

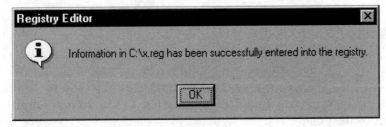

Figure 3.17   Invoking registry editor scripts.

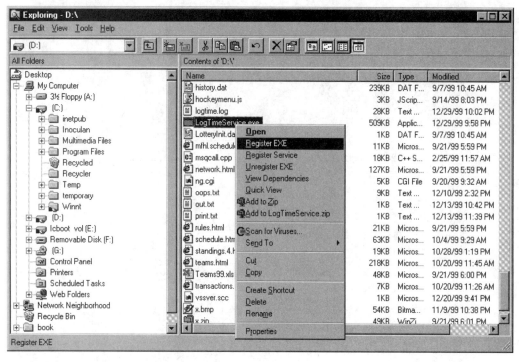

Figure 3.18 Register COM module in Windows Explorer.

the Register Service menu item for an EXE that ignores command-line parameters, then the EXE will launch itself. That can be dangerous.

Beyond DLLs and EXEs another module that is often neglected for registration in the Windows Registry is the type library (.tlb). One reason that type libraries may be quite often neglected is the lack of preinstalled tools for registering them.

In order to facilitate this registration, many developers wrote utilities called RegTypeLib, RegTlb, and so forth. The source code for these tools is always similar to the code shown in Listing 3.49.

Users can paste this code into their favorite C++ IDE and create their own type library registration utility. These RegTLB utilities are very similar to the RegSrv32 utility, except they register TLBs whereas RegSrv32 registers DLLs. Programmers can also configure the utility to be run from Windows Explorer as I did with RegSrv32 earlier in this chapter. Listing 3.50 shows the Windows Registry script that will configure RegTLB to run from Windows Explorer context menus.

```cpp
#include <windows.h>
#include <io.h>
#include <sstream>

std::wstring ToWide(const std::string & str)
{
 WCHAR * sz = new WCHAR[str.length()+1];
 ::MultiByteToWideChar(CP_ACP, 0, str.c_str(), -1,
            sz, str.length()+1);
 std::wstring ws = sz;
 delete[] sz;
 return ws;
}

int WINAPI WinMain( HINSTANCE hInstance,
    HINSTANCE hPrevInstance,
    LPSTR lpCmdLine,
    int nCmdShow)
{
 ::CoInitialize(NULL);
 if ( ( lpCmdLine == NULL ) ||
    ( ::lstrlen(lpCmdLine) == 0) ||
    ( _access( lpCmdLine, 0 ) == -1 ) )
 {
  ::MessageBox(NULL, "Usage: REGTLB.EXE yourtlb.tlb",
      "Type library does not exist",
      MB_OK+MB_ICONERROR);
  return 0;
 }

 ITypeLib * typelib = NULL;
 HRESULT hresult = ::LoadTypeLibEx(ToWide(lpCmdLine).c_str(),
            REGKIND_REGISTER, &typelib);
 if ( FAILED(hresult) )
 {
  std::stringstream ss;
  ss << "File = " << lpCmdLine << ". HRESULT = " << hresult;
  ::MessageBox(NULL, ss.str().c_str(),
            "Error while registering type library",
            MB_OK+MB_ICONERROR);
  return 0;
 }
 typelib->Release();
 ::CoUninitialize();
 return 0;
};
```

Listing 3.49   RegTypeLib.

```
REGEDIT4

[HKEY_CLASSES_ROOT\.tlb]
@="tlbfile"

[HKEY_CLASSES_ROOT\tlbfile]
@="Type Library"

[HKEY_CLASSES_ROOT\tlbfile\shell\Register TLB\command]
@="REGTLB.EXE %1"
```

Listing 3.50   RegTypeLib shell.

I can copy the listing to a .REG file and double-click the file to add these entries to the Windows Registry.

Dynamic Link Libraries

What I've described so far is how to create an out-of-process COM server. They are called out-of-process COM servers because they are loaded into their own processes. If a COM object is created in an out-of-process COM server, a separate process is started, if it has not already started, and the COM object is created within this process space. Calls are then marshaled between the calling client and the COM object.

Another type of COM server is the in-process COM server. These are DLLs (dynamic link libraries) that implement COM classes that are loaded in-process when created, that is, into the same process as the calling client. The advantages of in-process COM servers is that when the COM object and client are in the same apartment, the method calls need not be marshaled. When methods calls are made direct rather than marshaled, performance can increase several hundredfold, depending on the amount and type of marshaling required.

Creating a DLL or in-process COM server is similar to creating an EXE or out-of-process COM server. The code to create the classes and class factories is identical. The differences lie in how the class factories are exposed to the outside world. In an out-of-process COM server, I expose the class factories by calling the CoRegisterClassObject function. In an in-process COM server, the class factory is exposed using a DLL export function. The function is called DllGetClassObject.

```
STDAPI DllGetClassObject(REFCLSID rclsid, REFIID riid,
                         LPVOID * ppv);
```

The DllGetClassObject function takes the class id and interface id as input parameters and returns a void * result. The void * return parameter is typically an IClassFactory pointer, but it can be any type of class factory interface. This class factory object can then be used to create new object instances. A sample implementation for DllGetClassObject is shown in Listing 3.51.

```
STDAPI DllGetClassObject(REFCLSID rclsid, REFIID riid,
    LPVOID* ppv)
{
 static MyClass myclass;
 if (rclsid == CLSID_MyClass)
 {
  return myclass.QueryInterface(riid, ppv);
 }

 *ppv = 0;
 return CLASS_E_CLASSNOTAVAILABLE;
}
```

Listing 3.51   Sample DllGetClassObject.

I don't have to call the DllGetClassObject entry point. The CoGetClassObject function calls the DLL entry point on my behalf. Earlier in the chapter, I called CoGetClassObject in order to obtain the class factory of an out-of-process COM class. The CoGetClassObject function would also be used to acquire the class factory of an in-process COM class. Listing 3.52 shows an example of acquiring the class factory and creating a COM object.

```
IClassFactory * factory = NULL;
::CoGetClassObject( CLSID_BeerBottle, CLSCTX_ALL, 0,
    IID_IClassFactory, (void **)&factory );
IBeerBottle * beer = NULL;
factory->CreateInstance(0, IID_IBeerBottle, (void **)&beer);
factory->Release();
// Do something with the interface, then release it
// ...
beer->Release();
```

Listing 3.52   Calling CoGetClassObject.

This example will work for both in-process and out-of-process COM classes. This is because I passed the CLSCTX_ALL parameter to CoGetClassObject. The CoGetClassObject function can take any of the parameters shown in Listing 3.53.

```
enum tagCLSCTX
  { CLSCTX_INPROC_SERVER = 0x1,
    CLSCTX_INPROC_HANDLER = 0x2,
    CLSCTX_LOCAL_SERVER = 0x4,
    CLSCTX_INPROC_SERVER16 = 0x8,
    CLSCTX_REMOTE_SERVER = 0x10,
    CLSCTX_INPROC_HANDLER16 = 0x20,
    CLSCTX_INPROC_SERVERX86 = 0x40,
    CLSCTX_INPROC_HANDLERX86 = 0x80
  } CLSCTX;

#define CLSCTX_ALL           (CLSCTX_INPROC_SERVER| \
                              CLSCTX_INPROC_HANDLER| \
                              CLSCTX_LOCAL_SERVER| \
                              CLSCTX_REMOTE_SERVER)

#define CLSCTX_SERVER        (CLSCTX_INPROC_SERVER| \
                              CLSCTX_LOCAL_SERVER| 
                              CLSCTX_REMOTE_SERVER)
```

Listing 3.53   CLSCTX.

So then, what does this CoGetClassObject function do? It's not hard to sur-
mise. For in-process COM servers, the CoGetClassObject simply loads the
appropriate DLL and calls the DllGetClassObject function. If I were attempting to write my own CoGetClassObject function, then it would look something like Listing 3.54.

The first thing the CoGetClassObject function does is convert the CLSID
object into its string representation. This is done using the StringFromCLSID
helper function. The second step is to read the module name of the in-process
COM server from the registry. This module name is located in the registry in
the HKEY_CLASSES_ROOT/CLSID/{clsid-as-string}/InProcServer32 key.
Once the module name is read, the module can be loaded using the Load
Library function. The address of the DllGetClassObject function can be acquired using the GetProcAddress function. This function can then be called
and the results returned.

This version of the CoGetClassObject function, of course, will only work for
in-process servers, as it ignores the CLSCTX parameter completely and
assumes the COM server is in-process.

The proxy-stub DLL in the previous example exported two functions, Dll-
RegisterServer and DllUnregisterServer, to provide for registration and
unregistration of the server. A DLL COM Server must also export these two

```
HRESULT CoGetClassObject(REFCLSID rclsid, DWORD dwClsCtx,
  COSERVERINFO * pcsi, REFIID riid, void ** ppv)
{
 LPOLESTR pszGUID = NULL;
 ::StringFromCLSID(iid, &pszGUID);

 std::stringstream ss;
 ss << "CLSID\\" << WideToAnsi(pszGUID)
  << "\\InProcServer32";
 HKEY hkey;
 ::RegOpenKey(HKEY_CLASSES_ROOT, ss.str().c_str(), &hkey);
 char szFilename[_MAX_PATH];
 DWORD dwSize = _MAX_PATH;
 DWORD dwType;
 ::RegQueryValueEx(hKeyInProc, "", NULL, &dwType,
         (BYTE*)szFilename, &dwSize);
 ::RegCloseKey(hKey);

 HINSTANCE hinstance = ::LoadLibrary(szFilename);
     HRESULT (STDAPICALLTYPE* dllgetclassobject)
         (REFCLSID rclsid, REFIID riid, LPVOID* ppv);
     dllgetclassobject = (HRESULT (STDAPICALLTYPE*)
         (REFCLSID rclsid, REFIID riid, LPVOID* ppv))
         ::GetProcAddress(hinstance, "DllGetClassObject);
 return (*dllgetclassobject) (rclsid, riid, ppv);
}
```

Listing 3.54   CoGetClassObject.

functions to perform registration of the in-process COM classes. Example registration and unregistration code in shown in Listing 3.55.

I registered the proxy stub using the RegSrv32 utility. This utility will also work on in-process COM servers. In this case, I've shown a very simple implementation of the DllRegisterServer and DllUnregisterServer functions.

```
STDAPI DllCanUnloadNow();
```

A DLL COM server may also export the DllCanUnloadNow function. The DllCanUnloadNow function is not a mandatory implementation. DLLs that do not export this function will not be unloaded until the process calls the CoUninitialize function. DLLs that do implement this function will be unloaded only if DllCanUnloadNow returns S_OK. If the DLL should not be unloaded, then it should return S_FALSE. An example of the DllCanUnload-Now function is shown in Listing 3.56.

```
STDAPI DllRegisterServer(void)
{
 char szModuleName[_MAX_PATH];
 ::GetModuleFileName(NULL, szModuleName, _MAX_PATH);

 std::stringstream ss;
 ss << "CLSID\\{clsid-as-guid}\\InProcServer32";
 HKEY hkey;
 ::RegOpenKey(HKEY_CLASSES_ROOT, ss.str().c_str(), &hkey);
 ::RegSetValue(hkey, NULL, REG_SZ, szModuleName,
  std::string(szModuleName).length());
 ::RegCloseKey(hkey);

 return S_OK;
}

STDAPI DllUnregisterServer(void)
{
 HKEY hkey;
 ::RegOpenKey(HKEY_CLASSES_ROOT, "CLSID", &hkey);
 ::RegDeleteKey(hkey, "{clsid-as-guid}");
 ::RegCloseKey(hkey);

 return S_OK;
}
```

Listing 3.55   Dll(Un)RegisterServer.

The first question I should be asking is what this lockcount variable is and when is it equal to zero? This lockcount must be implemented and maintained in the DLL's code. The typical solution is to increase the lockcount by one in calls to the AddRef method of non-class factory COM classes and decrease the lockcount by one in calls to the Release method of non-class factory COM classes. This is exemplified in Listing 3.57.

Instead of calling the DllCanUnloadNow function directly, I should always call the CoFreeUnusedLibraries function. The CoFreeUnusedLibraries will call the DllCanUnloadNow function and free the DLL if it returns S_OK.

```
STDAPI DllCanUnloadNow(void)
{
 return g_lockcount == 0 ? S_OK : S_FALSE;
}
```

Listing 3.56   DllCanUnloadNow.

```
ULONG STDMETHODCALLTYPE AddRef()
{
 ::InterlockedIncrement(&g_lockcount);
 ::InterlockedIncrement(&m_references);
 return m_references;
}
ULONG STDMETHODCALLTYPE Release()
{
 ::InterlockedDecrement(&g_lockcount);
 ::InterlockedDecrement(&m_references);
 if (m_references == 0)
 {
 delete this;
 }
 return m_references;
}
```

Listing 3.57   AddRef and Release lockcount.

That's pretty much everything about in-process COM servers. What I've uncovered for you so far is simply the basics behind the in-process COM server. In the next couple of sections, I show you how to take the next step and add some late 1990s flavor COM into your application. Technologies such as MTS and COM+ are built using in-process, not out-of-process, COM servers; that's why I spent so much time explaining them.

Surrogate Servers

MTS and COM+ components are developed as in-process COM servers. Though these components will surely be used to cross process boundaries, there is a reason why they are not developed as out-of-process COM servers. The reason they are developed as in-process COM servers is so that the operator can choose which in-process COM classes will reside in which processes.

If MTS or COM+ components were out-of-process COM servers, then the developer would be indicating programmatically which and how COM objects were to be grouped into processes. That is, the out-of-process COM servers would be logically grouped into processes as defined by the modules in which they were contained.

Since MTS and COM+ components are developed as in-process COM servers, the choice as to grouping of COM components into processes becomes less constrained by the developer and allows the operator to define these relationships. A more complete explanation is that a COM object defined within an EXE must be in a process of the same name as the EXE, whereas a COM object defined within a DLL can be in a process of the name of any EXE.

In order to complete the theory where an in-process COM object may be contained within any process, Microsoft developed the concept of a surrogate process. A surrogate process is some EXE or process that can contain in-process COM objects. Any number of surrogates across any number of NT machines may distribute the in-process COM objects as designated by the operator.

Windows NT ships with a standard surrogate process with the filename dllhost.exe. This surrogate will contain any in-process COM object in such a manner that it will behave as an out-of-process COM object. The benefit is that disastrous process behaviors that kill the process only affect the COM objects in the surrogate process, and clients in the calling process are not affected. This type of process insulation has many benefits but the one disadvantage is that out-of-process calls are less efficient than equivalent in-process calls.

Two other surrogate processes have become or will become popular over the next few years. The first such surrogate is MTS. It is already in widespread usage and has moved COM development into the scalable Internet age. The second such surrogate is COM+. As of this writing, COM+ is still in beta, but it will soon catch on as the preferred surrogate process for developers. In fact, the COM+ surrogate process is a more advanced replacement for the MTS surrogate process. The COM+ surrogate is also an aggregation of the previous standard surrogate and the MTS surrogate.

For the rest of this section, I describe how to configure an in-process COM class to be loaded into the default surrogate and then how to load an in-process COM class into a remote default surrogate. The steps to loading the COM class into the default surrogate are twofold.

The first step is to call the CoGetClassObject or CoCreateInstance(Ex) function with the CLSCTX_LOCAL_SERVER class context parameter. This is what enables surrogate usage from the client creation call. If I specify the CLSCTX_INPROC_SERVER, CLSCTX_SERVER, or CLSCTX_ALL class context parameters, then the COM class will be created in-process.

The second step is to mark the COM class as being activated with the default surrogate. This can be done with the OLEView utility. I find the in-process COM class in the left-pane treeview of OLEView and select it. In the right pane of OLEView, I select the Implementation tab and check the Use Surrogate Process checkbox (see Figure 3.19).

If the COM class cannot be found in OLEView, the COM DLL likely has not been registered. Also, since the COM class will be accessed out-of-process, I

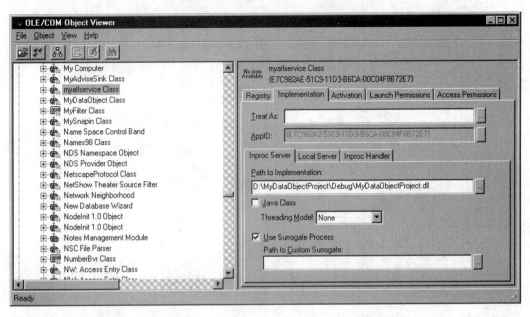

Figure 3.19 Use Surrogate Process.

can't forget that it now has marshaling requirements. The COM DLL must have an embedded type library, a type library file (.TLB), an embedded proxy stub, or a proxy-stub DLL. This marshaling component must also be registered either using the RegSrv32 utility or an equivalent type library registration utility.

If I wanted to load the COM class in a surrogate process other than the default surrogate, I could have specified the path to the surrogate process module name in the Path to Custom Surrogate edit box.

Checking the Use Surrogate Process checkbox has the effect of setting the Dll-Surrogate value name in the COM class's AppID subkey in the Windows Registry. I've shown an example of the DllSurrogate value name in Figure 3.20.

If the DllSurrogate value name of the AppID subkey is a zero-length string, then COM assumes that the COM class will be loaded in the default surrogate process. If I selected to load the COM class in an alternate surrogate with OLEView, then the path to this surrogate module would be specified in place of the zero-length string.

NOTE Since most DLLs do not register an AppID in the Windows Registry, how was the AppID derived? The AppID subkey was created by the OLEView utility for the COM module. The Global Unique Identifier (GUID) used to represent the AppID is identical to the GUID of the COM class configured to run in the default surrogate.

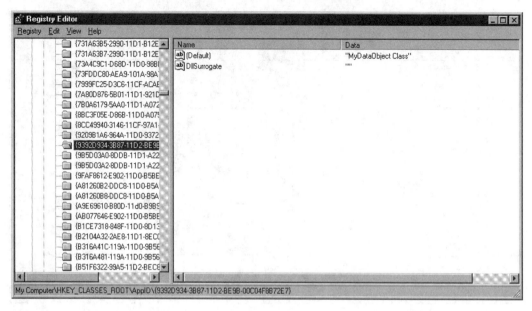

Figure 3.20 DllSurrogate in Windows Registry.

A major advantage of the default surrogate, or any surrogate for that matter, is that developers can also configure the COM class to load in a remote surrogate process. Before I begin loading a COM DLL remotely, I must remember that the DLL must be registered on the server machine and the marshaling component (type library of proxy stub) must be registered on both the server and client machine.

To load the COM class remotely, I start OLEView on the client machine, find the COM class in the left-pane treeview of OLEView, and select it. Then I switch to the Activation tab in the right pane of OLEView and enter the Remote Machine Name (see Figure 3.21).

This will add the RemoteServerName value name in the AppID subkey for the COM module. The value will be the name I entered as the remote machine. I also must remember to check the Use Surrogate Process on the server machine as I did in the previous example.

The first thing I want to do once I've loaded a remote COM DLL is to check that the COM class is actually running on the server machine. Checking that the task list on the remote server includes at least one dllhost.exe process can validate that it is running remotely.

One issue I'm not going to try to resolve in this section is configuring the COM security so that remote surrogate activation can happen. It is likely that while attempting to run my remote surrogate I'll encounter security issues

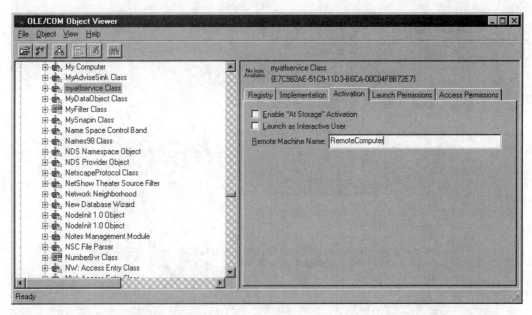

Figure 3.21   Remote Machine Name.

and the big E_ACCESSDENIED 0x80070005 error message from the CoGet-ClassObject or CoCreateInstance(Ex) functions. If it causes many problems, then, like everything else, COM security can be disabled.

To disable COM security, I start DCOMCNFG, select the Default Properties tab, and select the (None) default authentication level (see Figure 3.22).

I may have to restart the computer before the changes to the Default Authentication Level take effect.

COM Internet Services

A limitation in the DCOM implementation over TCP/IP and UDP/IP was that that communication between computers was done over a large set of ports. This was not always possible, and even when it was possible, it was extremely difficult. This is because the Internet is littered with firewalls limiting a lot of traffic that occurs outside a standard set of ports. DCOM over TCP/IP did not use these standard ports and, thus, DCOM over the Internet was either not possible or required reconfiguring one or more firewalls.

The solution to this limitation was to redirect DCOM traffic over a standard port. The most widely used IP port is port 80. This is the port where almost all Internet traffic occurs. This is the page where non-secured HTTP generally occurs. COM Internet Services allows DCOM traffic to be tunneled through

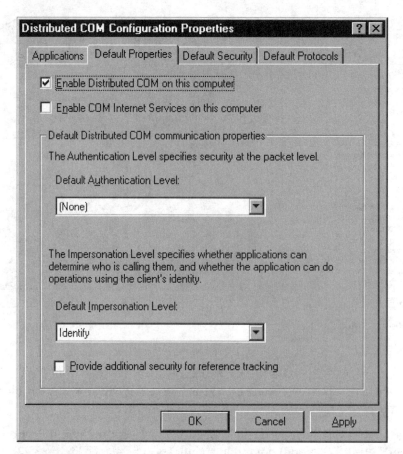

Figure 3.22 Disable COM security.

TCP/IP over port 80. Since almost all firewalls are configured to pass-through all port 80 traffic, the limitation would be removed.

Microsoft introduced COM Internet Services (CIS) in the NT 4 SP (Service Pack) 4. Along with IIS, an NT machine could be configured to transport DCOM traffic over port 80. The configuration for transporting DCOM traffic over TCP/IP port 80 is shown in Figure 3.23.

CIS allows almost any COM server to be activated and manipulated over TCP/IP port 80. This includes both out-of-process COM servers and in-process COM servers (running as surrogates).

NOTE

The instructions I'm about to give on how to configure CIS are also available in almost identical form in the readme.txt files for both NT 4 Service Packs 4 and 5. It's a good idea to print section 3.12 of either file and double-check that I'm explaining things correctly and that the implementation is correct.

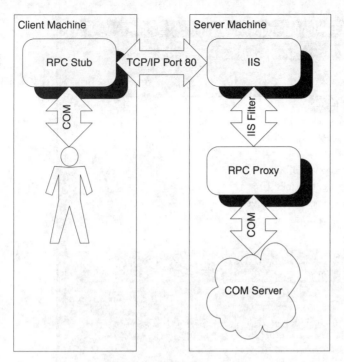

Figure 3.23 Configuration of DCOM port 80.

Setting up a client NT machine to use DCOM HTTP tunneling is the easy part. To do this, I start up DCOMCNFG again and select the Default Protocols tab (see Figure 3.24).

From the Default Protocols tab, I click the Add button and the Select DCOM protocol and endpoint dialog appears (see Figure 3.25).

I select Tunneling TCP/IP in the Protocol Sequence drop-down combo box and click on OK. The protocol will then be added to my set of default protocols. The ordering of the protocols is also the order that the COM run time will use when attempting to connect to a remote server. I can adjust this ordering by selecting a protocol and using the MoveUp and MoveDown buttons. For this example, I will move the Tunneling TCP/IP protocol to the top of the protocol list. This will ensure that remote connections occur quite quickly. If I don't specify the correct protocol sequence, the COM run time may actually connect with a protocol higher in the protocol list.

Configuring the server side of a CIS implementation is much more difficult. I must install Microsoft's IIS Web server. This is a free download in the NT Options Pack. The NT Options Pack may be downloaded from www.microsoft .com/ntserver/nts/downloads/recommended/NT4OptPk/default.asp.

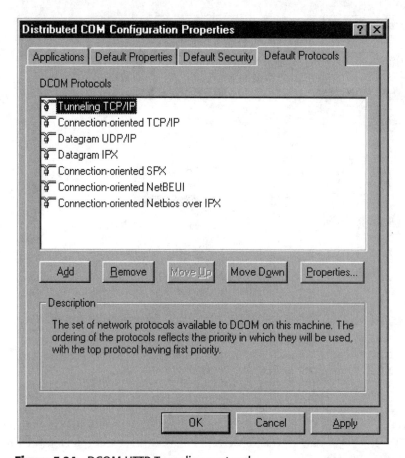

Figure 3.24 DCOM HTTP Tunneling protocol.

TIP

A common problem in many DCOM implementations is a 30- to 45-second delay when the initial connection between a DCOM client and server is attempted. This is caused by the COM run time walking the list of protocols until the one protocol succeeds. The client DCOM machine may be attempting protocols that are not supported by the server DCOM machine. The first protocol in this protocol list is UDP in the standard NT 4.0 installation, and the UDP protocol is not implemented on DCOM95-98 or DCOM-Unix. The UDP protocol times out only after 30 to 45 seconds, producing this delay. This delay can be removed by moving the UDP protocol further down in the protocol list.

Returning to DCOMCNFG, I select the Default Properties tab. From this tab, I check the Enable COM Internet Services on this computer checkbox (see Figure 3.26).

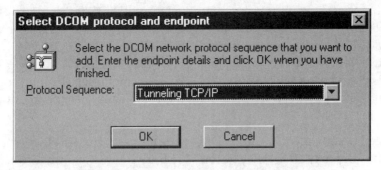

Figure 3.25 Select DCOM protocol and endpoint dialog.

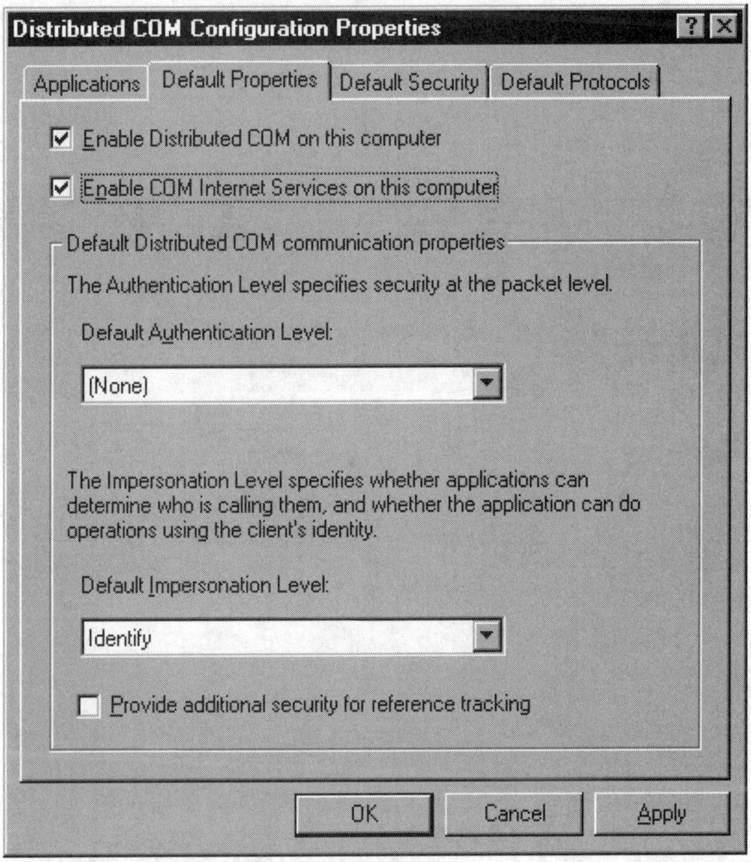

Distributed COM Configuration Properties [?][X]

| Applications | Default Properties | Default Security | Default Protocols |

☑ Enable Distributed COM on this computer

☑ Enable COM Internet Services on this computer

┌─ Default Distributed COM communication properties ─┐

The Authentication Level specifies security at the packet level.

Default Authentication Level:

[(None) ▼]

The Impersonation Level specifies whether applications can determine who is calling them, and whether the application can do operations using the client's identity.

Default Impersonation Level:

[Identify ▼]

☐ Provide additional security for reference tracking

[OK] [Cancel] [Apply]

Figure 3.26 Enable COM Internet Services.

I won't forget to click OK when exiting the DCOMCNFG utility or Apply to save the changes in the Windows Registry. When this checkbox is selected, the DCOMCNFG changes the HKEY_LOCAL_MACHINE\SOFTWARE\Microsoft\Ole subkey. The value name EnableDCOMHTTP is set to "Y" when this checkbox is selected and "N" when it is not selected. If this option has never previously been selected, then the value name may be missing and assumed to be "N."

Next, I need to copy the RPC-proxy DLL to the Inetpub\rpc directory on my IIS server. The Rpcproxy.dll file may be found in the windows system directory. The Inetpub directory is the directory where I installed IIS. It is highly likely that the rpc directory does not exist and I have to manually create this directory.

The next step is to create a virtual root for the rpc directory. This is done using IIS's MMC snap-in, also known as Internet Service Manager. The Internet Service Manager may be started from the Start menu (Programs | Windows NT 4.0 Options Pack | Microsoft Internet Information Server | Internet Service Manager).

In the left pane of the Microsoft Management Console, I select Console Root | Internet Information Server | [my server name] | Default Web Site (see Figure 3.27).

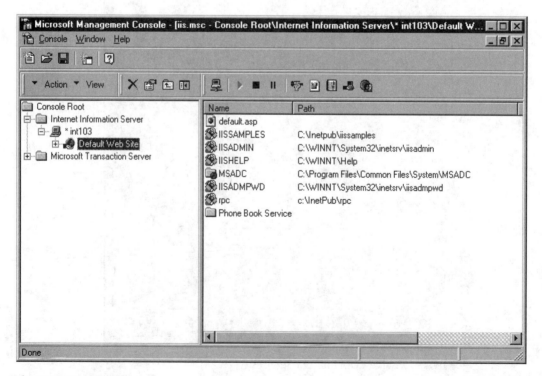

Figure 3.27 MMC IIS.

I then right-click on the Default Web Site node and select New | Virtual Directory from the floating context menu. This will initiate the New Virtual Directory Wizard.

The first page of the wizard asks for the virtual directory alias (see Figure 3.28).

The alias should be rpc. I add this in the edit box and click the Next button. The next page of the wizard asks for the path of the directory where the virtual directory content is found (see Figure 3.29).

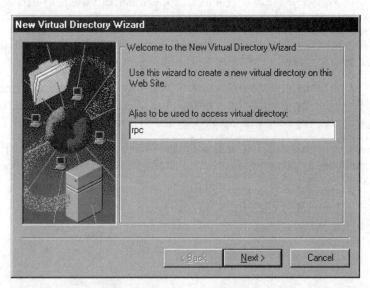

Figure 3.28 Virtual Directory Wizard alias.

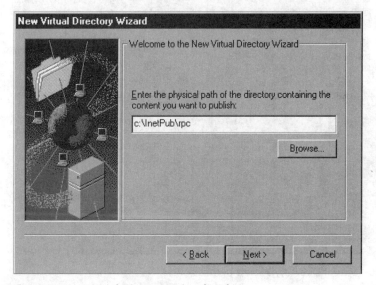

Figure 3.29 Virtual Directory Wizard path.

This should be the path to the directory where I copied the Rpcproxy.dll module. I click the Next button to move to the last page of the wizard. The final page of the New Virtual Directory Wizard asks for the directory permissions (see Figure 3.30).

I check the Allow Execute Access checkbox on this last page and click the Finish button to add the virtual directory to my Web server configuration.

Once I've returned to the Microsoft Management Console, I right-click again on the Default Web Site node and select Properties from the pop-up menu. This displays the Web Site Properties tab (see Figure 3.31).

From the Web Site tab, I set the Connection Timeout to 300 seconds. Then I click OK to return again to the Microsoft Management Console.

Now there's one last step. Again, from the Microsoft Management Console, I right-click this time on the machine name and select Properties from the pop-up menu. This displays the Master Properties dialog (see Figure 3.32).

In the Master Properties dialog, I click on the Edit button. The Master Properties property sheet appears again. Next, I change to the ISAPI Filters tab (see Figure 3.33).

In the ISAPI Filters tab, I click the Add button and the Filter Properties dialog pops up (see Figure 3.34).

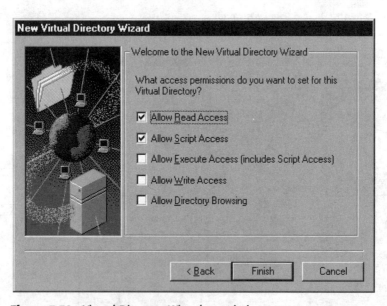

Figure 3.30 Virtual Directory Wizard permissions.

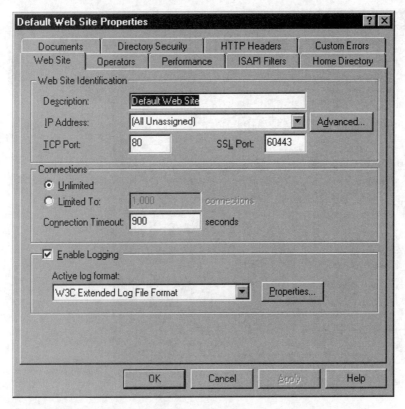

Figure 3.31 MMC Web site Connection Timeout.

I set the Filter Name to Rpcproxy and the Executable to the Rpcproxy.dll module I copied into the rpc directory. I must make certain I select the DLL that I copied to the rpc directory and not the DLL located in the system directory. I click OK when I have typed these values and this adds the ISAPI filter that converts HTTP traffic into DCOM traffic.

The last thing I need to do is restart the client and server NT machines, as some of the changes I have made will not take effect until the computers are restarted.

Once all these properties are set, I should be able to access any COM servers registered on the IIS box from my client using TCP/IP and port 80. I can verify that a DCOM connection is occurring over port 80 by reviewing the detail output by the netstat utility. The netstat utility should only have connections between the client and server IP address over port 80. If there are other connections, they may be from various sources such as a connected drive.

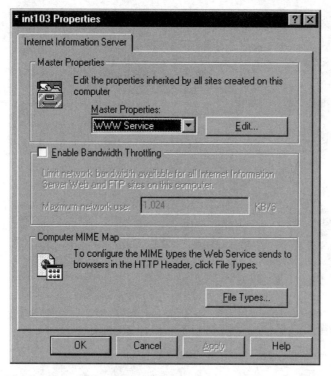

Figure 3.32 MMC Master Properties.

Microsoft Transaction Service

Microsoft Transaction Service (MTS) is an extension of Microsoft's Distribute Transaction Coordinator (DTC) into the world of COM. MTS was introduced in order to provide transaction context similar to a database transaction to COM objects. With the transaction context, it is therefore possible for COM objects to perform two-phase commits across multiple database servers. It also becomes possible to perform server-side lifetime management of COM objects in order to improve efficiency and scalability. The architecture of MTS is presented in Figure 3.35.

MTS introduced a new surrogate process similar to the dllhost.exe default surrogate process but with extensions that give developers distributed transactions and object pooling. The MTS surrogate process is the mtx.exe module.

Microsoft Transaction Service and the Microsoft Management Console

MTS, like many of Microsoft's emerging technologies, is configured and managed using the Microsoft Management Console (mmc.exe). Technologies

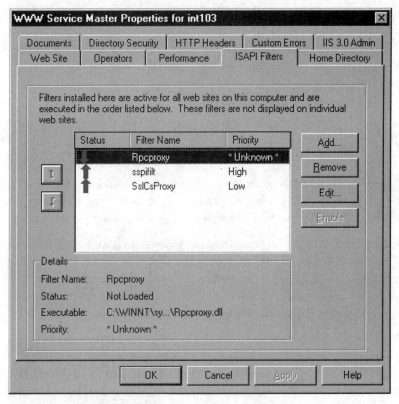

Figure 3.33 MMC ISAPI Filters.

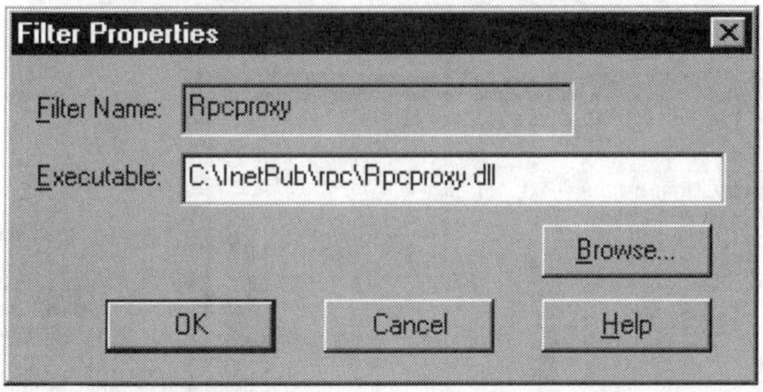

Figure 3.34 Filter Properties dialog.

that make themselves configurable through the MMC do so by registering a snap-in with the MMC. The MTS snap-in is shown in Figure 3.36.

The MTS MMC snap-in goes by many names including the MTS Explorer and the MTS Catalog. In fact, the MTS Explorer and the MTS snap-in are the same, while the MTS Catalog is the database where the information presented in the MTS Explorer is persisted.

Installing a COM class into the MTS Catalog is quite simple: I right-click on the Console Root | Microsoft Transaction Server | Computers | [my computer name] | Packages Installed treeview item in the left pane of the MTS Explorer. Then, I select New | Package from the pop-up menu.

Microsoft Transaction Service Scalability

Among other features that MTS provided to the maturing COM feature base was the ability to perform object pooling and just-in-time activation. These features were added in order to increase the scalability of MTS components.

In Chapter 1, I wrote that statelessness leads to scalability. Here's an instance where this is true. MTS uses a context object to verify the transactional state of a COM object. The context object's interface is presented in Listing 3.58.

The CreateInstance method creates a new object instance that will continue to use the current IObjectContext object. The DisableCommit and EnableCommit methods allow the programmer to toggle between operations that are transactional and those that are not. The IsCallerInRole, IsInTransaction, and IsSecurityEnabled return the state information of the context.

The last two methods, SetAbort and SetComplete, are similar to the SQL statements ROLLBACK and COMMIT. The programmer should call the SetAbort method when a transaction fails and should be aborted. The programmer should call the SetComplete method when a transaction succeeds.

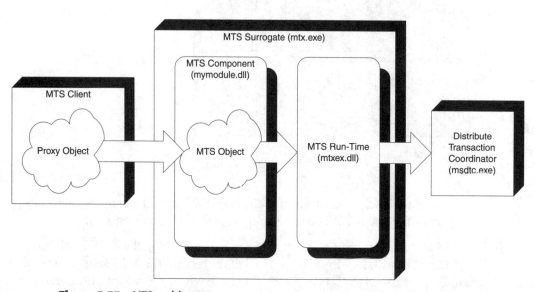

Figure 3.35　MTS architecture.

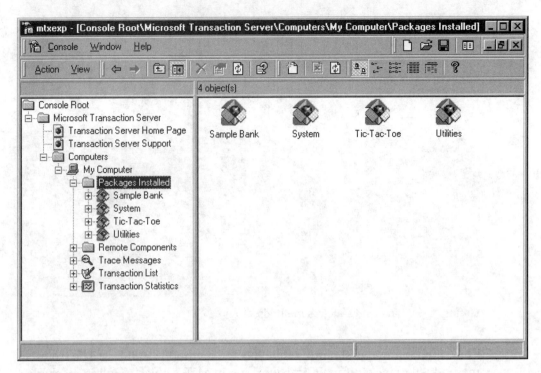

Figure 3.36   MMC snap-in.

This allows a resource manager such as SQL Server to determine when it should do a two-phase rollback or commit on the database transactions associated with this context.

Components that maintain state information make this model very difficult to manage. Listing 3.59 shows a class with two methods.

```
interface IObjectContext : IUnknown
{
HRESULT CreateInstance([in] REFCLSID rclsid,
 [in] REFIID riid,
[retval][iid_is][out] LPVOID __RPC_FAR *ppv);
HRESULT SetComplete(void);
HRESULT SetAbort(void);
HRESULT EnableCommit(void);
HRESULT DisableCommit(void);
BOOL IsInTransaction(void);
BOOL IsSecurityEnabled(void);
HRESULT IsCallerInRole([in] BSTR __MIDL_0000,
[retval][out] BOOL __RPC_FAR *__MIDL_0001);
};
```

Listing 3.58   IObjectContext IDL.

```
class A
{
 int m_i;
public:
 A()
   : m_i(0)
 {};

 int Count()
 {
 return ++m_i;
 };

 int Ten()
 {
 return 10;
 };
}
```

Listing 3.59 State and stateless methods.

The Count method is stateful, while the Ten method is stateless. The Count method will have a difficult time working in MTS's object-pooling mechanics. The reason is that states maintained from one method call to another, making it impossible for MTS to reuse the object between calls. If the object were reused to call the Count method, the state of the object would change and this would have an effect on the client calling the method. This effect may be good or may be bad, but if it is bad, then this state makes pooling this object very unlikely.

The second method, Ten, is stateless and makes the object very poolable. If this method were written as a COM method, then it would probably resemble Listing 3.60.

Now, in order to make the object work with MTS transactions, I add code to retrieve the object's context and mark it complete. The code to perform this action is summarized in Listing 3.61.

```
STDMETHODIMP A::Ten(int * i)
{
 *i = 10;
 return S_OK;
};
```

Listing 3.60 Stateless method.

```
void SetObjectComplete()
{
 IObjectContext * context;
 if (SUCCEEDED(::GetObjectContext(&context)))
 {
  context->SetComplete();
  context->Release();
 }
};
```

Listing 3.61 SetObjectComplete.

An MTS implementation of the Ten method would have the SetObjectComplete function called prior to returning S_OK.

```
STDMETHODIMP A::Ten(int * i)
{
 *i = 10;
 ::SetObjectComplete();
 return S_OK;
};
```

What the SetObjectComplete method does is tell MTS that it must return the object on the server to the pool. MTS will actually call the Release method on the server object. The next time the proxy object is used, MTS can then create a new object and use it. The reason MTS deletes objects that are marked complete is to free up any memory used by the object.

By freeing the memory, MTS adds scalability to the object. The scalability is added by the fact that developers can now have an increased amount of proxy objects that don't require instances on the server. So, if they could support a thousand server objects, they could support several thousand proxy objects. Depending on the utilization of the server object, they may be able to support millions of proxy objects.

Now imagine if the COM class also supported the Count method as shown in Listing 3.62.

```
STDMETHODIMP A::Count(int * i)
{
 *i = ++m_i;
 ::SetObjectComplete();
 return S_OK;
};
```

Listing 3.62 Count method.

After this method called SetObjectComplete and returned, the MTS run time would also delete the server object. The proxy object would continue to exist, but to what end? The state has been removed from the server object. If I called the MTS method over and over, it would always return 1.

MTS does provide a way of maintaining state between method calls. The IObjectControl interface, if implemented by an MTS object, allows the server object to receive notification when the object is activated or deactivated. The IObjectControl interface is presented in Listing 3.63.

```
interface IObjectControl : IUnknown
{
    HRESULT STDMETHODCALLTYPE Activate( void);
    void Deactivate( void);
    BOOL CanBePooled( void);
};
```

Listing 3.63 IObjectControl IDL.

When an object is activated, the Activate method is called on the object. Activating an object happens when a proxy object is bound to the server object. Now I can support state, since the object's state can be reset during the call to the Activate method.

The Deactivate method is called when the proxy object is unbound from the server object. Any state in the server object can be persisted into some form of storage for later retrieval when the object is reactivated.

Another set of COM classes provides the ability to persist this state. The Shared Property Manager (SPM) provides the ability to temporarily store object state in a database.

The last method of the IObjectControl method is CanBePooled. Returning true from this method tells the MTS run time that it does not have to allocate and deallocate the objects between method calls. Instead, the MTS run time allocates a pool of such objects and binds proxy objects to server objects in this pool. This also requires control of the object's state, since the object's state will be passed between multiple proxy objects.

Microsoft Transaction Service Transactions

MTS transactions are pretty much automatic. Configuring an MTS class's transactional behavior is easy with MTS Explorer. I simply right-click on the class in MTS Explorer and select Properties. Then I switch to the Transaction tab and am presented with the transaction options for the class (see Figure 3.37).

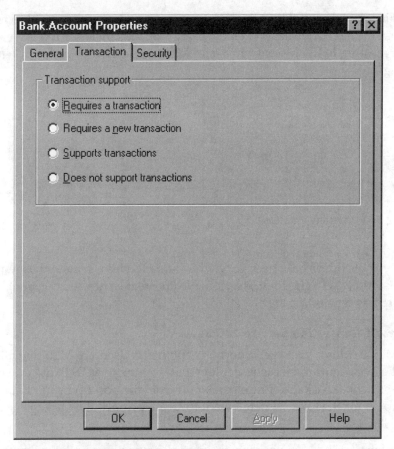

Figure 3.37 MTS Transaction tab.

One problem with this model is that clients that do not support MTS transactions cannot create classes that support MTS transactions. In order for a non-MTS client to create MTS objects within a transaction, an additional interface was created called ITransactionContextEx. This interface is borrowed directly from MS-DTC and is shown in Listing 3.64.

```
interface ITransactionContextEx : IUnknown
{
    HRESULT STDMETHODCALLTYPE CreateInstance([in] REFCLSID cid,
        [in] REFIID rid,
        [iid_is][retval][out]
        void __RPC_FAR *__RPC_FAR *pObject);
    HRESULT STDMETHODCALLTYPE Commit( void);
    HRESULT STDMETHODCALLTYPE Abort( void);
};
```

Listing 3.64 ITransactionContextEx IDL.

The client can then call the CreateInstance method to create MTS objects that will use the MTS transaction I create using CoCreateInstance(Ex). An example of creating MTS objects from a base MTS transaction object is shown in Listing 3.65.

```
ITransactionContextEx * transaction;
::CoCreateInstance( CLSID_TransactionContextEx, NULL,
  CLSCTX_INPROC, IID_ITransactionContextEx,
  (void **)&transaction);
transaction->CreateInstance(???);
```

Listing 3.65 Starting a transaction.

This type of code is only necessary when an MTS class is marked as requiring a transaction. MTS classes that automatically create a new transaction do not require this type of coding.

Microsoft Transaction Service Packages

The MTS Explorer Package Exporter is another godsend of MTS that allows COM components to be easily deployed. Returning to MTS Explorer, I can right-click on a package and select Export from the pop-up menu. I am then prompted for the folder where I want to create (export) the package (see Figure 3.38).

When I export the MTS package, the modules associated with the package are copied to the folder along with a configuration file (*.pak) that describes the settings of the package on the local computer. This makes it very easy to call the COM component from various computers without having to worry about duplicating the COM proxy configuration on the various client computers.

Without the Package Exporter, I will be required to register the component with RegSvr32.exe and one of either DComCnfg.exe or OleView.exe. Removing the step of manually configuring COM components makes installation a breeze. It also removes the human element, that is, mistakes.

COM+

The MTS product eventually was re-released with an entire set of new features as COM+. Beyond what was already provided by MTS, COM+ also included an event service and load balancing.

The event service was an integration of asynchronous decoupled method calls (hint: MSMQ) with COM. With the event service, it is possible to create a

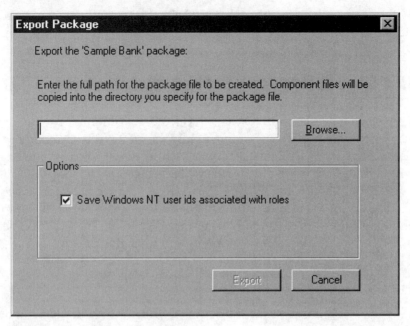

Figure 3.38 Export Package dialog.

construct that decouples the source of events and the sink of events, that is, the source that triggers events from the sink that receives event notifications.

I'm not going to go into much detail on COM+, as the technology doesn't really exist just yet. But I'll explain what COM+ is generally all about. In the mid-1990s, Microsoft had two separate development strategies. One was its core COM technology and the second was its distributed transaction technology. Eventually (around 1997), Microsoft decided to merge these two strategies and incorporate all the distributed transaction features of MTS into its core-COM technology. This gave birth to COM+.

Fail-Over and Load Balancing

COM+, which will be fully released with Windows 2000 (and most likely before this book hits the shelves), includes the ability to load balance COM objects. Again, I'll note that this technology is still in beta and that nobody has any real experience using this it yet.

COM without COM+ provides no inherent ability to perform fail-over or load balancing. This does not mean that COM cannot be made to perform fail-over and load balancing. Developers who don't trust the beta technology may decide to write custom fail-over and load-balancing frameworks for COM. This may sound like a difficult task, but if they take a similar approach to what is currently available in beta COM+, then they'll surely have some confidence that this can be done.

Common Object Request Broker Architecture

Object Management Group (OMG) was created in order to provide for an object-oriented version of RPC. Eventually the OMG introduced a standard called Common Object Request Broker Architecture (CORBA). The largest failing of this undertaking is that the OMG was unable to adopt RPC as the underlying transport for CORBA. The CORBA-specific transport is actually TCP/IP. This means that vendors are unable to reuse existing RPC implementations that were discussed earlier in this chapter. The CORBA specification did reuse one important feature of DCE RPC, that is, IDL.

Visibroker

Just as DCE RPC is only a standard, so is CORBA. Many implementations, mostly incompatible, exist across a multitude of platforms. My discussions will pertain to the most commonly used CORBA implementation, Inprise's Visibroker.

Interface Definition Language for CORBA

CORBA IDL is an object-oriented implementation of DCE IDL. The vendor provides a vendor- and language-specific compiler that can generate code called the stub and skeleton of the object (see Figure 3.39). The stub code, which is very similar to the proxy code generated by DCE IDL, is linked with the client, and the skeleton code, which is very similar to DCE IDL stub code, is linked with the server.

Earlier in this chapter (see Listing 3.27), I defined a COM IDL interface for the BeerBottle class. This interface is rewritten in CORBA IDL in Listing 3.66.

Once I have a CORBA IDL file, I can compile the IDL into stubs and skeletons using an IDL2CPP compiler. Each CORBA vendor will ship their own IDL2CPP compiler with its development kit. Figure 3.40 shows the command-line options for Visibroker's IDL2CPP compiler.

I can use the hdr_suffix and src_suffic options to change the generated source to comply with my group's file extension conventions. The version command-line option is also useful for checking the version of the IDL2CPP compiler. If I want to include an alternate CORBA header file, this is done using the

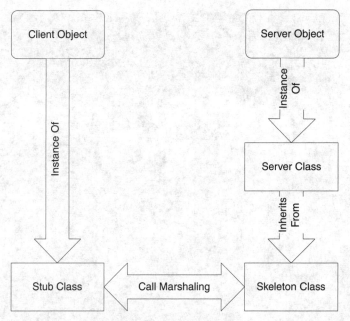

Figure 3.39   CORBA stub and skeleton.

corba_inc option. Last, it may be a good idea to consider disabling ties where possible using the no_tie option and retaining comments using the C command-line option.

If I execute IDL2CPP not using command-line options on the file in Listing 3.64, I will generate four files: beerbottle_c.hh, beerbottle_c.cc, beerbottle_s.hh, and beerbottle_s.cc.

The beerbottle_c.hh file contains the type definitions that are required to use the BeerBottle interface. Abbreviations of these types are shown in Listing 3.67.

```
module BeerModule
{
  interface IBeerBottle
  {
   void Open();
   void Drink();
   long GetMiliLiters();
  };
};
```

Listing 3.66   CORBA IBeerBottle interface.

```
C:\WINNT\System32\cmd.exe                                                _ □ ✕

D:\>idl2cpp
usage: idl2cpp [-options] files...

where options are:
  -version                   Print version
  -root_dir<dir_string>      Specify directory to write all generated code to
  -hdr_dir<dir_string>       Specify directory to write generated headers to
  -src_dir<dir_string>       Specify directory to write generated source to
  -client_ext<ext_string>    Specify client file extension -'none' for none,defaul
t:'_c'
  -server_ext<ext_string>    Specify server file extension -'none' for none,defaul
t:'_s'
  -hdr_suffix<suf_string>    Specify header file suffix - default:'hh'
  -src_suffix<suf_string>    Specify source file suffix - default:'cc'
  -no_exceptions             Suppress exception generation
  -no_tie                    Suppress generation of tie code
  -ptie                      Generate ptie code
  -obj_wrapper               Generate typed object wrapper code
  -no_stdstream              Suppress generation of class stream operators
  -pretty_print              Generate _pretty_print methods
  -type_code_info            Generate type code information
  -virtual_impl_inh          Generate virtual interface impl. inheritance
  -export<tag_string>        Generate export tags (WinNT/95)
  -export_skel<tag_string>   Generate export tags in skeletons (WinNT/95)
  -incl_files_code           Generate code for included files
  -corba_inc<include_file>   Use include_file instead of 'corba.h'
  -impl_base_object<o_str>   Use o_str instead of 'CORBA::Object'
  -map_keyword<keyword> <replacement> Replace 'keyword' with 'replacement'
  -preprocess_only           Send preprocessed source to stdout; do not compile
  -no_preprocess             Do not preprocess the source
pre-processor options:
  -C                         Retain comments in output
  -D                         Define a macro
  -H                         Print the pathnames of included files
  -I<directory>              Specify an[other] directory in the include path
  -P                         Suppress #line pragmas
  -U                         Undefine a macro

D:\>_
```

Figure 3.40   IDL2CPP command-line options.

I've excluded a lot of the content of the beerbottle_c.hh file and marked snipped areas with ellipsis notations. The complete declarations were unreadable without the snipping. The complete declarations may be viewed by running IDL2CPP on the beerbottle.idl file and opening the files with the editor.

The important classes to note are IBeerBottle_ptr, IBeerBottle_var, and IBeer-Bottle. The IBeerBottle_ptr type is simply a pointer to an IBeerBottle object. The IBeerBottle_var type is a smart pointer to an IBeerBottle object. The IBeerBottle type is the stub class.

The beerbottle_c.cc file contains the stub routines. The details of these stub routines are not that important in this discussion, so I'll leave their explanation to a more in-depth CORBA book. In short, the stub wraps method calls from the calling client, marshals the function parameters, and transmits the marshaled call over the network or to another local process.

```
#include "corba.h"
 class IBeerBottle;
 typedef IBeerBottle* IBeerBottle_ptr;
 class IBeerBottle_var: public CORBA::_var {
 ...
 };

 class IBeerBottle : public virtual CORBA_Object {
  ...
 public:
  static const CORBA::TypeInfo *_desc();
  virtual const CORBA::TypeInfo *_type_info() const;
  virtual void *_safe_narrow(const CORBA::TypeInfo& ) const;
  static CORBA::Object *_factory();
  IBeerBottle_ptr _this();
 protected:
  IBeerBottle(const char *obj_name = NULL)
     : CORBA_Object(obj_name, 1);
 public:
  virtual ~IBeerBottle() {}
  static IBeerBottle_ptr _duplicate(IBeerBottle_ptr _obj);
   { if ( _obj ) _obj->_ref(); return _obj; }
  static IBeerBottle_ptr _nil()
     { return (IBeerBottle_ptr)NULL; }
  static IBeerBottle_ptr _narrow(CORBA::Object *_obj);
  static IBeerBottle_ptr _clone(IBeerBottle_ptr _obj) {
   CORBA::Object_var _obj_var(_clone(_obj));
   return _narrow(_obj_var); }
  static IBeerBottle_ptr _bind(
    const char *_object_name = NULL,
    const char *_host_name = NULL,
    const CORBA::BindOptions* _opt = NULL,
    CORBA::ORB_ptr _orb = NULL);

  virtual void Open();
  virtual CORBA::Long GetMiliLiters();
  virtual void Drink();
  ...
 };
 };
 #endif
```

Listing 3.67   beerbottle_c.hh.

The beerbottle_s.hh file contains the type definitions necessary to implement a class that exposes the IBeerBottle interface. The header contains two types: _sk_IBeerBottle and BeerModule_tie_IBeerBottle<class T>. The _sk_IBeerBottle is an abstract class from which a class that exposes the IBeerBottle interface inherits. Listing 3.68 shows the generated _sk_IBeerBottle class definition.

```cpp
class _sk_IBeerBottle : public BeerModule::IBeerBottle {
protected:

  _sk_IBeerBottle(const char *_obj_name = (const char *)NULL);
  _sk_IBeerBottle(
    const char *_service_name,
    const CORBA::ReferenceData& _data);
  virtual ~_sk_IBeerBottle() {}

public:
  static const CORBA::TypeInfo _skel_info;

  // No op function to force base skeletons to be linked in
  static void __noop();
  // The following operations need to be implemented

  virtual void Open() = 0;
  virtual CORBA::Long GetMiliLiters() = 0;
  virtual void Drink() = 0;

  // Skeleton Operations implemented automatically

  static void _Open(
    void *_obj,
    CORBA::MarshalInBuffer &_istrm,
    CORBA::Principal_ptr _principal,
    const char *_oper,
    void *_priv_data);

  static void _GetMiliLiters(
    void *_obj,
    CORBA::MarshalInBuffer &_istrm,
    CORBA::Principal_ptr _principal,
    const char *_oper,
    void *_priv_data);

  static void _Drink(
    void *_obj,
    CORBA::MarshalInBuffer &_istrm,
    CORBA::Principal_ptr _principal,
    const char *_oper,
    void *_priv_data);

};
```

Listing 3.68 _sk_IBeerBottle class definition.

Table 3.3 Call Stack for IBeerBottle::Drink

PROCESS/MODULE	FUNCTION NAME
Server	BeerBottleImpl::Drink
Server	_sk_IBeerBottle::_Drink
ORB	
Client	IBeerBottle::Drink
Client	main

Marshaled calls from the stub objects are passed to the static routines of the skeleton class. That is, calls to the stub IBeerBottle::Drink method eventually turn into calls to the _Drink skeleton method. The call is unmarshaled and forwarded to the pure virtual Drink method. Since the concrete implementation would have implemented the virtual Drink method, the call will be directed through the v-table to this method. Table 3.3 shows a sample call stack from client to server CORBA object.

Implementing a CORBA class is easier than it might have been assumed. I've explained a lot of details that developers need not understand when implementing a CORBA class. To implement a CORBA class, they simply inherit from the skeleton class, implement a constructor that takes an object name, and implement the pure virtual functions of the interface. Listing 3.69 shows the class declaration that I will use in implementing my CORBA class.

The class implementation needs to implement a constructor and the interface methods, and it must inherit from the skeleton interface implementation. This inherited skeleton gives me all the default behavior I require for mar-

```
class BeerBottleImpl : public _sk_BeerModule::_sk_IBeerBottle
{
 bool m_open;
 int m_mililiters;
 int m_references;
public:
 BeerBottleImpl(const char * objectname);
 virtual ~BeerBottleImpl();

 virtual void Open();
 virtual CORBA::Long GetMiliLiters();
 virtual void Drink();

};
```

Listing 3.69 CORBA class declaration.

shaling call parameters, passing the object name to the naming service, and directing incoming calls to the appropriate object instance.

TIP

Convention calls for developers to suffix their class names with **Impl** when implementing a CORBA class. I find this convention helps a lot in determining whether a class is a CORBA class or not.

The class definition is just as simple (see Listing 3.70).

An important point is to pass the object name constructor function parameter to the superclass skeleton constructors. Everything else in the class definition is implementation-dependent.

The last step is to create a simple Win32 shell application that exposes the BeerBottle object. Listing 3.71 is a minimal CORBA server implementation.

A CORBA server or client should call the CORBA::ORB_init static method to start the CORBA run time. Any subsequent calls to the CORBA::ORB_init

```
BeerBottleImpl::BeerBottleImpl(const char * objectname)
: _sk_IBeerBottle(objectname),
m_open(false), m_mililiters(350), m_references(0)
{

}

BeerBottleImpl::~BeerBottleImpl()
{

}

void BeerBottleImpl::Open()
{
m_open = true;
};

CORBA::Long BeerBottleImpl::GetMiliLiters()
{
 return m_mililiters;
};

void BeerBottleImpl::Drink()
{
 if (m_open)
 {
  m_mililiters -= 50;
 }
};
```

Listing 3.70   CORBA class definition.

```
int WINAPI WinMain(HINSTANCE hinstance,
 HINSTANCE /* hprevious */, LPSTR lpCmdLine, int /* nShowCmd */)
{
 try
 {
  TRACE("CORBA::ORB_init");
  CORBA::ORB_ptr orb = CORBA::ORB_init();
  TRACE("orb->BOA_init");
  CORBA::BOA_ptr boa = orb->BOA_init();

  TRACE("new BeerBottleImpl");
  BeerModule::IBeerBottle_ptr object
    = new BeerBottleImpl("BeerBottle");

  TRACE("boa->obj_is_ready");
  boa->obj_is_ready(object);

  TRACE("boa->impl_is_ready");
  boa->impl_is_ready();
 }
 catch(const CORBA::Exception & e)
 {
  // Add error handling here
  std::stringstream ss;
  ss << "Corba Exception: " << e._name();
  TRACE(ss.str().c_str());
 }
 catch(...)
 {
  // Add error handling here
 }
 return 0;
}
```

Listing 3.71 CORBA server.

method will return the ORB object that was initialized in the first call. Once I have a pointer to the ORB object, I want to acquire a pointer to the BOA (Basic Object Adaptor).

Basic Object Adaptor

The BOA does a lot of things, but its most important task is to allow a CORBA server to activate an object so that clients may use it. In Listing 3.71, you'll see that I call the BOA::obj_is_ready method. It is this call that makes a CORBA object available to calling clients. There is also a BOA::deactivate_obj method that deactivates a CORBA object.

Finally, I call the BOA::impl_is_ready method. This last method blocks the current thread until the shutdown method is called or the server terminates.

Dynamic Interface Invocation

An interesting feature of CORBA is Dynamic Interface Invocation (DII). This is very similar to COM's Automation capability in that the client need not know the implementation of the server at compile time. For a discussion of the advantages of postcompile binding of functions, see the section on COM automation earlier in this chapter.

Internet Inter-ORB Protocol

In order to provide interoperability between CORBA implementations, the OMG created an inter-ORB protocol known as Internet Inter-ORB Protocol. IIOP is derived from the General Inter-ORB Protocol (GIOP) standard. GIOP is a more generic standard for inter-ORB communication, whereas IIOP is a TCP/IP implementation of GIOP.

Many make the mistake of thinking that all IPC (Inter-Process Communication) in CORBA happens over IIOP. This is not true. Many CORBA ORBs will implement a proprietary IPC mechanism to transmit marshaled calls between two processes that are local to the same computer. There is also no reason why a CORBA ORB could not implement a more efficient IPC mechanism than IIOP even when calls are made across computer boundaries.

Integrated Transaction Service

Integrated Transaction Service (ITS) is to CORBA as MTS is to COM. That is, ITS provides for transaction behavior in distributed objects just like MTS. Unfortunately, like MTS, it is a very budding technology and it does not have many implementations. Inprise's ITS implementation only works for Oracle and Sybase databases. This is very similar to the lack of support for MTS.

I won't go into much detail on ITS as I don't have the experience myself to describe anything revolutionary about the product. But I want to make certain developers know that if they are implementing a CORBA system, these technologies are available for CORBA.

Sample CORBA Service

Now that I've described how to build a CORBA server, I can combine that knowledge with the NT Service framework and make a CORBA service. This is easily done by copying the code from the WinMain function in Listing 3.71 to the run method. Listing 3.72 is the completed CORBA service.

```cpp
class CORBAService : public NtService::Service
{
 DWORD dw;
public:
 CORBAService()
   :NtService::Service("CORBAService") {};
 virtual void OnRun()
 {
 try
 {
  TRACE("CORBA::ORB_init");
  CORBA::ORB_ptr orb = CORBA::ORB_init();
  TRACE("orb->BOA_init");
  CORBA::BOA_ptr boa = orb->BOA_init();

  TRACE("new BeerBottleImpl");
  BeerModule::IBeerBottle_ptr object
   = new BeerBottleImpl("BeerBottle");

  TRACE("boa->obj_is_ready");
  boa->obj_is_ready(object);

  TRACE("boa->impl_is_ready");
         boa->impl_is_ready();
 }
 catch(const CORBA::Exception & e)
 {
  // Add error handling here
  std::stringstream ss;
  ss << "Corba Exception: " << e._name();
  TRACE(ss.str());
 }
 catch(...)
 {
  // Add error handling here
 }
 }
};

int WINAPI WinMain(HINSTANCE hinstance,
 HINSTANCE /* hprevious */, LPSTR lpCmdLine, int /* nShowCmd */)
{
 CORBAService().Start(lpCmdLine);
 return 0;
}
```

Listing 3.72 CORBA service.

The CORBA service is not that different, again, from the earlier CORBA server. This is because the framework developed in Chapter 2 is doing all the real work. I have to link this class and the WinMain function with my class implementation, the skeleton implementation, the stub implementation, and the orb_r.lib library.

Sample CORBA Client

Now that a CORBA service is running in the background, it would be nice if I could grab one of its objects and do a little IPC. Listing 3.73 is the code for the CORBA client.

The code of a CORBA client starts off just like the CORBA server, by initializing the ORB and BOA. Once they are initialized, I bind to the existing object instance by calling the _bind static method of stub class.

```
int main(int argc, char* argv[])
{
 try
 {
  TRACE("CORBA::ORB_init");
  CORBA::ORB_ptr orb = CORBA::ORB_init();
  TRACE("orb->BOA_init");
  CORBA::BOA_ptr boa = orb->BOA_init();

  TRACE("BeerModule::IBeerBottle::_bind");
  BeerModule::IBeerBottle_var beer
   = BeerModule::IBeerBottle::_bind("BeerBottle");

  beer->Open();
  beer->Drink();
  std::cout << "Liters left = " << beer->GetMiliLiters()
   << std::endl;
  beer->_release();

 }
 catch(const CORBA::Exception & e)
 {
  TRACE(e._name());
 }
 catch(...)
 {
  TRACE("Unhandled Exception");
 }

 return 0;
}
```

Listing 3.73 CORBA client.

NOTE **The _bind method is a proprietary implementation in Visibroker. It is not part of the general CORBA standard.**

Once I have bound my stub object to the object in the CORBA service, I can then freely call the method in the IBeerBottle interface. When I have finished using the stub object, I should call the _release method. The _bind method increased the reference count in the stub object by one. When I call _release the reference, the reference count is reduced by one, and if the count reaches zero, then the stub is freed.

A reference count is maintained when working with CORBA objects. The reference count is held by the stub and determines the life of the stub object. Calling _release on the stub only decreases the reference count in the stub. This makes reference counting somewhat more complicated that what exists in COM.

For singleton objects, this is usually not a problem. Singleton objects usually live for the lifetime of the server. So, the reference counts held by clients have no effect on the life of the singleton. On the other hand, the client usually controls the lives of objects that are not singletons. In order to implement nonsingleton classes in CORBA, I can use a class factory design.

Factory Objects

The class factory is one of the fundamental building blocks of COM. This design is not as popular in CORBA circles, but has been growing in popularity as experienced COM developers crowd onto the CORBA bandwagon.

The design pattern for a class that is created using a class factory is well known. A C++ template for the class factory is given in Listing 3.74.

```
template<class T>
class ClassFactory
{
public:
 T * Create()
 {
  return new T;
 };
};
```

Listing 3.74 Class factory template.

The dependent class T must have two features to work in the class factory design. The class must make all constructors private and must implement a release method that destroys the class instances. The template in Listing 3.75 is a good but insufficient attempt to encapsulate both requirements.

```
class Ware
{
protected:
 Ware(){};
 Ware(const Ware & rhs){};
 virtual ~Ware(){};
public:
 void Release(){delete this;};
};
```

Listing 3.75   Template for class.

The Release method in the Ware class differs from the _release method in all CORBA classes. The CORBA _release method, as I've previously explained, only decreases the reference count in the stub object. This new Release method should call through the interface to the server object and destroy the server object.

This template does not make all constructors private in subclasses. It does help in that subclasses of Ware will not have any compiler-generated public constructors. It is the responsibility of an implemented subclass not to explicitly expose any public constructors. Listing 3.76 shows a class that inherits from Ware and implements a class factory.

Definition: Ware

Ware is something that is manufactured in a factory.

```
class Hello : public Ware
{
 friend ClassFactory<Hello>;
 Hello(){};
public:
 int x;
};
```

Listing 3.76   Ware of class factory.

I had to create a private default constructor and make friends with the class factory, so that only the class factory can create a new instance.

CORBA IDL doesn't implement templates, so moving this design pattern to a CORBA implementation is not straightforward. I must explicitly declare each class factory object in IDL. Listing 3.77 shows the IDL for an implementation that follows the class factory design pattern.

```
module BeerModule
{
 interface IBeerBottle
 {
  void Open();
  void Drink();
  long GetMiliLiters();

  void Release();
 };

 interface IBeerFactory
 {
  IBeerBottle * Create();
 };
};
```

Listing 3.77   Class factory IDL.

The lifetime of the BeerBottle object is now managed by creating new instances with the Create method of the class factory and destroying existing instances with the Release method of the object instances. One problem that might crop up now is garbage collection. If a server is terminated without the object being released, I'll have a dangling object in my server. In order to manage the dangling objects, I either have to design such that the impact of the dangling objects in minimized or perform some additional lifetime management function.

Inprise Application Server

An extension of the Visibroker CORBA implementation is a product called Application Server that provides a great deal of distributed component management. The Application Server comes with a GUI called Developer Console (see Figure 3.41) which enables developers to manage their servers graphically.

From the Developer Console, I can manage my core CORBA infrastructure services. These include location services, naming services, interface repositories, implementation repositories, and the transaction server.

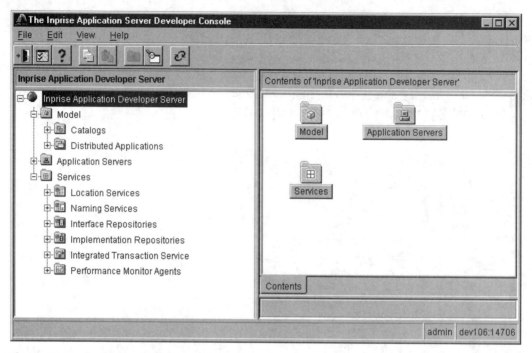

Figure 3.41 Application Server console.

Individual Visibroker objects and servers can also be graphically managed using Inprise's AppCenter utility (see Figure 3.42).

The AppCenter Management Console is very similar to the Microsoft Management Console, but not quite as flexible. The AppCenter Management Console does provide a lot of functionality not yet available in the Microsoft alternative. AppCenter also allows developers to start and stop their CORBA and non-CORBA servers, view activity in their servers, create events that respond to conditions in their application, and schedule maintenance utilities.

Fail-Over and Load Balancing

With Application Server, fail-over and load balancing are trivial. The infrastructure provided by Application Server automatically provides all that is needed. If Application Server is not installed, then fail-over and load balancing must be manually implemented using some sort of location service.

A common technique for programmatically providing for fail-over and load balancing is to use a location service to query information about object instances in the environment and balance the load against these instances. Visibroker's Application Server provides for fail-over and load balancing using a Smart Agent that is shipped with the Application Server product. The

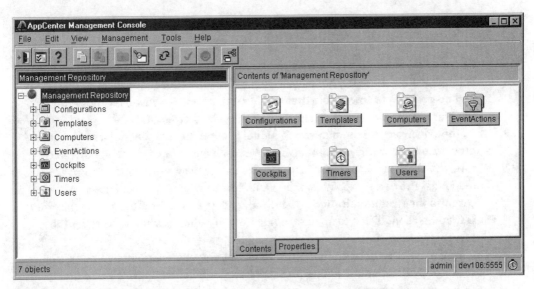

Figure 3.42 AppCenter.

Smart Agent queries the Location Service and performs static load balancing against the table of object instances.

If developers do decide to implement their own smart agents, they should attempt to follow Visibroker's lead and use the Location Service to query object instances in their server environments. Also, in order to fully implement fail-over and load balancing, their best bet is to create stateless objects. With stateless objects, developers can rebind their objects without fear of losing this state, because there isn't any. This allows them the freedom to rebind at any time, which in turn allows the location service to provide its complete range of facilities (fail-over and load balancing) at any time.

Microsoft Message Queue

The function and object-oriented protocols I've discussed are all somewhat limited in that they are synchronous communications protocols. Microsoft Message Queue (MSMQ) differs from these protocols in that it provides for asynchronous communication, not synchronous communication.

MSMQ can be installed from the NT Options Pack. The NT Options Pack may be downloaded from www.microsoft.com/ntserver/nts/downloads/recommended/NT4OptPk/default.asp.

MSMQ is a communication protocol based on messages and queues. Producers can place messages on queues and consumers can retrieve messages on queues (see Figure 3.43).

Synchronous versus Asynchronous

I've done a lot of talking about the advantages of synchronous and asynchronous communication models. Those who are familiar with these models probably have had no problem following the theoretical discussions. However, for those not familiar with these models, a short description is in order.

The *synchronous* communication model is when the two endpoints of a communication take turns communicating over the wire. In a client-server architecture, the client sends a transmission to the server, then waits until the server responds. The server responds, then waits for the client. The two endpoints synchronize their communications. The disadvantage of synchronous communication is that the client is in a wait state, doing next to nothing, while it waits for the server response.

In the *asynchronous* communication model, the two endpoints do not synchronize their communications. The client may send communications to the server at any time and does not need to wait for a response. The server may send communications to the client at any time and does not need to wait for a client request. The disadvantage of asynchronous communication is that it is much more complex.

The disadvantages of the synchronous communication model can be overcome by maintaining more than one thread that talks over more than one communication channel. When there is more than one thread and more than one communication channel, even while one thread is blocked waiting for its turn, the other threads can continue utilizing the CPU. Two threads may use two communication channels to send simultaneous communications.

An advantage of the message queue model is that the producer is loosely coupled with the consumer. This is because the producer need only know how to place messages on the queue and the form of those messages. The consumer also need only know how to retrieve messages from the queue and the form of those messages.

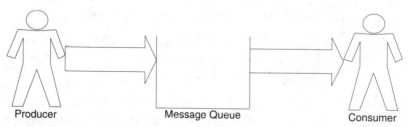

Figure 3.43 Producers, queues, and consumers.

A disadvantage of the message queue model is that the additional layer of indirection serves to slow communication between the producer and consumer.

Microsoft Message Queue Programming

There are two separate sets of functions used in programming MSMQ: queue definition and queue manipulation. Queue definition functions include all the functions that are used to create and destroy queues. Queue manipulation functions include all the functions that are used to open queues, queue messages, retrieve messages, and close queues.

There are two queue definition functions: MQCreateQueue and MQDeleteQueue.

```
HRESULT MQCreateQueue(
    SECURITY_DESCRIPTOR * pSecurityDescriptor,
    MQQUEUEPROPS * pQueueProps, LPWSTR lpwcsFormatName,
    LPDWORD lpdwFormatNameLength );
```

Instead of introducing a new set of functions each with 20 or more parameters, Microsoft chose a much simpler solution of passing a set of properties as an array to the functions. This greatly simplifies MSMQ programming, as developers need only worry about those properties that they are consuming. To provide for the array of properties, Microsoft introduced a property structure.

```
typedef struct tagMQQUEUEPROPS
{
 DWORD cProp;
 QUEUEPROPID aPropID[];
 PROPVARIANT aPropVar[];
 HRESULT aStatus[];
} MQQUEUEPROPS;
```

The MQQUEUEPROPS::cProp member is the number of properties that will be contained in the array. The MQQUEUEPROPS::aPropID member is an array of identifiers identifying the content of each property in the array. The MQQUEUEPROPS::aPropVar is the actual content of each member of the property array. The MQQUEUEPROPS::aStatus on return to a function will contain an array of result codes.

The MQCreateQueue function has four parameters: a security descriptor, the properties array, the returned format name of the queue, and the length of the format name. When creating a simple message queue, developers need only worry about one property in the property array, the pathname of the queue. Listing 3.78 shows an example of creating a message queue.

```
void CreateQueue(const std::wstring & name)
{
std::wstringstream ss;
ss << L".\\" << name;

QUEUEPROPID keys[1];
keys[0] = PROPID_Q_PATHNAME;
PROPVARIANT values[1];
values[0].vt = VT_LPWSTR;
values[0].pwszVal = const_cast<unsigned short *>(ss.str().c_str());

MQQUEUEPROPS properties;
properties.cProp = 1;
properties.aPropID = keys;
properties.aPropVar = values;
properties.aStatus = NULL;

WCHAR formatname[64];
DWORD dw = 64;
::MQCreateQueue( NULL, &properties, formatname, &dw );
};
```

Listing 3.78   Create a message queue.

Deleting a queue is even easier than creating one.

```
HRESULT MQDeleteQueue( LPCWSTR lpwcsFormatName );
```

The only complication is that the MQDeleteQueue function requires one
parameter, which is the format name of the queue.

NOTE

Format names do not have a one-to-one correspondence with message queue path-
names. What I mean is that, for instance, I can create two message queues on two
separate machines with the same pathname and both will have different format
names. I can also create a message queue, destroy it, and re-create the message
queue using the same pathname, and the format name will have changed.

A very common problem that most new MSMQ users encounter is saving a format
name for later use, re-creating the queues, thus changing the format name, and
stumbling over why they can no longer access the message queue with the older format name.

Listing 3.79 shows an example of deleting a message queue.

The four primary queue manipulation functions are MQOpenQueue,
MQSendMessage, MQReceiveMessage, and MQCloseQueue.

```
void DeleteQueue(const std::wstring & name)
{
  std::wstringstream ss;
  ss << L".\\" << name;

  WCHAR formatname[64];
  DWORD dw = 64;
  ::MQPathNameToFormatName( ss.str().c_str(), formatname &dw ):
  ::MQDeleteQueue(formatname);
};
```

Listing 3.79 Deleting a message queue.

```
HRESULT MQOpenQueue( LPCWSTR lpwcsFormatName, DWORD dwAccess,
 DWORD dwShareMode, LPQUEUEHANDLE phQueue );
```

The MQOpenQueue function has four parameters. The first parameter is the format name of the queue. The second parameter is a bit mask of desired access rights. The enumeration of access rights is shown in Listing 3.80.

```
//
// MQOpenQueue - Access values
//
#define MQ_RECEIVE_ACCESS        0x00000001
#define MQ_SEND_ACCESS           0x00000002
#define MQ_PEEK_ACCESS           0x00000020
```

Listing 3.80 Message queue access rights.

The receive access right enables me to pop messages from the queue. The send access right enables me to push messages onto the queue. The peek access right enables me to browse the list of messages on the queue.

The third parameter of the MQOpenQueue function determines the sharing options of the opened queue. Listing 3.81 shows these sharing options.

```
//
// MQOpenQueue - Share values
//
#define MQ_DENY_NONE             0x00000000
#define MQ_DENY_RECEIVE_SHARE    0x00000001
```

Listing 3.81 Message queue sharing options.

The sharing option when set to deny will not allow me to open the queue in receive or peek mode unless it is not opened in receive or peek mode by any other users. And once I do successfully open the queue in deny mode, no other users will be allowed to open the queue in receive or peek mode until I close it.

The fourth parameter of the MQOpenQueue function is a return parameter that will contain the handle to the queue that I will use when calling other queue manipulation functions. Listing 3.82 shows an example of using the MQOpenQueue function to open a queue.

```
QUEUEHANDLE OpenQueue(const std::wstring & name)
{
 WCHAR formatname[64];
 DWORD dw = 64;
 std::wstringstream ss;
 ss << L".\\" << name;
 ::MQPathNameToFormatName(ss.str().c_str(),formatname &dw );
 QUEUEHANDLE queue;
 ::MQOpenQueue(formatname, MQ_SEND_ACCESS+MQ_RECEIVE_ACCESS,
        MQ_DENY_NONE, &queue );
 return queue;
};
```

Listing 3.82 Opening a message queue.

Once I've opened a queue, I can place messages on the queue and retrieve messages from the queue.

```
HRESULT MQSendMessage( QUEUEHANDLE hDestinationQueue,
 MQMSGPROPS *pMessageProps, ITransaction *pTransaction );
```

The MQSendMessage function is used to place messages on a queue. The function has three parameters: the queue handle, the property array, and a transaction handle. The NULL transaction means that transactioning is not being used for this operation. The simplest call to MQSendMessage has one property, the message body.

Listing 3.83 shows an example of a minimal MQSendMessage call.

I can use MQReceiveMessage to retrieve messages from the message queue.

```
HRESULT MQReceiveMessage( QUEUEHANDLE hSource, DWORD dwTimeout,
    DWORD dwAction, MQMSGPROPS pMessageProps,
    LPOVERLAPPED lpOverlapped,
    PMQRECEIVECALLBACK fnReceiveCallback, HANDLE hCursor,
    Transaction *pTransaction );
```

```
void SendMessage(QUEUEHANDLE queue, const std::wstring body)
{
 MSGPROPID keys[1];
 PROPVARIANT values[1];
 keys[0] = PROPID_M_BODY;
 values[0].vt = VT_VECTOR | VT_UI1;
 values[0].caub.pElems = (LPBYTE) body.c_str();
 values[0].caub.cElems = body.length() * sizeof(WCHAR);

 MQMSGPROPS properties;
 properties.cProp = 1;
 properties.aPropID = keys;
 properties.aPropVar = values;
 properties.aStatus = NULL;
 ::MQSendMessage( queue, &properties, NULL );
};
```

Listing 3.83 Placing a message on the queue.

This function has eight function parameters. The first parameter is the queue handle. The second parameter is a timeout. The timeout is an integer denoting the maximum amount of milliseconds the function will wait for a message before it returns. The constant INFINITE will cause the function to wait infinitely for a message. The third parameter is the type of retrieval to perform. Listing 3.84 shows the different operation constants.

The fourth parameter of the MQReceiveMessage function is the property array. The fifth parameter is an OVERLAPPED structure, and the sixth is a pointer to a callback function. Both can be set to NULL if I'm not intending to use them. These last two parameters provide for only redundant functionality.

In the MQReceiveMessage function, I do not believe it is necessary to provide three methods for waiting for incoming messages. I should use the timeout parameter provided in the function to provide for a wait state. Using an event handle or callback function is simply an alternate means of accomplish-

```
//
// MQReceiveMessage - Action values
//
#define MQ_ACTION_RECEIVE      0x00000000
#define MQ_ACTION_PEEK_CURRENT 0x80000000
#define MQ_ACTION_PEEK_NEXT    0x80000001
```

Listing 3.84 MQReceiveMessage operation types.

ing a wait state in a function. Providing three ways of accomplishing the same thing only makes the design complex.

TIP

The redundant implementation of notification is another example of Microsoft's use of the Swiss Army Knife anti-design pattern (see the book, *Anti-Patterns,* William J. Brown, Wiley, April 1999). As I've stressed many times, Keep It Simple, Stupid. A rule following the KISS law of programming is to only provide the simplest implementation. If a complete implementation is necessary, then so be it. But don't confuse a complete implementation with a complex implementation or redundant implementation. A complete implementation is often simple when it is minimally complete.

The seventh parameter can be used with the third parameter to scan the message queue without removing messages. The last parameter is the transaction handle. The last four parameters can be set to NULL. Listing 3.85 shows an example of using the MQReceiveMessage.

The last queue manipulation function is MQCloseQueue and is used to close a handle to a queue.

```
HRESULT MQCloseQueue( QUEUEHANDLE hQueue );
```

```cpp
std::wstring ReceiveMessage(QUEUEHANDLE queue)
{
 MSGPROPID keys[2];
 PROPVARIANT values[2];
 keys[0] = PROPID_M_BODY;
 values[0].vt = VT_VECTOR | VT_UI1;
 WCHAR body[256];
 values[0].caub.pElems = (LPBYTE) body;
 values[0].caub.cElems = 256 * sizeof(WCHAR);

 keys[1] = PROPID_M_BODY_SIZE;
 values[1].vt = VT_UI4;
 values[1].ulVal = 256 * sizeof(WCHAR);

 MQMSGPROPS properties;
 properties.cProp = 2;
 properties.aPropID = keys;
 properties.aPropVar = values;
 properties.aStatus = NULL;
 ::MQReceiveMessage( queue, INFINITE, MQ_ACTION_RECEIVE,
        &properties, NULL, NULL, NULL, NULL );
 return body;
};
```

Listing 3.85 Retrieving message from a queue.

The function takes one parameter, the handle that is to be closed. Listing 3.86 shows an example of using this function.

```
::MQCloseQueue(queue);
```

Listing 3.86   Closing a queue handle.

Earlier when I discussed the MQReceiveMessage function, I ignored a couple of parameters that could be used to read an entire message queue. In order to read an entire message queue, I need to use an MQ cursor.

```
HRESULT MQCreateCursor( QUEUEHANDLE hQueue, PHANDLE phCursor );
HRESULT MQCloseCursor( HANDLE hCursor );
```

MQCreateCursor and MQCloseCursor are needed in order to read an entire message queue. Listing 3.87 shows an example of using these functions to read an entire queue.

```
int main(int argc, char * argv[])
{
 if (argc != 2)
 {
  std::cout << "Usage:\tReadQueue [queuename]"
               << std::endl;
  return 1;
 }

 std::wstringstream ss;
 ss << L".\\" << AnsiToWide(argv[1]);
 std::cout << "Reading Queue ñ " << argv[1] << std::endl;

 WCHAR formatname[64];
 DWORD dw = 64;
 ::MQPathNameToFormatName(ss.str().c_str(),formatname, &dw);
 QUEUEHANDLE queue;
 ::MQOpenQueue(formatname, MQ_SEND_ACCESS+MQ_RECEIVE_ACCESS,
        MQ_DENY_NONE, &queue );
 HANDLE cursor;
 ::MQCreateCursor(queue, &cursor);

 MSGPROPID keys[2];
 PROPVARIANT values[2];
 keys[0] = PROPID_M_BODY;
```

Continues

Listing 3.87   Reading a queue.

```
values[0].vt = VT_VECTOR | VT_UI1;
WCHAR body[256];
values[0].caub.pElems = (LPBYTE) body;
values[0].caub.cElems = 256 * sizeof(WCHAR);

keys[1] = PROPID_M_BODY_SIZE;
values[1].vt = VT_UI4;
values[1].ulVal = 256 * sizeof(WCHAR);

MQMSGPROPS properties;
properties.cProp = 2;
properties.aPropID = keys;
properties.aPropVar = values;
properties.aStatus = NULL;

DWORD dwAction = MQ_ACTION_PEEK_CURRENT;
for (int i=0;;i++)
{
 HRESULT hresult = ::MQReceiveMessage( queue, 0,
              dwAction, &properties, NULL, NULL, cursor, NULL);
 if (hresult == MQ_ERROR_IO_TIMEOUT)
 {
 break;
 }
 std::cout << "Message #" << i << " = " << body
              << std::endl;
 dwAction = MQ_ACTION_PEEK_NEXT;
};

::MQCloseCursor(cursor);
::MQCloseQueue(queue);

return 0;

};
```

Listing 3.87 Reading a queue *(Continued)*.

In order to read the queue, I had to open it with at least MQ_RECEIVE_
ACCESS access rights. I then create a cursor for the queue and use that cursor
to traverse the queue in the repeated calls to the MQReceiveMessage function. I know there are no more messages when the MQReceiveMessage fails
with the MQ_ERROR_IO_TIMEOUT error message. Once I am finished with
a cursor, I will not forget to close it.

Transactions

MSMQ transactions are accomplished using the ITransaction interface. The
pseudo-IDL for this interface is presented in Listing 3.88.

```
interface ITransaction : IUnknown
{
    HRESULT Commit( [in] BOOL fRetaining,
        [in] DWORD grfTC, [in] DWORD grfRM);
    HRESULT Abort( [unique][in] BOID __RPC_FAR *pboidReason,
        [in] BOOL fRetaining, [in] BOOL fAsync);
    HRESULT GetTransactionInfo(
        [out] XACTTRANSINFO __RPC_FAR *pinfo);
};
```

Listing 3.88 Pseudo ITransaction interface.

Once I've started a transaction and acquired an ITransaction interface, I can call the Commit method to commit the transaction or the Abort method to abort the transaction. To retrieve an ITransaction interface and start an MSMQ transaction, I should call the MQBeginTransaction function.

```
HRESULT MQBeginTransaction(ITransaction **ppTransaction);
```

If I wanted to wrap a single call to an MQSendMessage function call, then I could write it as shown in Listing 3.89.

```
ITransaction * transaction;
::MQBeginTransaction (&transaction);
::MQSendMessage(queue, &msgprops, transaction);
transaction->Commit(0,0,0);
transaction->Release();
```

Listing 3.89 Using ITransaction.

But this code is redundant since calls to MQSendMessage and MQReceive-Message that do not use explicit transactions will use implicit transactions that are committed before the function returns.

Microsoft Message Queue ActiveX Component

Another method of programming with MSMQ is using the MSMQ ActiveX component. I find the ActiveX component quite confusing to use and prefer using the API, but the ActiveX component has a great advantage in that it can be used from any programming tool that is Automation-capable. For this reason, I will demonstrate the use of the ActiveX component from Visual Basic.

Creating a new queue from Visual Basic is trivial. Create a QueueInfo ActiveX object, set the pathname, and call the Create method. Listing 3.90 shows an example of creating message queues from Visual Basic.

```
Set info = CreateObject("MSMQ.MSMQQueueInfo");
info.PathName = ".\MyQueue";
info.Create
```

Listing 3.90   Create queue from Visual Basic.

Destroying a queue is just as easy as creating one. Listing 3.91 shows an example of deleting message queues from Visual Basic.

```
Set info = CreateObject("MSMQ.MSMQQueueInfo");
info.PathName = ".\MyQueue";
info.Delete
```

Listing 3.91   Destroy queue from Visual Basic.

Placing messages on a queue is a little more complicated, but nonetheless easy. Create the QueueInfo object, set the pathname, and call the Open method. The Open method will return a queue object. Then create a new message object and set the Body property. Last, call the Send method of the message object and pass the queue object as a parameter. Listing 3.92 shows an example of putting a message on a queue using this technique.

```
Set info = CreateObject("MSMQ.MSMQQueueInfo");
info.PathName = ".\MyQueue";
Set queue = info.Open(MQ_SEND_ACCESS+MQ_RECEIVE_ACCESS, MQ_DENY_NONE);
Set message = CreateObject("MSMQ.MSMQMessage");
message.Body = "Hello";
message.Send queue
queue.Close
```

Listing 3.92   Put message from Visual Basic.

To retrieve a message from a message queue, create the QueueInfo object, set the pathname, and call the Open method. The Open method will return a queue object. Then call the Receive method on the queue object. The method will return a message object. Listing 3.93 shows an example of retrieving a message on a queue using this technique.

```
Set info = CreateObject("MSMQ.MSMQQueueInfo");
info.PathName = ".\MyQueue";
Set queue = info.Open(MQ_SEND_ACCESS+MQ_RECEIVE_ACCESS, MQ_DENY_NONE);
Set message = queue.Receive
queue.Close
```

Listing 3.93 Get message from Visual Basic.

Sample Microsoft Message Queue Service

I personally have a lot of experience with request-response messaging and will only be addressing MSMQ as it relates to request-response messaging. This most likely has a lot do to with my fear of asynchronous communication models.

The MSMQ Service I present in this section simply receives a Unicode text message and responds with the same Unicode text message. The sample can easily be slightly modified into something more useful. The MSMQ Service is presented in its entirety in Listing 3.94.

```
class MSMQService : public NtService::Service
{
public:
 MSMQService()
  :NtService::Service("MSMQService") {};

 virtual void OnRun()
 {
  QUEUEHANDLE requestqueue, responsequeue;
  {
   WCHAR formatname[64];
   DWORD dw = 64;
   ::MQPathNameToFormatName( L".\\MyServiceRequestQueue",
         formatname, &dw );
```

Continues

Listing 3.94 MSMQ Service.

```
  ::MQOpenQueue( formatname, MQ_RECEIVE_ACCESS, MQ_DENY_NONE,
   &requestqueue );
}
{
 WCHAR formatname[64];
 DWORD dw = 64;
 ::MQPathNameToFormatName( L".\\MyServiceResponseQueue",
  formatname, &dw );
 ::MQOpenQueue( formatname, MQ_SEND_ACCESS, MQ_DENY_NONE,
  &responsequeue );
}
while(true)
{
 UCHAR szMessageID[20];

 MSGPROPID keys[3];
 PROPVARIANT values[3];
 keys[0] = PROPID_M_BODY;
 values[0].vt = VT_VECTOR | VT_UI1;
 WCHAR body[256];
 values[0].caub.pElems = (LPBYTE) body;
 values[0].caub.cElems = 256*sizeof(WCHAR);

 keys[1] = PROPID_M_BODY_SIZE;
 values[1].vt = VT_UI4;
 values[1].ulVal = 256*sizeof(WCHAR);

 keys[2] = PROPID_M_MSGID;
 values[2].vt = VT_VECTOR | VT_UI1;
 values[2].caub.pElems = (LPBYTE) szMessageID;
 values[2].caub.cElems = 20*sizeof(UCHAR);

 MQMSGPROPS properties;
 properties.cProp = 3;
 properties.aPropID = keys;
 properties.aPropVar = values;
 properties.aStatus = NULL;
 HRESULT hresult = ::MQReceiveMessage( requestqueue,
        INFINITE, MQ_ACTION_RECEIVE, &properties, NULL, NULL,
          NULL, NULL );

 std::wstring str = std::wstring(body, values[0].1Val);

 if (SUCCEEDED(hresult))
 {
  MSGPROPID keys[2];
  PROPVARIANT values[2];
  keys[0] = PROPID_M_BODY;
```

Continues

Listing 3.94 MSMQ Service *(Continued)*.

```
      values[0].vt = VT_VECTOR | VT_UI1;
      values[0].caub.pElems = (LPBYTE) str.c_str();
      values[0].caub.cElems = str.length() * sizeof(WCHAR);

      keys[1] = PROPID_M_CORRELATIONID;
      values[1].vt = VT_VECTOR | VT_UI1;
      values[1].caub.pElems = (LPBYTE) szMessageID;
      values[1].caub.cElems = 20*sizeof(UCHAR);

      MQMSGPROPS properties;
      properties.cProp = 2;
      properties.aPropID = keys;
      properties.aPropVar = values;
      properties.aStatus = NULL;
      ::MQSendMessage( responsequeue, &properties, NULL );
    }
  };
  ::MQCloseQueue(requestqueue);
  ::MQCloseQueue(responsequeue);
}

virtual void OnInstall()
{
  Service::OnInstall();

  // Create the request queue
  {
    QUEUEPROPID keys[1];
    keys[0] = PROPID_Q_PATHNAME;
    PROPVARIANT values[1];
    values[0].vt = VT_LPWSTR;
    values[0].pwszVal = L".\\MyServiceRequestQueue";

    MQQUEUEPROPS properties;
    properties.cProp = 1;
    properties.aPropID = keys;
    properties.aPropVar = values;
    properties.aStatus = NULL;

    WCHAR formatname[64];
    DWORD dw = 64;
    ::MQCreateQueue( NULL, &properties, formatname, &dw );
  }

  // Create the response queue
  {
    QUEUEPROPID keys[1];
    keys[0] = PROPID_Q_PATHNAME;
    PROPVARIANT values[1];
```

Continues

Listing 3.94

```
      values[0].vt = VT_LPWSTR;
      values[0].pwszVal = L".\\MyServiceResponseQueue";

      MQQUEUEPROPS properties;
      properties.cProp = 1;
      properties.aPropID = keys;
      properties.aPropVar = values;
      properties.aStatus = NULL;

      WCHAR formatname[64];
      DWORD dw = 64;
      ::MQCreateQueue( NULL, &properties, formatname, &dw );
    }
  }

  virtual void OnUninstall()
  {
   Service::OnUninstall();

    // Delete the request queues
    {
     WCHAR formatname[64];
     DWORD dw = 64;
     ::MQPathNameToFormatName( L".\\MyServiceRequestQueue",
       formatname, &dw );
     ::MQDeleteQueue(formatname);
    }

    // Delete the response queues
    {
     WCHAR formatname[64];
     DWORD dw = 64;
     ::MQPathNameToFormatName( L".\\MyServiceResponseQueue",
       formatname, &dw );
     ::MQDeleteQueue(formatname);
    }
  }
};

int WINAPI WinMain(HINSTANCE hinstance,
 HINSTANCE /* hprevious */, LPSTR lpCmdLine, int /* nShowCmd */)
{
 MSMQService().Start(lpCmdLine);
 return 0;
}
```

Listing 3.94 MSMQ Service *(Continued)*.

I overrode the OnRun virtual method and started the method by acquiring handles to the request and response queues.

```
QUEUEHANDLE requestqueue, responsequeue;
{
 WCHAR formatname[64];
 DWORD dw = 64;
 ::MQPathNameToFormatName( L".\\MyServiceRequestQueue", formatname,
  &dw );
 ::MQOpenQueue( formatname, MQ_RECEIVE_ACCESS, MQ_DENY_NONE,
  &requestqueue );
}
{
 WCHAR formatname[64];
 DWORD dw = 64;
 ::MQPathNameToFormatName( L".\\MyServiceResponseQueue",
  formatname, &dw );
 ::MQOpenQueue( formatname, MQ_SEND_ACCESS, MQ_DENY_NONE,
  &responsequeue );
}
```

I used the MQPathNameToFormatName to turn a human-readable name into a format name. Again, I suggest that format names be used only temporarily as they can change if someone decides to reset the queue by deleting and re-creating it. I then use the format name to acquire the queue handle.

Note that I explicitly opened the queues with restricted access. The one queue was opened with receive access and the other with send access. I do this in order to prevent myself from inadvertently writing or reading from the wrong queue. Inadvertent writes and reads caused by confusing one queue handle with another can be very difficult to debug, so it's just as well to prevent this by opening the queues with restricted access.

Once I've opened handles to the request and response queues, I can loop endlessly reading from the request queue and writing to the response queue.

```
UCHAR szMessageID[20];

MSGPROPID keys[3];
PROPVARIANT values[3];
keys[0] = PROPID_M_BODY;
values[0].vt = VT_VECTOR | VT_UI1;
WCHAR body[256];
values[0].caub.pElems = (LPBYTE) body;
values[0].caub.cElems = 256*sizeof(WCHAR);

keys[1] = PROPID_M_BODY_SIZE;
values[1].vt = VT_UI4;
values[1].ulVal = 256*sizeof(WCHAR);

keys[2] = PROPID_M_MSGID;
```

```
values[2].vt = VT_VECTOR | VT_UI1;
values[2].caub.pElems = (LPBYTE) szMessageID;
values[2].caub.cElems = 20*sizeof(UCHAR);

 MQMSGPROPS properties;
 properties.cProp = 3;
 properties.aPropID = keys;
 properties.aPropVar = values;
 properties.aStatus = NULL;
 HRESULT hresult = ::MQReceiveMessage( requestqueue,
     INFINITE, MQ_ACTION_RECEIVE, &properties, NULL, NULL,
     NULL, NULL );
```

Note that I've also acquired the message ID by providing the output message ID property in the MQReceiveMessage function call. After calling the MQ-ReceiveMessage MSMQ function and receiving a successful HRESULT, I copy the received message to a local STL string.

```
std::wstring str;
 if (SUCCEEDED(hresult))
 {
  str = std::wstring(body, values[0].1Val);
 }
```

Again, if I receive a successful HRESULT from the MQReceiveMessage function, I copy the local STL string onto the response queue. I also specify the message ID as the correlation ID in the call to the MQSendMessage function.

```
 if (SUCCEEDED(hresult))
 {
 MSGPROPID keys[2];
 PROPVARIANT values[2];
 keys[0] = PROPID_M_BODY;
 values[0].vt = VT_VECTOR | VT_UI1;
 values[0].caub.pElems = (LPBYTE) str.c_str();
 values[0].caub.cElems = str.length() * sizeof(WCHAR);

 keys[1] = PROPID_M_CORRELATIONID;
 values[1].vt = VT_VECTOR | VT_UI1;
 values[1].caub.pElems = (LPBYTE) szMessageID;
 values[1].caub.cElems = 20*sizeof(UCHAR);

 MQMSGPROPS properties;
 properties.cProp = 2;
 properties.aPropID = keys;
 properties.aPropVar = values;
 properties.aStatus = NULL;
  ::MQSendMessage( responsequeue, &properties, NULL );
 }
```

In order to match the response and request, I tag the outgoing response with a correlation ID that matches the message ID of the incoming request. I can later use this in the client code to match up responses to the request.

The MQCloseQueue function calls will never be reached because I never break from the while-true loop. But in a production-quality application, I should check the returned HRESULTs for conditions for which I should be calling a break.

```
::MQCloseQueue(requestqueue);
::MQCloseQueue(responsequeue);
```

In the OnInstall overridden method, I create the queue. This ensures that the queues are available when the application is installed. It might be tempting in creating the queues to use scripts outside of the server. This is an acceptable alternative, but requires an extra deployment module (the script).

```
virtual void OnInstall()
{
 Service::OnInstall();

 // Create the request queue
 {
  QUEUEPROPID keys[1];
  keys[0] = PROPID_Q_PATHNAME;
  PROPVARIANT values[1];
  values[0].vt = VT_LPWSTR;
  values[0].pwszVal = L".\\MyServiceRequestQueue";

  MQQUEUEPROPS properties;
  properties.cProp = 1;
  properties.aPropID = keys;
  properties.aPropVar = values;
  properties.aStatus = NULL;

  WCHAR formatname[64];
  DWORD dw = 64;
  ::MQCreateQueue( NULL, &properties, formatname, &dw );
 }

 // Create the response queue
 {
  QUEUEPROPID keys[1];
  keys[0] = PROPID_Q_PATHNAME;
  PROPVARIANT values[1];
  values[0].vt = VT_LPWSTR;
  values[0].pwszVal = L".\\MyServiceResponseQueue";

  MQQUEUEPROPS properties;
  properties.cProp = 1;
  properties.aPropID = keys;
  properties.aPropVar = values;
  properties.aStatus = NULL;
  WCHAR formatname[64];
  DWORD dw = 64;
  ::MQCreateQueue( NULL, &properties, formatname, &dw );
 }
}
```

In the OnUninstall overridden method, I delete the queue. I always deploy these routines as I've encountered situations during development, testing, and installation in which I want to remove pollution in the queues before I attempt to start the server.

```
virtual void OnUninstall()
{
 Service::OnUninstall();

 // Delete the request queues
 {
  WCHAR formatname[64];
  DWORD dw = 64;
  ::MQPathNameToFormatName( L".\\MyServiceRequestQueue",
   formatname, &dw );
  ::MQDeleteQueue(formatname);
 }

 // Delete the response queues
 {
  WCHAR formatname[64];
  DWORD dw = 64;
  ::MQPathNameToFormatName( L".\\MyServiceResponseQueue",
   formatname, &dw );
  ::MQDeleteQueue(formatname);
 }
}
```

The code in the OnInstall and OnUninstall methods to create and destroy the queues is pretty simple. Call MQCreateQueue with one property, the queue pathname. Call MQDeleteQueue with the format name acquired temporarily from MQPathNameToFormatName.

Sample Microsoft Message Queue Client

The MSMQ client is no more complex than the server is. Listing 3.95 shows the source code for the MSMQ client.

Fail-Over and Load Balancing

As mentioned earlier, the advantage of the message queue model is that the producer is loosely coupled with the consumer. This has some enormous advantages in fail-over and load balancing. Because they are not coupled, the consumer may crash without affecting the producer. The reverse situation is also true.

```
int main(int argc, char * argv[])
{
 // open the request and response queues
 QUEUEHANDLE requestqueue = OpenQueue(L"MyServiceRequestQueue");
 QUEUEHANDLE responsequeue = OpenQueue(L"MyServiceResponseQueue");

 std::wstring str = "Hello";

 MSGPROPID keys[2];
 PROPVARIANT values[2];
 keys[0] = PROPID_M_BODY;
 values[0].vt = VT_VECTOR | VT_UI1;
 values[0].caub.pElems = (LPBYTE) str.c_str();
 values[0].caub.cElems =
  str.length() * sizeof(WCHAR);

 MQMSGPROPS properties;
 properties.cProp = 1;
 properties.aPropID = keys;
 properties.aPropVar = values;
 properties.aStatus = NULL;
 ::MQSendMessage(responsequeue,&properties, NULL);

 {
  MSGPROPID keys[3];
  PROPVARIANT values[3];
  keys[0] = PROPID_M_BODY;
  values[0].vt = VT_VECTOR | VT_UI1;
  WCHAR body[256];
  values[0].caub.pElems = (LPBYTE) body;
  values[0].caub.cElems = 256*sizeof(WCHAR);

  keys[1] = PROPID_M_BODY_SIZE;
  values[1].vt = VT_UI4;
  values[1].ulVal = 256*sizeof(WCHAR);

  MQMSGPROPS properties;
  properties.cProp = 2;
  properties.aPropID = keys;
  properties.aPropVar = values;
  properties.aStatus = NULL;
  ::MQReceiveMessage( requestqueue, INFINITE,
   MQ_ACTION_RECEIVE, &properties, NULL,
   NULL, NULL, NULL );
 };
 ::MQCloseQueue(requestqueue);
 ::MQCloseQueue(responsequeue);
}
```

Listing 3.95 MSMQ client.

It is also possible to have a series of consumers working in parallel that read from the same queues. Since the consumers will only process messages as they are freed, the load balancing is quite dynamic and optimized.

The consumers could also be implemented in separate processes and on separate machines. If they are on separate processes, then failures in one process will be isolated and will not affect the other consumers.

Both fail-over and load balancing are easily implemented in MSMQ. No additional coding is required when there is a design that allows users to scale to multiple consumers across multiple processes and machines.

MQ Series

MSMQ was designed as an alternative to IBM's MQ Series for message queue basic communication on NT Servers. IBM's MQ Series product is a much more mature product that is considered extremely stable. Many of the concepts that I have introduced apply equally well to MQ Series.

Standard Generalized Markup Language

One of the fastest-growing development standards is SGML (Standard Generalized Markup Language)-based messaging. It's actually quite amazing how fast SGML has become one of the most used standards in software development. Every time users retrieve a page on the World Wide Web they are downloading text in a format known as HTML (HyperText Markup Language). HTML is an implementation of this SGML standard.

An SGML document is a hierarchical representation of data. The document contains one root element and each element may contain any number of attributes, child elements, or data. This is an oversimplification, but for this discussion it is appropriate. Each element begins with a tag of the form <element-name>. An element may also have an optional terminating tag. Listing 3.96 shows an SGML document with one element.

The node in the single-element SGML document is named MyDoc. It contains no child elements, no data, and no attributes.

```
<MyDoc>
</MyDoc>
```

Listing 3.96   Single-element SGML document.

Attributes are key-value pairs that are contained with the start tag. Each key-value pair is delimited by spacing and the key and value are delimited by the equality character (=). Listing 3.97 shows an SGML document with one element and multiple attributes.

```
<MyDoc name=mydoc.sgml type=mymarkup>
</MyDoc>
```

Listing 3.97   Single element with multiple attributes.

The MyDoc node in this SGML document now has two attributes. The key name has the value mydoc.sgml. The key type has the value mymarkup.

Child elements are exactly similar to the root element in that they may also contain attributes, data, and child elements. Listing 3.98 shows an SGML document with several levels of elements.

```
<MyDoc name=mydoc.sgml type=mymarkup>
 <Text>
  <Content></Content>
  <Content></Content>
 </Text>
 <Text>
  <Content></Content>
 </Text>
 <Binary>
  <Content></Content>
 </Binary>
</MyDoc>
```

Listing 3.98   Multilevel SGML document.

It is important to note that any element may contain multiple child elements that have the same name. In this last document, the MyDoc element has three child elements; two have the name Text and one has the name Binary.

Elements may also contain data. Listing 3.99 continues the example by adding data to the content tags.

Because elements that have no child elements are not required to have end tags, it is conventional to disregard the end tag when an element has data and no child elements.

SGML documents are defined by their DTD (document type definition). The DTD defines the attributes, data, and child elements that are found in each

```
<MyDoc name=mydoc.sgml type=mymarkup>
 <Text>
  <Content>Hello Guy
  <Content>How are you doing
 </Text>
 <Text>
  <Content>Roger
 </Text>
 <Binary>
  <Content>0x00060004
 </Binary>
</MyDoc>
```

Listing 3.99   Multilevel SGML document with data.

element. The DTD for this growing SGML example might be similar to Listing 3.100.

```
<!ELEMENT MyDoc ((Text | Binary)*)>
<!ELEMENT Text (Content*)>
<!ELEMENT Binary (Content*)>
<!ELEMENT Content (#PCDATA)>
```

Listing 3.100   SGML DTD example.

The first line of the DTD says that the MyDoc element may have any number of Text and Binary elements that are child elements. The second and third lines indicate that the Text and Binary elements have any number of Content elements. The last line indicates that the Content element contains character data.

History

SGML has a long history. The entire markup language story began over 30 years ago at IBM. Charles Goldfarb, Edward Mosher, and Raymond Lorie invented a language called GML (Generalized Markup Language). GML evolved for years before it was standardized. Listing 3.101 shows an example of the GML notation.

The SGML standard was first published nearly 20 years ago. The early adopters were the U.S. IRS (Internal Revenue Service) and DoD (Department of Defense).

```
::h1.Chapter 1 Introduction
:p. The biggest development in Microsoft Windows in the last few years
is the introduction of Windows NT application servers.
```

Listing 3.101   GML example.

SGML really hadn't made much of a splash yet. Then came this language called HTML. HTML is in fact an implementation of SGML for delivery of content over the Internet. Listing 3.102 shows a very small HTML sample document.

```
<HTML>
<HEAD>
<TITLE>KBCafe.COM</TITLE>
</HEAD>
<BODY>
<TABLE>
<TR><TD WIDTH=20% VALIGN=TOP>
 <FONT SIZE=+2 COLOR=RED><B>KBCafe.COM Homepage</B></FONT>
</TD><TD VALIGN=TOP>
 Hello
</TD></TR>
</TABLE>
</BODY>
</HTML>
```

Listing 3.102   HTML example.

Most HTML documents are much more complex, as HTML has evolved into a very rich content delivery format. An HTML document always begins with an HTML start tag and ends with an HTML end tag. The document is split in two parts: the HEAD and the BODY. The HEAD contains a TITLE among other things. The BODY may contain a very large amount of different tags to represent the rich content delivery format. In my example, I have a table with two rows.

Eventually, the Internet started moving toward thinner and thinner clients and is now today moving toward mobile clients. Yes, now users can surf the Web on their mobile phones. The problem with SGML and HTML is that the parsing rules are very heavy and require a lot of memory. To reduce the parsing requirements, the SGML language was reduced into a new standard called XML.

eXtensible Markup Language

XML (eXtensible Markup Language) is a subset of the SGML standard. The biggest difference between XML and SGML from the perspective of most software developers is that XML requires end tags even when the element has no child elements.

Because XML requires end tags, developers do not have to interpret a DTD in order to parse an XML document. Most developers have a hard time understanding that last sentence. In old SGML days, the end tags were not required, so it was difficult to figure out which elements were children of which when the author failed to use end tags everywhere. Listing 3.103 shows an example of this type of confusing SGML.

```
<MyDoc name=mydoc.sgml type=mymarkup>
<Text>
<Content>Hello Guy
<Content>How are you doing
<Text>
<Content>Roger
<Binary>
<Content>0x00060004
</MyDoc>
```

Listing 3.103   Confusing SGML.

It is not clear at all in the preceding document whether the Content elements are children of the Text and Content elements or whether they are children of the more global MyDoc element. But the SGML parser could read the DTD and figure out the real truth behind this SGML document.

In XML this confusion doesn't exist because the end tags are now required. Similar XML would look like Listing 3.104.

Fallacy

Some software developers actually think that the difference in end tags between SGML and XML is that SGML does not allow end tags when no child elements are present. This belief is simply not true. SGML end tags are always optional. XML end tags are never optional and are always required.

```
<MyDoc name=mydoc.sgml type=mymarkup>
<Text>
<Content>Hello Guy</Content>
<Content>How are you doing</Content>
</Text>
<Text>
<Content>Roger</Content>
</Text>
<Binary>
<Content>0x00060004</Content>
<≠Binary>
</MyDoc>
```

Listing 3.104   Unconfusing XML.

The XML document is clear as to which elements are children of which. This removes the responsibility of reading the DTD from the markup language parser. This is why XML is so great for smaller (and thinner) devices.

Summary

For more detailed information on topics covered in this chapter, I suggest readers dive into books on their favorite IPC mechanisms. Chapter 4 is about using the NT Event Log to turn an NT Service into something very professional.

The Event Log

Because NT Services do not readily interact with interactive users, a mechanism was needed to provide feedback to interactive users in order to communicate the health of an NT Service. The NT Event Log was chosen as the standard mechanism for communicating this information. The NT Event Log itself is an NT Service that is started by the SCM when the NT Workstation Server is booted and is terminated when the NT Workstation Server is shut down.

An obvious requirement is that the NT Event Log be started prior to any NT Services that require the services of the NT Event Log. In order to ensure that the NT Event Log starts before any client NT Services that use it, users can specify the NT Event Log short name as a dependent service when they install their services with the CreateService function. This was done throughout the previous chapters.

The NT Event Log is not one event log. NT Workstation Server is actually installed with three default event logs and more can easily be added. The three default event logs installed with NT Workstation Server are the System, Security, and Application event logs. Application servers will typically write log entries in the Application event log although they should also be enabled to write System and Security event logs when appropriate.

Application servers can create and write to additional event logs beyond the three event logs installed with NT Workstation Server. I discuss adding and writing to additional event logs later in this chapter.

Event Viewer

The most important utility to become familiar with before writing applications that use the NT Event Log is the Event Viewer. This application is installed with NT Workstation Server and allows the interactive or remote user to view event logs.

In the following section, I demonstrate how to use the Event Viewer. I start the Event Viewer by selecting Programs | Administrative Tools | Event Viewer from the Start menu (see Figure 4.1).

The Event Viewer can be used to read any of the three standard event logs. To switch from reading one event log to another, I select Log from the menu bar (see Figure 4.2). Then I select the Application, Security, or System menu items to switch to viewing the particular event log.

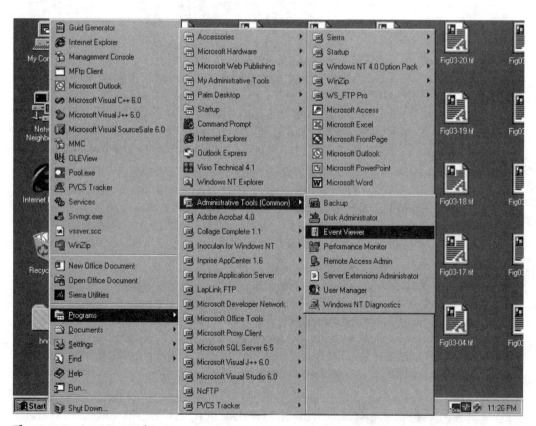

Figure 4.1 Start Event Viewer.

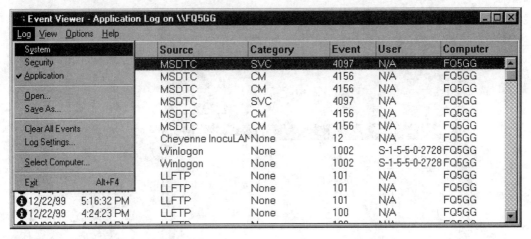

Figure 4.2   Switching event logs.

It is not possible to read any event logs beyond the three standard logs with the Event Viewer. If users do create their own event logs, then they'll also have to write a custom viewer for them. Later in this chapter I describe exactly how to write a custom viewer.

Reading Remote Event Logs

I can also read the Application, Security, or System event logs on remote computers. I select Log | Remote from the menu bar and the Select Computer dialog appears (see Figure 4.3).

I can type the computer name or select the computer from the combo box drop-down list and then click the OK button. The event logs on the remote computer are then be displayed in the Event Viewer client area.

Filtering Event Logs

Another feature of the Event Viewer is its ability to filter the message displayed in the Event Viewer client area. By selecting View | Filter Events from the menu bar, the Filter dialog appears (see Figure 4.4).

The filtering may occur by date, source, severity, or many other criteria. I typically filter on events that have the error severity. On an application server that generates a large amount of informational and warning logs, filtering on error logs makes it easier to find appropriate log entries in crisis situations.

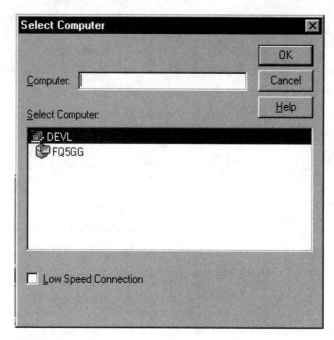

Figure 4.3 Select Computer dialog.

If you select (All) in the Source combo box, then only (All) may be selected from the Category combo box. To select a Category other than (All), users must first select a Source that implements categories.

View Event Details

I can view event details by double-clicking on a log entry or by selecting a log entry and pressing the Enter key. The Event Detail dialog shows me all details of the particular log entry (see Figure 4.5).

The Date and Time fields are the date and time when the entry was placed in the log. The User field is usually NULL, but you can set this to any user for any message. The Computer field is the computer name where the entry was placed in the log. This can change over time, if users write to logs from more than one computer.

The Event ID and Source are used to construct the message description. I discuss message sources and how they can used to format messages later in the chapter. The Type may be any of Error, Warning, Information, Success audit, or Failure audit.

The Category is usually None, but some event sources do implement cate-

Figure 4.4 Filter dialog.

gories in order to facilitate filtering of events by category. Many of the Security event sources implement event categories.

The Description field is a composite of the Event ID, Source, and message parameters. Each Source defines its Event IDs and they are combined with the message parameters to form the full Descriptions. This may seem a bit complex, but there is logic behind this madness.

The Data field is binary data. This binary data is usually not present in most log entries. Even when present, it is very difficult for the operator to make any sense of binary data. But when an event occurs, it may be helpful for an experienced operator to receive this additional binary data, as a diagnostic aid. As an example, if an error occurred when a SQL query was sent to a database, an operator may wish to report the description "Error Querying Database" and place the query and results in the Data field.

Reading the Event Log

Operators can read the NT Event Log using the Event Viewer, but sometimes a more programmatic method is needed. Functions are also available for

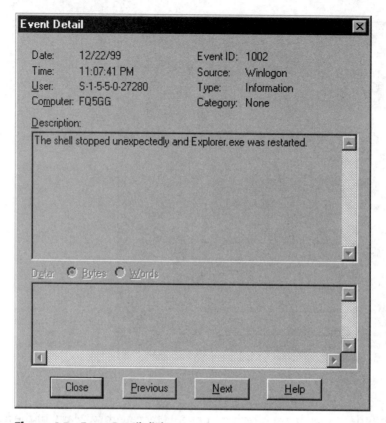

Figure 4.5 Event Detail dialog.

reading the NT Event Log. Listing 4.1 shows the code necessary to read the Application event log.

I've introduced three new functions in the listing: OpenEventLog, Close-EventLog, and ReadEventLog. The OpenEventLog and CloseEventLog functions are trivial.

```
HANDLE OpenEventLog( LPCSTR lpUNCServerName, LPCSTR lpSourceName );
BOOL CloseEventLog( HANDLE hEventLog );
```

The two parameters to OpenEventLog function are the computer name and log name. If I call OpenEventLog with the first parameter equal to NULL, the parameter defaults to the local computer. The log name can be any of the standard event logs (System, Security, or Application) or a nonstandard event log. The OpenEventLog function returns a handle that is used in calls to ReadEventLog. When I am finished using the handle, I should call CloseEventLog to free it.

```
int main(int argc, char* argv[])
{
HANDLE handle = ::OpenEventLog(NULL, "Application");
DWORD dwRecord = 0;
static const int c = 65536;
DWORD dwRead, dwNext;
BYTE by[c];
while (true)
{
 if (!::ReadEventLog(handle, EVENTLOG_BACKWARDS_READ+
                     EVENTLOG_SEQUENTIAL_READ, 1, by, c,
                     &dwRead, &dwNext))
 {
 break;
 }
 DWORD dw = 0;
 while (dwRead > dw)
 {
 EVENTLOGRECORD * p;
 p = (EVENTLOGRECORD *) (by+dw);
 char * sz = (char *) (by+dw+56);
 TCHAR * tchar = (TCHAR *) (by+dw+p->StringOffset);
 std::cout << "Source Name = " << sz << std::endl;
 std::cout << "String = " << tchar << std::endl;
 dw += p->Length;
 }
}
::CloseEventLog(handle);
return 0;
}
```

Listing 4.1   Reading the Event Log.

```
BOOL ReadEventLog( HANDLE hEventLog, DWORD dwReadFlags,
   DWORD dwRecordOffset, LPVOID lpBuffer,
     DWORD nNumberOfBytesToRead, DWORD *pnBytesRead,
     DWORD *pnMinNumberOfBytesNeeded );
```

The ReadEventLog function is not trivial at all. The hEventLog parameter is the handle I retrieved from the call to the OpenEventLog function.

The dwReadFlags parameter is a bit mask that determines the direction and searching that should be used in the call. I include the EVENT_LOG_ BACKWARDS_READ mask to read the event log from the most recent to the least recent entry or the EVENTLOG_FORWARDS_READ mask to read the event log from least recent to most recent entry. EVENTLOG_SEQUENTIAL_ READ is used to perform sequential reading of the event log, and EVENTLOG_

SEEK_READ is used to jump to the record denoted by the dwRecordOffset parameter. The dwRecordOffset parameter is ignored if EVENTLOG_SEEK_READ is not specified.

```
#define EVENTLOG_SEQUENTIAL_READ    0X0001
#define EVENTLOG_SEEK_READ          0X0002
#define EVENTLOG_FORWARDS_READ      0X0004
#define EVENTLOG_BACKWARDS_READ     0X0008
```

The lpBuffer out parameter should point to the location where the function will place the EVENTLOGRECORD record. Since the EVENTLOGRECORD record has dynamic size, I must specify the size of my buffer in the nNumberOfBytesToRead parameter. The pnBytesRead out parameter will contain the size in bytes of the EVENTLOGRECORD record copied to my buffer. The pnMinNumberOfBytesNeeded out parameter is filled when the ReadEventLog function fails because the nNumberOfBytesToRead parameter was too small. It will contain the required size of the EVENTLOGRECORD record. If the nNumberOfBytesToRead parameter is too small, the ReadEventLog function will return zero and the GetLastError function will return ERROR_INSUFFICIENT_BUFFER.

The EVENTLOGRECORD structure is not very typical. It contains some fixed-length members, but also contains variable-length members. To calculate the location of the variable-length members, I can use the offsets provided in the header of the EVENTLOGRECORD structure.

```
typedef struct _EVENTLOGRECORD {
  DWORD Length;
  DWORD Reserved;
  DWORD RecordNumber;
  DWORD TimeGenerated;
  DWORD TimeWritten;
  DWORD EventID;
  WORD  EventType;
  WORD  NumStrings;
  WORD  EventCategory;
  WORD  ReservedFlags;
  DWORD ClosingRecordNumber;
  DWORD StringOffset;
  DWORD UserSidLength;
  DWORD UserSidOffset;
  DWORD DataLength;
  DWORD DataOffset;
  //
  // Then follow:
  //
  // WCHAR SourceName[]
  // WCHAR Computername[]
  // SID UserSid
```

```
// WCHAR Strings[]
// BYTE  Data[]
// CHAR  Pad[]
// DWORD Length;
//
} EVENTLOGRECORD,  *PEVENTLOGRECORD;
```

An important part of the structure, since it is variable-length, is to include a Length member at both the start and end of the structure. This makes it possible to traverse a contiguous array of these structures in physical memory. Once I establish the beginning of one structure, I could use its internal offset to find the variably positioned members (those that were commented out) and use the Length member to move to the next and previous contiguous structures.

I've written a small class that encapsulates the offsets so that the members are more easily retrieved. The class is shown in Listing 4.2.

Most of this class is a simple implementation of pointer arithmetic. The most difficult method implementation is the String method. In this method, I step through the entire list of strings and load them into a return vector.

Using this EventLogRecord class is quite simple. Listing 4.3 is a reimplementation of reading the entire Application log using this class.

Comparing this last code listing to previous ones, this one is much cleaner and doesn't require the same level of pointer arithmetic since this arithmetic is hidden in the class implementation.

Looking at the output of this dump and comparing it to the NT Event Viewer, I see that the text output is not the same. This is because the Event Viewer is formatting the strings of the log entries using a message source.

Formatting Log Entries

The message formatting of event log entries is quite complex. The Event ID, message source name, and parameter message strings are combined with external resources to derive the message description. Using the message source name, a lookup occurs in the Registry to determine the event message file and the parameter message file. The event message file is then queried to determine the template message string. The template message string is then scanned for parameter message file strings. These parameter message file strings are loaded from the parameter message file and, along with the parameter message strings, are substituted into the template message string to derive a complete message.

In this section, I address only the substitution of parameter message strings into the template message string. Later in this chapter, I readdress formatting of message descriptions using the parameter message file. Listing 4.4 shows a

```
class EventLogRecord
{
  const EVENTLOGRECORD * m_p;
  EventLogRecord()
    :m_p(NULL) { };
public:
  EventLogRecord(const EVENTLOGRECORD * p)
    :m_p(p) { };
  DWORD Length() { return m_p->Length; };
  DWORD RecordNumber() { return m_p->RecordNumber; };
  DWORD TimeGenerated() { return m_p->TimeGenerated; };
  DWORD TimeWritten() { return m_p->TimeWritten; };
  DWORD EventID() { return m_p->EventID; };
  WORD EventType() { return m_p->EventType; };
  WORD EventCategory() { return m_p->EventCategory; };
  std::string SourceName() { return (TCHAR*)m_p+56; };
  std::string ComputerName()
  { return (TCHAR*)m_p+56+SourceName().length()+1; };
  SID * UserSid() { return (SID*)m_p+m_p->UserSidOffset; };
  DWORD UserSidLength() { return m_p->UserSidLength; };
  std::vector<std::string> Strings()
  {
    std::vector<std::string> v;
    DWORD offset = m_p->StringOffset;
    for (int i=0;i<m_p->NumStrings;i++)
    {
      std::string str = (TCHAR*)m_p+offset;
      v.push_back(str);
      offset += str.length()+1;
    }
    return v;
  }
  BYTE * Data() { return (BYTE*)m_p+m_p->DataOffset; };
  DWORD DataLength() { return m_p->DataLength; };

};
```

Listing 4.2 EventLogRecord class.

class I've created that formats log entries using the appropriate message source.

The steps to formatting an event log message description are quite numerous. First, I must construct the Registry key string using the event log name and the message source name. This is a simple substitution equivalent to SYS-TEM\\CurrentControlSet\\Services\\Eventlog\\, plus the event log name, plus another \\ delimiter, plus the message source name.

```cpp
int main(int argc, char* argv[])
{
 HANDLE handle = ::OpenEventLog(NULL, "Application");
 DWORD dwRecord = 0;
 static const int c = 65536;
 DWORD dwRead, dwNext;
 BYTE by[c];
 while (true)
 {
  if (!::ReadEventLog(handle, EVENTLOG_BACKWARDS_READ+
     EVENTLOG_SEQUENTIAL_READ, 1, by, c,
     &dwRead, &dwNext))
  {
  break;
  }
  DWORD dw = 0;
  while (dwRead > dw)
  {
  EventLogRecord rec((EVENTLOGRECORD *)(by+dw));
  std::cout << "Record Number = "
              << rec.RecordNumber() << "\n";
  std::cout << "Time Generated = "
              << rec.TimeGenerated() << "\n";
  std::cout << "Time Written = "
              << rec.TimeWritten() << "\n";
  std::cout << "Event ID = " << rec.EventID() << "\n";
  std::cout << "Event Type = "
              << rec.EventType() << "\n";
  std::cout << "Event Category = "
              << rec.EventCategory() << "\n";
  std::cout << "Source Name = "
              << rec.SourceName() << "\n";
  std::cout << "Computer Name = "
              << rec.ComputerName() << "\n";
  std::vector<std::string> v = rec.Strings();
  for (std::vector<std::string>::iterator i = v.begin();
   i!=v.end();i++)
  {
   std::cout << "String = " << *i << "\n";
  }
  std::cout << std::endl;

  dw += rec.Length();
  }
 }
 ::CloseEventLog(handle);
 return 0;
}
```

Listing 4.3 Reading the Event Log with EventLogRecord class.

```
class FormatEventLogRecord
{
 std::string m_eventlog;
 FormatEventLogRecord()
  { };
public:
 FormatEventLogRecord(const std::string & eventlog)
 {
        m_eventlog =
        "SYSTEM\\CurrentControlSet\\Services\\Eventlog\\"
                    + eventlog;
    };
 std::string Format(const EVENTLOGRECORD * record)
 {
  std::stringstream ss;
  EventLogRecord rec(record);
  ss << m_eventlog << "\\" << rec.SourceName();
  HKEY hkey;
  if (::RegOpenKey(HKEY_LOCAL_MACHINE, ss.str().c_str(),
                   &hkey) != ERROR_SUCCESS)
  {
   return "";
  };
  char sz[256*256];
  DWORD dw = sizeof(sz);
  if (::RegQueryValueEx(hkey, "EventMessageFile", NULL,
                   NULL, (BYTE*)sz, &dw) != ERROR_SUCCESS)
  {
   ::RegCloseKey(hkey);
   return "";
  }
  ::RegCloseKey(hkey);
  ::ExpandEnvironmentStrings(std::string(sz).c_str(),
   sz, sizeof(sz));
  HINSTANCE handle = ::LoadLibraryEx(sz, NULL, 0);
  if (handle == NULL)
  {
   return "";
  }
  DWORD dwArgs[16] = {0};
  DWORD offset = record->StringOffset;
  for (int i=0;i<record->NumStrings && i<16;i++)
  {
   dwArgs[i] = ((DWORD)record)+offset;
   std::string str = (TCHAR *)dwArgs[i];
   offset += str.length()+1;
```

Continues

Listing 4.4   FormatEventLogRecord class.

```
        }
    dw = ::FormatMessage(FORMAT_MESSAGE_FROM_HMODULE |
     FORMAT_MESSAGE_ARGUMENT_ARRAY,
     handle, rec.EventID(), 0, sz, 1024,
                    (va_list*)dwArgs);
    if (dw == 0)
    {
      dw = ::GetLastError();
    }
    ::FreeLibrary(handle);
    return sz;
    };
};
```

Listing 4.4

```
m_eventlog = "SYSTEM\\CurrentControlSet\\Services\\Eventlog\\"
     + eventlog;
std::stringstream ss;
ss << m_eventlog << "\\" << rec.SourceName();
```

The next step is to read the EventMessageFile value from this Registry key.

```
HKEY hkey;
::RegOpenKey(HKEY_LOCAL_MACHINE, ss.str().c_str(), &hkey)
char sz[256*256];
DWORD dw = sizeof(sz);
::RegQueryValueEx(hkey, "EventMessageFile", NULL, NULL, (BYTE*)sz, &dw)
::RegCloseKey(hkey);
```

Once I have the filename with path, I must expand any environment macros that exist in the value. The most likely environment macro is %SystemRoot%. In order to expand this macro into the Windows directory, I can call the ExpandEnvironmentString function.

```
::ExpandEnvironmentStrings(std::string(sz).c_str(), sz,
sizeof(sz));
```

The next step is to load the message source file so that I can load the message string and format it using the FormatMessage function.

```
HINSTANCE handle = ::LoadLibraryEx(sz, NULL, 0);
```

Once I've acquired a handle to the message source file, I can use this handle in the call to FormatMessage to complete the compilation of the event description.

```
DWORD dwArgs[16] = {0};
DWORD offset = record->StringOffset;
for (int i=0;i<record->NumStrings && i<16;i++)
{
```

```
 dwArgs[i] = ((DWORD)record)+offset;
 std::string str = (TCHAR *)dwArgs[i];
 offset += str.length()+1;
}
dw = ::FormatMessage(FORMAT_MESSAGE_FROM_HMODULE |
   FORMAT_MESSAGE_ARGUMENT_ARRAY,
   handle, rec.EventID(), 0, sz, 1024, (va_list*)dwArgs);
```

I could also have manually loaded the message string and performed the substitution myself, but the FormatMessage is quite convenient in this task. Later in this chapter I show how formatting event messages is even more complex once I introduction the parameter message file.

Event Viewer

Now that I've formatted event descriptions with parameter strings, I can enhance the event viewer to account for these substitutions. If I compile and run the event viewer in Listing 4.5, it will format nearly all message descriptions in the same manner as the NT Event Viewer.

```
int main(int argc, char* argv[])
{
 HANDLE handle = ::OpenEventLog(NULL, "Application");
 FormatEventLogRecord format("Application");
 DWORD dwRecord = 0;
 static const int c = 65536;
 DWORD dwRead, dwNext;
 BYTE by[c];
 while (true)
 {
  if (!::ReadEventLog(handle, EVENTLOG_BACKWARDS_READ+
         EVENTLOG_SEQUENTIAL_READ, 1, by, c, &dwRead, &dwNext))
  {
  break;
  }
  DWORD dw = 0;
  while (dwRead > dw)
  {
  EventLogRecord rec((EVENTLOGRECORD *)(by+dw));
  std::cout << "Record Number = "
            << rec.RecordNumber() << "\n";
  std::cout << "Time Generated = "
            << rec.TimeGenerated() << "\n";
  std::cout << "Time Written = "
            << rec.TimeWritten() << "\n";
```

Continues

Listing 4.5 Formatting event log entries.

```
std::cout << "Event ID = " << rec.EventID() << "\n";
std::cout << "Event Type = "
            << rec.EventType() << "\n";
std::cout << "Event Category = "
            << rec.EventCategory() << "\n";
std::cout << "Source Name = "
            << rec.SourceName() << "\n";
std::cout << "Computer Name = "
            << rec.ComputerName() << "\n";
std::cout << "Formatted = "
 << format.Format((EVENTLOGRECORD *)(by+dw))
            << "\n";
std::cout << std::endl;

dw += rec.Length();
}
}
::CloseEventLog(handle);
return 0;
}
```

Listing 4.5

In comparison to the code in Listing 4.3, the complexity of this code remains very constant, as the details of formatting the event log entry are now encapsulated in the FormatEventLogRecord class.

Writing to the Event Log

Writing to the Application event log is quite trivial. Listing 4.6 shows the code necessary to write a Hello log in the Application event log.

I begin by registering the event source in the call to the RegisterEventSource function. This is a HANDLE creation function.

```
char * psz[] = {"Hello", NULL};
HANDLE handle = ::RegisterEventSource(NULL, "ProprietarySource");
::ReportEvent(handle, EVENTLOG_INFORMATION_TYPE, 0, 1, NULL,
 1, 0, (const char **)psz, NULL);
::DeregisterEventSource(handle);
return 0;
```

Listing 4.6   Writing to the Event Log.

```
HANDLE RegisterEventSource(LPCTSTR lpUNCServerName,
    LPCTSTR lpSourceName );
BOOL ReportEvent(HANDLE hEventLog, WORD wType, WORD wCategory,
    DWORD dwEventID, PSID lpUserSid, WORD wNumStrings,
    DWORD dwDataSize, LPCTSTR *lpStrings, LPVOID lpRawData);
BOOL DeregisterEventSource(HANDLE hEventLog);
```

Once I have this handle, I can repeatedly write to the event log using the ReportEvent function. When I am finally finished writing events to the event log, I can free the handle I acquired by calling the DeregisterEventSource function.

Message Sources

By using the Event Viewer to view the logs I just wrote to the Application event log, I'd see that they contain a warning. This is because the NT Event Log entries must contain a message source and message identifier that describe the formatting of the log entry. Because I didn't provide the formatting, the Event Viewer displays the warning shown in Figure 4.6.

To remove this warning, I have to provide a message source for the message. I'll build the message source using the Message Compiler.

Message Compiler

The Message Compiler (Mc.exe) is a utility provided with most Win32 development tools that is used solely to develop message sources that are interpreted by the FormatMessage function and Event Viewer.

The input to the Message Compiler is a text file with one or more entries denoting the various message texts that will be saved in the message source. Lines that contain a period and nothing else delimit the individual message text entries. A minimal Message Compiler input file is shown in Listing 4.7.

```
MessageID=10
SymbolicName=MRS_TEXT
Language=English
%1
.
```

Listing 4.7 Minimal Message Compiler input file.

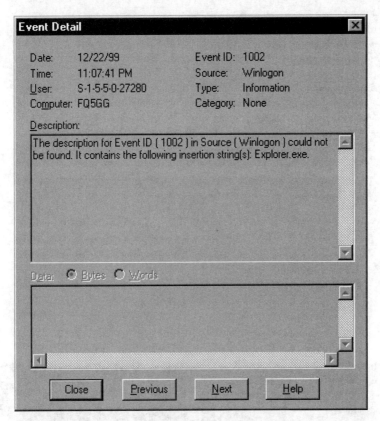

Figure 4.6 Event Log entry missing an event source.

I've used this Message Compiler input file on many projects that needed basic NT Event Log capabilities. Typically, users should provide a comprehensive use of the NT Event Log by using Event Identifiers to denote events explicitly.

This has the advantage of requiring less log space per log entry since part of the log text is saved once in the message source instead of once per occurrence in the NT Event Log. Another advantage is that the log entries can easily be localized or internationalized by modifying the message source. A more complex Message Compiler input file is shown in Listing 4.8.

Once a Message Compiler source file is saved, it can be run through the message compile. The -c compiler option must be used to set the appropriate customer code bit in the generated header file (see Figure 4.7). Most books and articles that address the NT Event Log or Win32 error handling fail to properly address the customer code bit in the Win32 error code. Users shouldn't make the same mistake; it's important when developing a complete error-handling implementation that these details be taken care of.

```
MessageID=10
SymbolicName=MRS_TEXT
Language=English
%1
.
MessageID=11
SymbolicName=MRS_STARTING
Language=English
Starting the Service
.
MessageID=12
SymbolicName=MRS_STOPPING
Language=English
Stopping the Service
.
```

Listing 4.8 Message Compiler input file.

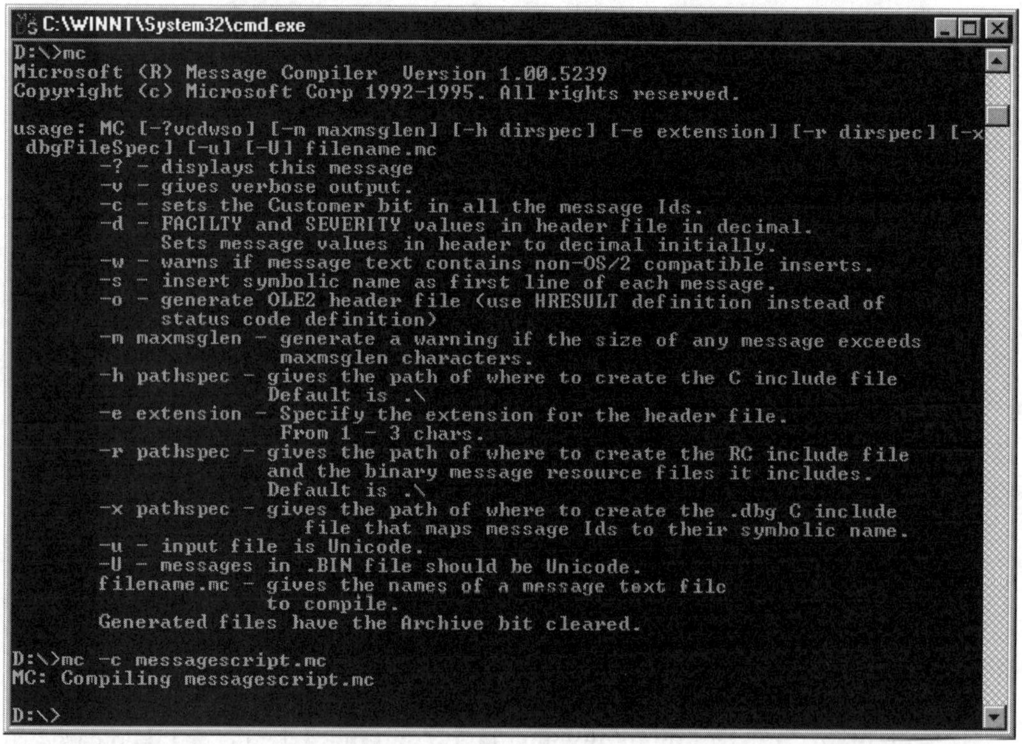

Figure 4.7 Compiling message scripts.

The output of the Message Compiler will be three files: a binary (.bin), a resource script (.rc), and a header file (.h).

The binary file contains the actual content of messages. This binary file is referenced in the resource script file (see Listing 4.9). The resource script (rc) file may be included directly in the project, or the contents of the message rc file may be copied to the master rc file, or the message rc file may be included in the master rc file using a preprocessor include directive.

```
LANGUAGE 0x9,0x1
1 11 MSG00001.bin
```

Listing 4.9 Resource script for message source.

The resource code is not very apparent, so I'll explain it. The LANGUAGE statement indicates that all resources that follow will be in the language 0x9, 0x1. This language ID is the default and equates to U.S. English. The message source may be translated to any language and included after a LANGUAGE statement which indicates the appropriate language. This could provide the ability to eventually port message sources to more than one language or events to more than one dialect.

The second line of the resource script indicates the name of the resource "1," the type of the resource "11," and the filename from which the resource is imported. The resource type 11 is defined in the Windows header files as RT_MESSAGETABLE.

```
/*
 * Predefined Resource Types
 */
#define RT_CURSOR           MAKEINTRESOURCE(1)
#define RT_BITMAP           MAKEINTRESOURCE(2)
#define RT_ICON             MAKEINTRESOURCE(3)
#define RT_MENU             MAKEINTRESOURCE(4)
#define RT_DIALOG           MAKEINTRESOURCE(5)
#define RT_STRING           MAKEINTRESOURCE(6)
#define RT_FONTDIR          MAKEINTRESOURCE(7)
#define RT_FONT             MAKEINTRESOURCE(8)
#define RT_ACCELERATOR      MAKEINTRESOURCE(9)
#define RT_RCDATA           MAKEINTRESOURCE(10)
#define RT_MESSAGETABLE     MAKEINTRESOURCE(11)
#define DIFFERENCE          11
#define RT_GROUP_CURSOR     MAKEINTRESOURCE((DWORD)RT_CURSOR + \
    DIFFERENCE)
#define RT_GROUP_ICON       MAKEINTRESOURCE((DWORD)RT_ICON + \
    DIFFERENCE)
#define RT_VERSION          MAKEINTRESOURCE(16)
```

```
#define RT_DLGINCLUDE      MAKEINTRESOURCE(17)
#define RT_PLUGPLAY        MAKEINTRESOURCE(19)
#define RT_VXD             MAKEINTRESOURCE(20)
#define RT_ANICURSOR       MAKEINTRESOURCE(21)
#define RT_ANIICON         MAKEINTRESOURCE(22)
#define RT_HTML            MAKEINTRESOURCE(23)
```

The last file generated by the Message Compiler is the header file. A sample is shown in Listing 4.10.

```
//
// Values are 32 bit values layed out as follows:
//
//3 3 2 2 2 2 2 2 2 2 2 2 1 1 1 1 1 1 1 1 1 1
//1 0 9 8 7 6 5 4 3 2 1 0 9 8 7 6 5 4 3 2 1 0 9 8 7 6 5 4 3 2 1 0
//---+-+-+---------------------------+-------------------------------
//Sev|C|R|   Facility        |            Code
//---+-+-+---------------------------+-------------------------------
//
// where
//
//   Sev - is the severity code
//
//     00 - Success
//     01 - Informational
//     10 - Warning
//     11 - Error
//
//  C - is the Customer code flag
//
//  R - is a reserved bit
//
//  Facility - is the facility code
//
//  Code - is the facility's status code
//
//
// Define the facility codes
//

//
// Define the severity codes
//

//
// MessageId: MRS_TEXT
//
```
                                                          Continues

Listing 4.10 Header file for message source.

```
// MessageText:
//
// %1
//
#define MRS_TEXT            0x2000000AL

//
// MessageId: MRS_STARTING
//
// MessageText:
//
// Starting the Service
//
#define MRS_STARTING        0x2000000BL

//
// MessageId: MRS_STOPPING
//
// Mes sageText:
//
// Stopping the Service
//
#define MRS_STOPPING        0x2000000CL
```

Listing 4.10

This file will likely not format very well in this book, but I wanted to present it in full because a good visual representation of a Win32 error code is in the comments of the header.

Once I've compiled the messages in a module, I can then register the message source by creating a couple of entries in the registry. Figure 4.8 shows example entries necessary for message source registration with the NT Event Log.

Under the EventLog hive, there is one key for each event log. The defaults of Application, Security, and System will always be there and more may also be present. Under each event log subkey are the message sources that are contained within the individual event logs.

Alternatively, I can write these entries using the Win32 API. Listing 4.11 shows generic code for registering a message source with the NT Event Log.

Creating a new key for the event source is done by first creating the subkey with the name of the event source. Then both the EventMessageFile and TypesSupported values, as a minimum, should be added. I've used the

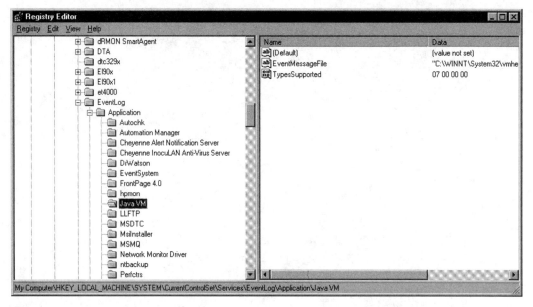

Figure 4.8 Message source registration.

actual preprocessor constant representations of the event log entry types to accurately portray in the code which event types (severities) I'm supporting.

When I do add these entries, the Event Log service is watching for changes in these Registry folders. As I add the entries, the Sources setting in the root of the individual event log subkeys will be updated to reflect the added event source.

```cpp
void RegisterEventSource(const std::string & str)
{
 HKEY hkey;
 std::stringstream ss;
 ss << "SYSTEM\\CurrentControlSet\\Services\\EventLog\\"
   << "Application\\" << str;
 ::RegCreateKey(HKEY_LOCAL_MACHINE, ss.str().c_str(), &hkey);
 char sz[MAX_PATH];
 ::GetModuleFileName(NULL, sz, MAX_PATH);
 ::RegSetValueEx(hkey, "EventMessageFile", 0, REG_EXPAND_SZ,
        (LPBYTE)sz, std::string(sz).length+1);
 DWORD dwData = EVENTLOG_ERROR_TYPE | EVENTLOG_WARNING_TYPE |
        EVENTLOG_INFORMATION_TYPE;
 ::RegSetValueEx(hkey, "TypesSupported", 0, REG_DWORD,
        (LPBYTE) &dwData, sizeof(DWORD));
 ::RegCloseKey(hkey);
};
```

Listing 4.11 Register message source with NT Event Log.

Event Logs

Some developers may consider creating event logs that exist independently of the NT Event Log. The reasoning for this type of action is typically that they don't want to pollute the existing event logs, primarily the Application log. This logic is sound, but they shouldn't be fooled into thinking that they can't use the NT Event Log to created additional event logs. If they want to create logs that are independent of the Application log, then the NT Event Log service already provides for creating additional logs.

The big disadvantage of creating new event logs is that they are not viewable in the NT Event Viewer. This can also be an advantage in that the log entries are not cluttering the three standard event logs. Additionally, there are security advantages of not allowing users to read an event log.

Developers can add additional event logs by creating new subkeys beneath the SYSTEM\CurrentControlSet\Services\EventLog Registry key (see Figure 4.9). To create this new subkey, they can right-click on the EventLog Registry key and select New | Key from the pop-up menu. Alternatively, they may select the EventLog Registry key and select Edit | New | Key from the menu bar.

As soon as they add the new subkey, the NT Event Log service creates a Source value beneath the key. Additionally, as message sources are added beneath the subkey, they will be added to the binary data contained in the Source Data.

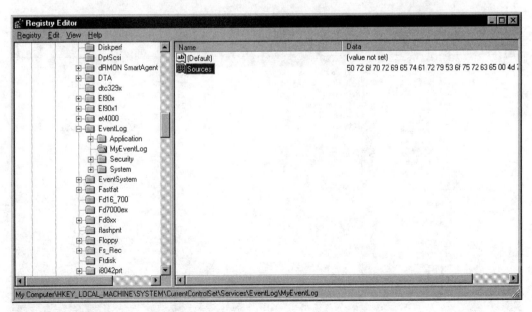

Figure 4.9 Additional event logs.

Beyond the Source value in the event log subkey, there are also additional values that can be used to configure the log. Under the EventLog\Security Registry key, very likely there is a very complete listing of what is available (see Figure 4.10).

The File value represents a path and filename to the location where the event log is saved. If this value is not present, then it defaults to %SystemRoot%\System32\config\{log-name}. When I added the MyEventLog Registry key, the Event Log service created a file called %SystemRoot%\System32\config\MyEventL.evt where entries to this log are saved.

NOTE
If the MyEventLog subkey was added manually, the Event Log service may also have created a file, %SystemRoot%\System32\config\New Key.evt temporary, before the subkey name could be corrected.

The MaxSize value in the event log's subkey represents the maximum size in kilobytes that the event log file will grow to. The default value is 512, meaning 512 kilobytes. The value must be in increments of 64 kilobytes.

The Retention value of the subkey is the number of seconds each log entry is retained before the Event Log service considers overwriting the log entry. The default value is 604,800 seconds or 7 days. There are several values for this field that have special meanings. A Retention of zero means the entries can be overwritten at will. A Retention of 0xFFFFFFFF (hexadecimal notation) means the entries can never be overwritten.

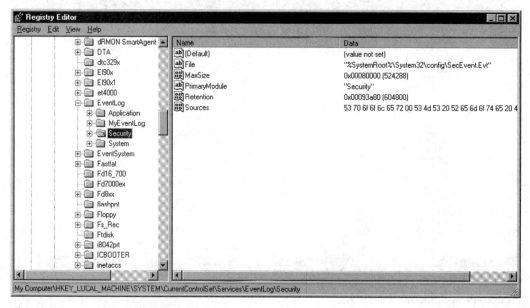

Figure 4.10 EventLog\{log-name} key.

The PrimaryModule value I've only seen used in the Security event log and is not documented. It seems to indicate which of the message sources can be used as a default message source for the event log.

Event Log COM Component

Now that I've discussed most all of the facets of the NT Event Log, I propose a reusable component for reading, writing, and managing the NT Event Log. I write the interface for the component in COM-IDL. I need one primary interface that will both read and write entries in the event log and one enumeration interface (see Listing 4.12).

The event log component has one type definition, three new interfaces, and one COM class created by a class factory. The type definition emulates the

```
typedef struct tagLOGENTRIES
 {
 BSTR datasource;
 int messageid;
 int category;
 int type;
 BSTR datetime;
 BSTR userid;
 BSTR computer;
 BSTR description;
 IStream * data;
} LOGENTRIES;

[
 object,
 uuid(1D332C80-6198-11d3-B6CD-00C04F8B72E7),
 pointer_default(unique)
]
interface IEnumLogEntries : IUnknown
{
// standard
 HRESULT Next([in] ULONG celt, [out] LOGENTRIES * rgelt,
     [out] ULONG * pceltFetched);
 HRESULT Skip([in] ULONG celt);
 HRESULT Reset();
 HRESULT Clone([out] IEnumLogEntries ** ppenum);
};

[
```

Continues

Listing 4.12 IDL for event log component.

```idl
object,
uuid(1D332C81-6198-11d3-B6CD-00C04F8B72E7),
pointer_default(unique)
]
interface IEnumStrings : IUnknown
{
//standard
HRESULT Next([in] ULONG celt, [out] BSTR * rgelt,
    [out] ULONG * pceltFetched);
HRESULT Skip([in] ULONG celt);
HRESULT Reset();
HRESULT Clone([out] IEnumStrings ** ppenum);
};

[
  object,
  uuid(6A4A3525-A78A-11D3-B6E7-00C04F8B72E7),
  helpstring("IEventLog Interface"),
  pointer_default(unique)
]
interface IEventLog : IUnknown
{
  [id(1), helpstring("method Read")] HRESULT Read(
              [in] BSTR log, [out] IEnumLogEntries ** e);
  [id(2), helpstring("method Write")] HRESULT Write(
              [in] BSTR source, [in] int message,
              [in] int category, [in] int type,
              [in] BSTR userid, [in] IEnumStrings * strings,
              [in] IStream * data);
};

[
uuid(6A4A3519-A78A-11D3-B6E7-00C04F8B72E7),
version(1.0),
helpstring("eventlogctrl 1.0 Type Library")
]
library EVENTLOGCTRLLib
{
importlib("stdole32.tlb");
importlib("stdole2.tlb");

  [
  uuid(6A4A3526-A78A-11D3-B6E7-00C04F8B72E7),
  helpstring("EventLog Class")
  ]
  coclass EventLog
  {
  [default] interface IEventLog;
  };
};
```

Listing 4.12 IDL for event log component *(Continued)*.

content of one event log entry. This structure is used in the IEnumLogEntries enumeration interface, in order to browse the list of entries in an event log. The IEnumStrings enumeration interface is used to provide an ordered container of strings.

The real interface behind this design is the IEventLog interface. It has six methods for working with the NT Event Log. It can both read and write to event logs.

```cpp
// EventLog.cpp : Implementation of CEventLog
namespace
{
 class MyEnumLogEntries : public IEnumLogEntries
 {
  std::wstring m_log;
  HANDLE m_handle;
  DWORD m_i;
  LONG m_references;
 public:
  MyEnumLogEntries()
   :m_i(0),
   m_handle(NULL)
  {
  }
  ~MyEnumLogEntries()
  {
   if (m_handle!=NULL)
   {
    ::CloseEventLog(m_handle);
   }
  }

  ULONG STDMETHODCALLTYPE AddRef()
  {
   ::InterlockedIncrement(&m_references);
   return m_references;
  }
  ULONG STDMETHODCALLTYPE Release()
  {
   ::InterlockedDecrement(&m_references);
   if (m_references == 0)
   {
    delete this;
   }
   return m_references;
```

Continues

Listing 4.13 Implementation for event log component.

```
}
STDMETHODIMP QueryInterface(REFIID riid, void ** ppv)
{
 if (riid == IID_IUnknown)
 {
  *ppv = static_cast<IUnknown*>(this);
  AddRef();
  return S_OK;
 }
 if (riid == IID_IEnumLogEntries)
 {
  *ppv = static_cast<IEnumLogEntries*>(this);
  AddRef();
  return S_OK;
 }
 *ppv = NULL;
 return E_NOINTERFACE;
};

void SetLogName(const std::wstring & log)
{
 m_log = log;
 m_handle = ::OpenEventLogW(NULL, log.c_str());
};

STDMETHODIMP Next(ULONG celt, LOGENTRIES * rgelt,
             ULONG * pceltFetched)
{
 if (celt != 1)
 {
  return S_FALSE;
 }
 if (pceltFetched != NULL)
 {
  *pceltFetched = 1;
 }
 char * buffer = new char[4];
 DWORD dw, next;
 ::ReadEventLog(m_handle,
                  EVENTLOG_SEQUENTIAL_READ+
                  EVENTLOG_BACKWARDS_READ, m_i, buffer, 0,
                  &dw, &next);
 delete[] buffer;
 buffer = new char[next];
 if (::ReadEventLog(m_handle,
                  EVENTLOG_SEQUENTIAL_READ+
                  EVENTLOG_BACKWARDS_READ, m_i, buffer, next,
                  &dw, &next) == 0)
```

Continues

Listing 4.13 Implementation for event log component *(Continued).*

```
{
 delete[] buffer;
 return FALSE;
};

EventLogRecord rec((EVENTLOGRECORD *)&buffer);
if (rgelt->datasource != 0)
{
 ::SysFreeString(rgelt->datasource);
}
rgelt->datasource = ::SysAllocString(
                 AnsiToWide(rec.SourceName()).c_str());
rgelt->messageid = rec.EventID();
rgelt->category = rec.EventCategory();
rgelt->type = rec.EventType();
if (rgelt->computer != 0)
{
 ::SysFreeString(rgelt->computer);
};
rgelt->computer = ::SysAllocString(
                 AnsiToWide(rec.ComputerName()).c_str());
FormatEventLogRecord format(WideToAnsi(m_log));
if (rgelt->description != 0)
{
 ::SysFreeString(rgelt->description);
}
rgelt->description = ::SysAllocString(
                 AnsiToWide(format.Format(
                 (EVENTLOGRECORD *)buffer)).c_str());
if (rgelt->data != NULL)
{
 ULONG l;
 rgelt->data->Write(rec.Data(),
                        rec.DataLength(), &l);
}
delete[] buffer;
m_i++;
return S_OK;
};
STDMETHODIMP Skip(ULONG celt)
{
 return S_OK;
};
STDMETHODIMP Reset()
{
 return S_OK;
};
STDMETHODIMP Clone(IEnumLogEntries ** ppenum)
```

Continues

Listing 4.13

```
  {
   return S_OK;
  };
};

class MyEnumStrings : public IEnumStrings
{
 std::vector<std::wstring> m_vstr;
 int m_i;
 LONG m_references;
public:
 MyEnumStrings()
   :m_i(0)
   {
};
ULONG STDMETHODCALLTYPE AddRef()
{
 ::InterlockedIncrement(&m_references);
 return m_references;
}
ULONG STDMETHODCALLTYPE Release()
{
 ::InterlockedDecrement(&m_references);
 if (m_references == 0)
  {
   delete this;
  }
 return m_references;
}
STDMETHODIMP QueryInterface(REFIID riid, void ** ppv)
{
 if (riid == IID_IUnknown)
  {
   *ppv = static_cast<IUnknown*>(this);
   AddRef();
   return S_OK;
  }
 if (riid == IID_IEnumStrings)
  {
   *ppv = static_cast<IEnumStrings*>(this);
   AddRef();
   return S_OK;
  }
 *ppv = NULL;
 return E_NOINTERFACE;
};

void AddLogName(const std::wstring & str)
```

Continues

Listing 4.13 Implementation for event log component *(Continued).*

```
{
 m_vstr.push_back(str);
}
STDMETHODIMP Next(ULONG celt, BSTR * rgelt,
            ULONG * pceltFetched)
{
 if (celt != 1)
 {
  return S_FALSE;
 }
 if (m_i+celt >= m_vstr.size())
 {
  return S_FALSE;
 }
 if (pceltFetched != NULL)
 {
  *pceltFetched = 1;
 }
 if (rgelt != NULL)
 {
  ::SysFreeString(*rgelt);
 }
 *rgelt = ::SysAllocString(m_vstr[m_i].c_str());
 m_i++;
 return S_OK;
};
STDMETHODIMP Skip(ULONG celt)
{
 m_i += celt;
 return S_OK;
};
STDMETHODIMP Reset()
{
 m_i = 0;
 return S_OK;
};
STDMETHODIMP Clone(IEnumStrings ** ppenum)
{
 MyEnumStrings * p = new MyEnumStrings;
 p->m_vstr = m_vstr;
 if (*ppenum != NULL)
 {
  (*ppenum)->Release();
 }
 *ppenum = p;
 return S_OK;
};
```

Continues

Listing 4.13

```cpp
};
}

/////////////////////////////////////////////////////////////////////
// CEventLog

STDMETHODIMP CEventLog::Read(BSTR log, IEnumLogEntries ** e)
{
if (*e != NULL)
{
  (*e)->Release();
}
  MyEnumLogEntries * p = new MyEnumLogEntries;
p->SetLogName(std::wstring(log));
*e = p;
  return S_OK;
}

STDMETHODIMP CEventLog::Write(BSTR source, int message,
    int category, int type, BSTR userid, IEnumStrings
*strings,
    IStream *data)
{
  // call ReportEvent
  BSTR bstr;
  std::vector<std::wstring> vstr;
  while (strings->Next(1, &bstr, NULL))
  {
   vstr.push_back(bstr);
  };
  LPCWSTR * psz = new LPCWSTR[vstr.size()];
  for (int i=0;i<vstr.size();i++)
  {
   psz[i] = vstr[i].c_str();
  }

  STATSTG statstg;
  data->Stat(&statstg, STATFLAG_NONAME);
  BYTE * byte = new BYTE[statstg.cbSize.LowPart];
  data->Read(byte, statstg.cbSize.LowPart, NULL);

  HANDLE handle = ::RegisterEventSourceW(NULL, source);
  ::ReportEventW(handle, type, category, message, userid,
          vstr.size(), statstg.cbSize.LowPart, psz, byte);
  ::DeregisterEventSource(handle);

  delete[] psz;

  return S_OK;
}
```

Listing 4.13 Implementation for event log component *(Continued)*.

Custom Event Viewer

A problem with creating a custom event log is that the NT Event Viewer cannot be used to read the custom log. To read a custom log, a custom event log reader must be written.

My custom event viewer will allow me to read any log that follows the display rules that are used by the NT Event Viewer and the three standard logs, Application, Security, and System. But I do suggest developers consider altering my implementation when they see advantages in doing so. I have previously considered encrypting the data saved in the Data portion of the custom log and implementing a custom viewer that decrypts this data for display. This type of implementation would be important when logging sensitive data.

As an experienced MFC developer, my best bet for implementing this custom event viewer GUI was with the tool that I'm most familiar with. I could also have developed this tool in ATL or VB, but it would have taken me twice the time. I won't present the code here, as the code has little real value other than manipulating MFC GUIs. (Since this book is about NT Services, I thought I should refrain from explaining MFC GUI code.) But the very simple event log viewer may be found on the distribution CD-ROM.

Category Message File

Event Log categories are an interesting breed. The only common implementation is in the Security event source, where log entries are broken into seven categories (see Listing 4.14).

Why There's No Generic Event Log Reader

I've thought about why Microsoft didn't write a generic event log reader and have decided that its intent must have been to allow maximum flexibility in the design of custom logs. What I mean is that Microsoft wanted to allow developers to create logs that had implementation rules that could not be handled by the NT Event Viewer. As an example, developers could potentially create a custom log that does not use message sources, or one that implements a secure description in the Data portion of the event log record. The potential for variations becomes quite endless.

```
typedef enum _POLICY_AUDIT_EVENT_TYPE {
  AuditCategorySystem,
  AuditCategoryLogon,
  AuditCategoryObjectAccess,
  AuditCategoryPrivilegeUse,
  AuditCategoryDetailedTracking,
  AuditCategoryPolicyChange,
  AuditCategoryAccountManagement,
  AuditCategoryDirectoryServiceAccess,
  AuditCategoryAccountLogon
} POLICY_AUDIT_EVENT_TYPE, *PPOLICY_AUDIT_EVENT_TYPE;
```

Listing 4.14   Security event categories.

If I specify a category ID when calling the ReportEvent function without creating a category message file, the Event Viewer will display the category ID in brackets (see Figure 4.11).

But I can also create short descriptions for my categories by creating a category message file for the event source (see Listing 4.15).

Category message files are very similar to event message files; in fact, a message file may serve as both a category and an event message file. This is true of the MsAuditE.dll module, which is both the category and the event message file for the Security event source.

The difference between the two message files is that category message files must contain a sequential list of category IDs beginning at 1.

```
MessageIdTypedef=WORD
MessageId=0x1
SymbolicName=CATEGORY_1
Category 1
.

MessageId=0x2
SymbolicName=CATEGORY_2
Category 2
.
```

Listing 4.15   Descriptive category.

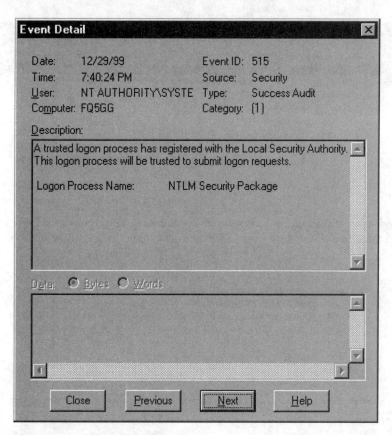

Figure 4.11   Integer category.

Audit Logging

In the typical installation, Security event logging is turned off. Systemwide audit logging can be enabled in the User Manager. I run the User Manager from the Start by selecting Start | Programs | Administrative Tools | User Manager (see Figure 4.12).

From the User Manager menu bar, I can select Policies | Audit, and the Audit Policy dialog appears (see Figure 4.13).

Most installations for NT will have the Do Not Audit radio button selected. In order to familiarize myself with the Security log and Categories, I can enable all the Failure Events and some Success Events.

In this section, I explain how to enable Windows Registry and the Windows NT file system (NTFS) directory-file audit logging.

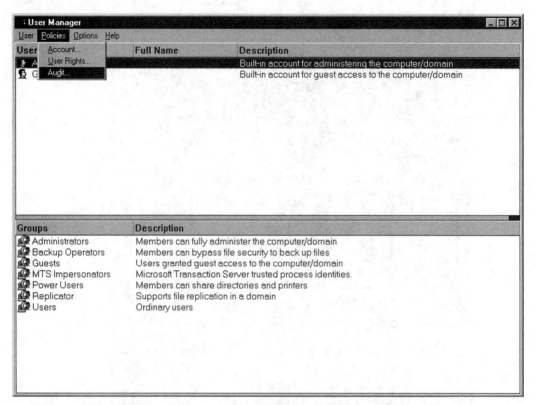

Figure 4.12 User Manager.

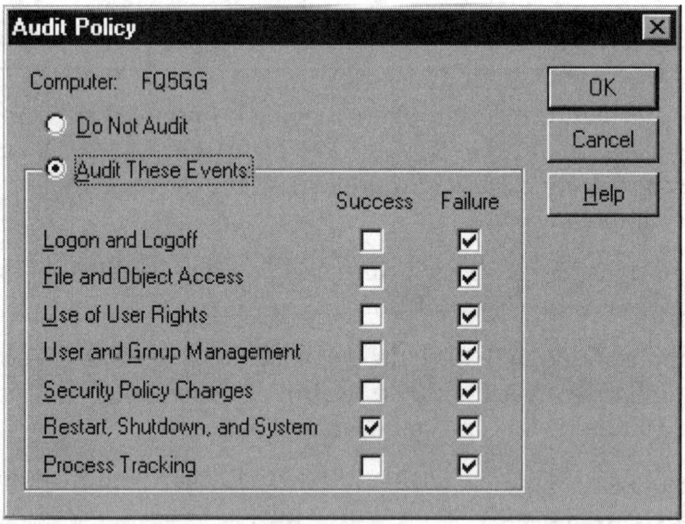

Figure 4.13 Audit Policy dialog.

Another place where additional Security logging may be enabled is in the Windows Registry. I can run the Regedt32 utility by selecting Start | Run from the Start menu, then typing *Regedt32* and clicking on OK (see Figure 4.14).

From the Regedt32 menu bar, I select Security | Auditing. The Registry Key Auditing dialog appears (see Figure 4.15).

I've never experimented with Windows Registry auditing, as I don't find it particularly useful. But I imagine somebody somewhere is using it. In a high-security production environment, I suggest the minimum auditing should be to log all Failure Events for all Users, all Registry hives, and all subkeys.

TIP

An interesting usage of Windows Registry auditing is to monitor activity in the Windows Registry. But this is more easily accomplished with a Windows Registry Monitor, explained in Chapter 5, Configuration.

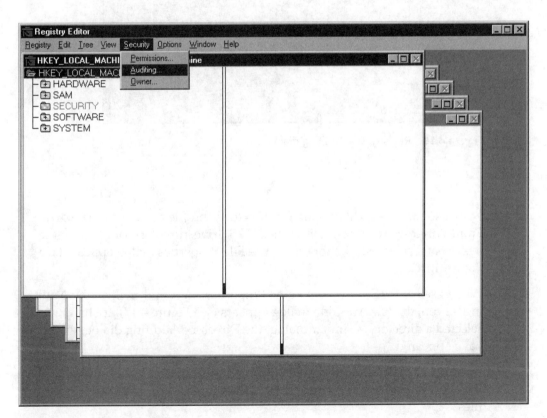

Figure 4.14   Regedt32 utility.

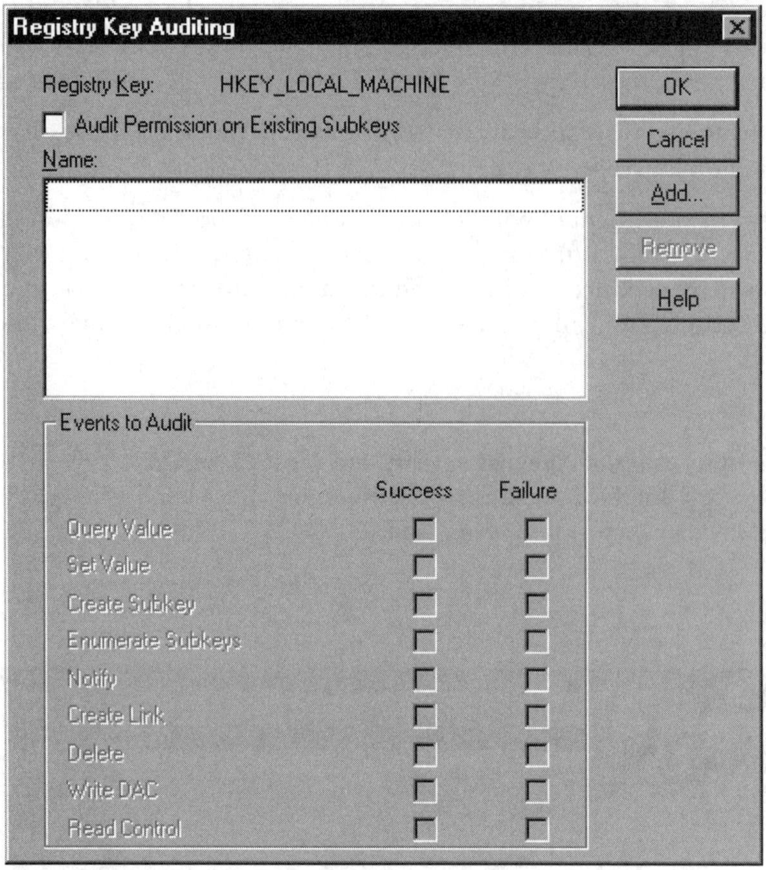

Figure 4.15 Registry Key Auditing dialog.

I can also turn on audit logging for directory and file access on NTFS drives. From Windows Explorer, I select the NTFS drive, directory, or file. From the menu bar, I select File | Properties. The File Properties dialog appears (see Figure 4.16).

When I select the Security tab in the Properties sheet and click on the Auditing button, the File Auditing dialog appears (see Figure 4.17). If I had selected a directory, a similar dialog, the Directory Auditing dialog, would have appeared.

In a high-security production environment, I suggest the minimum auditing should be to log all Failure Events for all Users, all directories, and files.

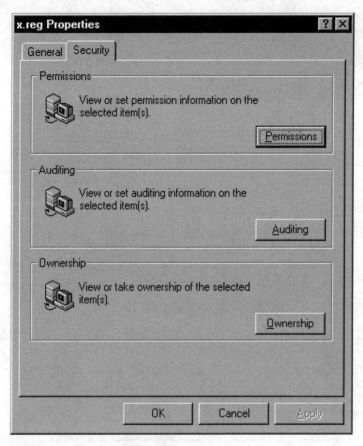

Figure 4.16   File Properties dialog.

Parameters Message File

EventMessageFiles and CategoryMessageFiles provide a large amount of discretion which makes constructing event log entries very flexible. But there's a third message file, the ParameterMessageFile, that provides yet another level of flexibility.

Using ParameterMessageFiles allows developers to provide replacement parameters for their event messages in a separate message file. I've yet to encounter a use for this type of replacement parameter, but I wanted to make the reader aware of this functionality. ParameterMessageFile replacement parameters are represented differently than replacement parameters supplied

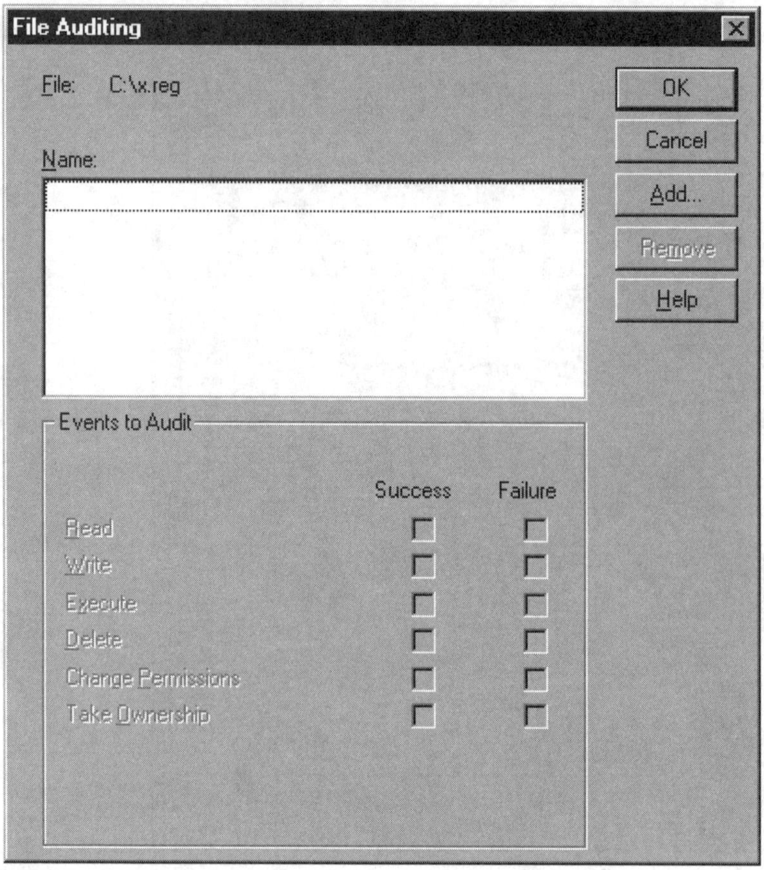

Figure 4.17 File Auditing dialog.

through the ReportEvent function by doubling up the % escape sequence. Where supplied replacement parameters have one % escape character, message file replacement parameters have two % escape characters.

Java Services

NT event logging with Java NT Services is accomplished by redirecting output from the standard output streams to the NT Event Log. This is very convenient in that most programmers would have already spent a lot of time sending debug output to the standard output streams. All of the debug output is now automatically redirected to the NT Event Log.

But with advantages also come disadvantages. All strings sent to the standard output stream are redirected to the NT Event Log, even that annoying debug statement that is buried deep in a third-party class. And it can't be gotten rid of. I've found that this redirecting, although convenient, makes an NT Service look very unprofessional.

Summary

Reporting events to the operator is an important part of the NT Service experience. Another part is receiving configuration information from the operator. Chapter 5 is all about how to make it easy for operators to configure NT Services.

Configuration

There are many ways of configuring an NT Service. Initialization files, the Windows Registry, a Control Panel applet, Microsoft's Management Console, system tray notification icons, and many more utilities may be used. In this chapter, I describe the various means of configuring an NT Service using these various techniques.

Windows Registry

The Windows Registry is a very convenient location for storing configuration information. Among the advantages of storing configuration information in the Windows Registry is that the user can back up the entire computer configuration using one common repository. Another advantage is that a lot of expertise exists in reading and writing to the Registry.

I find a lot of people don't consider existing expertise when determining the best solution to a problem. My own humble opinion is that expertise is the first consideration when undertaking a development. People can spend hundreds of hours researching a new technique when their development team does not have the necessary expertise. Many development efforts have failed because too many hundreds of hours were spent researching unknown techniques, rather than working with known expertise.

Working with the Windows Registry is one of the easier programming endeavors in Windows. The API is reasonably small. The individual functions tend to be complex with way too many function parameters. But once users understand that most of the parameters are avoidable, the API becomes quite simple.

NOTE

Most APIs, including many of the Windows APIs, suffer from a very common design flaw known as the Swiss-Army Knife design pattern. This means that the API attempts to satisfy all possible client requirements at the expense of simplicity. The Windows Registry API suffers from this anti-design pattern. A simpler technique may have been to provide more functions with fewer parameters per function. Loading a function with more than four or five parameters greatly complicates the API. I would understand if one or two functions had a large amount of function parameters, but nearly all the Windows Registry API functions have a large amount of parameters.

The Windows Registry is organized as a hierarchy of keys. Each key contains zero or more subkeys and zero or more values. One of the values is called the default value, because it is not named. All other values and all subkeys are named. There are few limitations in this hierarchy, but it is advised that structures greater than one or two kilobytes should not be saved in the Registry. Instead, they should be saved in a file and the file should be referenced in the Registry.

At the base of the Windows Registry hierarchy are two separate keys, known as HKEY_LOCAL_MACHINE and HKEY_USERS. In addition to the two base keys, there are two predefined shortcut keys that simply reference subkeys of the base keys. They are HKEY_CLASSES_ROOT (a subkey of HKEY_LOCAL_MACHINE) and HKEY_CURRENT_USER (a subkey of HKEY_USERS).

- HKEY_LOCAL_MACHINE. Used to save the local machine's configuration.

- HKEY_CLASSES_ROOT. Used to save OLE and shell configuration. This key is a shortcut to the HKEY_LOCAL_MACHINE\SOFTWARE\Classes subkey.

- HKEY_USERS. Used to save user configuration.

- HKEY_CURRENT_USER. Used to save user configuration for the current user.

I am concerned only with the HKEY_LOCAL_MACHINE key. Under this key is a subkey called SOFTWARE, which contains all the configuration information for the various software components on a computer system. Generally, the SOFTWARE subkey is organized by company; that is, the immediate sub-keys below SOFTWARE are keyed by the name of the organization that created the software component. Below the organization name subkey is the individual software component subkey. An example of this hierarchical implementation using McAfee's VirusScan software is shown in Figure 5.1.

Regedit and Regedt32

Two utilities that I refer to quite often are Regedit and Regedt32. These utilities provide a very effective user interface for reading and writing information to the Windows Registry. Each has its own advantages and disadvantages.

I typically use Regedit when I want to view Windows Registry contents. I don't really have a valid reason why I use Regedit over Regedt32, except that I'm programmed to type Regedit from the Start | Run dialog and the command prompt. Figure 5.2 shows the Regedit program.

Regedt32 has more functionality than Regedit. The most important distinguishing feature of Regedt32 is that it is organized as an MDI application. Regedit is an SDI application. In addition, Regedt32 provides access to the Windows Registry security, whereas Regedit does not. Figure 5.3 shows the Regedt32 program.

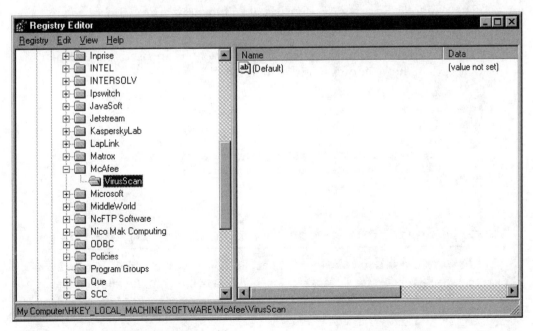

Figure 5.1 Microsoft Word Registry subkey.

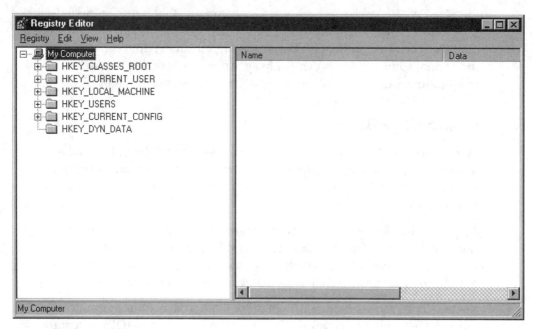

Figure 5.2 Regedit.

Programming the Windows Registry

The Windows Registry API consists of 26 functions. These functions are described in the next few sections.

The RegCreateKey and RegCreatcKeyEx functions are used to create new subkeys in the Windows Registry hierarchy.

```
LONG RegCreateKey(HKEY hKey,LPCTSTR lpSubKey,PHKEY phkResult);
LONG RegCreateKeyEx( HKEY hKey, LPCTSTR lpSubKey,
    DWORD Reserved, LPTSTR lpClass, DWORD dwOptions,
    REGSAM samDesired,
    LPSECURITY_ATTRIBUTES lpSecurityAttributes,
    PHKEY phkResult, LPDWORD lpdwDisposition );
```

Single Document Interface and Multiple Document Interface

An SDI (or single document interface) application is an application that provides one single window for viewing one single document. An MDI (or multiple document interface) application is an application that provides several child windows for viewing more than one document at a time.

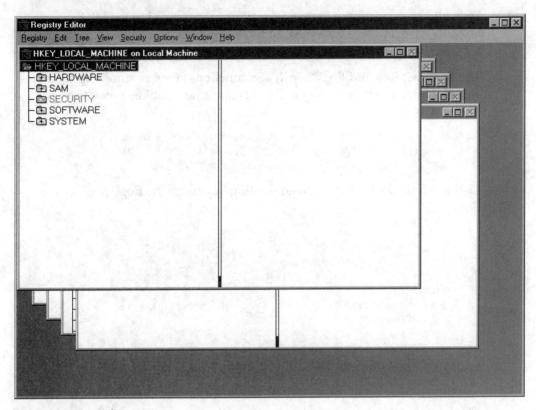

Figure 5.3 Regedt32.

Both functions will open the existing keys, if the key already exists. Listing 5.1 shows how to create a new key or open an existing key using the Reg-CreateKey function.

The RegCreateKey function takes three parameters: an HKEY value that may be any of the root level keys, the name of the subkey that will be created beneath the first parameter HKEY, and a return parameter that will contain the HKEY for the newly created key.

```
HKEY CreateKey(const std::string & key)
{
    HKEY hkey;
    ::RegCreateKey(HKEY_LOCAL_MACHINE, key.c_str(), &hkey);
    return hkey;
};
```

Listing 5.1 Using RegCreateKey.

Typically, software settings that span all users are saved in the HKEY_ LOCAL_MACHINE\SOFTWARE hive. Settings that are specific to the current user are saved in the HKEY_CURRENT_USER\Software hive.

The RegOpenKey and RegOpenKeyEx functions are very similar to their create key counterparts, but they will not create a new subkey when the key does not exist.

```
LONG RegOpenKey(HKEY hKey, LPCTSTR lpSubKey, PHKEY phkResult );
LONG RegOpenKeyEx( HKEY hKey, LPCTSTR lpSubKey,
    DWORD ulOptions, REGSAM samDesired, PHKEY phkResult );
```

Listing 5.2 shows how to open an existing key using the RegOpenKey function.

```
HKEY OpenKey(const std::string & key)
{
   HKEY hkey;
   ::RegOpenKey(HKEY_LOCAL_MACHINE, key.c_str(), &hkey);
   return hkey;
};
```

Listing 5.2   Using RegOpenKey.

The RegOpenKey function takes the same three parameters as the RegCreateKey function, that is, an HKEY, the key to open beneath the first parameter HKEY, and a return parameter that will contain the HKEY for the opened subkey.

Whenever users create a new subkey or open an existing subkey, they acquire a handle to the subkey. Eventually they should close the handle to the subkey by calling the RegCloseKey function.

```
LONG RegCloseKey( HKEY hKey );
```

The RegCloseKey function takes one parameter, the HKEY of the key being closed. Listing 5.3 shows how to close a key handle using RegCloseKey after it has been opened using RegOpenKey.

```
HKEY hkey;
::RegOpenKey(HKEY_LOCAL_MACHINE, "SOFTWARE\\NTServices", &hkey);
...
::RegCloseKey(hkey);
```

Listing 5.3   Using RegCloseKey.

The RegSetValue and RegSetValueEx functions are used to write information to the registry.

```
LONG RegSetValue( HKEY hKey, LPCTSTR lpSubKey, DWORD dwType,
    LPCTSTR lpData, DWORD cbData );
LONG RegSetValueEx( HKEY hKey, LPCTSTR lpValueName,
    DWORD Reserved, DWORD dwType, CONST BYTE *lpData,
    DWORD cbData );
LONG RegFlushKey( HKEY hKey );
```

Both of these functions attempt to optimize the performance of the Registry by lazy-writing data into the permanent Registry database. The RegFlushKey function is used to force the data written in active memory to be written to the permanent Registry database.

Listing 5.4 shows how to use RegSetValue to write information to the Registry.

```
void SetValue(const std::string & key, const std::string & name,
    const std::string & value)
{
    HKEY hkey;
    ::RegOpenKey(HKEY_LOCAL_MACHINE, key.c_str(), &hkey);
    ::RegSetValue(hkey, name.c_str(), REG_SZ, value.c_str(),
        value.length());
    ::RegCloseKey(hkey);
};
```

Listing 5.4   RegSetValue.

The RegQueryInfoKey, RegQueryMultipleValues, RegQueryValue, and Reg-QueryValueEx functions are used to read information from the Registry.

```
LONG RegQueryInfoKey ( HKEY hKey, LPTSTR lpClass,
    LPDWORD lpcbClass, LPDWORD lpReserved,
    LPDWORD lpcSubKeys, LPDWORD lpcbMaxSubKeyLen,
    LPDWORD lpcbMaxClassLen, LPDWORD lpcValues,
    LPDWORD lpcbMaxValueNameLen, LPDWORD lpcbMaxValueLen,
    LPDWORD lpcbSecurityDescriptor,
    PFILETIME lpftLastWriteTime );
LONG RegQueryMultipleValues( HKEY hKey, PVALENT val_list,
    DWORD num_vals, LPTSTR lpValueBuf, LPDWORD ldwTotsize );
LONG RegQueryValue( HKEY hKey, LPCTSTR lpSubKey,
    LPTSTR lpValue, PLONG lpcbValue );
LONG RegQueryValueEx( HKEY hKey, LPTSTR lpValueName,
    LPDWORD lpReserved, LPDWORD lpType, LPBYTE lpData,
    LPDWORD lpcbData );
```

Listing 5.5 shows how to use RegQueryValue to read information from the Registry.

```cpp
std::string GetValue(const std::string & key,
    const std::string & name)
{

    HKEY hkey;
    ::RegOpenKey(HKEY_LOCAL_MACHINE, key.c_str(), &hkey);
    char sz[128];
    LONG 1 = sizeof(sz);
    ::RegQueryValue(hkey, name.c_str(), sz, &l);
    ::RegCloseKey(hkey);
    return sz;
};
```

Listing 5.5 RegQueryValue.

It is also important in order to navigate the Windows Registry that the programmer is able to enumerate all subkeys and values that make up a Registry key. To provide for enumerating keys, three functions, RegEnumKey, RegEnumKeyEx, and RegEnumValue, can be used.

```cpp
LONG RegEnumKey( HKEY hKey, DWORD dwIndex, LPTSTR lpName,
    DWORD cbName );
LONG RegEnumKeyEx( HKEY hKey, DWORD dwIndex, LPTSTR lpName,
    LPDWORD lpcbName, LPDWORD lpReserved, LPTSTR lpClass,
    LPDWORD lpcbClass, PFILETIME lpftLastWriteTime );
LONG RegEnumValue( HKEY hKey, DWORD dwIndex,
    LPTSTR lpValueName, LPDWORD lpcbValueName,
    LPDWORD lpReserved, LPDWORD lpType,
    LPBYTE lpData, LPDWORD lpcbData );
```

Listing 5.6 shows a small program that enumerates using RegEnumKey and RegEnumValue to perform a search and replace on the entire Windows Registry.

The previous program scans the entire HKEY_LOCAL_MACHINE and HKEY_USERS Windows Registry hives for a pattern. If it finds the pattern, it asks the user whether it should replace it with replacement text. This is done by enumerating all the keys in the trees of these Windows Registry hives.

This key enumeration program works by maintaining a queue of unvisited keys. As new keys are uncovered as users drill up the tree, they are added to the queue. The queue is emptied one key at a time until it is completely empty, that is, until users have visited the entire tree.

```
int main(int argc, char* argv[])
{
  char c = 'n';

  if (argc < 2)
  {
    std::cout << "Usage:\n\th12yp find replace" << std::endl;
    return 0;
  }

  int x=0;
  for (HKEY key = HKEY_LOCAL_MACHINE; x<2; key = HKEY_USERS,x++)
  {
    std::queue<std::string> q;
    int i = 0;
    char buffer[MAX_PATH+1];
    while (::RegEnumKey(key, i, buffer, sizeof(buffer))
             == ERROR_SUCCESS)
    {
      q.push(buffer);
      i++;
      if (i>100)
      {
        break;
      }
    };

    while (!q.empty())
    {
      std::string keyname = q.front();
      q.pop();

      HKEY hkey;
      std::cout << "Open Keyname = " << keyname << std::endl;
      if (::RegOpenKey(key, keyname.c_str(), &hkey)
          == ERROR_SUCCESS)
      {
        i = 0;
        char valuename[MAX_PATH+1];
        DWORD lvaluename = sizeof(valuename);
        char data[MAX_PATH+1];
        DWORD ldata = sizeof(data);
        DWORD dw;
        while (::RegEnumValue(hkey, i, valuename, &lvaluename,
          NULL, &dw, (BYTE*)data, &ldata) == ERROR_SUCCESS)
        {
          if (dw != REG_SZ)
          {
```

Continues

Listing 5.6 Enumerate a Registry key.

```
        continue;
      }
    std::string str = data;
    int pos;
    int j=0;
    while ((pos = str.find(argv[1])) != str.npos)
    {
      std::cout << "Found Keyname = " << keyname
        << " Valuename = " << valuename
        << " Data = " << data;
      if (argc == 2)
      {
        break;
      }
      str.replace(pos, std::string(argv[1]).length(),
         argv[2]);
      j++;
      if (j>100)
      {
        break;
      }
      std::cout << " Newdata = " << str << std::endl;
      if (c != 'a' && c != 'A')
      {
        std::cout << "y=replace a=replaceall "
          "(please respond) ";
        std::cin >> c;
        std::cout << std::endl;
      }
      if (c == 'y' || c == 'Y' || c == 'a' || c == 'A')
      {
        ::RegSetValue(hkey, valuename, REG_SZ, str.c_str(),
                      str.length());
      };
    };
    i++;
    if (i>100)
    {
      break;
    }
  }
  i = 0;
  while (::RegEnumKey(hkey, i, buffer, sizeof(buffer))
         == ERROR_SUCCESS)
  {
```

Continues

Listing 5.6 Enumerate a Registry key (*Continued*).

```
            std::string name = keyname + "\\" + buffer;
            q.push(name);
            i++;
            if (i>100)
            {
               break;
            }
         };
         ::RegCloseKey(hkey);
      };
   };
};
   return 0;
}
```

Listing 5.6

I've found this program to be quite useful for doing global searches and replaces on the Windows Registry. From what I've heard, it works. But in the wrong hands, this program could severely damage a computer's configuration.

```
LONG RegDeleteKey( HKEY hKey, LPCTSTR lpSubKey );
LONG RegDeleteValue( HKEY hKey, LPCTSTR lpValueName );
```

Deleting Registry keys and values is done using the RegDeleteKey and RegDeleteValue functions. Listing 5.7 shows two functions that delete keys given their location.

```
void DeleteKey(const std::string & key)
{
    ::RegDeleteKey(HKEY_LOCAL_MACHINE, key.c_str());
};
```

Listing 5.7 Delete keys.

In Chapter 3, I described how the Event Log service automatically created some Registry values when I added a key to represent a new Event Log. I don't know the internals of the Event Log service, but I do know that this type of notification can be accomplished using the RegNotifyChangeKey-Value function.

```
LONG RegNotifyChangeKeyValue( HKEY hKey, BOOL bWatchSubtree,
    DWORD dwNotifyFilter, HANDLE hEvent, BOOL fAsynchronous);
```

There are two ways in which users can implement Registry notification. The first is to use an event object to receive notification when a change occurs in the Registry. This is accomplished by passing an event handle to the Reg-NotifyChangeKeyValue function (see Listing 5.8).

The second is to call the RegNotifyChangeKeyValue function in synchronous mode. When the function is called in synchronous mode, the function does not return until a notification is received (see Listing 5.9).

A very important feature of the Windows Registry is that it provides for security. Users can easily modify a key's security descriptor to secure a Registry key against tampering. Two Registry functions are provided to retrieve and save a key's security descriptor: RegGetKeySecurity and RegSetKeySecurity.

```
LONG RegGetKeySecurity( HKEY hKey,
 SECURITY_INFORMATION SecurityInformation,
 PSECURITY_DESCRIPTOR pSecurityDescriptor,
 LPDWORD lpcbSecurityDescriptor );
LONG RegSetKeySecurity( HKEY hKey,
 SECURITY_INFORMATION SecurityInformation,
 PSECURITY_DESCRIPTOR pSecurityDescriptor );
```

```
int main(int argc, char* argv[])
{
    if (argc != 2)
    {
        std::cout << "Usage:\n\tnotify [key]\n\n\t\t\t"
            "where key is a subkey of HKEY_LOCAL_MACHINE"
            << std::endl;
        return 1;
    }

    HKEY hkey;
    ::RegOpenKey(HKEY_LOCAL_MACHINE, argv[1], &hkey);
    HANDLE event = ::CreateEvent(NULL, FALSE, FALSE, NULL);
    while (true)
    {
        ::RegNotifyChangeKeyValue(hkey, TRUE,
            REG_NOTIFY_CHANGE_NAME+
            REG_NOTIFY_CHANGE_ATTRIBUTES+
            REG_NOTIFY_CHANGE_LAST_SET+
            REG_NOTIFY_CHANGE_SECURITY, event, TRUE);
        ::WaitForSingleObject(event, INFINITE);
        std::cout << "Subkey " << argv[1] << " was modified"
            << std::endl;
    }
    return 0;
}
```

Listing 5.8 Asynchronous Registry notification.

```
int main(int argc, char* argv[])
{
    if (argc != 2)
    {
        std::cout << "Usage:\n\tnotify [key]\n\n\t\t"
                "where key is a subkey of HKEY_LOCAL_MACHINE"
                << std::endl;
        return 1;
    }

    HKEY hkey;
    ::RegOpenKey(HKEY_LOCAL_MACHINE, argv[1], &hkey);
    while (true)
    {
        ::RegNotifyChangeKeyValue(hkey, TRUE,
                REG_NOTIFY_CHANGE_NAME+
                REG_NOTIFY_CHANGE_ATTRIBUTES+
                REG_NOTIFY_CHANGE_LAST_SET+
                REG_NOTIFY_CHANGE_SECURITY, NULL, FALSE);
        std::cout << "Subkey " << argv[1] << " was modified"
    << std::endl;
    }
    return 0;
}
```

Listing 5.9 Synchronous Registry notification.

Another important feature of the Windows Registry is the ability to save and restore keys to and from registration (.REG) files. Users can then easily import new Registry key hierarchies with one call, rather than calling RegCreateKey and RegSetValue repeatedly.

```
LONG RegLoadKey( HKEY hKey, LPCTSTR lpSubKey, LPCTSTR lpFile );
LONG RegReplaceKey( HKEY hKey, LPCTSTR lpSubKey,
    LPCTSTR lpNewFile, LPCTSTR lpOldFile );
LONG RegRestoreKey( HKEY hKey, LPCTSTR lpFile, DWORD dwFlags );
LONG RegSaveKey( HKEY hKey, LPCTSTR lpFile,
    LPSECURITY_ATTRIBUTES lpSecurityAttributes );
LONG RegUnLoadKey( HKEY hKey, LPCTSTR lpSubKey );
```

The last function that I wish to describe is the RegConnectRegistry function.

```
LONG RegConnectRegistry( LPTSTR lpMachineName, HKEY hKey,
 PHKEY phkResult );
```

Using this function, users can actually acquire HKEY handles on remote computers, thus enabling the entire Registry API to be invoked remotely.

No Template

I'm unsure why Microsoft left this one important class outside of the template-inline paradigm. It may be because there is some code in the IRegistrar object that Microsoft does not want to make public, or it may also be that the designer intended that this class be made available to more than just ATL efforts.

IRegistrar

The ActiveX Template Library (ATL) provides a small COM object for registering and unregistering keys and values in the Registry. The COM object is known as the Registrar and is implemented in the atl.dll module. Experienced ATL developers know that everything in ATL works without the atl.dll module except registration (and unregistration). This is because ATL classes are templated and/or inline except the IRegistrar object.

```
interface IRegistrar : IUnknown
{
 [id(100)] HRESULT AddReplacement([in] LPCOLESTR key,
                    [in] LPCOLESTR item);
 [id(101)] HRESULT ClearReplacements();
 [id(102)] HRESULT ResourceRegisterSz(
                    [in] LPCOLESTR resFileName,
                    [in] LPCOLESTR szID,
                    [in] LPCOLESTR szType);
 [id(103)] HRESULT ResourceUnregisterSz(
                    [in] LPCOLESTR resFileName,
                    [in] LPCOLESTR szID,
                    [in] LPCOLESTR szType);
 [id(104)] HRESULT FileRegister([in] LPCOLESTR fileName);
 [id(105)] HRESULT FileUnregister([in] LPCOLESTR fileName);
 [id(106)] HRESULT StringRegister([in] LPCOLESTR data);
 [id(107)] HRESULT StringUnregister([in] LPCOLESTR data);
 [id(120)] HRESULT ResourceRegister(
                    [in] LPCOLESTR resFileName,
                    [in] UINT nID, [in] LPCOLESTR szType);
 [id(121)] HRESULT ResourceUnregister(
                    [in] LPCOLESTR resFileName,
                    [in] UINT nID, [in] LPCOLESTR szType);
};
```

Listing 5.10 IRegistrar IDL.

The IRegistrar interface is most likely the best interface I've ever seen some-one at Microsoft put together. The first time I looked at it, I knew the function of every method of the interface. There are two sets of functions, one set to work with replacement parameters and one set to execute Windows Registry registration.

The first set has two functions, AddReplacement and ClearReplacements. This refers to replacement parameters that exist in the Registry scripts. Listing 5.11 is a simple Registry script with one replacement parameter.

```
HKCR
{
 NoRemove CLSID
 {
 ForceRemove {3D4F3C83-9C9B-11D1-9F4E-00805F5307DA}
               = s 'My Class'
  {
   ForceRemove 'Programmable'
   InprocServer32 = s '%MODULE%'
   {
    val ThreadingModel = s 'Apartment'
   }
  }
 }
}
```

Listing 5.11   Registry script with replacement macro.

The assumption is that the programming calling the Registrar COM object would have set up a replacement parameter for the %MODULE% replace-ment macro. The implementations calling the Registrar in ATL do this auto-matically.

The second set of functions provided by the IRegistrar interface are the func-tions to invoke registration and unregistration in the Windows Registry. This can be done from several sources: an RGS file, a BSTR string, or a resource embedded in a module. Listing 5.12 shows a small program that takes an RGS file as a parameter and invokes the Registry script using the Registrar object.

This program does not add any replacement parameters, so RGS files that have replacement parameters will not work. It is possible to enhance the current RGS program by adding the capability to provide the replacement parameters on the command line.

The last thing I should mention is that the Registrar object is contained with the ATL.DLL module. Users must register this DLL (regsvr32 atl.dll) before they can use the Registrar object.

```
#include <iostream>
#include <windows.h>

int main(int argc, char * argv[])
{
 if (argc != 2 &&
  (argc !=3 || std::string("-u") == argv[1]) )
 {
  std::cout << "Usage:\tRegRGS [-u] filename\n"
    "\twhere filename is name of the RGS file\n"
    "\twhere optional parameter -u unregisters "
                "the file\n" << std::end;
  return 0;
 }

 ::CoInitialize(NULL);

 IRegistrar * registrar;
 ::CoCreateInstance(CLSID_Registrar, NULL, CLSCTX_ALL,
  IID_IRegistrar, (void **)&registrar);

 if (argc == 2)
 {
  registrar->FileRegister(AnsiToWide(argv[1]).c_str());
 }
 else
 {
  registrar->FileUnregister(AnsiToWide(argv[1]).c_str());
 }

 registrar->Release();
 ::CoUninitialize();

 return 0;
}
```

Listing 5.12 Executing RGS scripts.

Windows Registry COM Component

Now that I've discussed the Windows Registry to death, I'll create a COM
component that performs the minimal amount of operations necessary to
encapsulate configuration information. One of the primary efforts in the
storing of configuration information in the last few years is the organization
of configuration data in hierarchical form. The Windows Registry is one configuration mechanism that organizes the data in such a form. The COM
interface that I will present for accessing the Windows Registry will be
abstracted such that any hierarchical configuration database can provide an
implementation for this interface. This will make it very easy to switch from
one hierarchical configuration database to another. The COM interface is
shown in Listing 5.13.

```
import "objidl.idl";
import "oaidl.idl";

interface INode;
[
 object,
 uuid(1D332C83-6198-11d3-B6CD-00C04F8B72E7),
 pointer_default(unique)
]
interface IEnumStrings : IUnknown
{
// standard
 HRESULT Next([in] ULONG celt, [out] BSTR * rgelt,
   [out] ULONG * pceltFetched);
 HRESULT Skip([in] ULONG celt);
 HRESULT Reset();
 HRESULT Clone([out] IEnumStrings ** ppenum);
};

[
 object,
 uuid(1D332C84-6198-11d3-B6CD-00C04F8B72E7),
 pointer_default(unique)
]
interface INode : IUnknown
{
 HRESULT Initialize([in]BSTR company, [in]BSTR product);
 HRESULT GetChildNode(BSTR name, INode ** child);
 HRESULT GetChildNodes(IEnumStrings ** nodes);
 HRESULT GetName(BSTR * name);
 HRESULT GetNames(IEnumStrings ** names);
 HRESULT GetValue(BSTR name, BSTR * value);
 HRESULT SetValue(BSTR name, BSTR value);
 HRESULT AddChild(BSTR name, INode ** child);
};

[
 uuid(795F3EB0-61A0-11d3-B6CD-00C04F8B72E7),
]
coclass WindowsRegistry
{
 [default] interface INode;
};
```

Listing 5.13 Hierarchical configuration database interface.

The IDL is divided into two interfaces and one COM class. The IEnumNodes interface is used to browse a list of zero or more nodes in a collection. The INode interface is used to read and write to one node. Both of these interfaces will remain the same for all the COM configuration components I write in this chapter.

The Windows Registry coclass (COM class) is the base Windows Registry key. In this case, I'll treat HKEY_LOCAL_MACHINE\SOFTWARE as the base key. I didn't use a real Windows Registry base key because that would require having knowledge of the Windows Registry when using the interface. My objective was to abstract the implementation from the interface and therefore this seemed like an appropriate manner of accomplishing that goal.

The next step is to generate the marshaling code with the MIDL compiler. I'll be implementing the server in-process, so I don't actually need the marshaling code, but I do need the C++ definitions for the CLSID, IID, and interfaces. Listing 5.14 shows the definitions that are required from MIDL.

I snipped the const IIDs and CLSID from the generated file with the _i.c suffix. The abstract classes were snipped from the generated header file.

```
const IID IID_IEnumNodes =
{0x1D332C83,0x6198,0x11d3,{0xB6,0xCD,0x00,0xC0,0x4F,0x8B,0x72,0xE7} };

const IID IID_INode =
{0x1D332C84,0x6198,0x11d3,{0xB6,0xCD,0x00,0xC0,0x4F,0x8B,0x72,0xE7}};

const CLSID CLSID_WindowsRegistry =
{0x795F3EB0,0x61A0,0x11d3,{0xB6,0xCD,0x00,0xC0,0x4F,0x8B,0x72,0xE7}};

MIDL_INTERFACE("1D332C83-6198-11d3-B6CD-00C04F8B72E7")
IEnumNodes : public IUnknown
{
public:
    virtual HRESULT STDMETHODCALLTYPE Next(
        /* [in] */ ULONG celt,
        /* [out] */ INode __RPC_FAR *rgelt,
        /* [out] */ ULONG __RPC_FAR *pceltFetched) = 0;

    virtual HRESULT STDMETHODCALLTYPE Skip(
        /* [in] */ ULONG celt) = 0;

    virtual HRESULT STDMETHODCALLTYPE Reset( void) = 0;

    virtual HRESULT STDMETHODCALLTYPE Clone(
        /* [out] */ IEnumNodes __RPC_FAR *__RPC_FAR *ppenum) = 0;

};

MIDL_INTERFACE("1D332C84-6198-11d3-B6CD-00C04F8B72E7")
INode : public IUnknown
{
public:
```

Continues

Listing 5.14 COM definitions.

```
    virtual HRESULT STDMETHODCALLTYPE GetChildren(
        /* [out] */ IEnumNodes __RPC_FAR *__RPC_FAR *e) = 0;

    virtual HRESULT STDMETHODCALLTYPE GetValue(
        /* [out] */ VARIANT __RPC_FAR *value) = 0;

    virtual HRESULT STDMETHODCALLTYPE GetName(
        /* [out] */ BSTR __RPC_FAR *bstr) = 0;

    virtual HRESULT STDMETHODCALLTYPE GetBranch(
        /* [out] */ BSTR __RPC_FAR *bstr) = 0;

    virtual HRESULT STDMETHODCALLTYPE AddChild(
        /* [in] */ BSTR name,
        /* [in] */ BSTR value) = 0;

    virtual HRESULT STDMETHODCALLTYPE AddChildNode(
        /* [in] */ INode __RPC_FAR *child) = 0;

    virtual HRESULT STDMETHODCALLTYPE SetValue(
        /* [in] */ VARIANT value) = 0;

    virtual HRESULT STDMETHODCALLTYPE SetName(
        /* [in] */ BSTR bstr) = 0;

};
```

Listing 5.14

The code for our COM Registry component is presented in Listings 5.15 and 5.16.

```
class WindowsRegistryNode : public INode
{
 HKEY m_hkey;
 std::wstring m_strName;
public:
 WindowsRegistryNode();
 ~WindowsRegistryNode();

 STDMETHODIMP Initialize(BSTR company, BSTR product);
 void Initialize(const std::wstring & name);

 STDMETHODIMP GetChildNode(BSTR name, INode ** child);
 STDMETHODIMP GetChildNodes(IEnumStrings ** nodes);
 STDMETHODIMP GetName(BSTR * name);
 STDMETHODIMP GetNames(IEnumStrings ** names);
 STDMETHODIMP GetValue(BSTR name, BSTR * value);
 STDMETHODIMP SetValue(BSTR name, BSTR value);
 STDMETHODIMP AddChild(BSTR name, INode ** child);
```

Continues

Listing 5.15   Registry class declaration.

```
long m_references;
ULONG STDMETHODCALLTYPE AddRef()
{
 ::InterlockedIncrement(&m_references);
 return m_references;
}
ULONG STDMETHODCALLTYPE Release()
{
 ::InterlockedDecrement(&m_references);
 if (m_references == 0)
 {
  delete this;
 }
 return m_references;
}
STDMETHODIMP QueryInterface(REFIID riid, void ** ppv)
{
 if (riid == IID_IUnknown)
 {
  *ppv = static_cast<IUnknown*>(this);
  AddRef();
  return S_OK;
 }
 if (riid == IID_INode)
 {
  *ppv = static_cast<INode*>(this);
  AddRef();
  return S_OK;
 }
 *ppv = NULL;
 return E_NOINTERFACE;
};
};
```

Listing 5.15 Registry class declaration *(Continued).*

```
namespace
{

class VStrings : public IEnumStrings
{
 std::wstring m_strKey;
 HKEY m_hkey;
 int m_i;
public:
```

Continues

Listing 5.16 Registry class definitions.

```
VStrings()
 :m_hkey(NULL), m_i(0), m_references(0)
{
}

~VStrings()
{
 if (m_hkey != NULL)
 {
  ::RegCloseKey(m_hkey);
 }
}

void Initialize(const std::wstring & key)
{
 m_strKey = key;
};

STDMETHODIMP Next(ULONG celt, BSTR * rgelt, ULONG * pceltFetched)
{
 if (celt != 1)
 {
  return S_FALSE;
 }

 if (m_hkey == NULL)
 {
  ::RegOpenKeyW(HKEY_LOCAL_MACHINE, m_strKey.c_str(), &m_hkey);
 }

 WCHARvaluename[MAX_PATH+1];
 DWORD lvaluename = sizeof(valuename);
 if (::RegEnumValueW(m_hkey, m_i, valuename, &lvaluename,
  NULL, NULL, NULL, NULL) != ERROR_SUCCESS)
 {
  return S_FALSE;
 }
 m_i++;

 if (*rgelt != NULL)
 {
  ::SysFreeString(*rgelt);
 }
 *rgelt = ::SysAllocString(valuename);
 *pceltFetched = 1;
 return S_OK;
};

STDMETHODIMP Skip(ULONG celt)
{
 m_i += celt;
```

Continues

Listing 5.16

```
  return S_OK;
};

STDMETHODIMP Reset()
{
 if (m_hkey != NULL)
 {
   ::RegCloseKey(m_hkey);
 }
 m_i = 0;
 return S_OK;
};

STDMETHODIMP Clone(IEnumStrings ** ppenum)
{
 VStrings * p = new VStrings;
 p->Initialize(m_strKey);
 if (*ppenum != NULL)
 {
   (*ppenum)->Release();
 }
 *ppenum = p;
 return S_OK;
};

 long m_references;
 ULONG STDMETHODCALLTYPE AddRef()
 {
   ::InterlockedIncrement(&m_references);
   return m_references;
 }
 ULONG STDMETHODCALLTYPE Release()
 {
   ::InterlockedDecrement(&m_references);
   if (m_references == 0)
   {
    delete this;
   }
   return m_references;
 }
 STDMETHODIMP QueryInterface(REFIID riid, void ** ppv)
 {
   if (riid == IID_IUnknown)
   {
    *ppv = static_cast<IUnknown*>(this);
    AddRef();
    return S_OK;
```

Continues

Listing 5.16 Registry class definitions *(Continued)*.

```
    }
    if (riid == IID_IEnumStrings)
    {
     *ppv = static_cast<IEnumStrings*>(this);
     AddRef();
     return S_OK;
    }
    *ppv = NULL;
    return E_NOINTERFACE;
  };

};

class KStrings : public IEnumStrings
{
 std::wstring m_strKey;
 HKEY m_hkey;
 int m_i;
public:

 KStrings()
  :m_hkey(NULL), m_i(0), m_references(0)
 {
 }

 ~KStrings()
 {
  if (m_hkey != NULL)
  {
   ::RegCloseKey(m_hkey);
  }
 }

 void Initialize(const std::wstring & key)
 {
  m_strKey = key;
 };

 STDMETHODIMP Next(ULONG celt, BSTR * rgelt, ULONG * pceltFetched)
 {
  if (celt != 1)
  {
   return S_FALSE;
  }

  if (m_hkey == NULL)
  {
   ::RegOpenKeyW(HKEY_LOCAL_MACHINE, m_strKey.c_str(), &m_hkey);
  }
```

Continues

Listing 5.16

```
    WCHAR valuename[MAX_PATH+1];
    if (::RegEnumKeyW(m_hkey, m_i, valuename, sizeof(valuename))
     != ERROR_SUCCESS)
    {
     return S_FALSE;
    }
    m_i++;

    if (*rgelt != NULL)
    {
     ::SysFreeString(*rgelt);
    }
    *rgelt = ::SysAllocString(valuename);
    *pceltFetched = 1;
    return S_OK;
    };

STDMETHODIMP Skip(ULONG celt)
{
 m_i += celt;
 return S_OK;
};

STDMETHODIMP Reset()
{
 if (m_hkey != NULL)
 {
  ::RegCloseKey(m_hkey);
 }
 m_i = 0;
 return S_OK;
};

STDMETHODIMP Clone(IEnumStrings ** ppenum)
{
 KStrings * p = new KStrings;
 p->Initialize(m_strKey);
 if (*ppenum != NULL)
 {
  (*ppenum)->Release();
 }
 *ppenum = p;
 return S_OK;
};

 long m_references;
 ULONG STDMETHODCALLTYPE AddRef()
 {
  ::InterlockedIncrement(&m_references);
```

Continues

Listing 5.16 Registry class definitions *(Continued).*

```
   return m_references;
  }
  ULONG STDMETHODCALLTYPE Release()
  {
   ::InterlockedDecrement(&m_references);
   if (m_references == 0)
   {
    delete this;
   }
   return m_references;
  }
  STDMETHODIMP QueryInterface(REFIID riid, void ** ppv)
  {
   if (riid == IID_IUnknown)
   {
    *ppv = static_cast<IUnknown*>(this);
    AddRef();
    return S_OK;
   }
   if (riid == IID_IEnumStrings)
   {
    *ppv = static_cast<IEnumStrings*>(this);
    AddRef();
    return S_OK;
   }
   *ppv = NULL;
   return E_NOINTERFACE;
  };

};

};

WindowsRegistryNode::WindowsRegistryNode()
 :m_hkey(NULL), m_references(0)
{
};

WindowsRegistryNode::~WindowsRegistryNode()
{
 if (m_hkey != NULL)
 {
  ::RegCloseKey(m_hkey);
 }
};

STDMETHODIMP WindowsRegistryNode::Initialize(BSTR company,
 BSTR product)
```

Continues

Listing 5.16

```
{
 std::wstringstream ss;
 ss << company << L"\\" << product;
 m_strName = ss.str();
 return S_OK;
};

void WindowsRegistryNode::Initialize(const std::wstring & name)
{
 if (m_hkey != NULL)
 {
  ::RegCloseKey(m_hkey);
 };
 m_strName = name;
};

STDMETHODIMP WindowsRegistryNode::GetChildNode(BSTR name,
 INode ** child)
{
 std::wstringstream ss;
 ss << m_strName << L"\\" << name;
 HKEY hkey;
 if (::RegOpenKeyW(HKEY_LOCAL_MACHINE, ss.str().c_str(), &hkey)
  != ERROR_SUCCESS)
 {
  return S_FALSE;
 };
 ::RegCloseKey(hkey);

 WindowsRegistryNode * retval = new WindowsRegistryNode;
 retval->Initialize(ss.str().c_str());
 if (*child != NULL)
 {
  (*child)->Release();
 }
 *child = static_cast<INode *>(retval);
 return S_OK;
};

STDMETHODIMP WindowsRegistryNode::GetChildNodes(IEnumStrings
** nodes)
{
 KStrings * e = new KStrings;
 e->Initialize(m_strName);
 if (*nodes != NULL)
 {
  (*nodes)->Release();
 }
```

Continues

Listing 5.16 Registry class definitions *(Continued).*

```
 *nodes = static_cast<IEnumStrings *>(e);
 return S_OK;
};

STDMETHODIMP WindowsRegistryNode::GetName(BSTR * name)
{
 if (*name != NULL)
 {
  ::SysFreeString(*name);
 }
 *name = ::SysAllocString(m_strName.c_str());
 return S_OK;
};

STDMETHODIMP WindowsRegistryNode::GetNames(IEnumStrings ** names)
{
 VStrings * e = new VStrings;
 e->Initialize(m_strName);
 if (*names != NULL)
 {
  (*names)->Release();
 }
 *names = static_cast<IEnumStrings *>(e);
 return S_OK;
};

STDMETHODIMP WindowsRegistryNode::GetValue(BSTR name, BSTR * value)
{
 HKEY hkey;
 std::wstringstream ss;
 ss << L"SOFTWARE\\" << name;
 ::RegOpenKeyW(HKEY_LOCAL_MACHINE, name, &hkey);

 wchar_t sz[1024];
 LONG l = sizeof(sz);
 ::RegQueryValueW(hkey, name, sz, &l);
 if (*value != NULL)
 {
  ::SysFreeString(*value);
 }
 *value = ::SysAllocString(sz);

 ::RegCloseKey(hkey);
 return S_OK;
};

STDMETHODIMP WindowsRegistryNode::SetValue(BSTR name, BSTR value)
{
 ::RegSetValueW(m_hkey, name, REG_SZ, value,
```

Continues

Listing 5.16

```
std::wstring(value).length());
 return S_OK;
};

STDMETHODIMP WindowsRegistryNode::AddChild(BSTR name, INode ** child)
{
 HKEY hkey;
 std::wstringstream ss;
 ss << L"SOFTWARE\\" << m_strName << L"\\" << name;
 ::RegCreateKeyW(HKEY_LOCAL_MACHINE, name, &hkey);
 ::RegCloseKey(hkey);

 {
  std::wstringstream ss;
  ss << m_strName << L"\\" << name;
  WindowsRegistryNode * node = new WindowsRegistryNode;
  node->Initialize(ss.str());
  if (*child != NULL)
  {
   (*child)->Release();
  }
  *child = node;
 }

 return S_OK;
};
```

Listing 5.16   Registry class definitions *(Continued).*

Initialization Files

In old 16-bit Windows, configuration information was not saved in the Windows Registry as it did not exist yet. Configuration information was saved in text files called initialization files. They were known as INI files because they almost always had the INI file extension. In order to support legacy systems that still use initialization files, the Win32 API has maintained and even enhanced the functions available for reading and writing INI files. The INI files are divided into sections. Each section would contain a set of key-value pairs.

The functions to read an INI file are GetPrivateProfileInt, GetPrivateProfileSection, GetPrivateProfileSectionNames, GetPrivateProfileString, and GetPrivateProfileStruct.

```
UINT GetPrivateProfileInt( LPCTSTR lpAppName,
    LPCTSTR lpKeyName, INT nDefault, LPCTSTR lpFileName );
DWORD GetPrivateProfileSection( LPCTSTR lpAppName,
```

```
    LPTSTR lpReturnedString, DWORD nSize,
        LPCTSTR lpFileName);
DWORD GetPrivateProfileSectionNames( LPTSTR lpszReturnBuffer,
 DWORD nSize, LPCTSTR lpFileName );
DWORD GetPrivateProfileString( LPCTSTR lpAppName,
        LPCTSTR lpKeyName, LPCTSTR lpDefault,
        LPTSTR lpReturnedString, DWORD nSize,
 LPCTSTR lpFileName );
BOOL GetPrivateProfileStruct( LPCTSTR lpszSection,
        LPCTSTR lpszKey, LPVOID lpStruct, UINT uSizeStruct,
        LPCTSTR szFile );
```

The five INI file get routines retrieve distinct types of information. The Get-PrivateProfileInt retrieves an integer value, the GetPrivateProfileString retrieves a string value, the GetPrivateProfileStruct retrieves a structure of values, the GetPrivateProfileSection retrieves all the names and values in a section, and the GetPrivateProfileSectionNames retrieves all the section names in the INI file.

The functions to write an INI file are WritePrivateProfileSection, Write-PrivateProfileString, and WritePrivateProfileStruct.

```
BOOL WritePrivateProfileSection( LPCTSTR lpAppName,
        LPCTSTR lpString, LPCTSTR lpFileName );
BOOL WritePrivateProfileString( LPCTSTR lpAppName,
        LPCTSTR lpKeyName, LPCTSTR lpString,
        LPCTSTR lpFileName );
BOOL WritePrivateProfileStruct( LPCTSTR lpszSection,
        LPCTSTR lpszKey, LPVOID lpStruct, UINT uSizeStruct,
        LPCTSTR szFile );
```

Just like their counterparts, the write routines put distinct types of information in the INI file. The WritePrivateProfileSection writes several names and values to one INI file section, the WritePrivateProfileString writes one name and value, and the WritePrivateProfileStruct writes a name and structure of values.

Initialization File COM Component

Listings 5.17 and 5.18 show the code for our COM INI file component.

```
class WindowsININode : public INode
{
 std::wstring m_strName;
 std::wstring m_strSection;
public:
```
Continues

Listing 5.17 INI class declaration.

```
WindowsININode();
~WindowsININode();

STDMETHODIMP Initialize(BSTR company, BSTR product);
void Initialize(const std::wstring & name,
 const std::wstring & section);

STDMETHODIMP GetChildNode(BSTR name, INode ** child);
STDMETHODIMP GetChildNodes(IEnumStrings ** nodes);
STDMETHODIMP GetName(BSTR * name);
STDMETHODIMP GetNames(IEnumStrings ** names);
STDMETHODIMP GetValue(BSTR name, BSTR * value);
STDMETHODIMP SetValue(BSTR name, BSTR value);
STDMETHODIMP AddChild(BSTR name, INode ** child);
};
```

Listing 5.17 INI class declaration *(Continued).*

```
namespace
{

class Strings : public IEnumStrings
{
 std::vector<std::wstring> m_vstr;
 int m_i;
public:

 Strings()
  :m_i(0), m_references(0)
 {
 }

 ~Strings()
 {
 }

 void Initialize(const std::vector<std::wstring> & vstr)
 {
 m_vstr = vstr;
 m_i = 0;
 };

 STDMETHODIMP Next(ULONG celt, BSTR * rgelt, ULONG * pceltFetched)
 {
  if (celt != 1)
```

Continues

Listing 5.18 INI class definitions.

```
{
 return S_FALSE;
}

if (m_vstr.size() <= m_i)
{
 return S_FALSE;
}

*rgelt = ::SysAllocString(m_vstr[m_i].c_str());
*pceltFetched = 1;
m_i++;
return S_OK;
};

STDMETHODIMP Skip(ULONG celt)
{
   m_i += celt;
   return S_OK;
};

STDMETHODIMP Reset()
{
 m_i = 0;
 return S_OK;
};

STDMETHODIMP Clone(IEnumStrings ** ppenum)
{
 Strings * p = new Strings;
 p->Initialize(m_vstr);
 if (*ppenum != NULL)
 {
  (*ppenum)->Release();
 }
 *ppenum = p;
 return S_OK;
};

 long m_references;
 ULONG STDMETHODCALLTYPE AddRef()
 {
  ::InterlockedIncrement(&m_references);
  return m_references;
 }
 ULONG STDMETHODCALLTYPE Release()
 {
  ::InterlockedDecrement(&m_references);
  if (m_references == 0)
```

Continues

Listing 5.18

```
   {
    delete this;
   }
   return m_references;
  }
  STDMETHODIMP QueryInterface(REFIID riid, void ** ppv)
  {
   if (riid == IID_IUnknown)
   {
    *ppv = static_cast<IUnknown*>(this);
    AddRef();
    return S_OK;
   }
   if (riid == IID_IEnumStrings)
   {
    *ppv = static_cast<IEnumStrings*>(this);
    AddRef();
    return S_OK;
   }
   *ppv = NULL;
   return E_NOINTERFACE;
  };
};

};

WindowsININode::WindowsININode()
{
};

WindowsININode::~WindowsININode()
{
};

STDMETHODIMP WindowsININode::Initialize(BSTR company, BSTR product)
{
 std::wstringstream ss;
 ss << company << L"." << product;
 m_strName = ss.str();
 return S_OK;
};

void WindowsININode::Initialize(const std::wstring & name,
        const std::wstring & section)
{
 m_strName = name;
 m_strSection = section;
};
```

Continues

Listing 5.18 INI class definitions *(Continued)*.

```
STDMETHODIMP WindowsININode::GetChildNode(BSTR name, INode ** child)
{
 if (!m_strSection.empty())
 {
  return S_FALSE;
 }

 WindowsININode * retval = new WindowsININode;
 retval->Initialize(m_strName, name);
 if (*child != NULL)
 {
  (*child)->Release();
 }
 *child = static_cast<INode *>(retval);
 return S_OK;
};

STDMETHODIMP WindowsININode::GetChildNodes(IEnumStrings ** nodes)
{
 if (!m_strSection.empty())
 {
  return S_FALSE;
 }

 WCHAR sz[1024];
 std::vector<std::wstring> vstr;
 ::GetPrivateProfileSectionNamesW(sz, sizeof(sz), m_strName.c_str());
 WCHAR * p = sz;
 for(;*p != NULL;p+=std::wstring(p).length()+1)
 {
  vstr.push_back(p);
 };

 Strings * e = new Strings;
 e->Initialize(vstr);
 if (*nodes != NULL)
 {
  (*nodes)->Release();
 }
 *nodes = static_cast<IEnumStrings *>(e);
 return S_OK;
};

STDMETHODIMP WindowsININode::GetName(BSTR * name)
{
 if (*name != NULL)
 {
  ::SysFreeString(*name);
```

Continues

Listing 5.18

```
}
*name = ::SysAllocString(m_strName.c_str());
return S_OK;
};

STDMETHODIMP WindowsININode::GetNames(IEnumStrings ** names)
{
 if (m_strSection.empty())
 {
  return S_FALSE;
 }

 WCHAR sz[1024];
 std::vector<std::wstring> vstr;
 ::GetPrivateProfileSectionW(m_strSection.c_str(), sz,
sizeof(sz), m_strName.c_str());
 WCHAR * p = sz;
 for(;*p != NULL;p+=std::wstring(p).length()+1)
 {
  vstr.push_back(p);
 };

 Strings * e = new Strings;
 e->Initialize(vstr);
 if (*names != NULL)
 {
  (*names)->Release();
 }
 *names = static_cast<IEnumStrings *>(e);
 return S_OK;
};

STDMETHODIMP WindowsININode::GetValue(BSTR name, BSTR * value)
{
 if (!m_strSection.empty())
 {
  return S_FALSE;
 }

 wchar_t sz[1024];
 ::GetPrivateProfileStringW(m_strSection.c_str(), name, L"",
 sz, sizeof(sz), m_strName.c_str());

 if (*value != NULL)
 {
  ::SysFreeString(*value);
 }
 *value = ::SysAllocString(sz);
```

Continues

Listing 5.18 INI class definitions *(Continued).*

```
    return S_OK;
};

STDMETHODIMP WindowsININode::SetValue(BSTR name, BSTR value)
{
  if (!m_strSection.empty())
  {
    return S_FALSE;
  }

  if (::WritePrivateProfileStringW(m_strName.c_str(),
m_strSection.c_str(),
    name, value) == FALSE)
  {
    return S_FALSE;
  };

  return S_OK;
};

STDMETHODIMP WindowsININode::AddChild(BSTR name, INode ** child)
{
  WindowsININode * node = new WindowsININode;
  node->Initialize(m_strName, name);
  if (*child != NULL)
  {
    (*child)->Release();
  }
  *child = node;
  return S_OK;
};
```

Listing 5.18

Control Panel Applets

The oldest and most widely used mechanism for configuring Windows is the through the Control Panel. TVs and phones have had control panels for decades and everyone knows how convenient they are. Microsoft attempted to duplicate this paradigm in Windows from its beginning. Even though the Windows Control Panel has been a complete success, Microsoft is considering better ways of doing the same thing.

So if Microsoft is abandoning this development stream, then why am I writing about it in a book? Because creating Control Panel applets is easy and most likely the best approach to provide for configuring services. An alternative would be to develop a Microsoft Management Console snap-in. The difference in complexity is enormous. Creating a Control Panel applet may be a half-hour endeavor. Creating a Microsoft Management Console snap-in is a half-week endeavor. Users can make the decision for themselves once they've read the next few sections on the Control Panel and Microsoft Management Console.

As I said, creating a Control Panel applet is easy. It's simply a DLL with the CPL extension that exports the CPlApplet function.

```
LONG CALLBACK CPlApplet(HWND hwnd, int msg, int lparam1,
    int lparam2);
```

The CPlApplet function has four parameters. The first parameter is the parent window that should be used when creating windows in the applet. The second parameter is the message that is being sent to the applet. The third and fourth parameters have different meanings depending on the message. There are nine possible messages.

- CPL_INIT. First message sent to the application. When users receive this message they should initialize the applet. Return non-zero if the applet initialized properly. The lparam1 and lparam2 parameters are not defined for this message.

- CPL_GETCOUNT. Second message sent. Return the number of applets that are supported by this module, which is almost always one. Again the lparam1 and lparam2 parameters are not defined for this message.

- CPL_INQUIRE. Third message sent. The lparam1 parameter is set to the applet number and the lparam2 parameter is a pointer to a CPLINFO structure. The lparam1 parameter will range from zero to one less than the value users return from the CPL_GETCOUNT message. That is, they'll receive one CPL_INQUIRE message for each applet supported.

```
typedef struct tagCPLINFO
{
    int      idIcon;
    int      idName;
    int      idInfo;
    LONG     lData;
} CPLINFO, *LPCPLINFO;
```

The idIcon is the resource ID of the icon that is to be displayed in the Control Panel. The idName and idInfo are string IDs that will be displayed in the Control Panel beneath the applet icon and in the status bar, respectively. The idIcon, idName, and idInfo resources must exist in the Control Panel applet's module resources.

The lData member is a LONG value that is passed to the CPlApplet function as the lparam2 parameter for the CPL_DBLCLK and CPL_STOP messages. If the lData value is set during initialization, the lData value will be passed like a cookie into the CPL_DBLCLK and CPL_STOP messages. This is a convenient place where users can maintain the state of their applets.

- CPL_NEWINQUIRE. Fourth message sent. The lparam1 parameter is set to the applet number and the lparam2 parameter is a pointer to a NEW-CPLINFO structure. Users receive one CPL_NEWINQUIRE message for each applet supported.

I don't suggest using the NEWCPLINFO structure unless for some reason the CPLINFO structure is not adequate.

```
typedef struct tagNEWCPLINFO {
    DWORD dwSize;
    DWORD dwFlags;
    DWORD dwHelpContext;
    LONG lData;
    HICON hIcon;
    TCHAR szName[32];
    TCHAR szInfo[64];
    TCHAR szHelpFile[128];
} NEWCPLINFO;
```

The dwSize member is set to the size in bytes of the NEWCPLINFO structure. The lData member has the same purpose as the lData member of the CPLINFO structure. The hIcon member is set to the handle of the Control Panel applets icon. The szName is set to the name of the Control Panel applet and szInfo is set to the long description of the Control Panel applet, as it should appear in the Control Panel status bar. The dwFlags, dwHelpContext, and szHelpFile members are not implemented.

- CPL_SELECT. This message is sent when someone selects the application in the Control Panel. This message is no longer sent to Control Panel applets.

- CPL_DBLCLK. This message is sent when someone double-clicks the application in the Control Panel. The lparam1 parameter is set to the applet number and the lparam2 parameter is a pointer to a lData value. If users set the lData value in CPL_INQUIRE, then the same value is passed to this function.

- CPL_STARTWPARMS. This message resembles the CPL_DBLCLK message, but is sent when the RUNDLL module starts the Control Panel applet directly. The lparam1 parameter is set to the applet number and the lparam2 parameter is a pointer to an LPSTR.

- CPL_STOP. Indicates that the Control is exiting. The lparam1 parameter is set to the applet number and the lparam2 parameter is a pointer to a lData value. If the lData value in CPL_INQUIRE was allocated, then it should be deallocated when this notification is received.

- CPL_EXIT. Sent prior to the applet being freed. The lparam1 and lparam2 parameters are not defined for this message.

Listing 5.19 shows a sample C++ implementation of the CPlApplet function.

```cpp
#include "cpl.h"

BOOL APIENTRY DllMain( HANDLE hModule,
                       DWORD ul_reason_for_call,
                       LPVOID lpReserved
    )
{
   switch (ul_reason_for_call)
   {
case DLL_PROCESS_ATTACH:
case DLL_THREAD_ATTACH:
case DLL_THREAD_DETACH:
case DLL_PROCESS_DETACH:
break;
   }
   return TRUE;
}

LONG APIENTRY CPlApplet( HWND hWnd, UINT uMsg, LONG lParam1,
    LONG lParam2 )
{
CPLINFO * cpl;
switch (uMsg)
{
case CPL_INIT:
 return TRUE;
case CPL_GETCOUNT:
 return 1;
case CPL_INQUIRE:
 cpl = (CPLINFO *)lParam2;
 cpl->lData = 0;
 cpl->idIcon = 100;
 cpl->idName = 100;
 cpl->idInfo = 101;
 return 0;
case CPL_NEWINQUIRE:
 return 0;
case CPL_DBLCLK:
 ::MessageBox(hWnd, "Applet", "Hello",
          MB_ICONINFORMATION);
 return 0;
case CPL_STARTWPARMS :
 ::MessageBox(hWnd, "Applet", "Hello",
          MB_ICONINFORMATION);
 return TRUE;
case CPL_STOP:
 return 0;
case CPL_EXIT:
 rcturn 0;
case CPL_SELECT:
default:
 return 0;
 }
 return 0;
};
```

Listing 5.19 Sample C++ CPlApplet.

Not really all that much code. The program has a DllMain like every other DLL. It also has the CPlApplet export function. In the CPL_INQUIRE, I set the values of the CPLINFO structure. These values map to the resources that I'll link to my DLL.

Next, I compile this listing and link it with a resource file (.RES) that has an icon numbered 100 and two strings numbered 100 and 101. I must also export the CPlApplet function by linking with a module definition file (.DEF) with content similar to that shown in Listing 5.20.

```
LIBRARY MyControlPanelApplet
DESCRIPTION 'My Control Panel Applet'
EXPORTS
 CPlApplet
```

Listing 5.20 Module definition file for CPlApplet.

Once I've created the Control Panel applet .dll, I should rename the .dll with a .cpl extension and install the library in the System32 folder. I can also do the same, by simply changing the linker settings to output the Control applet with a .cpl extension and to put it into the System32 folder.

Control Panel Applet Component

Now that I've created a very simple Control Panel applet, I'm now going to propose a general framework that developers can use to create their own Control Panel applets. The definition of this framework is presented in Listing 5.21.

The virtual functions in this class can be overridden to do processing when the associated control panel notification event is fired. The design of this framework closely resembles the NtService service framework I presented in Chapter 2, Programming NT Services. The implementation of the framework is shown in Listing 5.22.

The framework revolves around allocating a global instance of the ControlPanel::ControlPanelApplet object when the dynamic link library is loaded.

```
ControlPanelApplet::ControlPanelApplet()
{
    applet = this;
};
```

```
namespace ControlPanel
{

class ControlPanelApplet
{
public:
 ControlPanelApplet();
 ControlPanelApplet(const ControlPanelApplet & rhs);
 ControlPanelApplet & operator= (
          const ControlPanelApplet & rhs);
 virtual bool OnInit();
 virtual int OnGetCount();
 virtual void OnInquire(CPLINFO & cpl);
 virtual void OnNewInquire(NEWCPLINFO & cpl);
 virtual void OnSelect();
 virtual void OnDblClk(HWND hwnd, int idApplet, LONG lData);
 virtual bool OnStart(HWND hwnd, int idApplet, LPSTR sz);
 virtual void OnStop(LONG lData);
 virtual void OnExit();
};

};
```

Listing 5.21   Control Panel framework declaration.

```
namespace
{
ControlPanel::ControlPanelApplet * applet = NULL;
};
LONG CALLBACK CPlApplet(HWND hwnd, int msg, int lparam1,
     int lparam2)
{
 switch (msg)
 {
 case CPL_INIT:
  return applet->OnInit();
 case CPL_GETCOUNT:
  return applet->OnGetCount();
 case CPL_INQUIRE:
  applet->OnInquire(*(CPLINFO *)lparam2);
  return 0;
 case CPL_NEWINQUIRE:
  applet->OnNewInquire(*(NEWCPLINFO *)lparam2);
  return 0;
```

Continues

Listing 5.22   Control Panel framework implementation.

```
 case CPL_SELECT:
  applet->OnSelect();
  return 0;
 case CPL_DBLCLK:
  applet->OnDblClk(hwnd, lparam1, lparam2);
  return 0;
 case CPL_STARTWPARMS:
  return (applet->OnStart(hwnd, lparam1,
                (char *)lparam2) ? TRUE : FALSE);
 case CPL_STOP:
  applet->OnStop(lparam2);
  return 0;
 case CPL_EXIT:
  applet->OnExit();
  return 0;
 }
 return 0;
};

namespace ControlPanel
{

ControlPanelApplet::ControlPanelApplet()
{
 applet = this;
};

ControlPanelApplet::ControlPanelApplet(
     const ControlPanelApplet & rhs)
{
 applet = this;
};

ControlPanelApplet & ControlPanelApplet::operator=(
     const ControlPanelApplet & rhs)
{
 return *this;
};

bool ControlPanelApplet::OnInit()
{
 return true;
};

int ControlPanelApplet::OnGetCount()
{
 return 1;
};
```

Continues

Listing 5.22

```
void ControlPanelApplet::OnInquire(CPLINFO & cpl)
{
 cpl.lData = 0;
 cpl.idIcon = 100;
 cpl.idName = 100;
 cpl.idInfo = 101;
}

void ControlPanelApplet::OnNewInquire(NEWCPLINFO & cpl)
{
};

void ControlPanelApplet::OnSelect()
{
};

void ControlPanelApplet::OnDblClk(HWND hwnd, int idApplet,
    LONG lData)
{
};

bool ControlPanelApplet::OnStart(HWND hwnd, int idApplet,
    LPSTR sz)
{
 return false;
}

void ControlPanelApplet::OnStop(LONG lData)
{
};

void ControlPanelApplet::OnExit()
{
};

};
```

Listing 5.22 Control Panel framework implementation *(Continued)*.

During the construction of the global instance, the applet variable is set in the implementation. This variable is then used to call the virtual functions.

```
namespace
{
ControlPanel::ControlPanelApplet * applet = NULL;
};
```

I've also provided a copy constructor and copy operator so that Control-Panel::ControlPanelApplet objects can be freely passed around without fear.

```
ControlPanelApplet::ControlPanelApplet(
     const ControlPanelApplet & rhs)
{
 applet = this;
};

ControlPanelApplet & ControlPanelApplet::operator=(
     const ControlPanelApplet & rhs)
{
 return *this;
};
```

The core of the implementation occurs, as expected, in the CPlApplet exported function. In this function, the message sent to the CPlApplet function is redirected to the appropriate virtual function for the applet instance.

```
LONG CALLBACK CPlApplet(HWND hwnd, int msg, int lparam1,
     int lparam2)
{
 switch (msg)
 {
 case CPL_INIT:
  return applet->OnInit();
 case CPL_GETCOUNT:
  return applet->OnGetCount();
 case CPL_INQUIRE:
  applet->OnInquire(*(CPLINFO *)lparam2);
  return 0;
 case CPL_NEWINQUIRE:
  applet->OnNewInquire(*(NEWCPLINFO *)lparam2);
  return 0;
 case CPL_SELECT:
  applet->OnSelect();
  return 0;
 case CPL_DBLCLK:
  applet->OnDblClk(hwnd, lparam1, lparam2);
  return 0;
 case CPL_STARTWPARMS:
  return (applet->OnStart(hwnd, lparam1,
               (char *)lparam2)? TRUE : FALSE);
 case CPL_STOP:
  applet->OnStop(lparam2);
  return 0;
 case CPL_EXIT:
  applet->OnExit();
  return 0;
 }
 return 0;
};
```

Each of the virtual functions has a default implementation. The default implementation is a .cpl module with one Control Panel applet whose icon has a resource ID of 100 and whose name and status bar descriptions have string IDs of 100 and 101, respectively. The default implementations do not handle the CPL_DBLCLK and CPL_STARTWPARMS messages.

```
bool ControlPanelApplet::OnInit()
{
 return true;
};

int ControlPanelApplet::OnGetCount()
{
 return 1;
};

void ControlPanelApplet::OnInquire(CPLINFO & cpl)
{
 cpl.lData = 0;
 cpl.idIcon = 100;
 cpl.idName = 100;
 cpl.idInfo = 101;
}

void ControlPanelApplet::OnNewInquire(NEWCPLINFO & cpl)
{
};

void ControlPanelApplet::OnSelect()
{
};

void ControlPanelApplet::OnDblClk(HWND hwnd, int idApplet,
     LONG lData)
{
};

bool ControlPanelApplet::OnStart(HWND hwnd, int idApplet,
     LPSTR sz)
{
 return false;
}

void ControlPanelApplet::OnStop(LONG lData)
{
};

void ControlPanelApplet::OnExit()
{
};
```

Implementing a .cpl module that uses this framework is quite simple. I simply derive a subclass from ControlPanel::ControlPanelApplet and override the OnDblClk virtual method. Listing 5.23 is an example of using the framework to create a very simple Control Panel applet.

```
HINSTANCE hmodule = NULL;
BOOL APIENTRY DllMain( HANDLE hModule,
                       DWORD ul_reason_for_call,
                       LPVOID lpReserved
     )
{
   switch (ul_reason_for_call)
 {
 case DLL_PROCESS_ATTACH:
 hmodule = (HINSTANCE)hModule;
 case DLL_THREAD_ATTACH:
 case DLL_THREAD_DETACH:
 case DLL_PROCESS_DETACH:
 break;
 }
 return TRUE;
}

BOOL CALLBACK MyDialogProc(HWND hwndDlg, UINT message,
     WPARAM wParam, LPARAM lParam)
{
 switch (message)
 {
  case WM_COMMAND:
  switch (LOWORD(wParam))
  {
   case IDOK:
   case IDCANCEL:
    EndDialog(hwndDlg, wParam);
    return TRUE;
  }
 }
 return FALSE;
}

class MyControlPanelApplet : ControlPanel::ControlPanelApplet
{
public:
 MyControlPanelApplet() {};
 virtual void OnDblClk(HWND hwnd, int idApplet, LONG lData)
 {
     ::DialogBox(hmodule, MAKEINTRESOURCE(100), hwnd,
      MyDialogProc);
 };
};

MyControlPanelApplet instance;
```

Listing 5.23 Use ControlPanelApplet framework.

As I'm linking in the previous framework, I don't have to worry about the nitty-gritty of creating the CPlApplet function. Instead, I can create a global instance of the derived applet object and implement one or more of the virtual functions of the ControlPanel::ControlPanelApplet class.

In the example, I've created a project that has four resources, an icon (resource ID of 100), two strings (resource ID of 100 and 101), and one dialog (resource ID of 100). I've provided these resources in .rc resource script in Listing 5.24.

I specified in the default implementation of the OnInquire method that the idIcon member of the CPLINFO structure was 100. This translates to the ICON in this resource script with the same ID. I also specified the idName and idInfo as 100 and 101. These translate to the STRINGTABLE strings with the same IDs.

```
/////////////////////////////////////////////////////////////////
/////////////////////////////////////
// Icon

// Icon with lowest ID value placed first to ensure application
// icon remains consistent on all systems.
100                         ICON    DISCARDABLE     "icon1.ico"

/////////////////////////////////////////////////////////////////
////// Dialog
//

100 DIALOG DISCARDABLE 0, 0, 186, 95
STYLE DS_MODALFRAME | WS_POPUP | WS_CAPTION | WS_SYSMENU
CAPTION "Dialog"
FONT 8, "MS Sans Serif"
BEGIN
    DEFPUSHBUTTON   "OK",IDOK,129,7,50,14
    PUSHBUTTON      "Cancel",IDCANCEL,129,24,50,14
END

/////////////////////////////////////////////////////////////////
////// String Table
//

STRINGTABLE DISCARDABLE
BEGIN
    100                     "My Control Panel Applet"
    101                     "My Description"
END
```

Listing 5.24 Resources for Control Panel applet.

If I link these resources with the module definition file in Listing 5.20, the ControlPanel::ControlPanelApplet class, and the implementation in Listing 5.23, I've got an instant Control Panel applet.

Running the Control Panel Applet

I can run the Control Panel applet without double-clicking its icon in the Control Panel by executing the control.exe application and passing the Control Panel applet's name as the first command-line parameter. As an example, I can execute the Printers Control Panel applet using the following command line:

```
control printers
```

There are eight primary Control Panel applets, as follows, and they all can be accessed directly using this syntax:

- Printers—control printers
- System—control ports
- Fonts—control fonts
- Mouse—control mouse
- Displays—control color
- Regional Settings—control international
- Data/Time—control date/time
- Keyboard—control keyboard

Delphi Control Panel Applets

Creating a Control Panel applet in C++ is quite simple and the same is true for almost every other Windows development tool. In this section, I demonstrate how to create a Control Panel applet in Delphi. Listing 5.25 shows a sample Delphi implementation of the CPlApplet function.

To complete this Delphi Control Panel applet, I create a TForm1 dialog class and three resources in the .RES file. The three resources are the icon, the applet name, and the applet description.

```
library MyControlPanelApplet;
uses Windows, WinTypes, WinProcs, SysUtils, form in "eform.pasi"
{Form1};
{$R *.RES}
function CPlApplet(hwnd: HWND; msg: Word;
```

Continues

Listing 5.25 Sample Delphi CPlApplet.

```
    lParam1, lParam2 : LongInt) : LongInt; export;
var cplinfo : PCPLInfo;
begin
  Result := 0;
  try
  case Msg of
    CPL_INIT:
    begin
      Result := 1;
    end;
    CPL_GETCOUNT:
    begin
      Result := 1;
    end;
    CPL_INQUIRE:
    begin
      cplinfo := PCPLInfo(lParam2);
      cplinfo^.lData := 0;
      cplinfo^.idIcon := 100;
      cplinfo^.idName := 100;
      cplinfo^.idInfo := 101;
    end;
    CPL_DBLCLK:
    begin
      Application.CreateForm(TForm1, Form1);
      Application.Run;
    end;
    CPL_STOP:
    begin
      Result := 0;
    end;
    CPL_EXIT:
    begin
      Result := 0;
    end;
  end;
  except
    on E:Exeption do
    begin
      ShowMessage(E.Message);
    end;
  end;
  cnd;
  exports
    CPlApplet;
begin
end.
```

Listing 5.25 Sample Delphi CPlApplet *(Continued)*.

Microsoft Management Console

Microsoft has pretty much abandoned development of Control Panel applets in favor of Microsoft Manage Control (MMC) snap-ins. The problem I have with MMC snap-ins is that they are more difficult than pulling teeth and passing rocks at the same time. Hopefully, I can pull enough teeth and pass enough rocks so that readers don't have to do the same. My goal in this section is to first explain how MMC snap-ins work and, second, provide a framework that will make implementing custom MMC snap-ins as simple as possible.

Microsoft's goal in developing the MMC console and framework is to provide a common tool to administer Windows and Windows applications. If all the administration tools worked with similar look and feel and could be grouped together, then administering a server would become much easier.

The first thing that developers should do is download the latest version of the MMC and begin understanding the console from the user's viewpoint. The MMC installation package, white paper, and more may be downloaded from www.microsoft.com/management/mmc/. Once the MMC is installed, users can run the console by selecting Run from the Start menu, typing *MMC*, and clicking on OK. Figure 5.4 shows the bare-bones MMC application.

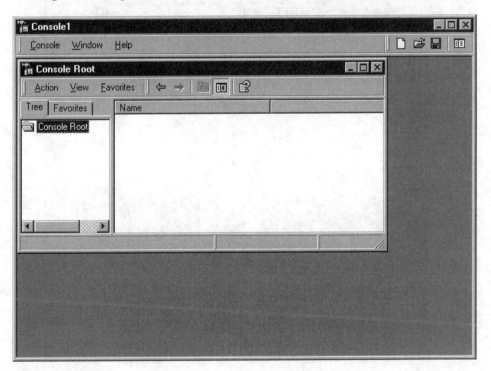

Figure 5.4   MMC.

Users should note that the MMC window is divided into two panes: the scope pane, or left pane, and the result pane, or right pane. In the same fashion as Windows Explorer, the scope pane is used for navigation and the result pane is used to view content.

The next step is to add a simple snap-in to the console. The simplest of snap-ins is the Link to Web Address snap-in. To add this snap-in, for instance, I select Console | Add/Remove Snap-in from the menu bar. The Add/Remove Snap-in dialog appears (see Figure 5.5).

This Add/Remove Snap-in dialog defines the snap-ins that are already included in a folder of the MMC. The listview is empty because I have not yet specified any snap-ins in the Console Root. If I click on the Add button, the Add Standalone dialog appears (Figure 5.6).

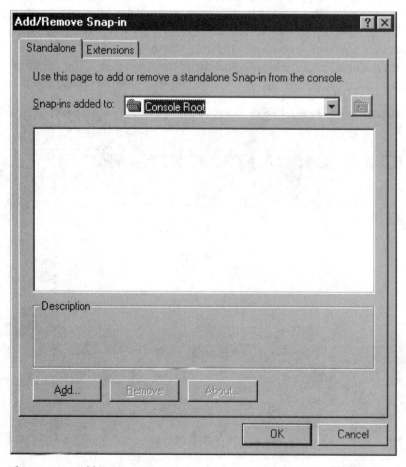

Figure 5.5 Add/Remove Snap-in.

Figure 5.6 Add Standalone snap-in.

Next, I select the Link to Web Address snap-in and click on the Add button. When the wizard prompts me for a Web address, I type *http://www .kbcafe.com*, and click Next (see Figure 5.7).

When the wizard prompts me for a name, I type http://www.kbcafe.com and click Finish | Close | OK (see Figure 5.8).

Now I've added a Web address snap-in to the management console. If I click on the Web address in the left pane, the right pane displays the associated Web page (see Figure 5.9).

A node has been added beneath the Console Root folder. This node has an Internet Explorer icon to denote that it is a link to a Web page. When I select the node, the Web page is loaded into the right view pane of the MMC. If I click on the MMC node and select Action | Properties from the menu bar, then the MMC Properties dialog is displayed (see Figure 5.10).

For the Link to Web Address node, the properties are the name and URL of the node. The MMC Properties dialog provides a convenient place for modifying console-specific data.

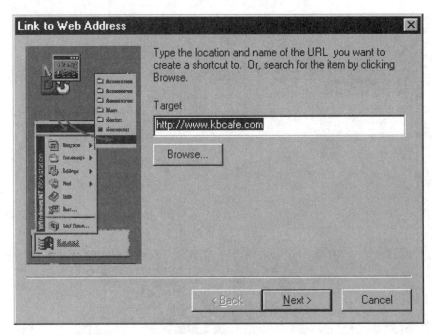

Figure 5.7 Link to Web Address URL entry.

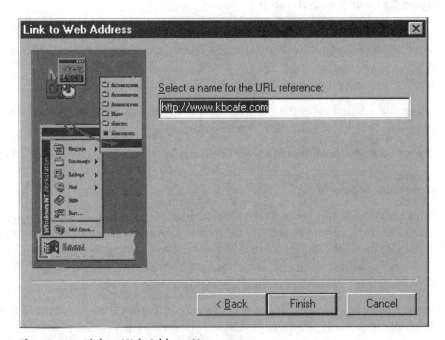

Figure 5.8 Link to Web Address Name entry.

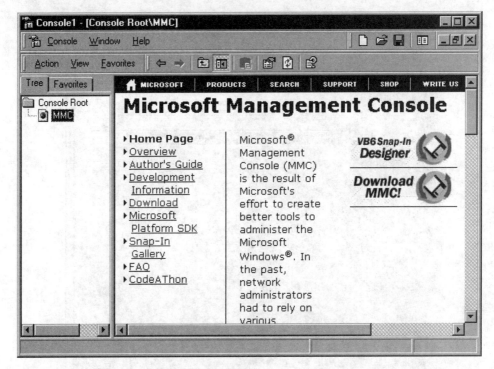

Figure 5.9 MMC Link to Web Address snap-in.

The most important feature of the MMC console is that it actually saves console settings, so that users don't have to re-create them each time they restart the MMC. In fact, users can save multiple console configurations so that they can load different configurations. To save a console configuration (.msc files), for instance, I simply select Console | Save from the menu bar. I can then load a console configuration by selecting Console | Open from the menu bar. I can also load a console configuration by double-clicking on the console configuration (.msc) file in Windows Explorer.

Microsoft Management Console Programming

The easiest way to create a MMC snap-in is to use the ATL COM AppWizard. First, I have to start the Visual C++ 6.0 IDE.

NOTE
These steps may change in future releases of Developer's Studio.

Then, I create a new ATL COM DLL by selecting File | New from the menu bar and switching to the Projects tab. I select ATL COM AppWizard, type a

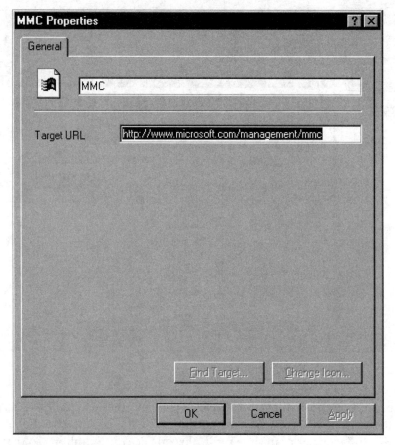

Figure 5.10 MMC Properties dialog.

Project name, and click the OK button. This will start the ATL COM App-Wizard. Next, I select Dynamic Link Library as the Server Type and click the Finish button. When the New Project Information dialog appears, I click on the OK button. Now I have created a new ATL DLL project.

Now I have to add my MMC snap-in objects. I select Insert | New ATL Object from the menu bar and the ATL Object Wizard appears (see Figure 5.11).

I'll select the Objects in the Category list, MMC snap-in in the Objects list, and click on the Next button. The ATL Object Wizard Properties dialog appears (see Figure 5.12).

I type a Short Name for my MMC object. All other properties are auto-filled by the wizard or are already in proper order. Then, I'll click on the OK button and the code for the snap-in is generated by the wizard. Next, I compile the snap-in project, and when it is compiled, the IDE will automatically register

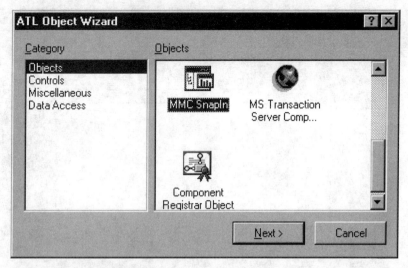

Figure 5.11 ATL Object Wizard.

the project with the MMC. If I decide to use this snap-in on another machine, I'll have to register the snap-in using RegSvr32.

```
RegSvr32 MyMmcSnapin.dll
```

If I run the MMC and add the new snap-in to the console, I see that all the wizard did was provide a folder (see Figure 5.13).

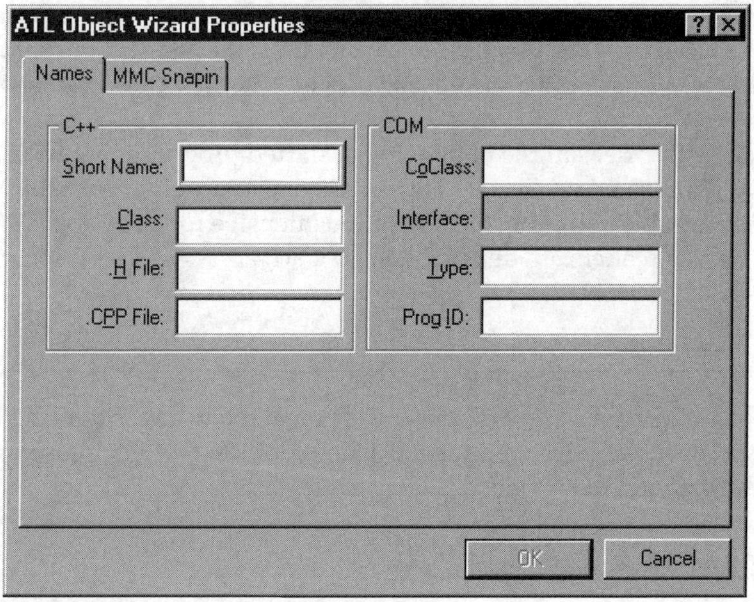

Figure 5.12 ATL Object Wizard Properties.

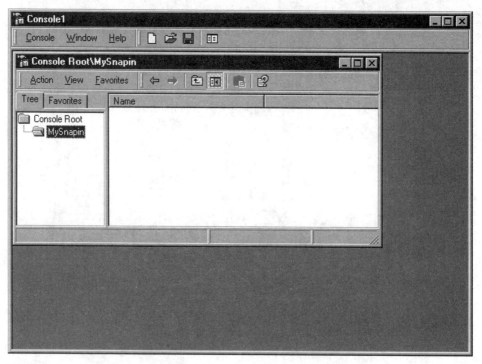

Figure 5.13 Wizard-generated snap-in.

TIP

To add a new snap-in to the console, users must select Console | Add/Remove Snap-in from the menu bar. Then they have to click on OK in the Add/Remove Snap-in dialog. Next, they must select the snap-in and click on Add, then Close, and finally OK.

I've given just a brief sample of how to get started programming with the Microsoft Management Console. The techniques to program with the MMC are quite extensive and probably a little too intensive for this book, but at least I've given readers an idea of where to start.

Tools

Now that I've described how to build additional tools for configuring NT Services, how about I describe some existing tools that will help users take full advantage of what NT Services has to offer?

Server Manager

The first tool is the Server Manager. This tool is distributed with NT Server and allows programmers to access the Services Control Panel applet remotely. I've found that I'm also able to install the Server Manager on NT Workstations by simply copying the executable in the System32 directory. To do this, I run the Server Manager (see Figure 5.14) and select the remote server in the listview.

From the menu bar, I select Computer | Services and the Remote Services Control Panel appears (see Figure 5.15).

Now I'm back to the Services Control Panel applet, except this time I am managing the services on a remote computer.

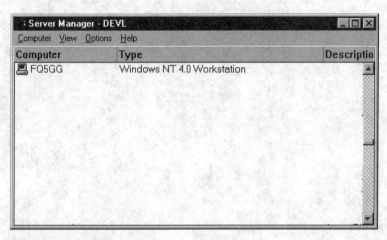

Figure 5.14   Server Manager.

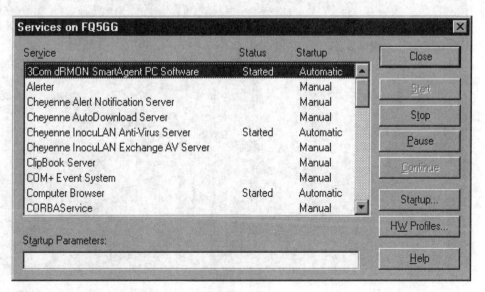

Figure 5.15   Remote Services Control Panel.

Service Controller

The Service Controller is not the easiest utility to get at. I've bookmarked it a few times without success, as it keeps moving around Microsoft's Web site. My latest bookmark is http://msdn.microsoft.com/library/techart/ msdn_scmslite.htm.

The service control utility pretty much does everything that is remotely possible with services. If I run the utility with no command-line parameters, then it will dump its usage text (see Figure 5.16).

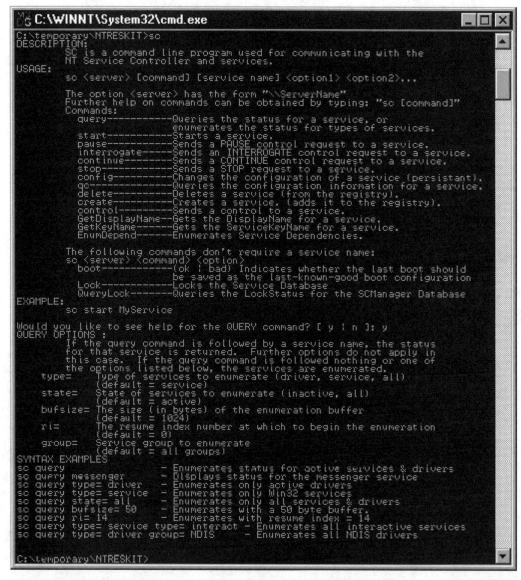

Figure 5.16 Service Controller.

Most users will likely be using the create, delete, start, and stop options of this utility. I've found it particularly useful when I want to programmatically perform these actions. Sometimes, calling CreateService or StartService is too much or is not accessible with the tool currently in use. In these cases, I recommend running a Service Controller command. This is particularly useful in batch files where users must start and stop services or in installation files where they must quickly install and uninstall services.

A particularly useful function of the Service Controller that I've not seen anywhere else is the ability to remotely create and start a service. This can be a little too powerful in very secure environments. A simple batch file (see Listing 5.26) could be created which copies files to a remote computer, creates the service, and starts it.

```
copy . \\RemoteComputerName\C$\.
sc \\RemoteComputerName create BadService C:\ServiceName.exe
sc \\RemoteComputerName start BadService
```

Listing 5.26   Create and start service.

Anybody with malicious intent and knowledge of this could do some damage. On the other hand, a little play at work never hurt anybody. Programmers could create a service that randomly performs funny behavior on a machine about once a week, then install it remotely using a similar batch file.

Winmsd

The Windows NT Diagnostic (Winmsd) utility is convenient for determining the configuration of an NT server. Winmsd is installed with most Windows NT installations. The utility may be started from the Start menu by selecting Programs | Administrative Tools | Windows NT Diagnostics.

The Winmsd utility has nine property pages, although this will likely change with new versions of the utility. The initial page is the Version tab (see Figure 5.17).

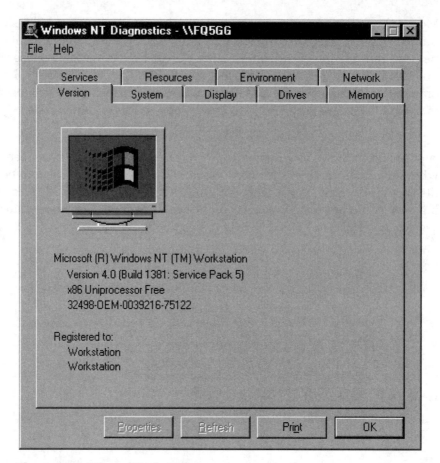

Figure 5.17 Winmsd Version tab.

I find this tab especially useful when I'm trying to determine the version and service pack of NT that the machine is running. I rarely visit all the Winmsd property pages, but I find the Memory tab useful for determining how much Physical Memory and Pagefile Space are on the machine (see Figure 5.18).

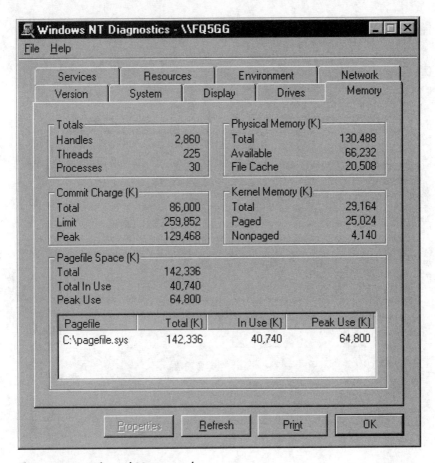

Figure 5.18 Winmsd Memory tab.

I've also found the Environment property page useful for determining the state of my system and user environment variables (see Figure 5.19).

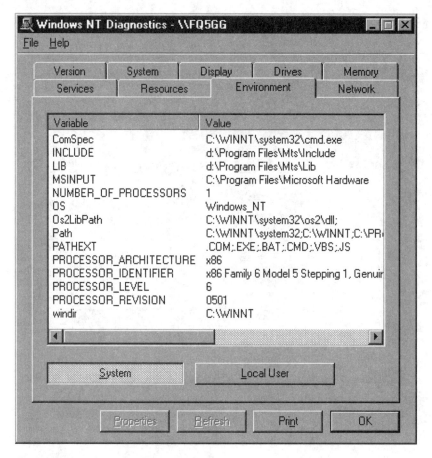

Figure 5.19 Winmsd Environment tab.

The last page I find useful is the one that most applies to this book. The Services property page lists all the services running on the machine and the state (whether running) of each service (see Figure 5.20).

Services are what this book is about, so users will likely be most interested in using Winmsd for quickly determining which services are running on any particular machine.

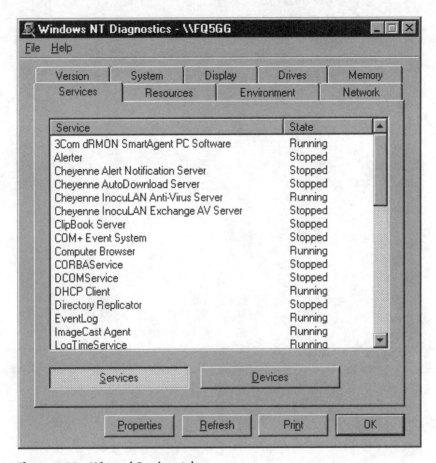

Figure 5.20   Winmsd Services tab.

Summary

Once readers have hit this point in the book, they are certified NT Service programming-capable. But if they're scared of shadows and ghosts, I suggest they skip the next chapter, for in Chapter 6, I hope to convert them to the dark side of security. Ahhh!

CHAPTER 6

Security

I magine a software developer has completed a 20-thousand-hour development effort and has got thousands of objects distributed over several physical servers. Under normal operations the interaction between these objects is not easily managed. The likelihood of rogue or even malicious objects performing some unintended behavior is extremely low. Or is it? If the system had Internet clients accessing its servers, then what's to stop some hacker from malicious activity? What of the server operators, who may be more clever than ethical? The solution to these problems is security.

Security is the firewall between the Internet client and the servers. Security is the authentication and authorization of activity between the thousands of objects. Security is the authentication and authorization of server operators. Security is the encryption of data. Security is the audit trail in the NT Event Log. Security is many other things. Security is good and security is bad.

The good thing about security is that it allows users to open up their servers to activity while limiting the liability. Without security, they'd allow only very trustworthy operators anywhere near their servers and they'd never connect those servers to the Internet.

The bad thing about security is that it usually is very difficult to properly configure. I don't know how many times I've heard that the application has stopped working because the firewall is misbehaving. (Yeah, right!) Or a system-user-account password changed. (Oops!)

System-User-Account Password

The following is a very popular post in the Usenet archives. Trust me, this happens everyday, all the time. Remember also that this is an example of one security problem and that it is a small subset of all security problems.

Question: I have been unable to remedy the following error message. DCOM got error "Logon failure: unknown user name or bad password." and was unable to log on {Domain}\{User-Id} in order to run the server: {GUID}. Please advise how I can locate the location that stores the invalid user ID [{Domain}\{User-Id}]. I have tried the registry and services in the control panel.

Answer: See DCOMCNFG.EXE

Only 10 years ago, security on a Windows computer was almost nonexistent. If programmers wanted security in their applications, then they had to program their own authentication and authorizing systems. Almost every application used a different security model and there was very little reuse. Users were almost always frustrated having to learn a new security model for each application, and this resulted in users turning off security.

Then Microsoft got serious about security. Its motivation was to get C2-level security compliance, and it got it.

NT Security

I don't know how many times I've been told about the relaxed security that is provided out-of-the-box for NT. It is true that a standard NT configuration has very little security. This was intentional so that less-experienced users would not have to deal with complex security issues when they install NT. This does not mean that an NT server is not secure.

Microsoft has provided a lot of techniques and settings that allow an NT machine to become a very secure NT machine. I explain these in brief so that readers are familiar with the techniques that turn an unsecured NT machine into something completely secure.

Enabling C2-Level Security

I start by describing what C2-level security is and what it means. C2-level security is an evaluation given by the National Computer Security Center (NCSC). NCSC is a U.S. government agency responsible for evaluating software security. The evaluation guidelines are described in the publication,

Department of Defense Trusted Computer System Evaluation Criteria, also known as the Orange Book. The entire publication is available online at www.radium .ncsc.mil/tpep/library/rainbow/5200.28-STD.txt.

A summary of this document is that it describes seven classes of computer security. The lowest class is level D and is equivalent to a failing grade. The next level is C1, then C2, B1, B2, B3, and finally A1.

Some of the criteria for acquiring the C1-level security are shown in Table 6.1.

Some of the criteria for acquiring the C2-level security are shown in Table 6.2.

The Department of Defense published a second book called *Trusted Network Interpretation of the Trusted Computer System Evaluation Criteria*, also known as the Red Book. This book, as the title suggests, is a reinterpretation of the Orange Book as it applies to computer networks.

An important thing to remember is that NT's certification as C2-level-compliant is for a very specific NT machine setup: the actual version of NT that was compliant was Windows NT Workstation and Server version 3.5 (not 4) with U.S. Service Pack 3. The evaluation guidelines are available

Table 6.1 C1-Level Security Criteria

Users must be capable of controlling access to resources by other users, groups of users, or both.
Users must be authenticated using usernames and passwords before performing any actions on the machine. The authentication data must be protected from access by unauthorized users.
The system must protect itself from external interference and tampering.
The system must be tested and there must not be any obvious ways of defeating the security mechanism.
The system must be documented.

Table 6.2 C2-Level Security Criteria

The access control described in C1-level security must also be capable of including and excluding access to individual users.
The representation of information shall not be made available in a reused object when it is reallocated. That is, programmers cannot allocate uninitialized memory and read the contents of its previous allocation. This applies to all reusable objects, not only memory.
The system must be capable of creating audit trails of individual user activity.
The audit data must be protected against access by unauthorized users.

online at www.radium.ncsc.mil/tpep/epl/entries/CSC-EPL-95-003.html and
are known as DoD 5200.28-STD.

The Windows NT 4.0 Resource Kit includes a utility called C2Config that
allows programmers to easily customize the security settings on their NT
machines (see Figure 6.1).

Many of the C2 security options that I describe in detail can be easily toggled
or configured using the C2 Configuration Manager.

The most basic security setting is to enable C2-level security for all system
objects. Setting the ProtectionMode value in the [HKEY_LOCAL_MACHINE\
System\CurrentControlSet\Control\SessionManager] Registry key to 1 (REG_
DWORD) enables C2-level security for all system objects.

Winlogon

Another technique of enhancing security is to add a warning notice prior to a
user's logon onto an NT machine. The warning notice was added as a legal
precaution. The legal thinking is that without the notice, the Winlogon dialog
seemed like an invitation to log on to the NT machine. The warning notice
should make it explicit that unauthorized logons are not permitted.

When a user attempts to log on to an NT machine, the warning notice is displayed before the Winlogon dialog. When the user clicks the OK button, the
warning notice disappears and the Winlogon dialog is displayed.

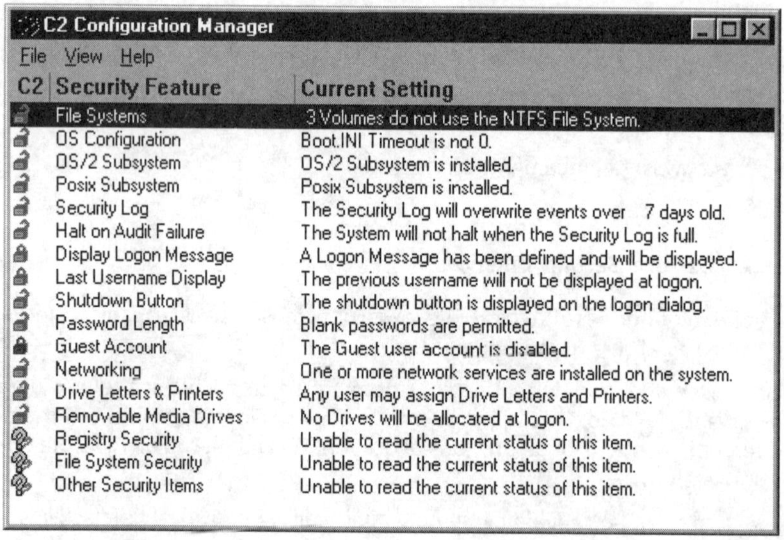

Figure 6.1   C2Config.

In the NT Registry key [HKEY_LOCAL_MACHINE\SOFTWARE\Microsoft\ Windows NT\Current Version\Winlogon], two settings are provided that allow programmers to configure the logon warning notice. The LegalNotice-Caption and LegalNoticeText keys contain plain text (REG_SZ) values that are displayed in the logon warning notice. Figure 6.2 shows these values in the RegEdit utility.

Developers might also consider removing write permissions to this Registry key for nonadministrators. I would generally allow Full Control to CREATE OWNER, Administrators, and SYSTEM, and only Read permissions for Everyone.

Another problem with winlogon's default configuration is that the username of the last user to log on is automatically displayed for the user, so that the user does not have to retype it. Some believe this is another security flaw. This can be disabled by setting the DontDisplayLastUserName value in the [HKEY_LOCAL_MACHINE\SOFTWARE\Microsoft\Windows NT\Current Version\Winlogon] Registry key to 1 (REG_SZ).

A third important setting in the Winlogon Registry key is ShutdownWithout-Logon. This value, when set to 0 (REG_SZ), restricts the ability to shut down

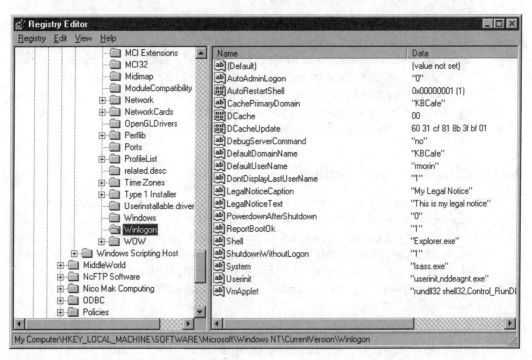

Figure 6.2 Warning notice Registry settings.

a server to a user that is logged on. This setting is quite important, as shutting down a server is about the easiest way to disable the application servers that are running on the server.

NT File System

Two file systems are commonly used on an NT machine. They are FAT (File Allocation Table) and NTFS (NT File System). FAT is the legacy file system that was inherited from NT's ancestor, DOS (Disk Operating System). NTFS is a secured file system with a full set of file access permissions that can be used to deny access rights to various users and user groups.

Remote Access to Windows Registry and Event Logs

The RegEdit Windows Registry editor allows remote access to the local Windows Registry. This can be perceived as a security hole and can also be plugged by creating the [HKEY_LOCAL_MACHINE\CurrentcontrolSet\ Control\SecurePipeServers\winreg] Registry key and setting the configuration permissions for this key. The configuration permissions of this key are also the configuration permissions for remote access to the entire Windows Registry of the local machine.

Developers can restrict access to each of the Event Log logs by setting the RestrictGuestAccess value in the [HKEY_LOCAL_MACHINE\System\CurrentControlSet\Services\EventLog\{LogName}] key to 1 (REG_DWORD). {LogName} is one of the following: Application, Security, System, or a custom log. This setting restricts access to the Event Log for guest accounts. This value is set in the default configuration for the Security event log.

Restricting Task Scheduling

A popular trick that I've pulled is to remotely start the task-scheduling service on a coworker's NT machine. Then, I remotely submit a new task that starts Notepad on his or her desktop every half hour. The first time Notepad starts, the user simply thinks he or she may have clicked some combination of hotkeys and started Notepad inadvertently. But after a while, the coworker shows his or her aptitude by either disabling the scheduler or becoming frustrated.

This is more than an anecdotal tale that developers can use to trick their own coworkers; it's also a security flaw. Imagine if any user could remotely start any task on a production NT server. Not good, right?

Fortunately, this can be disabled. By setting the access rights to the [HKEY_LOCAL_MACHINE\System\CurrentControlSet\Services\Schedule], programmers also set the permissions for who can schedule services. They can remove Full Control and give Read permissions to any users that should not be able to submit tasks to the scheduler service.

Clean the Page File

Another important part of NT that should be secured is the page file. Virtual memory can be swapped to and from the NT page file. That memory may contain sensitive data. In order to prevent users from reading the page file, developers should delete the page file when the system is shut down. If they set the ClearPageFileAtShutdown value in the [HKEY_LOCAL_MACHINE\SYSTEM\CurrentControlSet\Control\SessionManager\Memory Management] key to 1 (REG_DWORD), then the page file is wiped clean when the system is shut down.

NOTE This does not wipe the page file clean when the system is shut down by switching off the computer power. If the system was then restarted on an alternate boot that did not secure it, then the page file could still be browsed for sensitive information.

Programmatic Security

The great advantage of this NT Security model, or any security model that is programmatically accessible, is the possibility of reuse. As new applications are developed, programmers can reuse the NT Security system instead of writing their own.

Millions of hours have been spent redundantly writing security components. I don't know how many times I've been asked to add security to the application I'm developing. Had the NT Security system been available to me, I would have saved hundreds of hours in each attempt.

A few things to remember are that NT Security is not a firewall and only operates on computers that are aware of the NT Security system. I will not be

Definition: Firewall

A *firewall* is component of a network gateway that secures the resources on a network behind the gateway-firewall from users outside the gateway-firewall.

addressing firewalls or security on computers other than NT Workstation Servers beyond this section of the book.

Providing for security between computers that don't implement a common security system is costly. I suggest that the quickest solution is to port one of the security systems. This solution usually means only half the development effort, but can sometimes mean more work in the long run. Whenever I run into this situation, I've found that effort spent in analysis will be regained tenfold.

NT Security Model

NT Security is the evolved LAN Manager security provider. In its evolution, it has undergone a complete transformation from a small security system for the network protocol to a very large and complete security system.

NT Security is based on SIDs (Security IDs), SDs (Security Descriptors), ACLs (Access Control Lists), and ACEs (Access Control Entries).

Security IDs

The SID, or Security ID, is a structure that uniquely identifies a security principle. The C++ definition of the SID is a multibyte unique identifier.

```
typedef struct _SID_IDENTIFIER_AUTHORITY {
    BYTE Value[6];
} SID_IDENTIFIER_AUTHORITY, *PSID_IDENTIFIER_AUTHORITY;

typedef struct _SID {
    BYTE  Revision;
    BYTE  SubAuthorityCount;
    SID_IDENTIFIER_AUTHORITY IdentifierAuthority;
    DWORD SubAuthority[ANYSIZE_ARRAY];
} SID, *PISID;
```

The SID is broken into four sections: the Revision, the SubAuthorityCount, the IdentifierAuthority, and a list of SubAuthorities. The Revision member is currently always one, but this could change. The SubAuthorityCount member is the number of entries in the SubAuthority list. The IdentifierAuthority member represents the authority agent that generates the SID and is one of the values in Listing 6.1.

The last member is a list of SubAuthorities or RIDs (Relative IDs). There are many standard RIDs that represent unique users or groups. The standard RIDs are shown in Listing 6.2.

```
#define SECURITY_NULL_SID_AUTHORITY        {0,0,0,0,0,0}
#define SECURITY_WORLD_SID_AUTHORITY       {0,0,0,0,0,1}
#define SECURITY_LOCAL_SID_AUTHORITY       {0,0,0,0,0,2}
#define SECURITY_CREATOR_SID_AUTHORITY     {0,0,0,0,0,3}
#define SECURITY_NON_UNIQUE_AUTHORITY      {0,0,0,0,0,4}
#define SECURITY_NT_AUTHORITY              {0,0,0,0,0,5}
```

Listing 6.1   IdentifierAuthority constants.

```
#define SECURITY_NULL_RID                      (0x00000000L)
#define SECURITY_WORLD_RID                     (0x00000000L)
#define SECURITY_LOCAL_RID                     (0x00000000L)
#define SECURITY_CREATOR_OWNER_RID             (0x00000000L)
#define SECURITY_CREATOR_GROUP_RID             (0x00000001L)
#define SECURITY_CREATOR_OWNER_SERVER_RID      (0x00000002L)
#define SECURITY_CREATOR_GROUP_SERVER_RID      (0x00000003L)
#define SECURITY_DIALUP_RID                    (0x00000001L)
#define SECURITY_NETWORK_RID                   (0x00000002L)
#define SECURITY_BATCH_RID                     (0x00000003L)
#define SECURITY_INTERACTIVE_RID               (0x00000004L)
#define SECURITY_SERVICE_RID                   (0x00000006L)
#define SECURITY_ANONYMOUS_LOGON_RID           (0x00000007L)
#define SECURITY_PROXY_RID                     (0x00000008L)
#define SECURITY_ENTERPRISE_CONTROLLERS_RID    (0x00000009L)
#define SECURITY_SERVER_LOGON_RID \
       SECURITY_ENTERPRISE_CONTROLLERS_RID
#define SECURITY_PRINCIPAL_SELF_RID            (0x0000000AL)
#define SECURITY_AUTHENTICATED_USER_RID        (0x0000000BL)
#define SECURITY_RESTRICTED_CODE_RID           (0x0000000CL)
#define SECURITY_LOGON_IDS_RID                 (0x00000005L)
#define SECURITY_LOCAL_SYSTEM_RID              (0x00000012L)
#define SECURITY_NT_NON_UNIQUE                 (0x00000015L)
#define SECURITY_BUILTIN_DOMAIN_RID            (0x00000020L)
```

Listing 6.2   Standard RIDs.

There is also a list of well-known RIDs (see Listing 6.3).

Putting an IdentifierAuthority and a list of RIDs together makes a SID. SIDs are often viewed in string format, where they have four or more sections separated by hyphen delimiters. The first section is always S. The second section is the revision number and is always 1, but may change in the future. The third section represents the identifier authority, while fourth and subsequent sections represent the individual RIDs.

```
#define DOMAIN_USER_RID_ADMIN          (0x000001F4L)
#define DOMAIN_USER_RID_GUEST          (0x000001F5L)
#define DOMAIN_USER_RID_KRBTGT         (0x000001F6L)
#define DOMAIN_GROUP_RID_ADMINS        (0x00000200L)
#define DOMAIN_GROUP_RID_USERS         (0x00000201L)
#define DOMAIN_GROUP_RID_GUESTS        (0x00000202L)
#define DOMAIN_GROUP_RID_COMPUTERS     (0x00000203L)
#define DOMAIN_GROUP_RID_CONTROLLERS   (0x00000204L)
#define DOMAIN_GROUP_RID_CERT_ADMINS   (0x00000205L)
#define DOMAIN_GROUP_RID_SCHEMA_ADMINS (0x00000206L)
#define DOMAIN_ALIAS_RID_ADMINS        (0x00000220L)
#define DOMAIN_ALIAS_RID_USERS         (0x00000221L)
#define DOMAIN_ALIAS_RID_GUESTS        (0x00000222L)
#define DOMAIN_ALIAS_RID_POWER_USERS   (0x00000223L)
#define DOMAIN_ALIAS_RID_ACCOUNT_OPS   (0x00000224L)
#define DOMAIN_ALIAS_RID_SYSTEM_OPS    (0x00000225L)
#define DOMAIN_ALIAS_RID_PRINT_OPS     (0x00000226L)
#define DOMAIN_ALIAS_RID_BACKUP_OPS    (0x00000227L)
#define DOMAIN_ALIAS_RID_REPLICATOR    (0x00000228L)
```

Listing 6.3   Well-known RIDs.

Some SIDs are called well-known SIDs because they represent distinct entities. These well-known SIDs are shown in string format in Listing 6.4.

NT Services typically run under the local system account. The SID for the local system account is S-1-5-18, revision 1, NT identifier authority, and local system RID. I'm unsure why this is not considered a well-known SID.

Looking at the NULL SID, users will note that it has the SECURITY_NULL_SID_AUTHORITY authority and SECURITY_NULL_RID subauthority (or RID). Logon ID SIDs have the NT authority and several subauthorities including the SECURITY_LOGON_IDS_RID subauthority.

The SID for the current user may be determined from the Registry in the HKEY_USERS hive. Viewing this hive using RegEdit, users will note it has only one viewable subkey, the interactive user. The subkey is keyed by the interactive user's SID (see Figure 6.3).

This SID may be broken down into its authority and subauthorities. SIDs, even in string format, are not particularly human-readable. In order to present human-readable descriptions of the security principal, two functions are provided that convert between SIDs and their English descriptions.

LookupAccountName converts a SID to a human-readable name and LookupAccountSid converts a human-readable name to a SID.

```
// Null SID                    S-1-0-0
// World                       S-1-1-0
// Local                       S-1-2-0
// Creator Owner ID            S-1-3-0
// Creator Group ID            S-1-3-1
// Creator Owner Server ID     S-1-3-2
// Creator Group Server ID     S-1-3-3
// (Non-unique IDs)            S-1-4
// NT Authority                S-1-5
// Dialup                      S-1-5-1
// Network                     S-1-5-2
// Batch                       S-1-5-3
// Interactive                 S-1-5-4
// Service                     S-1-5-6
// AnonymousLogon              S-1-5-7
// Proxy                       S-1-5-8
// ServerLogon                 S-1-5-9
// Self                        S-1-5-10
// Authenticated User          S-1-5-11
// Restricted Code             S-1-5-12
// (Logon IDs)                 S-1-5-5-X-Y
// (NT non-unique IDs)         S-1-5-0x15-...
// (Built-in domain)           S-1-5-0x20
```

Listing 6.4   Well-known SIDs.

```
BOOL LookupAccountName( LPCTSTR lpSystemName,
    LPCTSTR lpAccountName,
    PSID Sid,
    LPDWORD cbSid,
    LPTSTR ReferencedDomainName,
    LPDWORD cbReferencedDomainName,
    PSID_NAME_USE peUse );
BOOL LookupAccountSid( LPCTSTR lpSystemName,
    PSID Sid,
    LPTSTR Name,
    LPDWORD cbName,
    LPTSTR ReferencedDomainName,
    LPDWORD cbReferencedDomainName,
    PSID_NAME_USE peUse );
```

Four functions are used for copying, validating, and comparing SIDs. The IsValidSid function determines whether a SID is valid. The EqualSid function compares two SIDs for equality. The EqualPrefixSid function compares two SIDs up to but not including the last SubAuthority item. The CopySid function copies the value of one SID onto another.

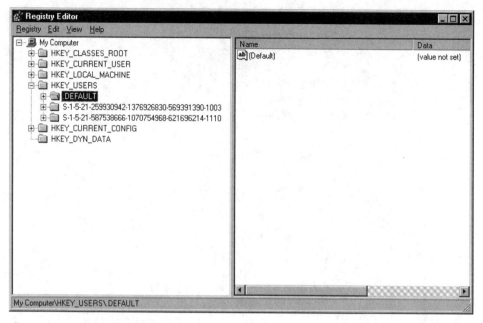

Figure 6.3 SID in HKEY_USERS.

```
BOOL IsValidSid ( PSID pSid );
BOOL EqualSid ( PSID pSid1, PSID pSid2 );
BOOL EqualPrefixSid ( PSID pSid1, PSID pSid2 );
BOOL CopySid ( DWORD nDestinationSidLength,
     PSID pDestinationSid, PSID pSourceSid );
```

Three functions are available for creating, initializing, and freeing SIDs. The AllocateAndInitializeSid and InitializeSid functions initialize SIDs with the function parameters. The AllocateAndInitializeSid function allocates a new SID, and the FreeSid function is used to deallocate the SID.

```
BOOL AllocateAndInitializeSid (
     PSID_IDENTIFIER_AUTHORITY pIdentifierAuthority,
     BYTE nSubAuthorityCount,
     DWORD nSubAuthority0,
     DWORD nSubAuthority1,
     DWORD nSubAuthority2,
     DWORD nSubAuthority3,
     DWORD nSubAuthority4,
     DWORD nSubAuthority5,
     DWORD nSubAuthority6,
     DWORD nSubAuthority7,
     PSID *pSid );
BOOL InitializeSid ( PSID Sid,
 PSID_IDENTIFIER_AUTHORITY pIdentifierAuthority,
     BYTE nSubAuthorityCount );
PVOID FreeSid( PSID pSid );
```

The SID structure is not something Microsoft advises using in development efforts. Using the SID structure directly opens developers up to incompatibilities when this structure changes. To avoid this potential future incompatibility, developers should use the SID access functions to acquire members of the SID structure.

```
PSID_IDENTIFIER_AUTHORITY GetSidIdentifierAuthority(PSID pSid);
PDWORD GetSidSubAuthority ( PSID pSid, DWORD nSubAuthority );
PUCHAR GetSidSubAuthorityCount ( PSID pSid );
DWORD GetLengthSid ( PSID pSid );
```

Putting the SID functions together, programmers can form a SID wrapper class (shown in Listing 6.5).

Now that I've demonstrated a class that makes working with SIDs easy, I thought it would be interesting to write a program that displays a user's SID in string format given a user ID (see Listing 6.6).

The SID Viewer takes the one command-line parameter and passes it as input to the SecurityID class constructor. The constructor attempts to interpret the argument as a String SID. If the argument is not a String SID, then it tries to construct the SID using the LookupAccountName function. Finally, it prints the user's SID in string format.

```cpp
class SecurityID
{
  PSID psid;
public:
  SecurityID();
  SecurityID(const SecurityID & rhs);
  SecurityID(const SID * rhs);
  SecurityID(const std::string & str);
  ~SecurityID();
  SecurityID & operator=(const SecurityID & rhs);
  bool operator==(const SecurityID & rhs) const;
  bool operator()() const;
  DWORD Length() const;
  SID_IDENTIFIER_AUTHORITY *
  GetSidIdentifierAuthority() const;
  DWORD * GetSidSubAuthority(DWORD nSubAuthority) const;
  UCHAR * GetSidSubAuthorityCount() const;
  SID * GetSID() const;
  std::string LookupAccountName(...) const;
  void LookAccountSID(...);
  std::string ToString() const;
};
```

Listing 6.5 SID class.

```
int main(int argc, char* argv[])
{
  if (argc != 2)
  {
   std::cout << "Usage:\n\tSIDViewer userid\n"
     "\t\twhere userid is a NT logon username"
               << std::endl;
   return 0;
  }
  SecurityID sid(argv[1]);
  std::cout << sid.ToString() << std::endl;
  return 0;
}
```

Listing 6.6 SID Viewer.

SECURITY_DESCRIPTOR

The SECURITY_DESCRIPTOR is a basic structure used in the NT Security model. This structure is usually wrapped in a SECURITY_ATTRIBUTE structure.

```
typedef struct _SECURITY_ATTRIBUTES
{
    DWORD nLength;
    LPVOID lpSecurityDescriptor;
    BOOL bInheritHandle;
} SECURITY_ATTRIBUTES;
```

There are two types of security descriptors: self-relative and absolute. A relative security descriptor is complete in itself in that system access control list (SACL) and discretionary access control list (DACL) members are contained within the structure. An absolute security descriptor does not contain the SACL and DACL members, but rather has pointers to SACL and DACL structures that exist outside of the structure. Both versions of the security descriptor are shown in Listing 6.7.

Only the fixed-length portion of the self-relative security descriptor is given in the SECURITY_DESCRIPTOR_RELATIVE structure. In self-relative form, the values of Owner, Group, Sacl, and Dacl are offsets into the security descriptor where these structures can be found. These offsets point beyond the last member of the fixed structure. To convert between the absolute and self-relative format of the security descriptor, programmers can use the MakeAbsoluteSD and MakeSelfRelativeSD functions.

```
typedef struct _SECURITY_DESCRIPTOR_RELATIVE {
    BYTE Revision;
    BYTE Sbz1;
    SECURITY_DESCRIPTOR_CONTROL Control;
    DWORD Owner;
    DWORD Group;
    DWORD Sacl;
    DWORD Dacl;
    } SECURITY_DESCRIPTOR_RELATIVE,
 *PISECURITY_DESCRIPTOR_RELATIVE;

typedef struct _SECURITY_DESCRIPTOR {
    BYTE Revision;
    BYTE Sbz1;
    SECURITY_DESCRIPTOR_CONTROL Control;
    PSID Owner;
    PSID Group;
    PACL Sacl;
    PACL Dacl;
    } SECURITY_DESCRIPTOR, *PISECURITY_DESCRIPTOR;
```

Listing 6.7   SECURITY_DESCRIPTOR.

```
BOOL MakeAbsoluteSD (
    PSECURITY_DESCRIPTOR pSelfRelativeSecurityDescriptor,
    PSECURITY_DESCRIPTOR pAbsoluteSecurityDescriptor,
    LPDWORD lpdwAbsoluteSecurityDescriptorSize,
    PACL pDacl, LPDWORD lpdwDaclSize,
    PACL pSacl, LPDWORD lpdwSaclSize,
    PSID pOwner, LPDWORD lpdwOwnerSize,
    PSID pPrimaryGroup, LPDWORD lpdwPrimaryGroupSize );
BOOL MakeSelfRelativeSD (
    PSECURITY_DESCRIPTOR pAbsoluteSecurityDescriptor,
    PSECURITY_DESCRIPTOR pSelfRelativeSecurityDescriptor,
    LPDWORD lpdwBufferLength );
```

The security descriptor has seven members. The Revision member is always 1. This value is actually defined in the Windows NT C header file as such. At some point, this value is expected to change and when it does, the Revision member will be used to interpret more than one version of the security descriptor.

```
#define SECURITY_DESCRIPTOR_REVISION     (1)
```

The Sbz1 member is set to zero and reserved for future use and is currently padding alongside the Revision member to form a full 16-bit WORD.

The Control member indicates how the structure of the security descriptor is composed.

```
#define SE_OWNER_DEFAULTED              (0x0001)
#define SE_GROUP_DEFAULTED              (0x0002)
#define SE_DACL_PRESENT                 (0x0004)
#define SE_DACL_DEFAULTED               (0x0008)
#define SE_SACL_PRESENT                 (0x0010)
#define SE_SACL_DEFAULTED               (0x0020)
#define SE_DACL_AUTO_INHERIT_REQ        (0x0100)
#define SE_SACL_AUTO_INHERIT_REQ        (0x0200)
#define SE_DACL_AUTO_INHERITED          (0x0400)
#define SE_SACL_AUTO_INHERITED          (0x0800)
#define SE_DACL_PROTECTED               (0x1000)
#define SE_SACL_PROTECTED               (0x2000)
#define SE_SELF_RELATIVE                (0x8000)
```

Most of the bits in the bit mask are not really relevant unless programmers plan on modifying security descriptors directly. The most important of these bits is the SE_SELF_RELATIVE bit. This bit, when set, indicates that the security descriptor is not absolute, but rather self-relative.

The Owner member is usually the SID of the security principal that created the securable object, but can be set to any SID. The Group member is similar to the Owner member but represents a collection of security principals that are owners of the securable object.

The Sacl member indicates the system ACL. The system ACL indicates the audit and alarm details when objects with the security descriptor are used. The Dacl member is a list of SIDs and rights that determine how a security principal (SID) may interact (rights) with the securable object.

In order to begin using a security descriptor, it should be constructed by calling the InitializeSecurityDescriptor function. This function generically sets the Revision member and NULLs the other members of the structure.

```
BOOL InitializeSecurityDescriptor (
    PSECURITY_DESCRIPTOR pSecurityDescriptor,
    DWORD dwRevision );
```

Because the SECURITY_DESCRIPTOR structure may take on more than one form, it is advisable that developers read and write this structure using the accessor and setter methods provided in the Win32 security API. These nine functions allow the programmer to get and set the last four members of the SECURITY_DESCRIPTOR structure and to retrieve the length of the structure.

```
BOOL GetSecurityDescriptorDacl (
    PSECURITY_DESCRIPTOR pSecurityDescriptor,
    LPBOOL lpbDaclPresent,
    PACL *pDacl, LPBOOL lpbDaclDefaulted );
```

```
BOOL GetSecurityDescriptorSacl (
    PSECURITY_DESCRIPTOR pSecurityDescriptor,
    LPBOOL lpbSaclPresent,
    PACL *pSacl, LPBOOL lpbSaclDefaulted );
BOOL GetSecurityDescriptorGroup (
    PSECURITY_DESCRIPTOR pSecurityDescriptor,
    PSID *pGroup, LPBOOL lpbGroupDefaulted );
DWORD GetSecurityDescriptorLength (
    PSECURITY_DESCRIPTOR pSecurityDescriptor );
BOOL GetSecurityDescriptorOwner (
    PSECURITY_DESCRIPTOR pSecurityDescriptor,
    PSID *pOwner, LPBOOL lpbOwnerDefaulted );
BOOL SetSecurityDescriptorDacl (
    PSECURITY_DESCRIPTOR pSecurityDescriptor,
    BOOL bDaclPresent, PACL pDacl, BOOL bDaclDefaulted );
BOOL SetSecurityDescriptorSacl (
    PSECURITY_DESCRIPTOR pSecurityDescriptor,
    BOOL bSaclPresent, PACL pSacl, BOOL bSaclDefaulted );
BOOL SetSecurityDescriptorGroup (
    PSECURITY_DESCRIPTOR pSecurityDescriptor,
    PSID pGroup, BOOL bGroupDefaulted );
BOOL SetSecurityDescriptorOwner (
    PSECURITY_DESCRIPTOR pSecurityDescriptor,
    PSID pOwner, BOOL bOwnerDefaulted );
```

It is very tempting to access the SECURITY_DESCRIPTOR structure directly, and trust me, it has been done many times, both accidentally and intentionally. Because of this, it is necessary to validate every security descriptor that is received from an unknown source. The IsValidSecurityDescriptor provides exactly this functionality.

```
BOOL IsValidSecurityDescriptor (
    PSECURITY_DESCRIPTOR pSecurityDescriptor );
```

Security descriptors are attached to securable objects. Most developers have probably passed them up many times when they create new NT objects. A partial list of the Win32 API functions that require or optionally require security descriptor parameters is shown in the following:

- CreateDirectory
- CreateDirectoryEx
- CreateEvent
- CreateFile
- CreateFileMapping
- CreateMailslot
- CreateMutex
- CreateNamedPipe

- CreatePipe
- CreatePrivateObjectSecurity
- CreateProcess
- CreateProcessAsUser
- CreateRemoteThread
- CreateSemaphore
- CreateThread
- CreateWaitableTimer
- DestroyPrivateObjectSecurity
- GetFileSecurity
- GetKernelObjectSecurity
- GetPrinter
- GetPrivateObjectSecurity
- GetUserObjectSecurity
- NetShareGetInfo
- NetShareSetInfo
- QueryServiceObjectSecurity
- RegGetKeySecurity
- RegSetKeySecurity
- SetFileSecurity
- SetKernelObjectSecurity
- SetPrinter
- SetPrivateObjectSecurity
- SetServiceObjectSecurity
- SetUserObjectSecurity

A very common security task is securing access to a file. A file can be secured during the call to the CreateFile function by passing an appropriate SECURITY_DESCRIPTOR. But a file can also be secured later by calling the GetFileSecurity and SetFileSecurity functions.

The last two members of the SECURITY_DESCRIPTOR structure are Access Control Lists (ACLs). Both the Security ACL and the Discretionary ACL have the same format.

```
typedef struct _ACL
{
```

```
    UCHAR AclRevision;
    UCHAR Sbz1;
    USHORT AclSize;
    USHORT AceCount;
    USHORT Sbz2;
} ACL;
```

The AclRevision member of the ACL structure is 2, not 1. And, again, the Sbz1 member is filler to pad the Revision to a full 16-bit WORD.

```
#define ACL_REVISION   (2)
```

The AclSize is the length in bytes of the ACL structure. Note again that I've only provided the structure of the fixed portion of the ACL. The AclSize provides an easy mechanism for managing the length in bytes of the variable-length ACL. The AceCount is the number of ACEs contained within the ACL variable-length structure. Since the fixed-length portion of the ACL structure does not fall exactly with a 32-bit DWORD boundary, the Sbz2 member is appended to pad the structure from 48 to 64 bits in length.

The ACLs are lists of SIDs and rights that determine how security principals may interact with the securable object. The individual items of the list are called Access Control Entries (ACEs). The list of ACEs begins immediately after the fixed-portion of the ACL structure.

Access Control Entries

The ACE structure is divided into halves, the ACE header and body.

```
typedef struct _ACE_HEADER {
    BYTE AceType;
    BYTE AceFlags;
    WORD AceSize;
} ACE_HEADER;
```

The ACE header has three members. The first is the AceType, which indicates the type of the ACE. The type can then be used to determine the content of the ACE's body.

```
//  The following are the predefined ace types that go into the
//  AceType field of an Ace header.
#define ACCESS_ALLOWED_ACE_TYPE          (0x0)
#define ACCESS_DENIED_ACE_TYPE           (0x1)
#define SYSTEM_AUDIT_ACE_TYPE            (0x2)
#define SYSTEM_ALARM_ACE_TYPE            (0x3)
```

The AceFlags member is a bit mask that indicates very low level details about the ACE.

```
//  The following are the inherit flags that go into the
//  AceFlags field of an Ace header.
#define OBJECT_INHERIT_ACE              (0x1)
#define CONTAINER_INHERIT_ACE           (0x2)
#define NO_PROPAGATE_INHERIT_ACE        (0x4)
#define INHERIT_ONLY_ACE                (0x8)
#define INHERITED_ACE                   (0x10)
#define VALID_INHERIT_FLAGS             (0x1F)
```

Just like the self-relative security descriptor and the ACL, the ACE is of varying length. The length in bytes of the ACE structure is indicated in the third member, AceSize.

The body of the ACE depends on the AceType member. Four ACE types are defined: access allowed, access denied, system audit, and system alarm.

```
typedef struct _ACCESS_ALLOWED_ACE {
    ACE_HEADER Header;
    ACCESS_MASK Mask;
    DWORD SidStart;
} ACCESS_ALLOWED_ACE;
typedef ACCESS_ALLOWED_ACE *PACCESS_ALLOWED_ACE;

typedef struct _ACCESS_DENIED_ACE {
    ACE_HEADER Header;
    ACCESS_MASK Mask;
    DWORD SidStart;
} ACCESS_DENIED_ACE;
typedef ACCESS_DENIED_ACE *PACCESS_DENIED_ACE;

typedef struct _SYSTEM_AUDIT_ACE {
    ACE_HEADER Header;
    ACCESS_MASK Mask;
    DWORD SidStart;
} SYSTEM_AUDIT_ACE;
typedef SYSTEM_AUDIT_ACE *PSYSTEM_AUDIT_ACE;

typedef struct _SYSTEM_ALARM_ACE {
    ACE_HEADER Header;
    ACCESS_MASK Mask;
    DWORD SidStart;
} SYSTEM_ALARM_ACE;
typedef SYSTEM_ALARM_ACE *PSYSTEM_ALARM_ACE;
```

Note that these structures actually contain the ACE header. The next field after the header is always the 32-bit access mask. After the access mask is the SID for the ACE. In these defined structures, the SID is presented as a DWORD. In fact, the SID is of varying length, as I indicated earlier in this chapter.

A full-access-allowed ACE could then be described in the pseudostructure in Listing 6.8.

```
typedef struct _ACCESS_ALLOWED_ACE {
  BYTE  AceType;
  BYTE  AceFlags;
  WORD  AceSize;
  ACCESS_MASK Mask;
  DWORD SidStart;
} ACCESS_ALLOWED_ACE;
```

Listing 6.8   Complete-access-allowed ACE.

All four ACE structures are identical, except in type name. The AceType member is one of the four types I've already defined (see Listing 6.9).

```
#define ACCESS_ALLOWED_ACE_TYPE    (0x0)
#define ACCESS_DENIED_ACE_TYPE     (0x1)
#define SYSTEM_AUDIT_ACE_TYPE      (0x2)
#define SYSTEM_ALARM_ACE_TYPE      (0x3)
```

Listing 6.9   ACE types.

The Mask member of the ACE structure is a bit mask of access rights.

```
//     typedef struct _ACCESS_MASK {
//          WORD   SpecificRights;
//          BYTE   StandardRights;
//          BYTE   AccessSystemAcl : 1;
//          BYTE   Reserved : 3;
//          BYTE   GenericAll : 1;
//          BYTE   GenericExecute : 1;
//          BYTE   GenericWrite : 1;
//          BYTE   GenericRead : 1;
//     } ACCESS_MASK;
```

All NT securable objects implement the three generic rights, GENERIC_READ, GENERIC_WRITE, and GENERIC_EXECUTE. The meaning of these rights depends entirely on the type of object being secured. Their meaning is quite obvious for files. Reading, writing, and executing files is easily understood. But the three generic rights do not always have obvious meaning. That is, it is not obvious what is meant by, for example, executing a printer.

There are also five standard rights: DELETE, READ_CONTROL, WRITE_DAC, WRITE_OWNER, and SYNCHRONIZE. Listing 6.10 shows a complete list of the NT Security predefined rights.

```
#define DELETE                       (0x00010000L)
#define READ_CONTROL                 (0x00020000L)
#define WRITE_DAC                    (0x00040000L)
#define WRITE_OWNER                  (0x00080000L)
#define SYNCHRONIZE                  (0x00100000L)
#define STANDARD_RIGHTS_REQUIRED     (0x000F0000L)
#define STANDARD_RIGHTS_READ         (READ_CONTROL)
#define STANDARD_RIGHTS_WRITE        (READ_CONTROL)
#define STANDARD_RIGHTS_EXECUTE      (READ_CONTROL)
#define STANDARD_RIGHTS_ALL          (0x001F0000L)
#define SPECIFIC_RIGHTS_ALL          (0x0000FFFFL)
#define ACCESS_SYSTEM_SECURITY       (0x01000000L)
#define MAXIMUM_ALLOWED              (0x02000000L)
#define GENERIC_READ                 (0x80000000L)
#define GENERIC_WRITE                (0x40000000L)
#define GENERIC_EXECUTE              (0x20000000L)
#define GENERIC_ALL                  (0x10000000L)
```

Listing 6.10   Generic and standard rights.

In addition to standard and generic rights, an object may also implement up to 16 specific rights. As an example, COM implements exactly one additional specific right, COM_RIGHTS_EXECUTE.

```
#define COM_RIGHTS_EXECUTE 1
```

The generic access rights often overlap the specific access rights. It is often understood that having GENERIC_READ access implies having a set of specific access rights. In order to encapsulate this concept into NT's security framework, NT allows developers to map the meaning of the three generic rights.

```
typedef struct _GENERIC_MAPPING {
    ACCESS_MASK GenericRead;
    ACCESS_MASK GenericWrite;
    ACCESS_MASK GenericExecute;
    ACCESS_MASK GenericAll;
} GENERIC_MAPPING;
```

In other words, if objects have generic read access rights, what specific rights does this imply? These types of mappings make it much easier to configure securable objects that have a large amount of specific rights. The operator can configure these rights using the simple approach of assigning read, write, and execute rights. Or the operator can give more fine-grain access rights control by turning the individual-specific rights on and off.

Remember that these structures may change at any time and developers should not modify the structure directly. Always use the provided functions to manipulate an ACE. The ACE accessor and setter functions are shown in Listing 6.11.

```
BOOL AddAccessAllowedAce ( PACL pAcl,
    DWORD dwAceRevision, DWORD AccessMask, PSID pSid );
BOOL AddAccessDeniedAce ( PACL pAcl,
    DWORD dwAceRevision, DWORD AccessMask, PSID pSid );
BOOL AddAce ( PACL pAcl, DWORD dwAceRevision,
    DWORD dwStartingAceIndex, LPVOID pAceList,
    DWORD nAceListLength );
BOOL AddAuditAccessAce( PACL pAcl, DWORD dwAceRevision,
    DWORD dwAccessMask, PSID pSid,
    BOOL bAuditSuccess, BOOL bAuditFailure );
BOOL DeleteAce ( PACL pAcl, DWORD dwAceIndex );
BOOL GetAce ( PACL pAcl, DWORD dwAceIndex, LPVOID *pAce );
BOOL GetAclInformation ( PACL pAcl, LPVOID pAclInformation,
    DWORD nAclInformationLength,
    ACL_INFORMATION_CLASS dwAclInformationClass );
BOOL InitializeAcl ( PACL pAcl, DWORD nAclLength,
    DWORD dwAclRevision );
BOOL IsValidAcl ( PACL pAcl );
BOOL SetAclInformation ( PACL pAcl, LPVOID pAclInformation,
    DWORD nAclInformationLength,
    ACL_INFORMATION_CLASS dwAclInformationClass );
```

Listing 6.11 ACE access and set functions.

Now that I've confused most readers with the details of the NT security objects, I'll present them with an easy choice. They can try and manage these structures and develop secure applications which call these structures using their encapsulation functions. Or they can use the ATL security descriptor class and leave all these details in the dust.

One of the best classes presented in the ATL class library is its security descriptor helper class. This class, presented in Listing 6.12, provides a large amount of insulation from the details that I've just described.

I still think it is important for readers to understand these basic security structures, but developing software with them can be quite a task. However, the CSecurityDescriptor class removes a lot of the headache from NT Security. The first thing to note is that this class can be found in atlcom.h header file. The class is presented in full with all functions provided inline within this header file. For presentation's sake, I've excluded most of those details in the preceding listing.

```
class CSecurityDescriptor
{
public:
 CSecurityDescriptor();
 ~CSecurityDescriptor();
 HRESULT Attach(PSECURITY_DESCRIPTOR pSelfRelativeSD);
 HRESULT AttachObject(HANDLE hObject);
 HRESULT Initialize();
 HRESULT InitializeFromProcessToken(
          BOOL bDefaulted = FALSE);
 HRESULT InitializeFromThreadToken(BOOL bDefaulted = FALSE,
          BOOL bRevertToProcessToken = TRUE);
 HRESULT SetOwner(PSID pOwnerSid, BOOL bDefaulted = FALSE);
 HRESULT SetGroup(PSID pGroupSid, BOOL bDefaulted = FALSE);
 HRESULT Allow(LPCTSTR pszPrincipal, DWORD dwAccessMask);
 HRESULT Deny(LPCTSTR pszPrincipal, DWORD dwAccessMask);
 HRESULT Revoke(LPCTSTR pszPrincipal);

    operator PSECURITY_DESCRIPTOR()
};
```

Listing 6.12   ATL security descriptor class.

Using the CSecurityDescriptor class is quite easy. For instance, all I have to do is create the object. Initialize it to some default state using one of the three provided initialization methods. Then, finally, call SetOwner, SetGroup, Allow, Deny, and Revoke to modify the security descriptor as I see fit. A very simple example is provided in Listing 6.13.

```
CSecurityDescriptor sd;
sd.InitializeFromThreadToken( );
sd.Allow("KBCAFE\\rmorin", GENERIC_ALL);
```

Listing 6.13   Using CSecurityDescriptor.

This example would initialize the security descriptor with the group and owner of the current thread and a NULL DACL. Remember that the NULL DACL allows open access. Then I modify the DACL to allow specific access to some username. By adding the one ACE to the DACL, I disallow all access except to the one specified user. This is because the DACL is no longer NULL.

Token

When I boot my NT machine, pop! upon my screen is presented a dialog that asks me for my username and password. This dialog is called the winlogon dialog. I enter my username and password, called credentials. But what is this logon dialog and what service pops this up on the desktop? The logon dialog is presented by a service called winlogon. When I enter my credentials into the winlogon dialog, the service presents these credentials to the Security Service Provider (SSP). The SSP is usually the NT LAN Manager (NTLM), which returns an access token in exchange for my validated security credentials. The access token is then used by all processes and threads created by the user. A set of functions is available that allows programmers to read and manipulate tokens.

```
BOOL OpenProcessToken ( HANDLE ProcessHandle,
    DWORD DesiredAccess, PHANDLE TokenHandle );
BOOL OpenThreadToken ( HANDLE ThreadHandle,
    DWORD DesiredAccess, BOOL OpenAsSelf,
    PHANDLE TokenHandle );
```

To acquire the token for a process or thread, I can use the OpenProcessToken and OpenThreadToken functions.

```
BOOL DuplicateToken( HANDLE ExistingTokenHandle,
    SECURITY_IMPERSONATION_LEVEL ImpersonationLevel,
    PHANDLE DuplicateTokenHandle );
```

A token can be copied using the DuplicateToken function.

```
BOOL GetTokenInformation ( HANDLE TokenHandle,
    TOKEN_INFORMATION_CLASS TokenInformationClass,
    LPVOID TokenInformation, DWORD TokenInformationLength,
    PDWORD ReturnLength );
```

Token information can be retrieved using the GetTokenInformation function.

```
BOOL SetTokenInformation ( HANDLE TokenHandle,
    TOKEN_INFORMATION_CLASS TokenInformationClass,
    LPVOID TokenInformation, DWORD TokenInformationLength );
BOOL AdjustTokenPrivileges ( HANDLE TokenHandle,
    BOOL DisableAllPrivileges, PTOKEN_PRIVILEGES NewState,
    DWORD BufferLength, PTOKEN_PRIVILEGES PreviousState,
    PDWORD ReturnLength );
BOOL AdjustTokenGroups ( HANDLE TokenHandle,
    BOOL ResetToDefault, PTOKEN_GROUPS NewState,
    DWORD BufferLength, PTOKEN_GROUPS PreviousState,
    PDWORD ReturnLength );
```

Token information can be modified using the SetTokenInformation, Adjust-TokenPrivileges, and AdjustTokenGroups functions.

Local System Account

NT Security has a special type of account called the local system account. The local system account is used to run NT Services. As this is a book about NT Services, the local system account is especially important in this chapter about security. The advantages of using the local system account when programming NT Services are enormous. But with advantages come disadvantages.

The big advantage of the local system account is that almost all securable objects on a local machine are configured for full access by the local system account. This configuration is invaluable as developers are almost assured that no additional configuration is necessary when accessing security objects on the local machine.

On the other hand, the local system account does not have credentials for authenticating itself on remote machines. This implies that it cannot gain access to any network resources. Period. But there are techniques for allowing services running under the local system account to access networked resources.

Security Service Provider Interface

Quite often developers talk about using NT Security. Well, that really doesn't mean that much. A statement like that needs to be qualified with either, "I'm using NTLM security," or "I'm using SSPI." NT 4.0 security is really the calls through the Security Service Provider Interface (SSPI) to the NT LAN Manager (NTLM) security.

Kerberos

The default security provider for Windows 2000 will no longer by NTLM, but will be Kerberos. Developers should be prepared to see a difference in security in Windows 2000. They'll log on and do a whole bunch of things and then think to themselves, "Wait, this looks and feels exactly like NTLM." That's because everything is happening through the SSPI interface and the change from NTLM to Kerberos should be very transparent.

Kerberos was born at the Massachusetts Institute of Technology. Since its birth, it's gone through a few revisions and the current version is called Kerberos 5. The standard is recognized by the IETF (Internet Engineering Task Force) under the name RFC (Request For Comments) 1510. This standard may be reviewed on the Web at www.ietf.org/rfc/rfc1510.txt.

Kerberos provides three unique security services: authentication, data integrity, and data privacy.

Authentication is the process of validating the identity of a user. When a user logs in using winlogon, the password is hashed into an encryption key. The client prepares a request for a Ticket Granting Ticket (TGT). The Key Distribution Center (KDC) receives the request. The KDC returns a TGT and a session key which is used for sending data between the client and the KDC. The TGT is encrypted with the private key of the KDC. Because it is encrypted using this private key, the client cannot decrypt the TGT. But the encrypted TGT can be used in the future to validate the client's identity with the KDC. The session key is encrypted with the client's hashed password. This is what guarantees that the client cannot acquire the session key without knowing the correct password. If the session key cannot be decrypted, then the logon fails, that is, wrong password. This process is depicted in Figure 6.4.

Now, if the client wants to prove its identity to a server other than the KDC, the client sends the new request encrypted with the KDC session key and the TGT back to the KDC. The KDC then prepares a ticket authenticating the client encrypted with the server's hashed password and a new session key encrypted with the KDC session key. Finally, the client sends the authentication ticket and new request encrypted with the new session key to the server. This process is depicted in Figure 6.5.

Data integrity is the process of validating that data was not modified while in transit between the source and destination. Once a session key is established between a client and server, the session key can be used to create a checksum encrypted with the session key. Any attempt to modify the data in transmission will invalidate the encrypted checksum. The checksum can then be used to verify that the data was not modified while in transit.

Data privacy is the process of encrypting data so that it cannot be interpreted by sources other than the source and destination. To provide for data privacy, all data transmitted between the client and server is encrypted using the session key. Because only the client, server, and KDC know the session key, no other servers can decrypt the data.

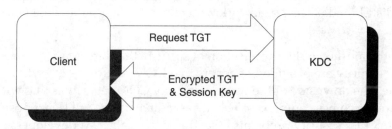

Figure 6.4   Kerberos user authentication.

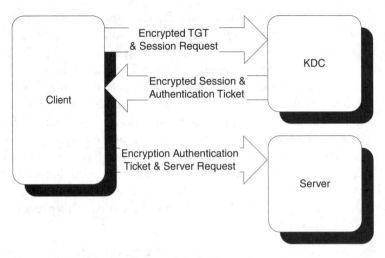

Figure 6.5 Kerberos client authentication.

The schema I've described in the preceding few paragraphs uses private key encryption. Kerberos is also capable of using public key encryption. Public key encryption uses a mathematical formula that allows one public key to encrypt data, but not to decrypt the data. Another secret key can be used to decrypt the data. This allows the source to encrypt data with a publicly available key without compromising the data privacy. The destination then uses its secret key to decrypt the data when received.

COM Security

Microsoft distributed technologies revolve around their COM framework. It is very important that such distributed technologies as COM are secure. For this reason, Microsoft introduced security to the COM protocol with the introduction of DCOM. In fact, the original release of DCOM had two specific enhancements to COM: COM could then be used in a distributed application and COM had security. These technologies were introduced together since a distributed object framework would be of little use if it were not secured.

COM is the most complete application of security that I'm aware of. Several layers of security are provided to ensure that COM security is everything to everyone. The downside of the completeness of COM security is that with completeness comes complexity. The neverending stream of Usenet posts related to COM security problems is scaring potential COM developers into using less complex and less complete technologies.

There are two ways of configuring a COM server. It can be configured using such tools as DCOMCNFG and OLEView, or it can be configured programmatically by calling the COM library functions.

DCOMCNFG and OLEView

Processwide COM security can be configured using the DCOMCNFG and OLEView utilities. DCOMCNFG is installed on a machine during the typical installation of Windows NT. OLEView is not normally installed on a machine, but can be downloaded from Microsoft's COM Web site (www.microsoft.com/com).

DCOMCNFG allows developers to configure general security that will apply to all COM objects on the machine. The DCOMCNFG utility may be started by selecting Run from the Start menu, typing DCOMCNFG, and clicking the OK button.

Machinewide security defaults may be configured from the Default Properties and Default Security tabs. The Default Properties tab is shown in Figure 6.6.

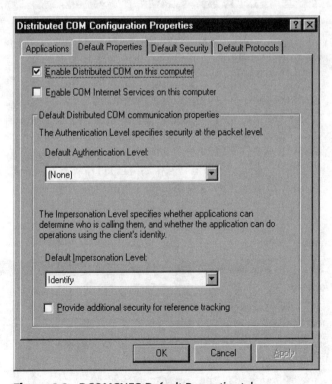

Figure 6.6   DCOMCNFG Default Properties tab.

From the Default Properties tab, developers can set three security-related properties: the Default Authentication Level, the Default Impersonation Level, and additional security for reference tracking. Each Default Authentication Level in the combo box is explained in Table 6.3.

Each Default Impersonation Level in the combo box is explained in Table 6.4.

If the Provide additional security for reference tracking checkbox is selected, then COM ensures that client calls to the AddRef and Release methods have some form of integrity, that is, that a client does not call the Release method more times than it calls the AddRef method.

As mentioned earlier, NT authorization is resolved using ACLs. The ACLs for COM applications can be modified in the Default Security tab of DCOMC-NFG (see Figure 6.7).

From this tab, developers can modify the ACLs for Default Access Permissions, Default Launch Permissions, and Default Configuration Permissions.

Table 6.3 Authentication Levels

LEVEL	DESCRIPTION
None	No authentication. Equivalent to disabling COM security.
Connect	Authentication once during connection. Only available if transport is connection-oriented.
Call	Authentication for every RPC function call.
Packet	Authentication for every packet transmitted.
Packet Integrity	Authentication for every packet transmitted. Plus each packet is verified to ensure that it was not modified during the transport.
Packet Privacy	Authentication for every packet transmitted. Plus each packet is verified to ensure that is was not modified during the transport. Plus the packets are encrypted.

Table 6.4 Impersonation Levels

LEVEL	DESCRIPTION
Anonymous	Impersonation is not allowed.
Identity	Server may impersonate client, but only to acquire access rights, not to read the client's access rights.
Impersonate	Server may impersonate client to acquire access rights and to read the client's access rights.
Delegate	Same as Impersonate, but also allows cloaking.

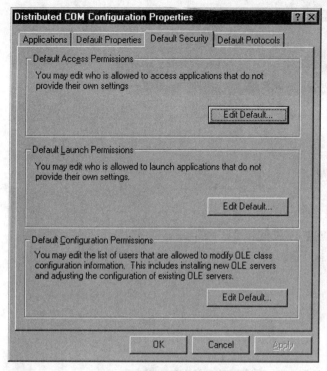

Figure 6.7 DCOMCNFG Default Security tab.

Each set of permissions can be modified by clicking the associated Edit Default button.

Access permissions allow a user to call methods on the object. Launch permissions allow a user to start up a COM application (EXE). The launch permissions are checked when a user creates an object whose application has not yet been launched. Configuration permissions allow a user to modify the access, launch, and configuration permissions.

TIP

Developers should avoid making the mistake of revoking too many default configuration permissions. Since configuration permissions are required to change the configuration permissions, they can find themselves in a situation where they (and many other users) no longer have permission to configure DCOM.

Clicking on the Edit Default button causes a Permissions dialog to appear (see Figure 6.8).

Using the Permissions dialog, developers can give and revoke access to particular users or user groups.

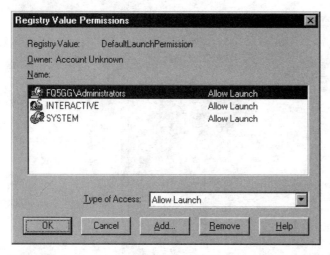

Figure 6.8 Permissions dialog.

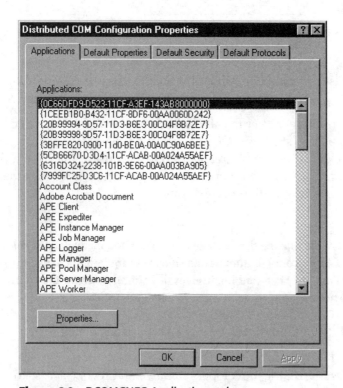

Figure 6.9 DCOMCNFG Applications tab.

DCOMCNFG also allows programmers to configure security specifically for an individual COM application. To configure application-specific COM security, they must double-click the COM application in the DCOMCNFG Applications tab (see Figure 6.9).

After double-clicking the COM application, the COM application-specific configuration property sheet appears (see Figure 6.10).

The initial General tab has only one configurable field, the Authentication Level. If this field is set to Default, then the value specified in the Default Properties tab will be used. Otherwise, the default value is overridden for this one COM application with the value specified in this field.

The second application tab that developers are concerned with is the Security tab (see Figure 6.11).

The Security tab allows operators to configure access, launch, and configuration permissions that override the default permissions specified in the Default Security tab. They can use the default security permissions by selecting the Use default permissions radio buttons. Or they can override the

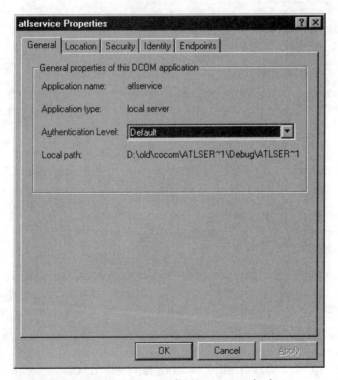

Figure 6.10 DCOMCNFG Application General tab.

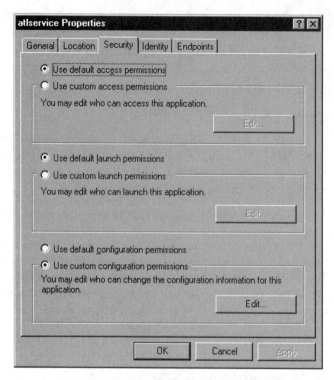

Figure 6.11 DCOMCNFG Application Security tab.

default by selecting the Use custom permissions radio buttons and clicking the Edit button. When they click the Edit button, they are presented with a permissions dialog.

Another way of modifying the security of a COM object is to change the identity (or credentials) used by the COM application. A server's identity may be changed using the Identity tab (see Figure 6.12).

Operators can run a COM application as the interactive user, the launching user, a specific user, or under the System Account. Only services can be configured to run using the System Account.

The *interactive user* is the user that owns the desktop, that is, the user who logged on to the machine. The *launching user* is the user that created the first object of the server and caused the COM application to be activated.

OLEView also allows developers to configure the access and launch permissions of a COM class. They may launch OLEView and select their COM class in the left pane of the OLEView utility. A set of tabs will be displayed for configuring the COM class (see Figure 6.13).

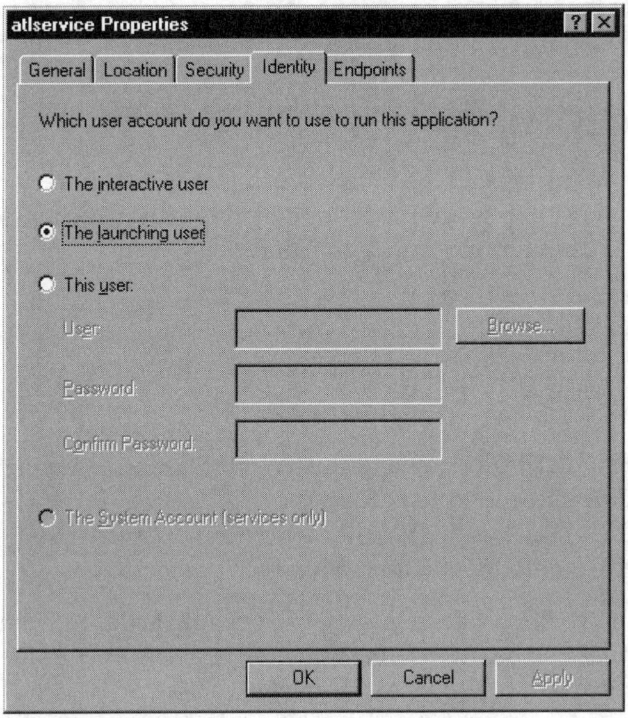

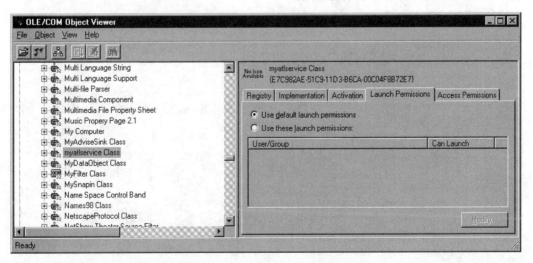

Figure 6.12 DCOMCNFG Application Identity tab.

Figure 6.13 OLE object permissions.

Developers can use the Launch Permissions and Access Permissions tabs to override the system default launch and access permissions.

Programmatic Security

A second way of configuring COM security is using the COM library functions. The first and most important function for configuring processwide COM security is the CoInitializeSecurity function.

```
HRESULT CoInitializeSecurity(PSECURITY_DESCRIPTOR pSecDesc,
 LONG cAuthSvc, SOLE_AUTHENTICATION_SERVICE *asAuthSvc,
 void *pReserved1, DWORD dwAuthnLevel, DWORD dwImpLevel,
 void *pReserved2, DWORD dwCapabilities,
     void *pReserved3 );
```

The SECURITY_DESCRIPTOR passed to the CoInitializeSecurity function is the ACL that will determine who can access the COM server. If the SECURITY_DESCRIPTOR's DACL is NULL, then everything is authorized; whereas if the DACL is zero length, then nobody is authorized.

The cAuthSvc and asAuthSvc parameters are used negotiate the authenticating-authorizing agent that will be used. Unless their objective is fine-grained security, developers rarely have to use these parameters. They can pass a –1 and NULL in place of these parameters to allow COM to select the authentication and authorization agent.

Ignoring the reserved parameters, the authentication and impersonation levels map to the authentication levels I used earlier with DCOMCNFG. I won't describe these levels again, but Listing 6.14 shows the constant values that can be passed to this function.

```
// authentication levels
#define RPC_C_AUTHN_LEVEL_DEFAULT 0
#define RPC_C_AUTHN_LEVEL_NONE 1
#define RPC_C_AUTHN_LEVEL_CONNECT 2
#define RPC_C_AUTHN_LEVEL_CALL 3
#define RPC_C_AUTHN_LEVEL_PKT 4
#define RPC_C_AUTHN_LEVEL_PKT_INTEGRITY 5
#define RPC_C_AUTHN_LEVEL_PKT_PRIVACY 6
// impersonation levels
#define RPC_C_IMP_LEVEL_ANONYMOUS      1
#define RPC_C_IMP_LEVEL_IDENTIFY       2
#define RPC_C_IMP_LEVEL_IMPERSONATE    3
#define RPC_C_IMP_LEVEL_DELEGATE       4
```

Listing 6.14 Authentication and impersonation constants.

The only other usable parameter of CoInitializeSecurity is the dwCapabilities. Typically I would pass EOAC_NONE, meaning no other capabilities required. But I may consider passing one or more of the other constants when security is very important.

```
typedef
enum tagEOLE_AUTHENTICATION_CAPABILITIES
{ EOAC_NONE = 0,
 EOAC_MUTUAL_AUTH = 0x1,
 EOAC_SECURE_REFS = 0x2,
 EOAC_ACCESS_CONTROL = 0x4
} EOLE_AUTHENTICATION_CAPABILITIES;
```

The SECURE_REFS constant is similar to the checkbox in the Default Properties tab of DCOMCNFG (see Figure 6.6).

The simple example of calling CoInitializeSecurity is to deny access to a COM server to everyone except one privileged user. Listing 6.15 presents this simple example.

```
CSecurityDescriptor sd;
sd.InitializeFromThreadToken( );
sd.Allow("KBCAFE\\rmorin", COM_RIGHTS_EXECUTE);
CoInitializeSecurity(sd, -1, NULL, NULL, RPC_C_AUTHN_LEVEL_PKT,
  RPC_C_IMP_LEVEL_IMPERSONATE, NULL, EOAC_NONE, NULL);
```

Listing 6.15 CoInitializeSecurity.

In this example, I've used the ATL security descriptor class to reduce the amount of code required. Note that I used the COM_RIGHTS_EXECUTE constant. As mentioned in the discussions on access rights, the COM_RIGHTS_EXECUTE access right is the one and only COM-specific right.

```
#define COM_RIGHTS_EXECUTE 1
```

Using the CoInitializeSecurity function allows developers to set processwide security. These settings override any security settings that may have been specified with DCOMCNFG or OLEView. Developers can also modify the security slightly from the COM server using the IServerSecurity interface (see Listing 6.16).

The first method of IServerSecurity interface, QueryBlanket, allows programmers to determine the security blanket that will be used for the method call. This may be different than the values specified in the call to the CoInitializeSecurity function because the COM run time will negotiate a security blanket with the client process. This negotiation usually leads to very little change

```
interface IServerSecurity : IUnknown
{
    HRESULT QueryBlanket
    (
        [out] DWORD    *pAuthnSvc,
        [out] DWORD    *pAuthzSvc,
        [out] OLECHAR **pServerPrincName,
        [out] DWORD    *pAuthnLevel,
        [out] DWORD    *pImpLevel,
        [out] void     **pPrivs,
        [out] DWORD    *pCapabilities
    );
    HRESULT ImpersonateClient();
    HRESULT RevertToSelf();
    BOOL IsImpersonating();
}
```

Listing 6.16   IServerSecurity IDL.

in the security blanket, but can result in tighter security, never looser security, than what may have been specified in the call to the CoInitializeSecurity function.

Programmers have to acquire the IServerSecurity interface using the CoGet-CallContent function before calling the methods of the IServerSecurity interface. This is done with the other method of the IServerSecurity interface, which is discussed in the next couple of paragraphs. But the GetBlanket method has a helper function that calls the GetBlanket method on behalf of the programmer. The helper function is called CoQueryClientBlanket and it removes the complexity of having to acquire the interface pointer. A CoQueryClientBlanket function has similar function to the code in Listing 6.17.

```
HRESULT CoQueryClientBlanket( DWORD* pAuthnSvc, DWORD* pAuthzSvc,
    OLECHAR ** pServerPrincName, DWORD * pAuthnLevel,
    DWORD * pImpLevel, RPC_AUTHZ_HANDLE * pPrivs,
    DWORD * pCapabilities)
{
 IServerSecurity * pss;
 ::CoGetCallContext(IID_IServerSecurity, (void **)&pss);
    HRESULT hresult = pss->QueryBlanket(pAuthnSvc, pAuthzSvc,
        pServerPrincName, pAuthnLevel, pImpLevel, pPrivs,
        pCapabilities);
 pss->Release();
 return hresult;
}
```

Listing 6.17   CoQueryClientBlanket.

The ImpersonateClient method takes zero parameters and allows the user to assume the identity of the calling client. Acquiring the IServerSecurity interface pointer and calling the function can be a little excessive, so Microsoft created a helper function called CoImpersonateClient. Although the contents of this function are unknown, developers can assume that it is similar to the code presented in Listing 6.18.

```
HRESULT CoImpersonateClient()
{
 IServerSecurity * pss;
 ::CoGetCallContext(IID_IServerSecurity, (void **)&pss);
 HRESULT hresult = pss->ImpersonateClient();
 pss->Release();
 return hresult;
}
```

Listing 6.18   CoImpersonateClient.

The RevertToSelf method is the opposite of the ImpersonateClient method. Normally, the application will assume the clients identity by calling the CoImpersonateClient function to perform some action on behalf of the client and revert back to its original identity by calling the CoRevertToSelf function. The CoRevertToSelf helper function can be assumed to be similar to the code presented in Listing 6.19.

```
HRESULT CoRevertToSelfClient()
 {
 IServerSecurity * pss;
 ::CoGetCallContext(IID_IServerSecurity, (void **)&pss);
 HRESULT hresult = pss->RevertToSelf();
 pss->Release();
 return hresult;
}
```

Listing 6.19   CoRevertToSelf.

Although there is not a CoIsImpersonating helper function that wraps calls to the IsImpersonating method of IServerSecurity, the code in Listing 6.20 can be used instead.

The IsImpersonating method returns TRUE, if the COM server is already impersonating a user, and FALSE otherwise.

The IServerSecurity can be called in the server to query the security blanket and to perform some impersonation. The IClientSecurity interface shown in Listing 6.21 is the equivalent interface that is used by the client.

```
BOOL CoIsImpersonating()
{
 IServerSecurity * pss;
 ::CoGetCallContext(IID_IServerSecurity, (void **)&pss);
 BOOL b = pss->IsImpersonating();
 pss->Release();
 return b;
}
```

Listing 6.20 CoIsImpersonating.

```
interface IClientSecurity : IUnknown
{
  HRESULT QueryBlanket
  (
      [in] IUnknown               *pProxy,
      [out] DWORD                 *pAuthnSvc,
      [out] DWORD                 *pAuthzSvc,
      [out] OLECHAR               **pServerPrincName,
      [out] DWORD                 *pAuthnLevel,
      [out] DWORD                 *pImpLevel,
      [out] void                  **pAuthInfo,
      [out] DWORD                 *pCapabilities
  );
  HRESULT SetBlanket
  (
      [in] IUnknown               *pProxy,
      [in] DWORD                   AuthnSvc,
      [in] DWORD                   AuthzSvc,
      [in] OLECHAR                *pServerPrincName,
      [in] DWORD                   AuthnLevel,
      [in] DWORD                   ImpLevel,
      [in] void                   *pAuthInfo,
      [in] DWORD                   Capabilities
  );
  HRESULT CopyProxy
  (
      [in] IUnknown *pProxy,
      [out] IUnknown **ppCopy
  );
}
```

Listing 6.21 IClientSecurity IDL.

The IClientSecurity interface is primarily concerned with querying and modifying the security blanket negotiated by the COM run time. The first method of the IClientSecurity interface, QueryBlanket is the equivalent of the Query-Blanket interface of the IServerSecurity interface. It allows programmers to query the security blanket that was negotiated for the particular proxy interface pointer.

The SetBlanket method allows programmers to renegotiate a new security blanket with a new set of input values. Before calling this method, programmers might consider first copying the proxy-interface pointer, as they'll be affecting all clients using the same proxy interface pointer. A proxy interface pointer may be copied using the last method, CopyProxy.

All three methods of the IClientSecurity interface have similar helper functions that remove the need to retrieve the interface pointer. These helper functions are CoQueryProxyBlanket, CoSetProxyBlanket, and CoCopyProxy. Again, the code behind these helper functions is not public, but is similar to the code shown in Listing 6.22.

```
HRESULT CoQueryProxyBlanket(IUnknown* pProxy, DWORD* pAuthnSvc,
    DWORD* pAuthzSvc, OLECHAR ** pServerPrincName,
    DWORD * pAuthnLevel, DWORD * pImpLevel,
    RPC_AUTH_IDENTITY_HANDLE* pAuthInfo,
    DWORD * pCapabilities)
{
 IClientSecurity * pss;
 ::CoGetCallContext(IID_IClientSecurity, (void **)&pss);
    HRESULT hresult = pss->QueryBlanket(pProxy, pAuthnSvc,
        pAuthzSvc, pServerPrincName, pAuthnLevel, pImpLevel,
        pAuthInfo, pCapabilities);
        pss->Release();
        return hresult;
}

HRESULT CoSetProxyBlanket(IUnknown * pProxy, DWORD dwAuthnSvc,
    DWORD dwAuthzSvc, WCHAR * pServerPrincName,
    DWORD dwAuthnLevel, DWORD dwImpLevel,
    RPC_AUTH_IDENTITY_HANDLE       pAuthInfo,
    DWORD dwCapabilities)
{
 IClientSecurity * pss;
 ::CoGetCallContext(IID_IClientSecurity, (void **)&pss);
    HRESULT hresult = pss->SetBlanket(pProxy, dwAuthnSvc,
```

Continues

Listing 6.22 IClientSecurity helper functions.

```
        dwAuthzSvc, pServerPrincName, dwAuthnLevel,
        dwImpLevel, pAuthInfo, dwCapabilities);
  pss->Release();
  return hresult;
};

HRESULT CoCopyProxy(IUnknown * pProxy, IUnknown ** ppCopy)
{
  IClientSecurity * pss;
  ::CoGetCallContext(IID_IClientSecurity, (void **)&pss);
      HRESULT hresult = pss->CopyProxy(pProxy, ppCopy);
  pss->Release();
  return hresult;
};
```

Listing 6.22   IClientSecurity helper functions. *(Continued)*

MTS Security

Another great feature added with Microsoft Transaction Server (MTS) was additional COM security. I can remember many times that people have asked me how to acquire the user name of the calling process because they wanted to perform some additional authorization.

In a distributed object environment, securing calls between objects can become very important. The solution was to impersonate the user and then find out its identity. The code in the solution was something similar to Listing 6.23.

```
std::string GetUserName()
{
  char buffer[UNLEN+1];
  DWORD dw = sizeof(buffer);
  ::CoImpersonateClient();
  ::GetUserName(buffer, &dw);
  ::CoRevertToSelf();
}
```

Listing 6.23   Impersonate and identify.

This solution had many limitations. In particular, users could only identify the one caller that they were also able to impersonate. This limitation does not exist in the new MTS security constructs. In MTS, the QueryInterface may be used to transform the IContextObject interface into an ISecurityProperty interface. The ISecurityProperty interface is shown in Listing 6.24.

```
interface ISecurityProperty : IUnknown
{
    HRESULT GetDirectCreatorSID(PSID __RPC_FAR *pSID);
    HRESULT GetOriginalCreatorSID(PSID __RPC_FAR *pSID);
    HRESULT GetDirectCallerSID(PSID __RPC_FAR *pSID);
    HRESULT GetOriginalCallerSID(PSID __RPC_FAR *pSID);
    HRESULT ReleaseSID(PSID pSID);
};
```

Listing 6.24   ISecurityProperty IDL.

Once this interface has been acquired, developers can acquire any of four
SIDs. (Remember that SIDs are unique identities of the security principals.)
By acquiring the SID, programmers can pretty much know all they need to
know in order to authorize the user. Listing 6.25 shows an example of using
the ISecurityProperty to display the calling user's SID.

```
void DisplaySID()
{
 IObjectContext * context;
 if (SUCCEEDED(::GetObjectContext(&context)))
 {
  ISecurityProperty * security;
  context->QueryInterface(IID_ISecurityProperty,
    (void **)&security);
  context->Release();
  PSID sid;
  security->GetDirectCallerSID(&sid);
  LPTSTR sz;
  ::ConvertSidToStringSid(sid, sz);
  std::cout << "SID = " << sz;
  ::LocalFree(sz);
  security->ReleaseSID(sid);
  security->Release();
 }
}
```

Listing 6.25   Display calling user SID.

Once the IObjectContext interface has been acquired, this interface can
be cast (using QueryInterface) into an ISecurityProperty interface. Then
any of the Get methods of ISecurityProperty may be called to perform
some authorization. To simplify this example, the SID is printed instead of
authorized.

The additional security that is provided through the ISecurityProperty interface is programmatic security. There is also another layer of declarative security in MTS that is not available in non-MTS classes. This security is made available in MTS Explorer. MTS components within packages contains a folder called Role Members. This is where the component's roles or membership in groups is defined.

Programmers can create new roles by right-clicking on the Roles folder in the package and selecting New | Role from the pop-up menu.

Summary

Okay, those readers who were scared of the dark can open their eyes now. I'm finished with this evil security subject.

Now I'll go into an important part of the development process, debugging. The book wasn't intended to get so gloomy near the end. (Hopefully, we can finish this last chapter without learning anything. We all know you developers are unfamiliar with such concepts as debugging, unit testing, and the like.)

Debugging

Debugging an NT Service tends to be a very complicated process. This is mainly caused by the fact that the startup code is only executed when the SCM starts the service. This obviously excludes the debugger from providing much feedback.

Another drawback when debugging NT Services is that they can run under the security context of the local system account user. Normally the debugger doesn't run under this security context, so it is sometimes difficult to simulate behavior that is security-related.

In this chapter, I explain all the little tricks that I've used over the years to debug NT Services. I've identified three techniques that help in debugging NT Services. The first technique is attaching the service at run time to a debugger. The second technique is using the Windows internal debug stream. The third technique is viewer network activity using a network monitor.

Using the Debugger

Just because a process cannot be started in the debugger doesn't mean it can't be imported into the debugger. In the next few sections, I demonstrate a few techniques for importing a running process into the debugger.

MsDev /P Command Line

The MsDev executable has a command-line switch that attaches the debugger to a running process. To attach a process to the debugger, the first thing I need to do is find the process ID of the running process. I can look up the process ID in the NT Task Manager (see Figure 7.1).

I can change the columns that are shown in the Processes tab of the Task Manager by selecting View | Select Columns from the menu bar. Once I've acquired the process ID, I can then start the debugger from a command prompt specifying process ID of the service I want to debug (see Figure 7.2).

I'm unsure why, but the command-line option to debug a process doesn't appear when you query for command-line help with the question mark switch. This technique works well but does require a lot of keystrokes to start the debugger. An even faster method is to task the debugger from the NT Task Manager.

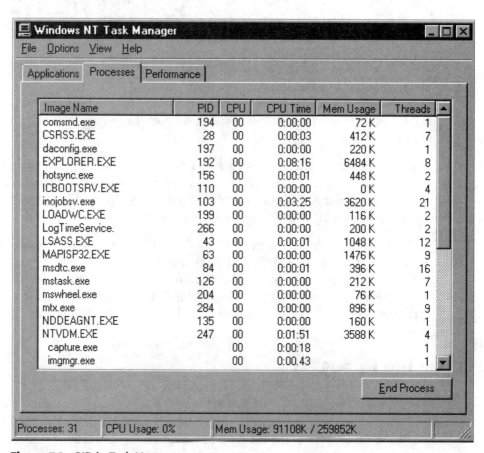

Figure 7.1 PID in Task Manager.

Figure 7.2 Start MsDev from the command line.

Debug from NT Task Manager

This technique only works if I have registered a default debugger. The advantage of this technique is that it is quick. I can simply right-click a process in the Processes tab of the Task Manager and select Debug and the debugger is started (see Figure 7.3).

A clear advantage of this technique is that it will work with most debuggers. Developers can simply configure their debuggers as the Windows default debugger. Most debuggers register themselves as the default debugger when they are installed.

MsDev Attach to Process

The Visual C++ IDE also provides a menu option for attaching to a running process. Select Build | Start Debug | Attach to Process from the menu bar (see Figure 7.4).

The Attach to Process dialog appears. Select the process to debug and click on OK (see Figure 7.5).

Users have to check the Show System Processes checkbox in order to view NT Services in the listview. If this checkbox is left unchecked, then they will not be able to see some of the processes, especially services. Select the process by name or process ID and click the OK button to begin debugging the process.

AT Commands

Attaching to an existing process is a good technique for debugging services. Especially when the problems are related to service-specific code or security

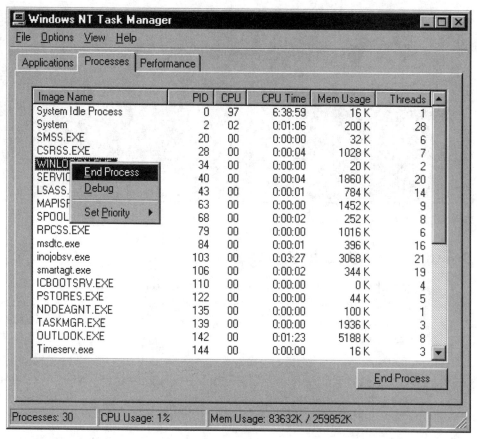

Figure 7.3 Debug from Task Manager.

problems because the service is running in the context of the Local System Account. But attaching to services can prove quite frustrating. Therefore, other techniques for debugging services are desired.

If developers know the problem is with running the service in the context of the Local System Account, another technique that can be used is to start MsDev with AT commands. How could this possibly help? The trick is the Task Scheduler which triggers AT commands usually runs under the Local System Account. In turn, all commands triggered by the Task Scheduler run under the Local System Account.

To run MsDev with the Task Scheduler, I can start a Command Prompt and add a task that will run the MsDev executable (see Figure 7.6). I schedule the task to run in one minute's time. I must also use the /INTERACTIVE command-line parameter. If I don't specify the /INTERACTIVE parameter, MsDev will run but the GUI will not be visible.

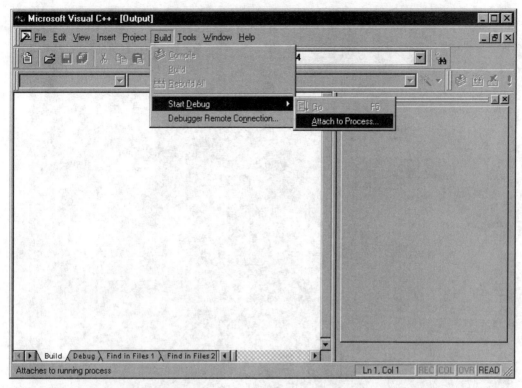

Figure 7.4 MsDev Attach to Process.

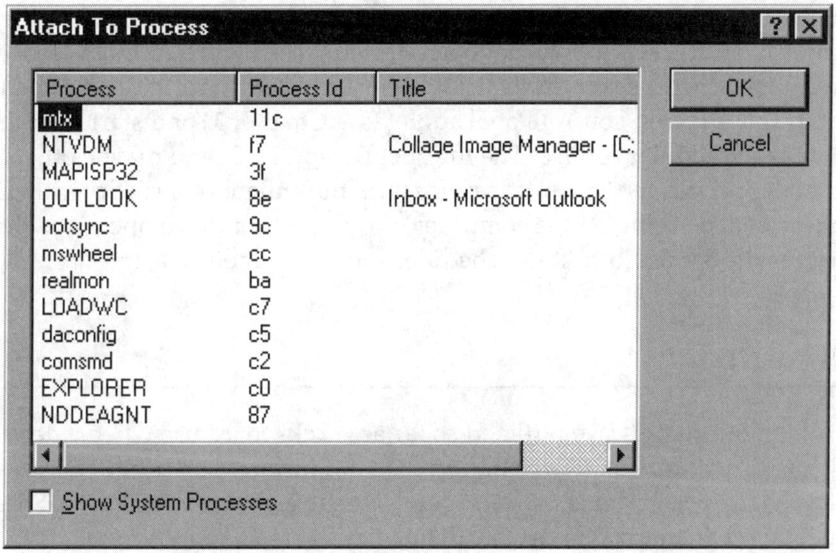

Figure 7.5 Attach To Process dialog.

Figure 7.6 Run MsDev using AT.

Sometimes when the AT commands are run, the system responds with the message, "The service has not been started" (see Figure 7.7). This is because the Task Scheduler service has not been started. To start the Task Scheduler, I start the Services Control Panel applet (see Chapter 1) and start the Schedule or Task Scheduler service. The Internet Explorer 5.0 (and maybe others) install replaces the Schedule service with the enhanced Task Scheduler service, so depending on the computer's configuration developers may have either the Schedule or Task Scheduler service on their machines.

Debug API

All the techniques I've outlined so far are tricks that I use when a debugger is available. Unfortunately, debuggers are not installed on production systems and many test systems. If I can't replicate the error on a system that has a debugger, then I use a portable debugger.

Figure 7.7 "The service has not been started" message.

Microsoft provides a small API for writing debuggers in Windows NT. I describe various functions of this API in this section. I explain only a subset of this API, the part of the API that is easily used in order to perform portable debugging.

Debug Stream Viewer

Not many developers are familiar with the OutputDebugString function, but I'm sure they've called many of the TRACE macros that exist in ATL and MFC.

```
VOID OutputDebugString(LPCTSTR lpOutputString);
```

Most of these TRACE macros are defined as calls to the OutputDebugString function. Listing 7.1 shows the definitions that convert an ATLTRACE macro call to an OutputDebugString function call.

These TRACE macro calls, which are calls to OutputDebugString, magically appear in the debug window. This magic is accomplished using Windows NT's debugging API.

DBMON is a great utility that Microsoft wrote that captures all TRACE statements sent with the OutputDebugString function using the debugging API.

```
#define ATLTRACE            AtlTrace
inline void _cdecl AtlTrace(LPCWSTR lpszFormat, ...)
{
    va_list args;
    va_start(args, lpszFormat);
    int nBuf;
    WCHAR szBuffer[512];
    nBuf = _vsnwprintf(szBuffer,
         sizeof(szBuffer) / sizeof(WCHAR), lpszFormat, args);
    ATLASSERT(nBuf < sizeof(szBuffer));
    OutputDebugStringW(szBuffer);
    va_end(args);
}
```

Listing 7.1 ATLTRACE definitions.

Readers shouldn't worry about downloading or installing this utility because in the next few pages I demonstrate how to write a custom debug stream viewer.

A call to OutputDebugString is directed to either the local process debugger or to the systemwide debugger. If a process debugger is attached, then the call to OutputDebugString will be directed to the debugger that attached to the process using either CreateProcess or DebugActiveProcess. Otherwise, calls to OutputDebugString are directed to a systemwide debugger. The implementation of the OutputDebugString function is private, but the code that directs the calls to the system debugger can be roughly estimated as something similar to the code in Listing 7.2.

The systemwide debugger works with three named objects. The DBWIN_BUFFER named file map is used to transfer content between the process that called the OutputDebugString function and the systemwide debugger. The DBWIN_BUFFER_READY named event is signaled when the systemwide debugger is ready to receive content. The DBWIN_DATA_READY named event is signaled when the DBWIN_BUFFER file map has content ready to be transferred from the process calling OutputDebugString to the systemwide debugger.

Now that I have the client portion of this protocol, I can determine the server portion of this protocol. Listing 7.3 shows an implementation of this simple systemwide debugger.

It is important that I initialize a new SECURITY_DESCRIPTOR with loose permissions, so that all other processes have complete access to the named objects.

```
VOID OutputDebugString(LPCTSTR output)
{
    HANDLE bufferready = ::OpenEvent(EVENT_MODIFY_STATE, FALSE,
        "DBWIN_BUFFER_READY");
    if (bufferready == NULL)
    {
        return;
    }

    HANDLE dataready = ::OpenEvent(EVENT_MODIFY_STATE, FALSE,
        "DBWIN_DATA_READY");
    if (dataready == NULL)
    {
        ::CloseHandle(bufferready);
        return;
    }

    HANDLE buffer = ::OpenFileMapping(FILE_MAP_ALL_ACCESS,
        TRUE, "DBWIN_BUFFER");
    if (buffer == NULL)
    {
        ::CloseHandle(bufferready);
        ::CloseHandle(dataready);
        return;
    }

    LPSTR memory = (LPSTR)::MapViewOfFile(buffer,
        FILE_MAP_WRITE, 0, 0, 4096);
    if (memory == NULL)
    {
        ::CloseHandle(buffer);
        ::CloseHandle(bufferready);
        ::CloseHandle(dataready);
        return;
    }

    ::WaitForSingleObject(bufferready, INFINITE);
    *((DWORD*) memory) = ::GetCurrentProcessId();
    ::wsprintf(memory + sizeof(DWORD), "%s", output);
    ::SetEvent(dataready);

    ::UnmapViewOfFile(memory);
    ::CloseHandle(buffer);
    ::CloseHandle(bufferready);
    ::CloseHandle(dataready);
    return;
}
```

Listing 7.2   OutputDebugString implementation.

```cpp
int main( int argc, char ** argv )
{
    SECURITY_ATTRIBUTES sa;
    SECURITY_DESCRIPTOR sd;
    sa.nLength = sizeof(SECURITY_ATTRIBUTES);
    sa.bInheritHandle = TRUE;
    sa.lpSecurityDescriptor = &sd;

    std::cerr << "**********************\n"
                 "Debug Monitor Started\n"
                 "**********************\n";

    if(::InitializeSecurityDescriptor(&sd,
            SECURITY_DESCRIPTOR_REVISION) == FALSE)
    {
        std::cout << "InitializeSecurityDescriptor failed"
            << std::endl;
        return 1;
    }

    if(::SetSecurityDescriptorDacl(&sd, TRUE, (PACL)NULL,
        FALSE)
            == FALSE)
    {
        std::cout << "SetSecurityDescriptorDacl failed"
            << std::endl;
        return 1;
    }

    HANDLE bufferready = ::CreateEvent(&sa, FALSE, FALSE,
                                    "DBWIN_BUFFER_READY");
    if (bufferready == NULL)
    {
        std::cout << "CreateEvent failed" << std::endl;
        return 1;
    }

    if (GetLastError() == ERROR_ALREADY_EXISTS)
    {
        std::cout << "Debugger Already Running" << std::endl;
        return 1;
    }

    HANDLE dataready = ::CreateEvent(&sa, FALSE, FALSE,
                                    "DBWIN_DATA_READY");
    if (dataready == NULL)
    {
        std::cout << "CreateEvent failed" << std::endl;
        ::CloseHandle(bufferready);
```

Continues

Listing 7.3 Debug stream viewer.

```
        return 1;
}

HANDLE buffer = ::CreateFileMapping(INVALID_HANDLE_VALUE,
    &sa, PAGE_READWRITE, 0, 4096, "DBWIN_BUFFER");
if (buffer == NULL)
{
    std::cout << "CreateFileMapping failed" << std::endl;
    ::CloseHandle(bufferready);
    ::CloseHandle(dataready);
    return 1;
}

void * str = ::MapViewOfFile(buffer, FILE_MAP_READ, 0, 0,
                             4096);

if (str == NULL)
{
    std::cout << "MapViewOfFile failed" << std::endl;
    ::CloseHandle(bufferready);
    ::CloseHandle(dataready);
    ::CloseHandle(buffer);
    return 1;
}

char * string = (char *)str + sizeof(DWORD);
DWORD lastpid = 0xffffffff;
bool cr = true;

while (true)
{
    if (::SetEvent(bufferready) == FALSE)
    {
        std::cout << "SetEvent failed" << std::endl;
        ::CloseHandle(bufferready);
        ::CloseHandle(dataready);
        ::UnmapViewOfFile(str);
        ::CloseHandle(buffer);
        return 1;
    };

    if (::WaitForSingleObject(dataready, INFINITE)
        != WAIT_OBJECT_0)
    {
        break;
    }
    else
    {
        DWORD pid = *(DWORD *)str;
```

Continues

Listing 7.3

```
                    if (lastpid != pid)
                    {
                        lastpid = pid;
                        if (!cr)
                        {
                            std::cerr << std::endl;
                            cr = true;
                        }
                    }

                    if (cr)
                    {
                        std::cerr << lastpid << ":";
                    }
                    std::cerr << (char*)string;
                    cr = (*string &&
                        (string[::strlen(string) - 1] == '\n'));
            }
        }

        std::cout << "WaitForSingleObject failed" << std::endl;
        ::CloseHandle(bufferready);
        ::CloseHandle(dataready);
        ::UnmapViewOfFile(str);
        ::CloseHandle(buffer);
        return 1;
    };
```

Listing 7.3 Debug stream viewer *(Continued).*

```
if(::InitializeSecurityDescriptor(&sd,
    SECURITY_DESCRIPTOR_REVISION) == FALSE)
{
    return 1;
}
if(::SetSecurityDescriptorDacl(&sd, TRUE, (PACL)NULL,
    FALSE) == FALSE)
{
    return 1;
}
```

Note that the DACL was set to NULL. As I explained in Chapter 6, a NULL DACL allows unrestricted access to the object. I require unrestricted access since all processes and threads are going to partake in sending debug strings via the OutputDebugString function.

Next, I create named objects using the SECURITY_DESCRIPTOR to make them available to all other processes. To create a named event, I call CreateEvent, and to create a named file map, I call CreateFileMapping. When I create the file named event, the function may succeed even though the named event already exists. I verify that I created and not opened the event by checking the GetLastError function. If this function returns ERROR_ALREADY_EXISTS, then my call to CreateEvent opened an existing named event and did not create a new named event. This is likely caused by already having a systemwide debugger running.

```
HANDLE bufferready = ::CreateEvent(&sa, FALSE, FALSE,
                            "DBWIN_BUFFER_READY");
if (GetLastError() == ERROR_ALREADY_EXISTS)
{
return 1;
}
HANDLE dataready = ::CreateEvent(&sa, FALSE, FALSE,
                            "DBWIN_DATA_READY");
HANDLE buffer = ::CreateFileMapping(INVALID_HANDLE_VALUE,
        &sa, PAGE_READWRITE, 0, 4096, "DBWIN_BUFFER");
```

Once these named resources are created, the next step is to create a view of the named file map. This is done using the MapViewOfFile. Both calls to CreateFileMapping and MapViewOfFile passed a maximum size of 4,096 because the protocol defines the map to be that size.

```
void * str = ::MapViewOfFile(buffer, FILE_MAP_READ, 0, 0, 4096);
```

Now that I've created all the necessary resources, I can loop endlessly reading all the debug messages. Setting the DBWIN_BUFFER_READY event and waiting on the DBWIN_DATA_READY event will initiate the data transfer. The client, as seen in Listing 7.2, will wait on the DBWIN_BUFFER_READY event. When the client receives this event, it will push data onto the DBWIN_BUFFER file map and set the DBWIN_DATA_READY event. This will trigger the debugger into processing the DBWIN_BUFFER file map. When the debugger is finished processing, it sets the DBWIN_BUFFER_READY event and continues in the loop.

```
while (true)
{
    if (::SetEvent(bufferready) == FALSE)
    {
        return 1;
    };
    if (::WaitForSingleObject(dataready, INFINITE)
            != WAIT_OBJECT_0)
    {
        break;
    }
        else
        {
            // do stuff with message
        }
}
```

This debugger is a great tool, especially for those on-site troubleshooting sessions. But like any tool, it is only useful when used properly. This means that the application should call OutputDebugString strategically in order to aid troubleshooting. If OutputDebugString is not called, then the debug stream viewer will be of little use.

NOTE

The systemwide debugger will not receive events for processes that are attached to a process debugger.

Remember that the TRACE macros are usually defined as calls to Output-DebugString in debug builds only. In releases builds, TRACE macros are usually defined as nothing, in order to speed the application.

Error Handling

TRACE macro facilities are a convenient method of communicating errors to the developer. But in order to communicate the proper information to the developer or to the operator, proper error handling must be implemented.

Most readers are likely writing production application servers that need to be perfect. This means they should check every single return code for possible errors and catch every single exception that is thrown. Failing to check return codes and catch exceptions is the most widespread cause of nonreproducible bugs.

Failing to check return codes or catch exceptions typically causes an error in the following few function calls, not necessarily immediately, but sometime down the road. Eventually, some error is going to get reported in the error log, but the error log will likely only contain symptoms and not the root cause of the error. Although symptoms can sometimes point developers in the right direction, it is always easier for them to diagnose bugs when they know the root cause.

Exception Handling

Catch all exceptions. Somewhere in the processing, developers have to catch all exceptions using the ellipsis notation (see Listing 7.4).

Definition: Bugs

Nonreproducible bugs are bugs that are reported but, because of lack of information, the bugs remain unverified and unsolved.

```
try
{
    // Do Stuff
    // ...
}
catch(...)
{
    DoReportEvent("Unhandled Exception");
}
```

Listing 7.4 Catch all exceptions.

Although catching the unhandled exception provides no benefit to operators in terms of understanding why the error occurs, it does provide them with some ability to log the error, beyond simply popping up that annoying Unhandled exception message box (see Figure 7.8).

An important point to remember is that these unhandled exceptions are not handled very well by NT Services. Listing 7.5 is a snippet of code that produces an exception in the NT Service.

Running this service causes a dialog similar to the one in Figure 7.9 to pop up on some machines. In a production environment, it is unlikely that the operator will be watching the screen for such errors, so the application server might find itself disabled for a long period of time before the operator finds the time to check the display.

The code in Listing 7.6 catches the exception and terminates the thread after reporting the error.

This technique is a little better, since it does report the error in the error log rather than with a popup or debugger. But a technique even more superior is to anticipate the kinds of exceptions that can be caught and to report them with as much relevant description as possible. A very common type of exception is the Standard Template Library (STL) exception. Listing 7.7 on page 382 shows how to handle a specific exception and report a relevant description.

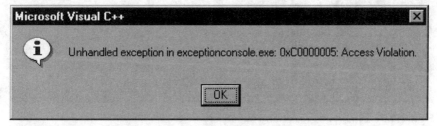

Figure 7.8 Unhandled exception message box.

```
class UnhandledExceptionService : public NtService::Service
{
public:
  UnhandledExceptionService()
     :NtService::Service("UnhandledExceptionService") {};
  virtual void OnRun()
  {
     ::Sleep(1000);
     std::string * p = NULL;
     p->c_str();
  }
};

int WINAPI WinMain(HINSTANCE hinstance,
  HINSTANCE /* hprevious */, LPSTR lpCmdLine, int /* nShowCmd */)
{
  UnhandledExceptionService().Start(lpCmdLine);
  return 0;
}
```

Listing 7.5 UnhandledExceptionService.

For testing purposes, I used the MessageBox function with the MB_SER-VICE_NOTIFICATION flag. This flag allows the NT Service to display message boxes on the desktop. Normally this would not be possible. I only recommend using this flag when developing code. In a production system, most developers should disable any calls to user interface (UI) objects in NT Services and report errors and problems in the NT Event Log. (I think I have repeated myself enough to convince you of this truth.)

GetLastError

Many Win32 API calls return a BOOL value that is TRUE when the function succeeds and FALSE when the function fails. Win32 factory-type functions

Figure 7.9 Unhandled exception in service.

```
class UnhandledExceptionService : public NtService::Service
{
public:
  UnhandledExceptionService()
     :NtService::Service("UnhandledExceptionService") {};
  virtual void OnRun()
  {
     try
     {
         ::Sleep(1000);
         std::string * p = NULL;
         p->c_str();
     }
     catch(...)
     {
         // Report the Error here
         // ...
     }
  }
};
```

Listing 7.6   Catch all exception handling.

return NULL when the function fails, instead of a handle. Whenever these errors occur, it is likely that the Win32 subsystem has a more complete description of the error than "it didn't work." This more complete error information is set using the SetLastError function.

```
VOID SetLastError( DWORD dwErrCode );
```

When SetLastError is called, the dwErrCode is set for the current thread using some form of TlsSetValue. The error value can later be retrieved by calling the GetLastError function.

```
DWORD GetLastError(VOID);
```

The DWORD that is set and retrieved using SetLastError and GetLastError has bit values that represent particular types of failures. The third most significant bit in the DWORD is set to zero by Win32 and one by all other servers calling SetLastError. This indicates to the client calling GetLastError whether the error is from the Win32 system or a client system. Failure to set this customer code bit can result in a client misinterpreting the error code.

FormatMessage

If an error code is a Win32 system error code, the error code can be easily turned into a human-readable error description by running it through the FormatMessage function (see Listing 7.8).

```
class UnhandledExceptionService : public NtService::Service
{
public:
  UnhandledExceptionService()
    :NtService::Service("UnhandledExceptionService") {};
  virtual void OnRun()
  {
    try
    {
        ::Sleep(1000);
        std::string str("Randy");
        str.substr(10, 200);
    }
    catch(std::exception & e)
    {
        // Report Event Here
        // Do not use MessageBox
        // Used only for demo purpose
        ::MessageBox(NULL, e.what(), "STL exception",
            MB_OK+MB_SERVICE_NOTIFICATION);
    }
    catch(...)
    {
        // Report Event Here
        // ...
    }
  }
};
```

Listing 7.7 Handling a common exception.

Debug Events

The debug stream viewer is a great portable debugger, but it is very limited in the information that it relays to the troubleshooter. If developers are not prepared to litter their programs with calls to the OutputDebugString function, then they might be interested in the portable debugger I describe in this next section.

In the previous section, I described the debug stream viewer utility as a systemwide debugger because it received debug events from all processes on a system. A process debugger uses a much more powerful set of functions (which can be found in the following list) that can retrieve a larger variety of information. But the process debugger is used to debug one process at a time and not on a systemwide basis.

- CreateProcess
- DebugActiveProcess

```
std::string GetLastErrorAndFormatMessage()
{
    DWORD dw = ::GetLastError();
    std::string str;
    if (dw && 0x20000000 == 0)
    {
        LPVOID lpMsgBuf = NULL;
        ::FormatMessage( FORMAT_MESSAGE_ALLOCATE_BUFFER |
            FORMAT_MESSAGE_FROM_SYSTEM |
            FORMAT_MESSAGE_IGNORE_INSERTS,
            NULL, dw, MAKELANGID(LANG_NEUTRAL,
            SUBLANG_DEFAULT), (LPTSTR) &lpMsgBuf, 0, NULL );
        str = static_cast<char *>(lpMsgBuf);
        ::LocalFree( lpMsgBuf );
    }
    return str;
};
```

Listing 7.8 Formatting Win32 error codes.

- WaitForDebugEvent
- ContinueDebugEvent

The CreateProcess and DebugActiveProcess functions are called from a debugger in order to debug a process being launched (CreateProcess) or a process that has already been launched (DebugActiveProcess).

Once I've attached the debugger to a process, I can then wait for debug events by calling the WaitForDebugEvent function. The WaitForDebugEvent function returns a DEBUG_EVENT structure that defines the event (See Listing 7.9).

```
typedef struct _DEBUG_EVENT {
    DWORD dwDebugEventCode;
    DWORD dwProcessId;
    DWORD dwThreadId;
    union {
        EXCEPTION_DEBUG_INFO Exception;
        CREATE_THREAD_DEBUG_INFO CreateThread;
        CREATE_PROCESS_DEBUG_INFO CreateProcessInfo;
        EXIT_THREAD_DEBUG_INFO ExitThread;
        EXIT_PROCESS_DEBUG_INFO ExitProcess;
        LOAD_DLL_DEBUG_INFO LoadDll;
        UNLOAD_DLL_DEBUG_INFO UnloadDll;
        OUTPUT_DEBUG_STRING_INFO DebugString;
        RIP_INFO RipInfo;
    } u;
} DEBUG_EVENT, *LPDEBUG_EVENT;
```

Listing 7.9 DEBUG_EVENT structure.

The dwProcessId and dwThreadId members are the process and thread IDs where this exception was thrown. The dwDebugEventCode member of DEBUG_EVENT is the debug event type and may be any of the constants defined in Listing 7.10.

```
#define EXCEPTION_DEBUG_EVENT        1
#define CREATE_THREAD_DEBUG_EVENT    2
#define CREATE_PROCESS_DEBUG_EVENT   3
#define EXIT_THREAD_DEBUG_EVENT      4
#define EXIT_PROCESS_DEBUG_EVENT     5
#define LOAD_DLL_DEBUG_EVENT         6
#define UNLOAD_DLL_DEBUG_EVENT       7
#define OUTPUT_DEBUG_STRING_EVENT    8
#define RIP_EVENT                    9
```

Listing 7.10 Debug event types.

The exception event is triggered with every exception regardless of whether the exception will be caught. The create thread and create process events are triggered when these resources are created, and the exit thread and exit process events are triggered as these resources are destroyed. The load and unload DLL events are triggered when new DLLs are loaded and old DLLs are unloaded. The output debug string event is triggered when the Output-DebugString function is called. The RIP event is not well documented.

The event type determines the union member of DEBUG_EVENT. For each of the event types, there is a different DEBUG_INFO structure (see Listing 7.11).

Developers might be tempted to use the lpImageName member of the LOAD_DLL_DEBUG_INFO structure to determine which DLLs are being loaded into the process. Unfortunately, this feature has been disabled in NT. It worked in Windows 95, but for one reason or another Microsoft has discontinued populating this field. Most debuggers determine the name of loaded DLLs by searching the module header of the loaded DLL for its filename.

The most interesting of the DEBUG_INFO structures is the EXCEPTION _DEBUG_INFO structure. The dwFirstChance member tells the debugger if it is the first time it has received this exception event. The ExceptionRecord member is an EXCEPTION_RECORD structure, shown in Listing 7.12.

The ExceptionCode member determines the exception type and may be any of the following exception constants:

- EXCEPTION_ACCESS_VIOLATION
- EXCEPTION_DATATYPE_MISALIGNMENT
- EXCEPTION_BREAKPOINT
- EXCEPTION_SINGLE_STEP

```
typedef struct _EXCEPTION_DEBUG_INFO {
    EXCEPTION_RECORD ExceptionRecord;
    DWORD dwFirstChance;
} EXCEPTION_DEBUG_INFO, *LPEXCEPTION_DEBUG_INFO;

typedef struct _CREATE_THREAD_DEBUG_INFO {
    HANDLE hThread;
    LPVOID lpThreadLocalBase;
    LPTHREAD_START_ROUTINE lpStartAddress;
} CREATE_THREAD_DEBUG_INFO, *LPCREATE_THREAD_DEBUG_INFO;

typedef struct _CREATE_PROCESS_DEBUG_INFO {
    HANDLE hFile;
    HANDLE hProcess;
    HANDLE hThread;
    LPVOID lpBaseOfImage;
    DWORD dwDebugInfoFileOffset;
    DWORD nDebugInfoSize;
    LPVOID lpThreadLocalBase;
    LPTHREAD_START_ROUTINE lpStartAddress;
    LPVOID lpImageName;
    WORD fUnicode;
} CREATE_PROCESS_DEBUG_INFO, *LPCREATE_PROCESS_DEBUG_INFO;

typedef struct _EXIT_THREAD_DEBUG_INFO {
    DWORD dwExitCode;
} EXIT_THREAD_DEBUG_INFO, *LPEXIT_THREAD_DEBUG_INFO;

typedef struct _EXIT_PROCESS_DEBUG_INFO {
    DWORD dwExitCode;
} EXIT_PROCESS_DEBUG_INFO, *LPEXIT_PROCESS_DEBUG_INFO;

typedef struct _LOAD_DLL_DEBUG_INFO {
    HANDLE hFile;
    LPVOID lpBaseOfDll;
    DWORD dwDebugInfoFileOffset;
    DWORD nDebugInfoSize;
    LPVOID lpImageName;
    WORD fUnicode;
} LOAD_DLL_DEBUG_INFO, *LPLOAD_DLL_DEBUG_INFO;

typedef struct _UNLOAD_DLL_DEBUG_INFO {
    LPVOID lpBaseOfDll;
} UNLOAD_DLL_DEBUG_INFO, *LPUNLOAD_DLL_DEBUG_INFO;

typedef struct _OUTPUT_DEBUG_STRING_INFO {
    LPSTR lpDebugStringData;
    WORD fUnicode;
    WORD nDebugStringLength;
} OUTPUT_DEBUG_STRING_INFO, *LPOUTPUT_DEBUG_STRING_INFO;
```

Continues

Listing 7.11   DEBUG_INFO structures.

```
typedef struct _RIP_INFO {
    DWORD dwError;
    DWORD dwType;
} RIP_INFO, *LPRIP_INFO;
```

Listing 7.11   DEBUG_INFO structures *(Continued)*.

```
typedef struct _EXCEPTION_RECORD {
    DWORD    ExceptionCode;
    DWORD ExceptionFlags;
    struct _EXCEPTION_RECORD *ExceptionRecord;
    PVOID ExceptionAddress;
    DWORD NumberParameters;
    UINT_PTR ExceptionInformation[EXCEPTION_MAXIMUM_PARAMETERS];
            } EXCEPTION_RECORD;
```

Listing 7.12   EXCEPTION_RECORD structure.

- EXCEPTION_ARRAY_BOUNDS_EXCEEDED
- EXCEPTION_FLT_DENORMAL_OPERAND
- EXCEPTION_FLT_DIVIDE_BY_ZERO
- EXCEPTION_FLT_INEXACT_RESULT
- EXCEPTION_FLT_INVALID_OPERATION
- EXCEPTION_FLT_OVERFLOW
- EXCEPTION_FLT_STACK_CHECK
- EXCEPTION_FLT_UNDERFLOW
- EXCEPTION_INT_DIVIDE_BY_ZERO
- EXCEPTION_INT_OVERFLOW
- EXCEPTION_PRIV_INSTRUCTION
- EXCEPTION_IN_PAGE_ERROR
- EXCEPTION_ILLEGAL_INSTRUCTION
- EXCEPTION_NONCONTINUABLE_EXCEPTION
- EXCEPTION_STACK_OVERFLOW
- EXCEPTION_INVALID_DISPOSITION
- EXCEPTION_GUARD_PAGE
- EXCEPTION_INVALID_HANDLE

After handling a debug event, developers should not forget to call Continue-DebugEvent to restart the thread that was stopped by the debug event. Listing 7.13 shows how to use the four process debug functions to construct a very portable debugger.

```
void ParameterError()
{
    ::MessageBox(NULL, "Usage:\nProcessDebug -c exectuable\n"
        "ProcessDebug -d processid", "Parameter Error",
        MB_OK);
}

std::string WideToAnsi(const std::wstring & str)
{
    char * sz = new char[str.length()+1];
    ::WideCharToMultiByte(CP_ACP, 0, str.c_str(), -1, sz,
        str.length()+1, NULL, NULL);
    std::string s = sz;
    delete[] sz;
    return s;
}

void HandleExceptionDebugEvent(const EXCEPTION_DEBUG_INFO & info)
{
    if (info.dwFirstChance != 0)
    {
        std::cout << "First Chance ";
    }
    switch(info.ExceptionRecord.ExceptionCode)
    {
    case EXCEPTION_ACCESS_VIOLATION:
        std::cout << "Access Violation Exception";
        break;
    case EXCEPTION_DATATYPE_MISALIGNMENT:
        std::cout << "Datatype Misalignment Exception";
        break;
    case EXCEPTION_BREAKPOINT:
        std::cout << "Breakpoint Exception";
        break;
    case EXCEPTION_SINGLE_STEP:
        std::cout << "Single Step Exception";
        break;
    case EXCEPTION_ARRAY_BOUNDS_EXCEEDED:
        std::cout << "Array Bounds Exception";
        break;
    case EXCEPTION_FLT_DENORMAL_OPERAND:
        std::cout << "Floating-Point Denormal Exception";
        break;
    case EXCEPTION_FLT_DIVIDE_BY_ZERO:
        std::cout << "Floating-Point Divide by Zero"
"Exception";
        break;
```

Continues

Listing 7.13   Portable debugger.

```
        case EXCEPTION_FLT_INEXACT_RESULT:
            std::cout << "Floating-Point Inexact Exception";
            break;
        case EXCEPTION_FLT_INVALID_OPERATION:
            std::cout << "Floating-Point Invalid Operation"
"Exception";
            break;
        case EXCEPTION_FLT_OVERFLOW:
            std::cout << "Floating-Point Overflow Exception";
            break;
        case EXCEPTION_FLT_STACK_CHECK:
            std::cout << "Floating-Point Stack Check Exception";
            break;
        case EXCEPTION_FLT_UNDERFLOW:
            std::cout << "Floating-Point Underflow Exception";
            break;
        case EXCEPTION_INT_DIVIDE_BY_ZERO:
            std::cout << "Integer Divide by Zero Exception";
            break;
        case EXCEPTION_INT_OVERFLOW:
            std::cout << "Integer Overflow Exception";
            break;
        case EXCEPTION_PRIV_INSTRUCTION:
            std::cout << "Privileged Instruction Exception";
            break;
        case EXCEPTION_IN_PAGE_ERROR:
            std::cout << "In Page Exception";
            break;
        case EXCEPTION_ILLEGAL_INSTRUCTION:
            std::cout << "Illegal Instruction Exception";
            break;
        case EXCEPTION_NONCONTINUABLE_EXCEPTION:
            std::cout << "Noncontinuable Exception";
            break;
        case EXCEPTION_STACK_OVERFLOW:
            std::cout << "Stack Overflow Exception";
            break;
        case EXCEPTION_INVALID_DISPOSITION:
            std::cout << "Invalid Disposition Exception";
            break;
        case EXCEPTION_GUARD_PAGE:
            std::cout << "Guard Page Exception";
            break;
        case EXCEPTION_INVALID_HANDLE:
            std::cout << "Invalid Handle Exception";
            break;
```

Continues

Listing 7.13 Portable debugger *(Continued).*

```
    }
    std::cout << std::endl;
}

int main(int argc, char* argv[])
{
    if (argc != 3)
    {
        ParameterError();
        return 0;
    }

    PROCESS_INFORMATION pi = {0};
    if (std::string(argv[1]) == "-c")
    {
        STARTUPINFO si = {0};
        si.cb = sizeof(STARTUPINFO);
        si.dwFlags = STARTF_FORCEONFEEDBACK |
            STARTF_USESHOWWINDOW;
        si.wShowWindow = SW_SHOWNORMAL;

        if (::CreateProcess(NULL, argv[2], NULL, NULL, FALSE,
            DEBUG_PROCESS, NULL, NULL, &si, &pi) == FALSE)
        {
            ParameterError();
            return 0;
        }
    }
    else if (std::string(argv[1]) == "-d")
    {
        std::stringstream ss;
        ss << std::string(argv[2]);
        DWORD dw;
        ss >> dw;
        if (::DebugActiveProcess(dw)==FALSE)
        {
            ParameterError();
            return 0;
        };
    }
    else
    {
        ParameterError();
        return 0;
    }
    DWORD dw;
    char buffer[4096*2] = {0};
```

Continues

Listing 7.13

```
while(true)
{
    DEBUG_EVENT debugevent;
    if (::WaitForDebugEvent(&debugevent, INFINITE)
        == FALSE)
    {
        break;
    }
    try
    {

        switch(debugevent.dwDebugEventCode)
        {
        case EXCEPTION_DEBUG_EVENT:
            HandleExceptionDebugEvent(
                debugevent.u.Exception);
            break;

        case CREATE_THREAD_DEBUG_EVENT:
            std::cout << "CreateThread Debug Event - "
                "Thread = " << debugevent.dwThreadId
                << std::endl;
            break;

        case CREATE_PROCESS_DEBUG_EVENT:
            std::cout << "CreateProcess Debug Event - "
                "Process = " << debugevent.dwProcessId
                << std::endl;
            break;

        case EXIT_THREAD_DEBUG_EVENT:
            std::cout << "ExitThread Debug Event - "
                "Thread = " << debugevent.dwThreadId
                << std::endl;
            break;

        case EXIT_PROCESS_DEBUG_EVENT:
            std::cout << "ExitProcess Debug Event - "
                "Process = " << debugevent.dwProcessId
                << std::endl;
            ::Sleep(10*1000);
            ::CloseHandle(pi.hProcess);
            ::CloseHandle(pi.hThread);
            return 0;

        case LOAD_DLL_DEBUG_EVENT:
            std::cout << "LoadLibrary Debug Event"
                << std::endl;
            break;
```

Continues

Listing 7.13 Portable debugger *(Continued)*.

```
                  case UNLOAD_DLL_DEBUG_EVENT:
                        std::cout << "FreeLibrary Debug Event"
                              << std::endl;
                        break;

                  case OUTPUT_DEBUG_STRING_EVENT:
                        ::ReadProcessMemory(pi.hProcess,
        debugevent.u.DebugString.lpDebugStringData,
                              buffer, sizeof(buffer), &dw);
                        if (debugevent.u.DebugString.fUnicode)
                        {
                              wchar_t * sz = (wchar_t *)buffer;
                              std::cout << WideToAnsi(sz)
                                    << std::endl;
                        }
                        else
                        {
                              std::cout << buffer << std::endl;
                        }
                        break;

                  case RIP_EVENT:
                        std::cout << "Rip Debug Event"
                              << std::endl;
                        break;

                  default:
                        std::cout << "Unknown Debug Event"
                              << std::endl;
                        break;
                  };
            }
            catch(...)
            {
            }

            ::ContinueDebugEvent(debugevent.dwProcessId,
                  debugevent.dwThreadId,
                  DBG_CONTINUE);
      }

      ::CloseHandle(pi.hProcess);
      ::CloseHandle(pi.hThread);
      return 0;
}
```

Listing 7.13

The listing as a whole doesn't really mean all that much, so I'll break it down into smaller snippets and explain what is happening in the debugger.

```
PROCESS_INFORMATION pi = {0};
if (std::string(argv[1]) == "-c")
{
        STARTUPINFO si = {0};
        si.cb = sizeof(STARTUPINFO);
si.dwFlags = STARTF_FORCEONFEEDBACK |
STARTF_USESHOWWINDOW;
        si.wShowWindow = SW_SHOWNORMAL;

        if (::CreateProcess(NULL, argv[2], NULL, NULL, FALSE,
            DEBUG_PROCESS, NULL, NULL, &si, &pi) == FALSE)
        {
                ParameterError();
                return 0;
        }
}
else if (std::string(argv[1]) == "-d")
{
        std::stringstream ss;
        ss << std::string(argv[2]);
        DWORD dw;
        ss >> dw;
        if (::DebugActiveProcess(dw)==FALSE)
        {
                ParameterError();
                return 0;
        };
}
else
{
        ParameterError();
        return 0;
}
```

This second snippet of code is where the debugger is initialized. If the first command-line parameter is –c, then I can create a new process using the second command-line parameter. In the call to CreateProcess, I passed the DEBUG_PROCESS flag. This indicates to the Win32 subsystems that I want to create this process and begin debugging it immediately.

If the first command-line parameter is –d, then I can attach the debugger to the process that is identified by the process ID, provided as the second command-line parameter. I connect the debugger to this process using the DebugActiveProcess function.

After the initialization is complete, I start a while loop so that I can repeat process debug events.

```
DEBUG_EVENT debugevent;
if (::WaitForDebugEvent(&debugevent, INFINITE) == FALSE)
{
    break;
}
```

Waiting for debug events is as simple as calling the WaitForDebugEvent function. If the function fails, then it will return a nonzero return value. When this happens, I exit the while loop by calling break. Otherwise, I use the returned DEBUG_EVENT structure to print out the message.

```
switch(debugevent.dwDebugEventCode)
{
case EXCEPTION_DEBUG_EVENT:
HandleExceptionDebugEvent(debugevent.u.Exception);
    break;

case CREATE_THREAD_DEBUG_EVENT:
    std::cout << "CreateThread Debug Event - "
        "Thread = " << debugevent.dwThreadId
<< std::endl;
    break;

case CREATE_PROCESS_DEBUG_EVENT:
    std::cout << "CreateProcess Debug Event - "
        "Process = " << debugevent.dwProcessId
<< std::endl;
    break;

case EXIT_THREAD_DEBUG_EVENT:
    std::cout << "ExitThread Debug Event - "
        "Thread = " << debugevent.dwThreadId
<< std::endl;
    break;

case EXIT_PROCESS_DEBUG_EVENT:
    std::cout << "ExitProcess Debug Event - "
        "Process = " << debugevent.dwProcessId
<< std::endl;
    ::Sleep(10*1000);
    ::CloseHandle(pi.hProcess);
    ::CloseHandle(pi.hThread);
    return 0;

case LOAD_DLL_DEBUG_EVENT:
    std::cout << "LoadLibrary Debug Event"
<< std::endl;
    break;

case UNLOAD_DLL_DEBUG_EVENT:
    std::cout << "FreeLibrary Debug Event"
<< std::endl;
    break;
```

```
    case OUTPUT_DEBUG_STRING_EVENT:
    ::ReadProcessMemory(pi.hProcess,
        debugevent.u.DebugString.lpDebugStringData,
            buffer, sizeof(buffer), &dw);
        if (debugevent.u.DebugString.fUnicode)
        {
            wchar_t * sz = (wchar_t *)buffer;
            std::cout << WideToAnsi(sz)
                << std::endl;
        }
        else
        {
            std::cout << buffer << std::endl;
        }
        break;

    case RIP_EVENT:
        std::cout << "Rip Debug Event"
<< std::endl;
        break;

    default:
        std::cout << "Unknown Debug Event"
<< std::endl;
        break;
    };
```

If the exception was an exception event, then I pass it to the HandleException-
DebugEvent function since there are many types of debug events and I don't
want to complete the code by introducing nested case statements.

For most of the events, I simply print out that the event happened. But for
some, I retrieve more information to make the debug output a little bit more
informative. In the create-exit thread-process events, I print the relevant
thread or process IDs. In the exit process thread, I wait 10 seconds (so I can
see the event), then I terminate the debugger.

The tricky event is the output debug string event. When this event is triggered, I know that the OUTPUT_DEBUG_STRING_INFO structure contains
a pointer to the debug string. But this string may be in either ANSI or UNI-
CODE format (single- or double-byte strings). I check the fUnicode flag to
determine which to output.

```
void HandleExceptionDebugEvent(const EXCEPTION_DEBUG_INFO & info)
{
    if (info.dwFirstChance != 0)
    {
        std::cout << "First Chance ";
    }
    switch(info.ExceptionRecord.ExceptionCode)
    {
```

```
case EXCEPTION_ACCESS_VIOLATION:
    std::cout << "Access Violation Exception";
    break;
...
}
std::cout << std::endl;
}
```

The HandleExceptionDebug event simply translates the exception constant into a more human-readable string that explains the error. The dwFirstChance member can be tested to find out if this is the first time that this exception instance has generated a debug event. If this member is nonzero, then it is the first time I am debugging this exception. If this member is zero, then I've previously handled the event and it was either continued or unhandled.

Now there's a simple and portable debugger. Programmers can load this on any computer and begin debugging an application without having to install a full debugger. To run this debugger against a running process, run the debugger with the –d and process ID command-line parameters. To run this debugger against a new process, run the debugger with the –c and the executable name command-line parameters.

Programmers may also register this portable debugger as the default debugger so that it can be launched from the Task Manager by right-clicking a process and selecting Debug from the pop-up menu. Listing 7.14 shows the Registry setting necessary to register this portable debugger as the default debugger.

It is usually very inefficient for applications to exhaustively call the debugger API, especially when there is no debugger present.

```
BOOL IsDebuggerPresent(VOID);
```

If the application is slowed by debug function calls, then developers can use the IsDebuggerPresent function to skip debug function calls when the application is not being debugged. The IsDebuggerPresent function returns TRUE when the current process is being debugged by another process.

```
REGEDIT4

[HKEY_LOCAL_MACHINE\SOFTWARE\Microsoft\Windows
NT\CurrentVersion\AeDebug]
"Debugger"="\"D:\\dbwin\\processdb\\Debug\\processdb.exe\" -p %ld"
```

Listing 7.14 Register default debugger.

Invoking the Debugger

If there is a debugger that is already configured as the default debugger, then I can call the DebugBreak function at run time to load the debugger with the current process.

```
VOID DebugBreak(VOID);
```

This function is invaluable during debugging and quality assurance as it provides a very effective way of retrieving important context information when those unexpected errors occur.

Calling this function stops the execution in-place and loads the debugger with all the process context information intact. A tester or developer can then take a snapshot of the call stack and related information which can later help guide the tracking of the defect.

PerfMon

The Windows Performance Monitor (PerfMon) is installed as a standard component with Windows NT. PerfMon provides a lot of functionality that is useful in the debugging and day-to-day operations of an NT Service. The PerfMon utility can be started from the Start menu by selecting Programs | Administrative Tools | Performance Monitor.

PerfMon's primary purpose is monitoring the activities of a Windows NT Server. Figure 7.10 shows the PerfMon utility monitoring the CPU usage of my laptop while I write this sentence.

I'm a pretty fast typist, so I was able to keep CPU utilization near 100 percent. Actually, WinWord continued to gobble near 100 percent CPU even when I wasn't typing. The programmers at Microsoft should have used PerfMon to diagnosis this unacceptably high CPU utilization.

The PerfMon utility has an array of values that it can monitor. Some of the more important values that should be monitored in a production operation are space utilization on each logical disk, percentage of committed memory bytes, percentage usage of the paging file, private bytes of each process, percentage processing time of each process, and the handle count of each process.

PerfMon Alerts

Monitoring these activities using the chart features of PerfMon would require that an operator glance at the results once in a while to find out if any of the values are out of the ordinary. It is best to set up PerfMon to automatically trigger activity when a particular condition arises. From the PerfMon menu bar, I select View Alert (see Figure 7.11).

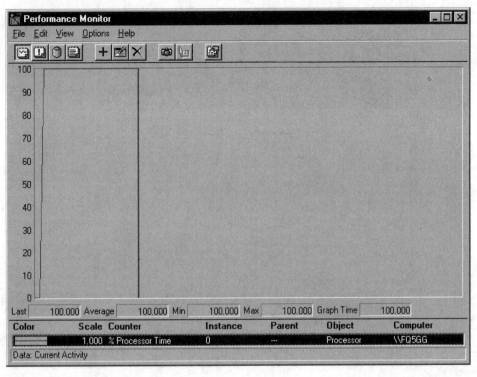

Figure 7.10 PerfMon chart view.

The alerts are a valuable feature of the tool. Programmers can set up various alerts to warn of potential critical behavior on a server. One of the basics of monitoring which should occur on any server is to monitor the level of disk usage on any logical disk. Programmers can set up an alert to trigger at a percentage utilization using PerfMon. To do this, from the menu bar, I select Edit | Add to Alert. The Add to Alert dialog appears (see Figure 7.12).

I select the Computer name whose logical disk I wish to monitor. Then I select Logical Disk from the Object drop-down combo box, % Free Space from the Counter combo box, and the logical drive instance in the Instance combo box. I select Over 20 in the Alert If group box and then First Time, and I type the program that will execute when the alert action is triggered.

For developers who have reliable e-mail, a very convenient action to take when an alert is triggered is to send e-mail to the operators using a utility such as sendmail. They may also run a batch file when an alert is triggered. This gives them the ability to perform several actions when an alert is triggered. And finally, they might also consider adding steps in their batch file that take corrective measures to remedy the problem. I've added many alerts that test whether a process's handle count is equal to zero and relaunch the process when the alert is triggered.

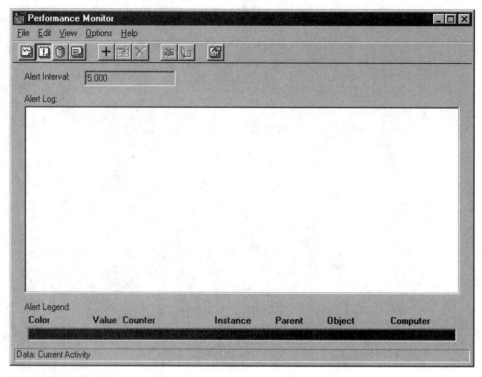

Figure 7.11 PerfMon alert view.

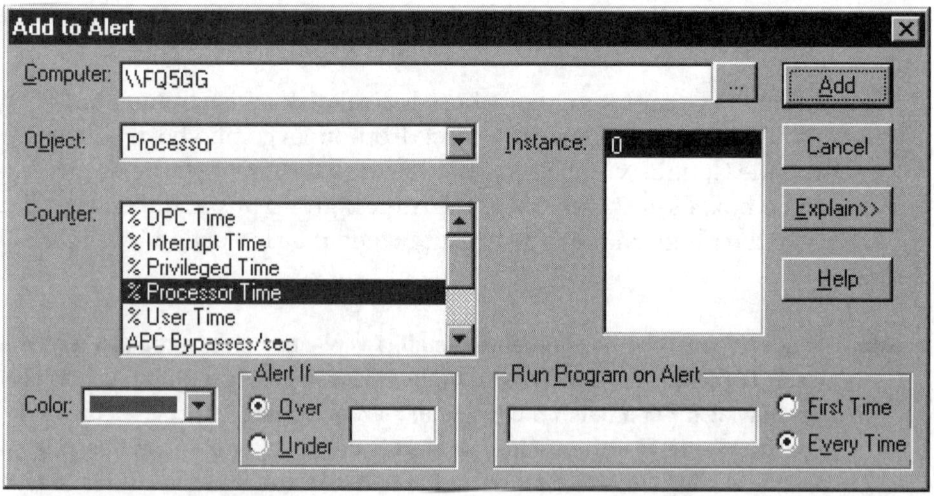

Figure 7.12 Add to Alert dialog.

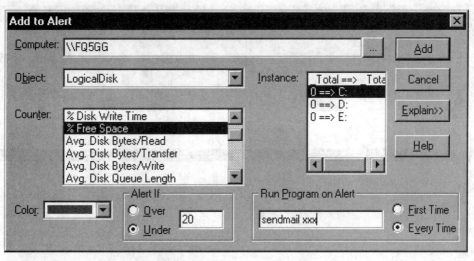

Figure 7.13   Monitor logical disk usage.

I click the Add button to add the alert and Done to exit the dialog. Figure 7.13 shows a completed Add to Alert dialog which will trigger e-mails when the disk utilization is in an unacceptable range.

When the disk utilization exceeds 80 percent, the sendmail program will be run.

Programmers should test whether the program will execute properly by setting the Alert If group box to Over 1%. Also, programmers can edit an existing alert by selecting the alert in the Alert Legend and selecting Edit | Edit Alert Entry from the menu bar.

When an alert is triggered, the Run Program will be executed and an entry will be added to the Alert Log (see Figure 7.14).

In a production operations environment, developers will be interested in saving the Alert Log. They can save it by selecting File | Export Alert from the menu bar. A sample exported Alert Log is shown in Listing 7.15.

The log files saved from PerfMon can then be saved and attached to the problem reports of incidents related to the triggered alerts.

PerfMon Alert Options

It is also important to set the appropriate Alert Options in the Alert Options dialog. I can display the Alert Options dialog by selecting Options | Alert from the menu bar (see Figure 7.15).

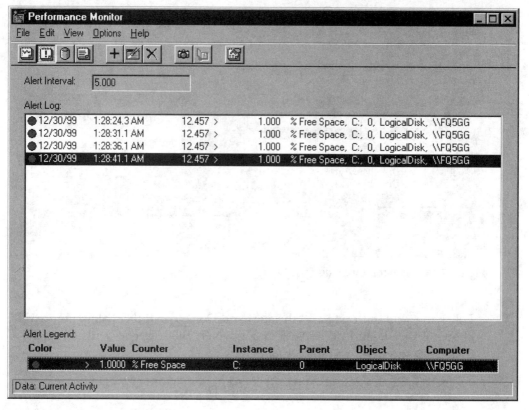

Figure 7.14 PerfMon Alert Log.

I suggest that developers always log the alert events in the application event log. This is done by checking the Log Event in the Application Log checkbox. A typical PerfMon event log entry is shown in Figure 7.16.

Developers should also reduce the Update Time Interval to a much larger number. I suggest 60 seconds. It can be quite annoying when the PerfMon

```
Reported on \\ZZ6SS
Date:   10/12/99
Time:   10:39:20 PM
Data:   Current Activity
Interval:   1.000 seconds

Date Time Value      Trigger Condition      Counter     Instance
      Parent    Object      Computer
10/12/99  10:39:06 PM          56.937        >          1.000     %
Free Space    C:   0    LogicalDisk      \\ZZ6SS
10/12/99  10:39:07 PM          56.937        >          1.000     %
Free Space    C:   0    LogicalDisk      \\ZZ6SS
```

Listing 7.15 Sample exported Alert Log.

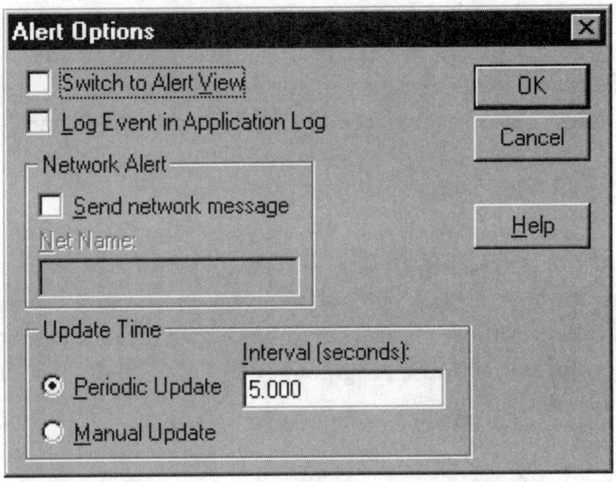

Figure 7.15 Alert Options.

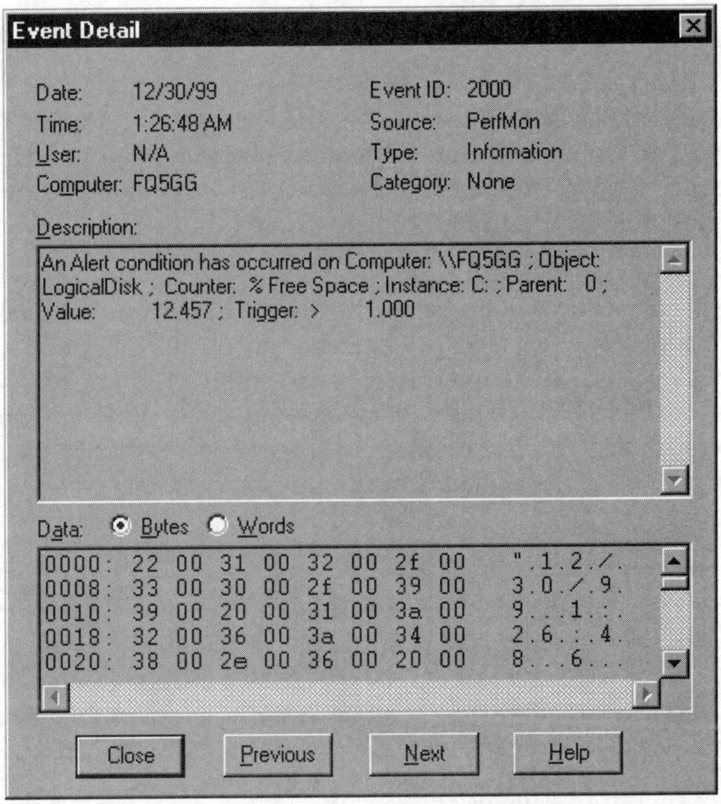

Figure 7.16 PerfMon event log entry.

utility spams a user's e-mail address with alerts. It's worth considering increasing this value or selecting the First Time radio button in the Add to Alerts or Edit Alert Entry dialogs. Selecting the First Time radio button ensures that an alert triggers a program only the first time the conditions are met.

WARNING
If the First Time radio button is selected and an alert is triggered, programmers must then remember to reset this alert or they will not receive anymore notifications. It is quite easy to receive an alert notification, fix the problem, and forget to reset the alert. The problem may continue after the programmer thinks it's been fixed but no more notifications will be sent.

PerfMon Logging

Another great feature of the PerfMon utility is the ability to log performance activity for later viewing. To configure logging in the PerfMon utility from the Log View, I select View | Log from the menu bar (see Figure 7.17).

To log activity, I select Edit | Add To Log from the menu bar and the Add To Log dialog appears (see Figure 7.18).

I select one of the objects that I want to log and click the Add button. Then I click the Done button when I am finished adding objects to be logged. In order to begin login, I must specify a filename that will contain the logged data; I select Options | Log from the menu bar and the Log Options dialog appears (see Figure 7.19).

I select the filename that will be used to log the information. I find that a small logging interval of 15 seconds generates too much log information and is sometimes very difficult to interpret. I usually set the logging interval for 10 minutes (or 600 seconds). This will add one log entry every 10 minutes. Almost every situation requires a different logging interval, and I can change the logging interval in the Update Time group box in the Log Options dialog.

Experience

It is a given that operators rarely follow procedures as documented by the server designers. Here's an important part of what the PerfMon utility provides for the developer: Designers can potentially set up an alert to programmatically gather all logs related to the incident that triggered an alert. Unfortunately, I'm not aware of any method to programmatically save the Alert Log.

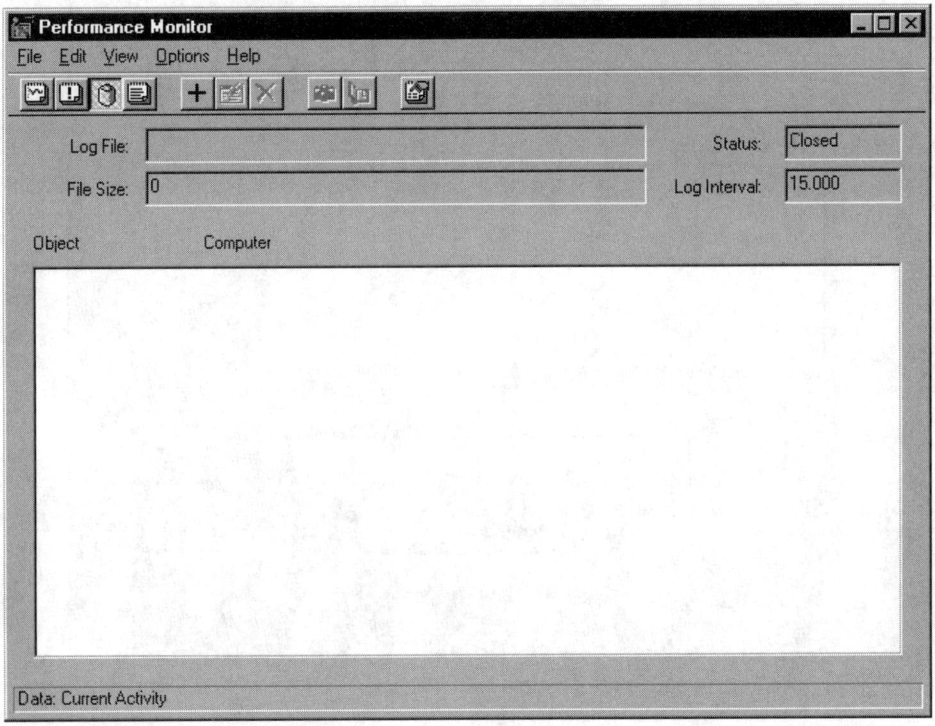

Figure 7.17 PerfMon log view.

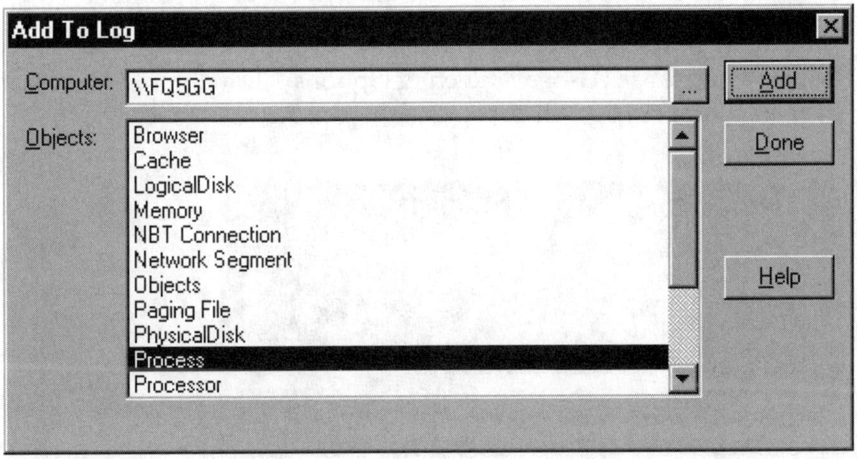

Figure 7.18 Add To Log dialog.

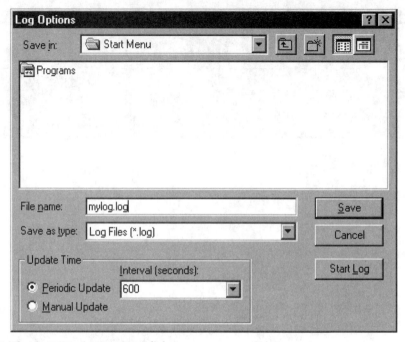

Figure 7.19 Log Options dialog.

Some versions of the PerfMon utility do not append a default extension to the log file, so programmers shouldn't forget to add the file extension if one is needed.

After I've selected the logging file and interval, I can click the Start Log button to initiate the logging of activity. To stop the logging activity, I must return to the Log Options dialog and click the Stop Log button.

I can view the log activity from the Chart View by selecting View | Chart from the menu bar. Also, by selecting Options | Data From in the menu bar, the Data From dialog will appear (see Figure 7.20).

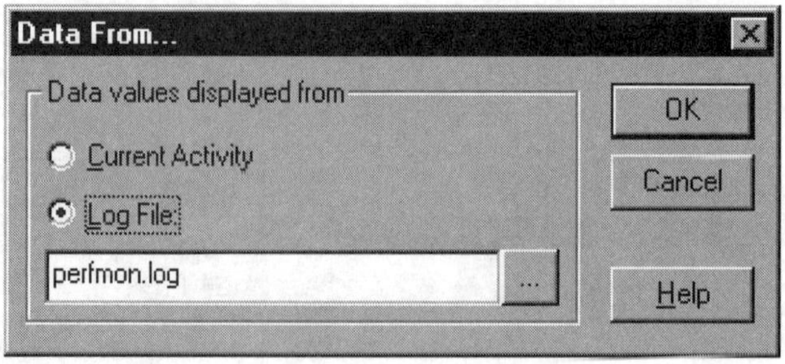

Figure 7.20 Data From dialog.

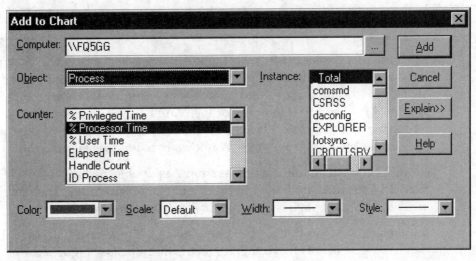

Figure 7.21   Add to Chart dialog.

I select the Log File radio button and place the log file name where I saved the log information in the Data values displayed from edit box. I click OK to return to the Chart View and go to the Add to Chart dialog (see Figure 7.21) to add items to the chart by selecting Edit | Add To Chart from the menu bar.

I select the Object, Counter, and Instance that I want to chart, click the Add button, and, finally, click the Done button. The chart will be displayed in the Chart View.

PerfMon in Production

I find that PerfMon is a great production utility for finding performance problems that exist in a server. Some application servers have small memory leaks that are not always apparent until the server is released in a production environment. I've found that monitoring the private bytes of a process using the Perf-Mon utility is a great way of determining whether these small memory leaks exist. PerfMon won't help find the leaks, but it can help determine if they exist.

One problem with using PerfMon in a production or near-production system is that most production machines are logged off most of the time. PerfMon cannot be run when nobody is logged into the system unless it is started using a utility such as SRVANY.

SRVANY

The SRVANY command-line utility can be used to convert any executable into a service.

Task Scheduler

With Internet Explorer 5.0 and NT Server 4.0 Service Pack 5, Microsoft packaged a new task-scheduling user interface that makes scheduling tasks easier than ever. Prior to this new task scheduler, programmers were required to use the AT command-line utility or the WinAT UI. Neither compare in ease of use to the new Scheduled Tasks shell extension. The shell extension is available under My Computer in the Windows Explorer (see Figure 7.22).

Adding a new scheduled task is as simple as double-clicking the Add Scheduled Task list item and filling in the presented wizard forms. The first Scheduled Task Wizard page is informational only (see Figure 7.23).

By clicking the Next button, the second page of the wizard will present a semicomplete list of all executables on the machine (see Figure 7.24).

I can select the application I want to schedule in the listview or I can click the Browse button to select an application that is not in the listview. By clicking Next, I move on to the next page (see Figure 7.25).

I've selected to run my task each time I log on. I click Next again to move to the username-password page (see Figure 7.26).

I've selected to run the task with my own user account. Assuming, of course, that the programmer knows the password, he or she can run the task with any user account. I click Next to move to the last page (see Figure 7.27).

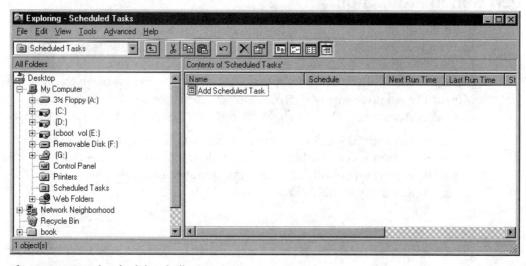

Figure 7.22 Task Scheduler shell extension.

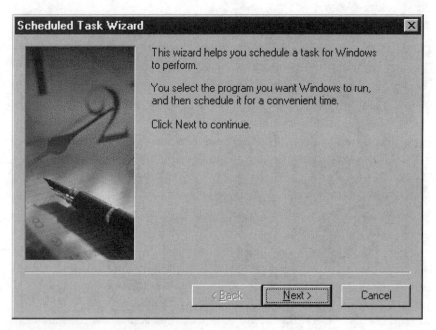

Figure 7.23   Scheduled Task Wizard, page 1.

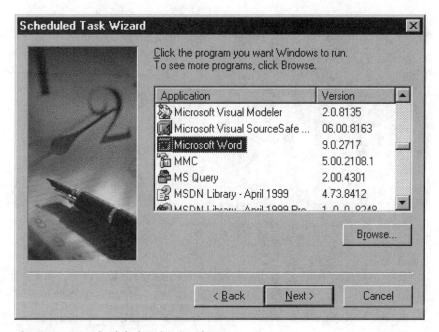

Figure 7.24   Scheduled Task Wizard, page 2.

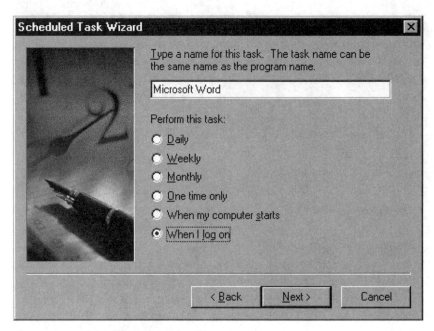

Figure 7.25 Scheduled Task Wizard, page 3.

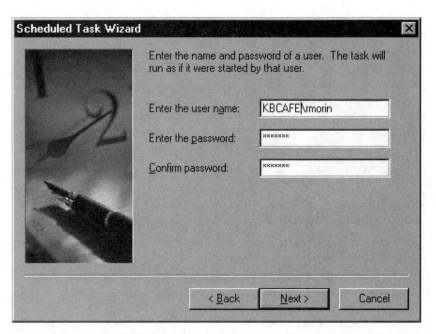

Figure 7.26 Scheduled Task Wizard, page 4.

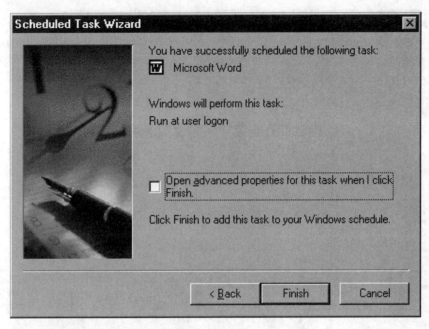

Figure 7.27 Scheduled Task Wizard, page 5.

Since I agree with all the information, I can simply click the Finish button and the task will be scheduled. Alternatively, I can click the Back button and change any previous item.

Scheduled Task Properties

I can also check the Open advanced properties for this task when I click Finish checkbox, click Finish, and I'll be presented with a property sheet detailing my scheduled task (see Figure 7.28).

The Scheduled Task property sheet has three tabs: Task, Schedule, and Settings. In the Task tab, I can change the command line, the starting directory, task comments, the run as user, and I can enable-disable the task. I find it particularly useful to use the Enabled checkbox to enable and disable a scheduled task for times when the task is not beneficial.

The Schedule tab, as shown in Figure 7.29, enables the user to configure when the task is scheduled.

I can configure a task to run daily, weekly, monthly, once, at system startup, at logon, and when idle. I can also check the Show multiple schedules check-

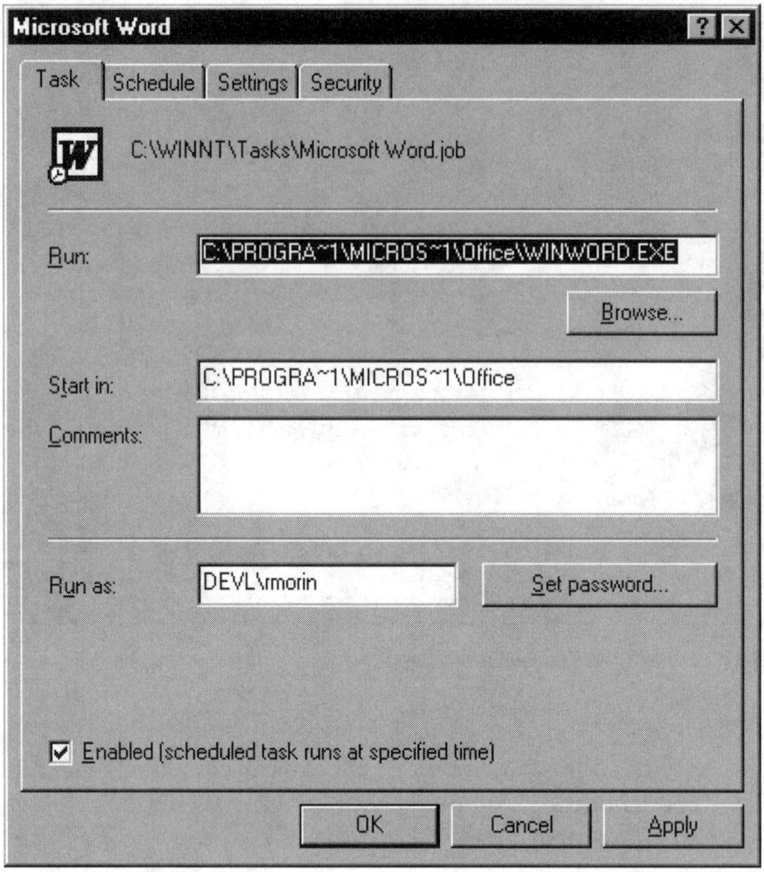

Figure 7.28 Scheduled Task task page.

box to provide for two or more of the previous alternatives. In order to schedule a task with a finer granularity than daily, I can click the Advanced button to achieve this granularity (see Figure 7.30).

To select an hourly schedule, I can check the Repeat Task checkbox and set the options as I've shown them in Figure 7.30. The last page of the Scheduled Task property sheet is the Settings tab (see Figure 7.31).

The Settings tab provides for some automatic management of tasks. I won't go into details on these options, as they are trivial and rarely used.

RegMon

Another interesting utility that helps debug applications is RegMon. This utility was created by System Internals (www.sysinternals.com/regmon.htm)

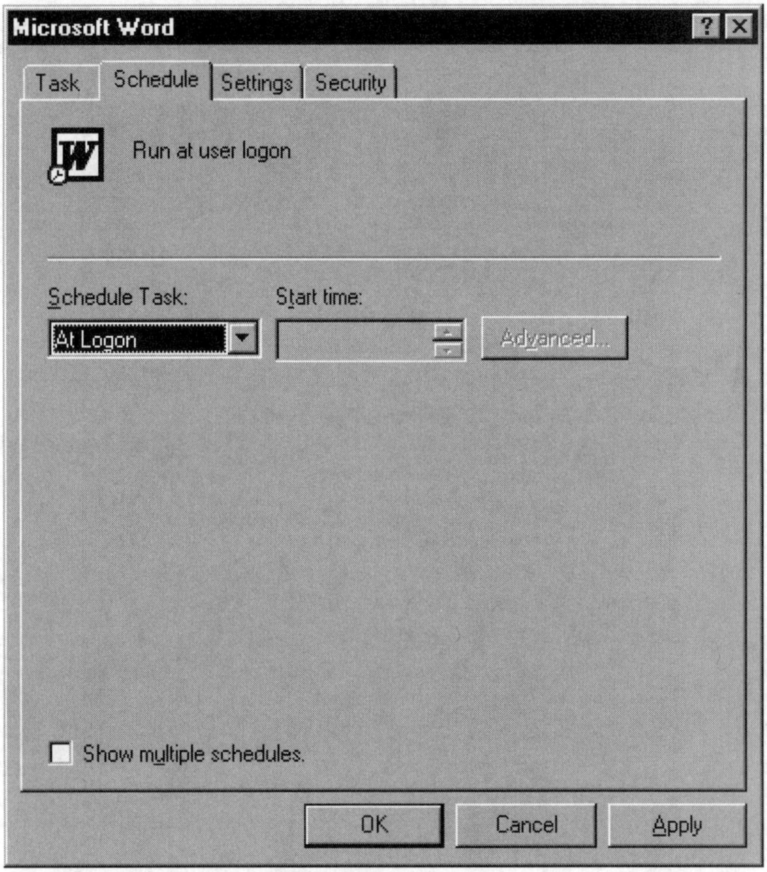

Figure 7.29 Scheduled Task schedule page.

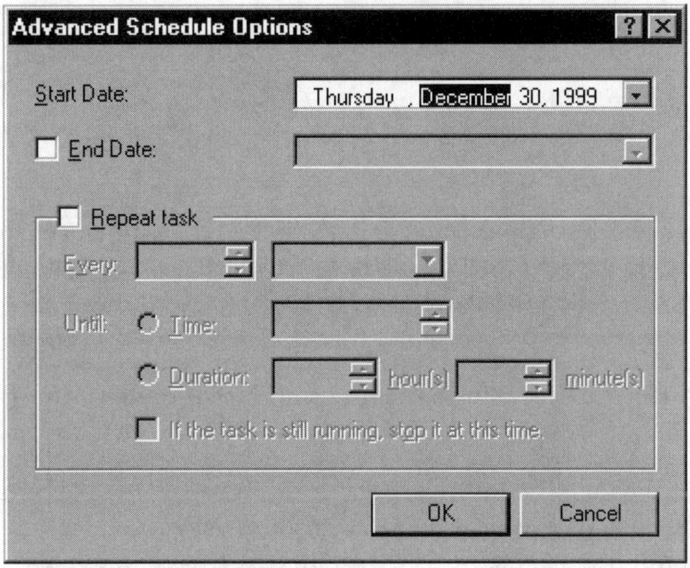

Figure 7.30 Advanced Schedule Options.

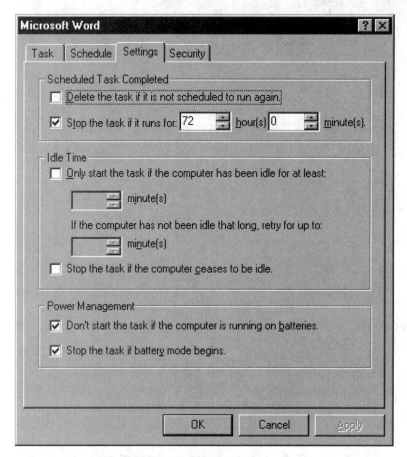

Figure 7.31 Scheduled Task settings page.

and performs a low-level hook into the Registry API. I would never suggest using such a utility in a production environment, but it can be invaluable in trying to track down Registry access problems.

Installing the utility is a breeze: I can simply unzip the files into any directory and run the executable. The user interface is quite simple (see Figure 7.32).

I don't explain the RegMon utility in detail, but I wanted to make certain readers are aware of its existence and power. I also suggest readers check out the unlimited utilities that are freely distributed by System Internals.

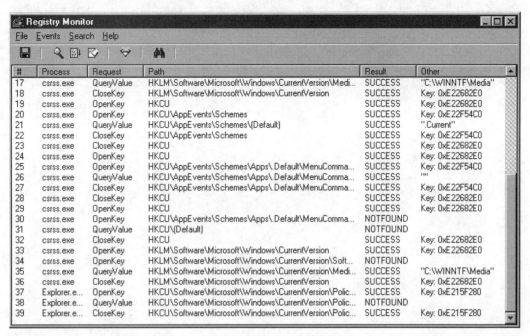

Figure 7.32 RegMon in action.

Summary

I guess we're finished. It's time to say goodbye. I hope you enjoyed this reading experience. Please do drop me an e-mail with your comments. Hopefully everything compiled, linked, and ran without a hitch. I don't compile my own code, so I wouldn't know :-)

What's on the CD-ROM?

The CD-ROM contains the source code used to code and test the sample listings throughout the book. The source code is contained within one archive file, Code.zip. The archive is organized into one large Visual C++ workspace, containing 59 Visual C++ projects.

Simple listings that cannot be compiled into a complete working example are contained in static libraries. Each chapter has one static library named ch0x, where x is the chapter number. More complex listings that can be compiled into a complete working example are contained in individual Visual C++ projects. The projects are named list0x0y, where x is the chapter number and y is the listing number.

You'll note that I've added code to the listing on the CD. The added code is there in order to make the listing compile. In the book, I refrained from placing include directives in the source listing to make the listings as simple as possible. This was not possible on the CD.

Hardware Requirements

To use this CD-ROM and the materials on the CD, your system must meet the following requirements:

Windows NT 4.0 or Windows 2000

Microsoft Visual C++ 6.0

User Assistance and Information

The software accompanying this book is being provided as is without warranty or support of any kind. Should you require basic installation assistance, or if your media is defective, please call our product support number at (212) 850-6194 weekdays between 9 am and 4 pm Eastern Standard Time. Or, we can be reached via e-mail at: **wprtusw@wiley.com**. Or you can contact the author via e-mail at: **rmorin@kbcafe.com**.

To place additional orders or to request information about other Wiley products, please call (800) 879-4539.